Can you imagine the USA without the States? Stephen H. Legomsky over-whelms the reader with this original, mind-blowing, and rarely discussed idea. A timely, novel, and provocative book for anyone troubled by the crisis of American democracy, with implications far beyond the US. Professor Legomsky is three in one: a visionary, a constitutional designer, and a policy planner. An intellectual ice-breaker!

Liav Orgad, European University Institute, author of
A Liberal Theory of Majority Rights

In this brilliant thought experiment, as in all his scholarship and congressional testimony, Professor Legomsky writes clearly, frankly, logically, and in a balanced way. We can't ask for a better guide to think through what governance structure is best for America well into her third century.

Andrew I. Schoenholtz, Georgetown University Law Center

Steve Legomsky is remarkable in the way he encourages us to think outside the box. In this groundbreaking book, he plants an idea, laying the seeds for changing public attitudes toward state government. While its message is primarily for the USA, it speaks to all federal countries using constitutional structures developed in centuries past and outdated.

Kim Rubenstein, University of Canberra and National University
of Australia, co-Series Editor of the Cambridge University Press
series Connecting International with Public Law

This pathbreaking book is an indispensable thought experiment to anyone thinking or teaching creatively about the allocation of power in our federalized constitu-tional order. Legomsky's vision is not one of simplistic nationalization or wooden uniformity; he persuasively shows how policy devolution and variation would be better delivered by enhancing local government power. It is a book I wish I had read decades ago at the start of my academic career, and I will incorporate it into my teaching and research going forward.

Theodore Ruger, Professor and former Dean, University
of Pennsylvania Carey Law School

REIMAGINING THE AMERICAN UNION

Reimagining the American Union challenges readers to imagine an America without state government. No longer a union of arbitrarily constructed states, the country would become a union of its people. The first book ever to argue for abolishing state government in the US, it exposes state government as *the* root cause of the gravest threats to American democracy. Some of those threats are baked into the Constitution; others are the product of state legislatures abusing their already-constitutionally-outsized powers through gerrymanders, voter suppression schemes, and other less-publicized manipulations that all too often purposefully target African-American and other minority voters. *Reimagining the American Union* also illustrates how having three levels of legislative bodies (national, state, and local) – and three levels of taxation, bureaucracy, and regulation – wastes taxpayer money and pointlessly burdens the citizenry. Two levels of government – national and local – would do just fine. After debunking the offsetting benefits typically claimed for state government, the book concludes with a portrait of what a new, unitary American republic might look like.

Stephen H. Legomsky is the John S. Lehmann University Professor Emeritus at the Washington University School of Law. Professor Legomsky has published scholarly books on immigration and refugee law, courts, and constitutional law, as well as a novel and a short story collection. His extensive professional background includes a post in the Obama Administration and other diverse experiences working with federal, state, local, UN, and foreign governments.

Reimagining the American Union

THE CASE FOR ABOLISHING STATE GOVERNMENT

STEPHEN H. LEGOMSKY

Washington University School of Law

Shaftesbury Road, Cambridge CB2 8EA, United Kingdom

One Liberty Plaza, 20th Floor, New York, NY 10006, USA

477 Williamstown Road, Port Melbourne, VIC 3207, Australia

314–321, 3rd Floor, Plot 3, Splendor Forum, Jasola District Centre, New Delhi – 110025, India

103 Penang Road, #05–06/07, Visioncrest Commercial, Singapore 238467

Cambridge University Press is part of Cambridge University Press & Assessment, a department of the University of Cambridge.

We share the University's mission to contribute to society through the pursuit of education, learning and research at the highest international levels of excellence.

www.cambridge.org
Information on this title: www.cambridge.org/9781009581431

DOI: 10.1017/9781009581424

When citing this work, please include a reference to the DOI 10.1017/9781009581424

First published 2025

A catalogue record for this publication is available from the British Library

A Cataloging-in-Publication data record for this book is available from the Library of Congress

ISBN 978-1-009-58143-1 Hardback
ISBN 978-1-009-58141-7 Paperback

With love, this book is dedicated to Lorraine, my dear departed wife and best friend.

No political dreamer was ever wild enough to think of breaking down the lines which separate the States, and of compounding the American people into one common mass.

Chief Justice John Marshall, writing for a unanimous Supreme Court in *McCulloch v. Maryland*, 17 U.S. (4 Wheat.) 316, 403 (1819)

* * *

States – What Are They Good For?
Absolutely Nothin'

With apologies to Edwin Starr, whose famous rendition of "War – What Is It Good For?" can be found at www.youtube.com/watch?v=ztZI2aLQ9Sw

Contents

Acknowledgments

For their thoughtful and invaluable comments while this book was in process, I extend my heartfelt thanks to Nick Almendares, Susan Appleton, Kathleen Clark, Conor Clarke, Danielle D'Onfro, John Drobak, Dan Epps, Sheldon Evans, Jens Frankenreiter, Trevor Gardner, Bill Henderson, David Konig, Aneil Kovvali, Jayanth Krishnan, JoAnne LaSala, Ron Levin, Asaf Lubin, Greg Magarian, Aviva Orenstein, Rafael Pardo, Bob Pollack, Adam Rosenzweig, Steve Sanders, Ken Dau Schmidt, Brian Tamanaha, India Thusi, Joe Tomain, Deborah Widiss, Peter Wiedenbeck, David Williams, Susan Williams, and all the participants in workshops at Washington University and Indiana University. Extra special thanks are owed to Carol Boggs, Travis Crum, Nora Demleitner, Andrea Katz, Liav Orgad, Srishti Prakash, Kim Rubenstein, Ted Ruger, Andy Schoenholtz, and Nikki Westra for their insightful comments on earlier drafts of this book, as well as the two anonymous Cambridge University Press peer reviewers for their painstaking appraisals and similarly thoughtful suggestions. I am also indebted to Washington University law librarians Wei Luo and Kathie Molyneaux, who cheerfully hunted down an unending stream of hard-to-find books. And I thank Cambridge University Press Executive Publisher and Acquisitions Editor Matt Gallaway for his strong and vital support of this project.

Introduction

This book is a thought experiment. It invites you to imagine an America without state government. The hypothesis it tests is that, all things considered, the national interest of the United States would be better served by a two-layer (national and local government) unitary system than by the current three-layer (national, state, and local) federation. In that hypothetical system, the functions currently performed by state government would be redistributed among the national government, the local governments, and various inter-government partnerships. The country would cease to be a union of states. It would become a union of its people.

This exercise – one that the scholarly literature has not yet undertaken – requires a careful, objective weighing of both the benefits and the costs of state government in the United States. That evaluation encompasses, but goes beyond, the traditional debates over federalism. The question considered here is not merely whether the US can do without federalism, but whether it can do without state government entirely. Those are different inquiries. While it is impossible to have federalism without political subdivisions, it is very possible to have political subdivisions without federalism. Indeed, unitary systems in which the subunits are mere subordinates of the central government are commonplace in today's world.[1] In such a unitary system, it seems fair to ask how many levels of subordinate units are optimal. This book suggests that for the United States, the answer is one – local government.[2]

After a brief historical summary of how the US came to be a federation of states, the book proceeds in two broad steps: The first step is to demonstrate the harms for

---

[1] As of 2024, the number of countries in the world ranges from 193 to 237, depending on one's definition of "country" and on certain international political judgments. The United Nations recognizes 195 countries. See, for example, Toby Saunders, BBC Science Focus, *How Many Countries Are There in 2024?* (Jan. 5, 2024), www.sciencefocus.com/planet-earth/how-many-countries-are-there. Of these, only about twenty-five are federations, though they account for approximately 40 percent of the world's population. Forum of Federations, *Federal Countries*, https://forumfed.org/countries/#:~:text=There%20 are%20roughly%2025%20federal,%2C%20Brazil%2C%20Germ*any%20and%20Mexico.

[2] For reasons detailed in Chapter 4, this book assumes that local government is indispensable. On that assumption, the one-subordinate-layer option would entail the elimination of state government rather than local government.

which state government can fairly be held responsible. Of these, by far the most serious is the continuing toll it has taken, and continues to take, on two of America's most sacred democratic norms – political equality and majority rule. Between the outsized status and powers that the US Constitution confers on the states (Chapter 2) and the ways in which state legislatures and state officials have deployed those powers (Chapter 3), state government will be shown to have become *the* root cause of many, if not most, of the gravest threats to US democracy. Examples are noted below. Chapter 4 will show that state government is also a source of fiscal waste. Three levels of legislative bodies, three levels of bureaucracy, three levels of regulation, and three levels of taxation will be shown to be unnecessary; two of each, it is submitted, would do just fine.

The second step in the argument is to identify and engage the many offsetting contributions that have been, or might be, claimed for state government. Most of those claimed benefits (Chapter 5) are modified versions of arguments drawn from the literature on federalism. That chapter demonstrates that the many virtues commonly ascribed to federalism, while facially attractive, become far less convincing under a microscope.

The elimination of state government would require several difficult secondary decisions. Who, for example, would decide which of the current state functions should be nationalized and which ones should be localized? Who would assume the states' current roles in national elections, in supplying the bulk of the country's judges, or in the constitutional amendment process? Chapter 6 identifies workable, if not ideal, answers to each of those questions. In the process, it offers a portrait of what a unitary American republic might look like without state government.

In the end, every experiment needs an outcome. Here, I submit, the conclusion will be clear: In today's America,[3] state government is an anachronism. Politically unavoidable as it was at the founding of the republic, it has outlived whatever value it ever added and in fact has become an impediment to both government efficiency and, more importantly, democracy itself. In an ideal world, it would be but a historical remnant, stuffing the same dustbin as monarchy, slavery, the disenfranchisement of women and people of color, and lawyers with wigs.

Ours, of course, is not an ideal world, and I do not labor under the delusion that the abolition of state government is anywhere on the immediate horizon. Given the combination of entrenched interests, culture wars, deep sentimental attachments, widespread distrust of the federal government, and both partisan and ideological differences that are unevenly distributed both among and within the various geographic regions, I must acknowledge that the constitutional transformation suggested here has no short-term political traction. At present, there is no conceivable

---

[3] Although this book contains scattered references to other countries' practices, it does not attempt a comparative study. I offer no opinions about the usefulness of states or their analogs in other federations.

path to the sweeping series of constitutional amendments that would be required. Among other barriers, I cannot foresee the necessary three-fourths of the state legislatures voting to abolish themselves any time soon.

Hence the humble description of this book as a thought experiment. But, unlike the book itself, the national conversation that it seeks to inspire would have both scholarly value and significant practical benefits.

The intended scholarly contributions are twofold. First, my goal is to expand the scope of the current debates over the fragile state of US democracy. The existing writings have collectively highlighted the substance of many of the looming dangers. Yet, amidst the plentiful scholarly and popular calls to heed the grave perils facing US democracy, no writing that I can find attempts to trace all or most of the problems to a common source. This book builds on that literature by highlighting state government as the root of the problem. The hope is that the arguments presented will spur a serious conversation about the wisdom of entrusting the core elements of US democracy to the states.

Second, and more broadly, the prolific body of federalism scholarship has elaborated the pros and cons of dividing government powers between a central authority and the sovereign states. In the process, it has offered diverse visions of federalism and other decentralization models. But the arguments of even the most impassioned federalism skeptics have generally focused either on matters of degree (what is the optimal division of power between the federal government and the states?) or on whether federalism should give way to a unitary, but still decentralized, system in which the states play subordinate, but still important, governance roles.[4] This book aims to expand that debate as well, by asking whether the benefits of decentralization could be more effectively achieved without state government – that is, by dividing power between the central government and the existing local governments.[5]

Theory aside, the national conversation that this book seeks to jump-start would have several potential practical benefits. First, while the states' immediate future is secure, history teaches us that the more distant future is full of surprises. Today's fantasies have a way of becoming tomorrow's realities. But those new realities don't materialize out of thin air. Gradual changes in public opinion are almost always a precondition for other fundamental changes. This book, therefore, takes a long-term view. By planting an idea, it seeks to lay the groundwork for an evolution in the

---

4 For an excellent article advocating decentralization without federalism (but retaining key roles for the states), see Edward L. Rubin & Malcolm Feeley, *Federalism: Some Notes on a National Neurosis*, 41 UCLA L. Rev. 903 (1994).

5 A word on terminology: In the United States today, the terms "federal government," "national government," and "central government" are commonly used interchangeably. This book similarly uses both terms when discussing the current US federal system. But without state government, the word "federal" would lose its meaning. When discussing the elements of a hypothetical unitary republic, therefore, this book will refer to either the "central government" or the "national government."

public's attitudes toward state government. In the long term, the prospects for even massive structural transformation should not be ruled out, as long as the arguments for change are compelling and the advocacy is patient but persistent.

Second, I hope to blunt the rhetorical impact of "states' rights" as a political slogan. Too often, these words have been nothing but code for the denial of individual rights – a perversion of the fundamental democratic principle that it is the job of the state to serve the people, not vice versa. When confederates raised the states' rights banner during the Civil War, no one was unaware that slavery was the particular "right" that the southern states felt they deserved to have – in fact, a right important enough to secede from the union over. *New York Times* columnist Jamelle Bouie has offered some dramatic examples of the democratic liberties that the legislatures of slave states were willing to extinguish in order to crush the antislavery movement.[6] Nor, as this book will demonstrate, did self-styled "states' rights" campaigns end with the Civil War; they continue to surface today in service of other troubling positions.

Third, greater skepticism about the value of state government will hopefully trigger more intensive public scrutiny of state legislators and governors. Ideally, that scrutiny will sharpen popular resistance to at least the more flagrant assaults on democratic rule.

Finally, in recognition of the reality that state government will be with us for some time to come, this book has an additional goal, one more modest and more immediate: to persuade you, the reader, that the social, economic, and political costs of state government are greater, and the benefits fewer, than is commonly assumed. The corollary hope is that those costs will then be weighed more seriously whenever the decision whether to entrust a specific function to the federal government or the states becomes a live issue. It often does. Today, for example, that "who decides?" question engulfs such controversial subjects as gun safety, immigration, abortion, environmental protection, and public health.

Primary attention will be focused on the democratic costs of state government, for those are both the weightiest and the most diverse of the harms. The decline of democracy in recent years is not, of course, limited to the United States; it is now a worldwide concern, especially in Europe, and it has multiple causes.[7] But the American case, when viewed against our historical and enduring embrace of a landmark experiment in democracy, is particularly unsettling.

---

[6] Jamelle Bouie, *The Real Threat to Freedom Is Coming from the States* (May 26, 2023), www.nytimes.com/2023/05/26/opinion/freedom-states-rights.html?campaign_id=39&emc=edit_ty_20230526&instance_id=93535&nl=opinion-today&regi_id=13788254&segment_id=133976&te=1&user_id=e16deb82e8516f294a4077a86c02f5c2. Bouie's powerful commentary is highlighted in Chapter 4, Section B.

[7] See, for example, Samuel Issacharoff *et al.*, The Law of Democracy – Legal Structure of the Political Process 44–46 (6th ed. 2022); Freedom House, *Democracies in Decline*, https://freedomhouse.org/issues/democracies-decline; Reuters, *Half of World's Democracies in Decline, Intergovernmental Watchdog Says*, www.reuters.com/world/half-worlds-democracies-decline-intergovernmental-watchdog-2022-11-30/.

Some of the current problems stem from the dominant role of state sovereignty baked into the US Constitution. These problems flow from the historical constitutional compromise between Antifederalists who believed that the national government should represent the sovereign states and Federalists who believed that in a democratic republic the national government should represent the people more directly. As others have observed, and as Chapter 2 will elaborate, the constitutional problems include the awarding of two senators to each state regardless of population; the Electoral College; the counter-majoritarian process for appointing federal judges; and the requirements for amending the Constitution.

Superimposed on those structural breaches of democratic norms are the many counter-majoritarian actions of state legislatures and state executive branch officials: state legislatures that gerrymander both congressional and their own state legislative districts with near impunity; the epidemic of ever more creative – and more ruthless – state voter suppression laws; the threats by state election officials and candidates for those offices to withhold certification of valid electoral outcomes; the ominous efforts to resuscitate the discredited "independent state legislature" theory, which has been invoked to place state legislatures' gerrymandering and voter suppression efforts beyond the reach of the federal courts and potentially even state courts[8]; state-enabled intimidation of voters and election officials; and state legislatures' usurpations of decisions traditionally, and wisely, left to local governments.

Too often, these efforts have purposely targeted African American and other minority voters, threatening to undo decades of social progress. Each of those features gives some citizens far more say than it gives others, undermining the goal of political equality and thereby simultaneously impeding the principle of majority rule. In part for those reasons, public faith in the institutions of government is at an all-time low. We have reached the point where, this book contends, we can no longer take for granted the long-term stability of the bedrock electoral and other institutions on which democracy rests.

I applaud the legions of thoughtful scholars who have called out many of these assaults on our democracy.[9] Several of these writers have offered constructive

---

[8]   As discussed in Chapter 3, Section C, the Supreme Court recently mitigated this danger but stopped short of extinguishing it.

[9]   In recent years, many books have highlighted the fragile state of democracy, both in the United States and worldwide. The long list of examples includes Jack M. Balkin, The Cycles of Constitutional Time (2020); Ari Berman, Minority Rule: The Right-Wing Attack on the Will of the People – and the Fight to Resist It (2024); James W. Ceaser, Presidential Selection: Theory and Development (1979); Tom Ginsburg & Aziz Z. Huq, How to Save a Constitutional Democracy (2018); Mark A. Graber, Sanford Levinson & Mark Tushnet (eds.), Constitutional Democracy in Crisis? (2018); Richard L. Hasen, A Real Right to Vote: How a Constitutional Amendment Can Safeguard American Democracy (2024); Steven Levitsky & Daniel Ziblatt, How Democracies Die (2018); Steven Levitsky & Daniel Ziblatt, Tyranny of the Minority (2023); Benjamin I. Page & Martin Gilens, Democracy in America? (2017); Ganesh Sitaraman, The Crisis of the Middle-Class Constitution (2017); and Cass Sunstein (ed.), Can It Happen Here? Authoritarianism in America (2018).

proposals to curb some of the more insidious abuses. But my view is that the problem runs deeper than even the sum of these transgressions. The fundamental problem, I argue, is state government itself. Without it, far fewer of these subversions could occur, as will be shown.

Yet, even those who have rightly raised the alarm have stopped short of proposing the abolition of state government.[10] And understandably so. They have chosen to operate within the political world we currently inhabit, not the world we wish we had.

Fair enough. To be sure, those proposals are more grounded than the abolition of state government. I get that. Throughout my own career, I have followed a similar path, unwilling to squander my finite time writing books or articles that advocate policies wildly beyond reach.

Until now. I fear we no longer have that luxury, for the illness has metastasized through our entire body politic. Think of this book as a mere theoretical exercise if you wish. Or, less charitably if you prefer, dismiss it as the mad ravings of an out of touch academic boomer. It doesn't matter. The perils to our democracy are now severe enough that radical surgery, however politically implausible in the near future, demands serious scholarly consideration.

But put aside states' relentless attack on our democracy. State government is also a source of fiscal waste. We don't need three levels of government – national, state, and local – all regulating us and all taxing us. The exhaustive research for this book could not unearth a single function that state governments typically perform – whether in the service realm or the representation realm – that they can do better than all other levels of government. In some subject areas the national government will be equally well or even better equipped; in others, the tasks could be performed at least as well

Several writers have more specifically criticized the multiple counter-majoritarian features that are built into the US Constitution: Robert A. Dahl, How Democratic Is the American Constitution? (2nd ed. 2003); Alexander Keyssar, The Right to Vote: The Contested History of Democracy in the United States (rev. ed. 2009); Sanford Levinson, Our Undemocratic Constitution: Where the Constitution Goes Wrong (And How We the People Can Correct It) (2006); and Levitsky & Ziblatt, Tyranny, above.

10 For example, Donald F. Kettl, The Divided States of America: Why Federalism Doesn't Work, chapter 11 (2020) (criticizing federalism but ultimately recommending specific reforms that retain the role of states); David Pepper, Laboratories of Autocracy: A Wake-Up Call from behind the Lines (2021); Rubin & Feeley, note 4, at 908 ("We are not arguing for the abolition of the states."). By way of exception, I have found two op-ed pieces that explicitly advocate the abolition of US states. They emphasize the inefficiency of three layers of government and the increased homogeneity of life in the United States, though not the adverse impact of states on American democracy. Lawrence R. Samuel, Washington Post, *States Are a Relic of the Past. It's Time to Get Rid of Them* (Nov. 15, 2016), www.washingtonpost.com/news/in-theory/wp/2016/11/15/states-are-a-relic-of-the-past-its-time-to-get-rid-of-them/; Daniel Greenwood, New York Newsday, *Why the States?* (Jan. 3, 1991), https://sites.hofstra.edu/daniel-greenwood/why-the-states/. In addition, one author has advocated the abolition of the Australian states. See Rodney Hall, Abolish the States – Australia's Future and a $30 Billion Answer to Our Tax Problem (1998). His proposal, focused on the waste and inefficiency of maintaining three levels of government, is discussed in Chapter 4.

by local governments, or national-local partnerships, or regional collaborations of local authorities. All of those scenarios avoid or substantially reduce the costs to the taxpayer of funding the duplicative legislative, bureaucratic, and judicial machinery, and the dizzying array of needlessly divergent laws, of fifty separate states.

Thus, the argument continues, we Americans are paying a hefty price – democratic and fiscal – for state government. What, exactly, are we getting in return? Does state government, for example, help avoid dangerous concentrations of power? Does it enable laws and policies more closely tailored to the needs and preferences of the fifty states' varying populations? Do policy differences among states empower individuals by giving every state's citizens the choice of moving to states with more agreeable laws? Does a system of fifty state governments stimulate economically beneficial competition for businesses? Are the states useful laboratories for social innovation? By being closer to the people than the national government is, do they foster citizen participation in our democracy? Does a state's muscle give its citizens a more effective voice in the formulation of national policy? Do state constitutions protect valuable individual rights that the US Constitution doesn't? Does state government furnish a sense of either personal or political community? Are the states essential partners in the implementation of federal laws?

Most of these benefits have long been asserted by others, in the somewhat different debates over the proper scope of federalism. Despite their initial appeal, Chapter 5 will show that some of these claimed benefits are nonexistent or greatly exaggerated, and that the others are real and important but replicable at least as well by the national government, local governments, or inter-government partnerships.

Before we go any further, and as Richard Nixon used to say, "Let me make one thing perfectly clear." *I am not proposing a wholesale transfer of power from the states to the national government.*[11] Rather, without state government, I propose reassigning *some* of the current state functions to the national government and the rest to the local governments – the cities, towns, and other political subdivisions that are geographically closer, and in most cases ideologically more closely attuned, to the people they represent.[12]

That said, I am also not proposing that the tens of thousands of local governments become ministates. That arrangement would still be a federation, one even more unwieldy than what we have now. I am urging that the US, like many of the world's other democracies, become a true unitary State. The national government

---

[11] I am sensitive to the many failings of the federal government, thoroughly analyzed by Peter Schuck in Why Government Fails So Often: And How It Can Do Better (2014).

[12] Chapter 4 proposes criteria and procedures for determining which of the functions currently performed by states would be reassigned to the national government and which ones to the local governments. Local governments, in turn, come in many shapes and sizes. They include not only municipalities, but also counties, townships, parishes, unincorporated areas, and special purpose entities such as school districts and sewer districts. Chapter 6, Section A therefore explores the processes that could be used to distribute the local functions among these various kinds of local governments.

would no longer be limited to a list of specific powers affirmatively referenced in the Constitution. It would still be constrained by everything else in the Constitution, including, most importantly, the provisions that protect individual rights. Each of the national government's three branches would remain further cabined by constitutionally enshrined separation of powers principles. And the political process – freed from its many state-related counter-majoritarian distortions – would remain the ultimate check.

Judged by world standards, that thesis is not as extreme as it might sound. The last several decades have seen a trend toward centralization in many other democracies and in the growth of supranational organizations as well. This trend is often ascribed to technological advances. One writer, Barry Friedman, emphasizes, in particular, the revolutions in transportation, communication, and industrialization – I would add homogenization – as forces that have expanded the scope of centralized regulation.[13] I agree and would suggest that these factors have not only explanatory value but normative value as well. They are simply another way of saying that as society's needs become more uniform, and as transportation and communication technologies have made geographic location within the country both less permanent and less important, it simply makes sense to adapt our governance structure accordingly.

A few disclaimers are required. First, defenders of state government will raise historical (among other) objections. They will assert the conventional wisdom[14] that the thirteen original colonies became sovereign states that in turn voluntarily created the federal government, not vice versa (though Congress indisputably created the other thirty-seven states). Moreover, I appreciate that many proponents of states' rights would find the notion of abolishing state government repugnant even if, as suggested here, it is substantially achieved by expanding the powers of local governments. Were the abolition of state government a live issue today, there would be impassioned popular opposition.

No matter. This book is not about whether the abolition of state government would be popular or whether it would be politically achievable in the near future or whether it would be in keeping with the model the founding fathers carefully constructed more than 200 years ago. I assume it would be none of those things. Rather,

---

[13] Barry Friedman, *Valuing Federalism*, 82 Minn. L. Rev. 317, 365–68 (1997). I push back, however, against Friedman's concession that "[i]ntuition certainly suggests that governance at the state and local level will have its benefits." *Ibid.*, at 380. Intuition, I would submit, suggests only that governance at *some* subnational level has benefits, not that that governance has to be by a combination of state and local authorities. This book argues that local jurisdictions and collaborative partnerships with either other local entities or the national government would be a beneficial substitute for the current fifty-state setup.

[14] Craig Green, in *The United/States: A Revolutionary History of American Statehood*, 119 Mich. L. Rev. 1 (2020), challenges that conventional wisdom. He points out that many scholars believe the Union came first and that only later did the former colonies attain statehood. Green himself rejects both theories, arguing that statehood for the original thirteen colonies and the birth of the union were accomplished simultaneously.

I am concerned here with only one question: In modern-day America, would we be better off without state government?

Additionally, I don't claim that every barrier to US democracy can be blamed on state government. With or without state government, our single-member district system for electing the US House of Representatives guarantees that the party that came in second in the national popular vote will frequently gain control of the House nonetheless.[15] With or without states, the US Senate could still cynically block the confirmation of Supreme Court and lower national court judges whenever that chamber is controlled by other than the president's party. Today's (relatively) internally cohesive and externally polarized political parties could still weaken the constraints imposed by traditional separation of powers principles.[16] The racial, social, and economic inequalities in wages, education, health care, infrastructure, and the environment obstruct equal practical access to, and equal benefit from, democratic institutions.[17] The excessive role of money – particularly dark money – in political campaigns means that not all Americans will have equal say.[18] Deep pocketed special interests and well-paid lobbyists will continue to influence legislative outcomes.[19] Human nature being what it is, there will always be unprincipled

---

[15] See the discussion in Chapter 3, Section A.

[16] See Daryl J. Levinson & Richard H. Pildes, *Separation of Parties, Not Powers*, 119 Harv. L. Rev. 2311 (2006), and the discussion in Chapter 5, Section A.

[17] For example, Kettl, note 10; Jamila Michener, Fragmented Democracy: Medicaid, Federalism, and Unequal Politics 13–14 (2018); Page & Gilens, note 9; Sitaraman, note 9; Jessica Bulman-Pozen & Miriam Seifter, *The Democracy Principle in State Constitutions*, 119 Mich. L. Rev. 859, 860 n.2 (2021).

[18] Grotesque sums of money are now spent on campaigns for both federal and state elective offices. See, for example, Federal Election Commission, *Statistical Summary of 24-Month Campaign Activity of the 2019–2020 Election Cycle* (Apr. 2, 2021), www.fec.gov/updates/statistical-summary-24-month-campaign-activity-2019-2020-election-cycle/; Page & Gilens, note 9. The contributions come disproportionately from a small number of extremely well-heeled individuals and corporations. See, for example, NPR (Nov. 10, 2022), www.npr.org/2022/11/10/1135718986/candidates-and-political-action-committees-spent-nearly-17-billion-on-midterms. The Supreme Court has largely blocked legislation that would have placed reasonable limits on campaign spending and required greater transparency as to the donors, thereby further easing the way for super-PACs and other organizations to gain preferential access to, and control of, political parties. See *Citizens United* v. *Federal Election Commission*, 558 U.S. 310 (2010); *Buckley* v. *Valeo*, 424 U.S. 1 (1976); Heather K. Gerken & Boden Lecture, *Boden Lecture: The Real Problem with Citizens United: Campaign Finance, Dark Money, and Shadow Parties*, 97 Marq. L. Rev. 904 (2014).

[19] Lobbying is protected by the First Amendment right "to petition the Government for a redress of grievances" and is an important element of participatory democracy. But "the vast majority of money spent on these activities comes from wealthy citizens and business interest groups. Moreover, and not surprisingly, studies find that businesses with the most to gain from favorable public policy engage in the most political activity. Worse, research indicates that campaign contributions and lobbying often help shape policy outcomes." John Craig & David Madland, *How Campaign Contributions and Lobbying Can Lead to Inefficient Economic Policy* (May 2, 2014), www.americanprogress.org/article/how-campaign-contributions-and-lobbying-can-lead-to-inefficient-economic-policy/. It is also big business. Daniel Weiser, while writing in defense of lobbying, acknowledges that "[i]n 2019 alone, lobbyists spent $3.47 billion on influencing political policy." Daniel Weiser, *Why Lobbying Is Legal and Important in the U.S.* (July 12, 2021), www.investopedia.com/articles/investing/043015/

presidents and members of Congress. And as we saw in the aftermath of the 2020 elections, there is the continuing danger of mob violence by supporters of the losing candidates, fanned by false claims of election fraud. Those factors will be acknowledged and discussed. But state government, it will be seen, remains the sine qua non of many of the most serious fissures in the foundations of American democracy.

I also accept that democracy does not require pure majoritarianism. Chapter 2 considers both the importance of majority rule and the concessions that must be made to assure that minority voices are also heard and meaningfully considered. For now, it is enough to acknowledge that, whether one's greater fear is tyranny of the majority or tyranny of the minority, the entrenched US Constitution commendably keeps certain rights and certain institutions beyond the reach of a simple majority. But it does not do this out of a belief that the will of the minority inherently deserves precedence over that of the majority. Rather, the particular rights and institutions that the Constitution deliberately insulates from a simple majority include those deemed essential to protecting popular sovereignty, political equality, other fundamental rights, or foundational structures of government.[20] Regrettably, however, as noted above, the Constitution also protects other institutions and processes that are anathema to these same values. Similarly antithetical to fundamental democratic norms are the various state actions catalogued above.

Finally, apart from the official, representational, and service functions that states perform, states hold sentimental value for many of their citizens. Those intangible ties must be conceded. Whether they are weighty enough to override the huge negative impact of states on both democracy and efficiency seems questionable enough. But even if they are, it seems more doubtful still that those affinities typically reflect a love of the state's *government*. If Alaskans were asked what they liked most about their state, I will go out on a limb here and guess that "the politicians in Juneau" would not make their top-ten list. Far more likely, one would assume, these attachments reflect affection for one's neighbors, a sense of community, perceptions of shared moral, cultural, or political values, or pride in the history, physical grandeur, or achievements of one's home state.

I would never disparage those attachments; they are quite real. The book therefore distinguishes between states and their governments, taking aim only at the latter.

---

why-lobbying-legal-and-important-us.asp. The Organisation for Economic Co-operation and Development (OECD) puts it best: "Although lobbying can be a positive force in democracy, it can also be a mechanism for powerful groups to influence laws and regulations at the expense of the public interest. This may result in undue influence, unfair competition and policy capture, to the detriment of effective policy making." OECD, *Lobbying*, www.oecd.org/corruption/ethics/lobbying/.

[20] On this subject, see the thoughtful treatment by Levitsky & Ziblatt, Tyranny, note 9, at 137–43. I refer here to the Constitution as it stands today. The original Constitution contained several counter-majoritarian provisions that cannot be explained as fostering popular sovereignty, political equality, or other fundamental rights. See, for example, U.S. Const. Art. I, § 2, Cl. 3 (counting only 3/5 of the slaves for purposes of state representation in the US House); Art. I, § 9, Cl.1 (permitting states to import slaves until 1808).

States themselves could continue to exist as geographic territories, with their current boundaries. They could remain on maps. Road signs that say "entering Ohio" could stay in place. The Arizona Diamondbacks and the Minnesota Twins could keep their names. Texans could still brag about how big their state is. States, in other words, could be preserved as geographic areas and as sources of identity, affiliation, and pride, even without the trappings of sovereignty, governments, and official legal recognition. Examples of such geographic areas abound: the American West,[21] the Deep South,[22] New Zealand's North and South Islands,[23] Chile's and Argentina's Patagonia,[24] and North and South Wales,[25] to name just a few.

It is time to expose state government as the single most formidable barrier to true democratic rule in the United States. And, more broadly, it is time to reevaluate whether our three-tier federal system really serves US interests better than a two-tier unitary system would. That dual mission plays out in the pages that follow.

[21] The American West is not a state or any other kind of political subdivision, but it has its own history and it has been popularized by books, television, film, and other forms of mass communication as a distinct geographic region. See, for example, Robert V. Hine *et al.*, The American West (2017) (recounting the distinctive history of the American West).

[22] Although different people might have different views of its precise boundaries, the Deep South has traditionally been understood to encompass the states "that were most dependent on plantation-agriculture" before the American Civil War, namely South Carolina, Georgia, Alabama, Mississippi, and Louisiana. Some would add Florida and Texas to this group. See, for example, New World Encyclopedia, *Deep South*, www.newworldencyclopedia.org/entry/Deep_South. The absence of official legal recognition has not prevented the *Deep South* from developing a distinctive culture and, for many of its residents, a sense of common identity. See, for example, Know Southern History, Southern Culture, www.knowsouthernhistory.net/Culture/.

[23] South Island is a specifically delineated land area of New Zealand. Travelers and residents alike admire its extraordinary beauty. See, for example, New Zealand, South Island, www.newzealand .com/us/south-island/. But it is not a political subdivision of any kind. Rather, within its space there exist several local authorities with jurisdiction over transport, the environment, sewage, and other local matters – precisely the structure advocated in this book. See Wikipedia, *South Island*, https:// en.wikipedia.org/wiki/South_Island.

[24] Patagonia has no legal or official status. It is simply the geographic region, within Chile and Argentina, that lies at the southern tip of the South American continent. See Wikipedia, *Patagonia*, https:// en.wikipedia.org/wiki/Patagonia.

[25] North and South Wales are familiar geographic regions of Wales. Their residents clearly identify with their respective regions, referring to themselves as "Gogs" and "Hwntws," the Welsh words for north and south, respectively. The populations of the two regions have different urban/rural balances and different speaking accents. But neither is its own political subdivision. Each region, in turn, is home to multiple counties and other local authorities. See Wikipedia, *Geography of Wales*, https:// en.wikipedia.org/wiki/North_Wales; Wikipedia, https://en.wikipedia.org/wiki/South_Wales; https:// en.wikipedia.org/wiki/Geography_of_Wales.

1

The Origins of American Federalism

A Tourist's Guide

A full historical treatment of the origination and evolution of American federalism would be a Herculean task for a single chapter of a book about whether twenty-first-century America needs states. Fortunately, a multitude of scholarly writings have collectively supplied the details of the varying events and perspectives that have got us to where we are today. I won't attempt to duplicate those discussions here.[1] But a few general observations are worth highlighting, both for overall context and for their specific relevance to the arguments offered in the ensuing chapters. Here, then, is a thumbnail sketch of the timeline from the colonial period to adoption of the US Constitution:

For much of the eighteenth century, relations between Britain and its American colonies were generally amicable.[2] Trans-Atlantic tensions began brewing – and escalating – during the several years that led up to the Revolutionary War. They came to a head when Britain imposed an import tax on tea that it shipped to the colonies. Objecting to taxation without any representation in the British Parliament, many Americans boycotted British tea. On December 16, 1773, a group of colonists took the protest to the next level. They boarded ships containing 342 chests of British tea and dumped the contents into Boston Harbor.[3]

Parliament's reaction to the Boston Tea Party was to pass what became known in the American colonies as "the Intolerable Laws." These laws, which imposed a series of new constraints on the colonies' economic and political powers, were intended to teach the colonists a lesson. Instead, they only fanned the flames. The colonists' reaction was to convene the First Continental Congress. Twelve of the thirteen colonies (all except Georgia) sent delegates. Among the more distinguished

---

[1] See especially Craig Green, *United/States: A Revolutionary History of American Statehood*, 119 Mich. L. Rev. 1 (2020).

[2] Adam E. Zielinski, American Battlefield Trust, Life in Colonial America Prior to the Revolutionary War, www.battlefields.org/learn/articles/life-colonial-america-prior-revolutionary-war.

[3] Constitution Center, On This Day, the Boston Tea Party Lights a Fuse (Dec. 16, 2023), https://constitutioncenter.org/blog/on-this-day-the-boston-tea-party-lights-a-fuse.

attendees were the men who would go on to become the first two US presidents – George Washington and John Adams.[4]

Meeting in Philadelphia between September 5 and October 26, 1774, this Congress took several bold steps. These included ordering people to refuse all British imports and endorsing the decision by Massachusetts to raise its own militia. Perhaps most importantly, this Congress created the Continental Association, which soon called for a ban on all trade with Britain. Finally, it arranged for a second Continental Congress to meet in the spring of 1775 if Britain had not satisfactorily addressed the colonists' grievances by then.[5]

Britain did little or nothing to address those grievances, and discontent continued to grow. When word leaked that British soldiers, already ensconced in Boston, were about to march to Concord to seize a rebel arms cache, the colonial militias began to assemble. Paul Revere (memorialized by Longfellow's epic poem[6]) and William Dawes[7] rode from Boston to Lexington to warn the militias.[8] By most accounts, the battles of Lexington and Concord, on April 19, 1775, marked the start of the Revolutionary War. It is generally believed that the colonists' successes in those battles gave them the confidence that they could win an all-out war against their militarily superior masters.[9]

As planned, the Second Continental Congress convened on May 10, 1775 (just three weeks after the battles of Lexington and Concord), again in Philadelphia[10] and again with delegates from every colony except Georgia. This Congress quickly assumed the functions of an unofficial national government, raising an army and directing the military strategy for the war, as well as appointing diplomats.[11]

Even though the war was raging, Congress had not yet gone so far as to declare independence from Britain. Neither the general public nor the governments of the individual colonies seemed quite ready to take that momentous step. Enter Thomas

---

[4] Katherine Horan, First Continental Congress, www.mountvernon.org/library/digitalhistory/digital-encyclopedia/article/first-continental-congress/.

[5] *Ibid.*

[6] Henry Wadsworth Longfellow, Poets.org, Paul Revere's Ride, https://poets.org/poem/paul-reveres-ride.

[7] Dawes, not having been included in Longfellow's poem, had been largely forgotten. But many years later, poet Helen F. Moore remedied the injustice by publishing "The Midnight Ride of William Dawes" in *Century Magazine*. Her poem can be found at 150 Years of "Paul Revere's Ride," www.paulreveresride.org/2010/01/response-midnight-ride-of-william-dawes.html. I am indebted to Carol Boggs for calling Moore's poem to my attention.

[8] Both attempted to continue on to Concord, but en route Revere was captured by British soldiers and Dawes was thrown off his horse. History.com Editors, "Battles of Lexington and Concord," (Jan. 14, 2020), www.history.com/topics/american-revolution/battles-of-lexington-and-concord.

[9] *Ibid.*

[10] Although Philadelphia was the site of their initial meeting, they had to relocate to other cities on several occasions to avoid the British army. Wikipedia, *Second Continental Congress*, https://en.wikipedia.org/wiki/Second_Continental_Congress.

[11] *Ibid.*

Paine. His eloquent pamphlet, "Common Sense,"[12] published on January 9, 1776, is best known for helping to persuade the residents of the colonies to take up arms to resist the tyranny of the King of England and fight for independence. "A government of our own is our natural right," he wrote. But as others have pointed out,[13] Paine also inspired them to create a new kind of government, one built (albeit very imperfectly) on the principle of rule by the people. In his words, "We have every opportunity and every encouragement before us, to form the noblest purest constitution on the face of the earth."

Like Paine's pamphlet, the "elegant" writing of Samuel Adams was credited by both John Adams and Thomas Jefferson as rousing public opinion in support of independence from Britain.[14] On July 4, 1776, with all thirteen colonies now in agreement, the Second Continental Congress approved the Declaration of Independence. At the same time, the Congress gave the new country its name: "the United States of America."[15]

On November 15, 1777, the Congress passed the Articles of Confederation.[16] They took effect on March 1, 1781, upon the approval of all thirteen states, and would remain in force until the adoption of the Constitution in 1789. Under Article II, each state retained "its sovereignty, freedom and independence," as well as every power that the Articles did not "expressly" delegate to the federal government. Article IV provided that each state was to have one vote in Congress. And Article XIII obliged each state to obey the laws passed by Congress as long as those laws were within the powers the Articles conferred upon Congress. As discussed more fully below, however, the powers that the Articles delegated to Congress were extremely limited, a weakness that ultimately led all thirteen states to replace them with the Constitution that in large part survives today.

The official end of the Revolutionary War came with the signing of the Treaty of Paris in 1783. In addition to ending armed hostilities, the treaty defined the boundaries of the United States and contained several other intensely negotiated (mainly by John Adams) provisions of contemporary importance.[17]

---

[12] Thomas Paine, The Project Gutenberg eBook of Common Sense, www.gutenberg.org/files/147/147-h/147-h.htm (Feb. 14, 1776).

[13] For example, Patrick J. Kiger, How Thomas Paine's "Common Sense" Helped Inspire the American Revolution (2021), www.history.com/news/thomas-paine-common-sense-revolution.

[14] Stacy Schiff, The Revolutionary Samuel Adams (2022).

[15] This name replaced "the United Colonies of America." Wikipedia, *Second Continental Congress*, https://en.wikipedia.org/wiki/Second_Continental_Congress.

[16] They are reproduced by the National Archives, in Articles of Confederation (1777), www.archives.gov/milestone-documents/articles-of-confederation.

[17] These included bilateral access to the Mississippi River, British surrender of all its military posts in the United States, payment of all prewar debts, and no retaliation against British loyalists. Amanda A. Mathews, Adams Papers, "Signed, Sealed and Delivered": The Treaty That Ended the Revolutionary War (May 8, 2019), www.masshist.org/beehiveblog/2014/09/signed-sealed-and-delivered-the-treaty-that-ended-the-revolutionary-war/.

It would be another four years before delegates from twelve of the thirteen states (all except Rhode Island) assembled in Philadelphia to draft a new constitution. From May 14 to September 17, 1787, some fifty-five delegates to the constitutional convention, George Washington presiding, labored to resolve fundamental disagreements and narrow issues alike. Among the former, the ones that dominated their discussions were the distribution of power between the national government and the states; congressional representation of the people and the states; and the inclusion or omission of a bill of rights. Their debates closely paralleled those that the Federalist and Antifederalist Papers would contain just months later; they are discussed later in this chapter. Although the delegates never achieved consensus, in the end thirty-nine of the fifty-five signed the draft constitution and sent it to the states for ratification.[18]

Under Article VII, once nine states had ratified the Constitution, it would go into effect – but only for those states. New Hampshire supplied the ninth ratification on June 22, 1788, and Congress made the Constitution effective as of March 9, 1789. By 1790, all thirteen states had ratified it. Under what became known as the Massachusetts Compromise, four states ratified the Constitution but made recommendations to Congress for a bill of rights.[19] "Inspired by Jefferson and drafted by James Madison," the Bill of Rights (the first ten amendments) became part of the Constitution in 1791. The first eight amendments protect various individual rights, and the tenth amendment confirms that all rights not granted to the central government remain with the states and the people.[20]

On the heels of both Continental Congresses, the publication of Thomas Paine's "Common Sense," the American Revolution, the Articles of Confederation, and finally the 1787 constitutional convention, came the Federalist Papers and the lesser-known Antifederalist Papers. As noted earlier, the debates they contain mirror those that had informed the drafting of the Constitution. Apart from their huge impact on public opinion and possibly on the ultimate ratification of the Constitution, these Papers are a rich source of the historical arguments for and against a strong national government.

The Federalist Papers are a series of eighty-five essays written by Alexander Hamilton, John Jay, and James Madison under the pen name "Publius."[21] They were published in various New York State newspapers in 1787 and 1788. Their

---

[18] ConstitutionFacts, The Constitutional Convention, www.constitutionfacts.com/us-constitution-amendments/the-constitutional-convention/#:~:text=The%20Constitutional%20Convention%20took%20place,delegates%20had%20much%20bigger%20plans; The White House, The Constitution, www.whitehouse.gov/about-the-white-house/our-government/the-Constitution/#:~:text=Delaware%20was%20the%20first%20State,begin%20operating%20under%20the%20Constitution.

[19] See the sources cited in note 18. See also Aaron N. Coleman & Christopher S. Leskiw (eds.), Debating Federalism: From the Founding to Today, Introductory Essay at xvi, (2019).

[20] ACLU, The Bill of Rights: A Brief History, www.aclu.org/other/bill-rights-brief-history#:~:text=The%20American%20Bill%20of%20Rights,the%20law%20of%20the%20l.

[21] They can be found, among other places, at Library of Congress, Full Text of the Federalist Papers, https://guides.loc.gov/federalist-papers/full-text.

immediate purpose was to sway public opinion in the State of New York in favor of ratifying the proposed Constitution, but their influence proved to be nationwide and long-lasting.

Unlike the Federalist Papers, which were an organized collection written by three men, the eighty-five Antifederalist Papers were written by a much greater number of authors acting independently and were assembled after the fact by numerous editors. Like the Federalist Papers, most of the Antifederalist Papers were published individually in various newspapers and later reproduced as collections. While historians differ as to the identities of the major authors, they include Cato (likely George Clinton), Brutus (likely either Melancton Smith, Robert Yates, or John Williams), Centinel (Samuel Bryan), the Federal Farmer (Melancton Smith, Richard Henry Lee, or Mercy Otis Warren), and Patrick Henry.[22] None of the authors disputed the need for some form of union, and most (not all) accepted the concept of a binding Constitution to replace the Articles of Confederation. But all had in common a passion for states' rights and a belief that the proposed Constitution gave the federal government power over too many subject areas. In addition, many of the Antifederalist writers fundamentally objected to the absence of a bill of rights.

Understanding these debates requires a brief detour. There was a menu of possible governmental models from which the constitutional framers could have chosen. Practically every country, and by definition every formal association of nations, has subunits of some sort – at the very least, cities and towns. When it comes to the status and powers of those subunits, and their relations to the whole, the possible governmental models span a continuous spectrum. In the case of the US, I find it helpful to think of four points that the states could have occupied along that spectrum, from their most dominant role down to their not existing at all.

The model that offers the constituent states their greatest power is what is often referred to as a confederation. As their name implies, the Articles of Confederation fit that model. More akin to an international treaty than to a national constitution, the Articles allowed the states to preserve their own individual sovereignties and retain their sole powers over the vast majority of subject areas. They created a common government but delegated only a few limited powers to it. Importantly too, Article XIII required the consent of every state to any amendment of the Articles. Tellingly, when referring to the union, the phrase "united states" was always in lower case letters, not the capitalized format that one would expect for the name of a real country.

[22] Wikipedia, *Anti-Federalist Papers*, https://en.wikipedia.org/wiki/Anti-Federalist_Papers. Different collectors of the Antifederalist Papers have varied somewhat in their selection of essays. In this book, all citations to the Antifederalist Papers refer to the essays compiled by Bill Bailey (ed.), The Anti-Federalist Papers (2012). A convenient hard copy of both sets of papers is "The Complete Federalist and Anti-Federalist Papers" (editor's name absent, Oct. 21, 2022).

A second point on the spectrum (a lower point for states' rights) would be the federation that the US Constitution ultimately created and that continues to exist today. While the states retained their individual sovereignties, they ceded far more power to the federal government than the Articles of Confederation had. Those federal powers are still limited to the ones affirmatively granted by the Constitution, but when the federal government exercises those powers, its decisions become the supreme law of the land, prevailing over any state actions with which they conflict. In subject areas that are not granted to the federal government, the Tenth Amendment to the US Constitution makes clear that the states (or the people) have the last word.[23] For me, that is the distinguishing feature of a true federation: There are at least some subject areas over which the national government has the last word and others over which the subunits have complete autonomy to make policy decisions without interference from the national government.

To be clear, the distinction between a confederation and a federation is not cut and dried. First, the difference is often just one of degree. The broader the range of subject areas over which the national government has exclusive authority, the more likely it is that the arrangement will be described as a federation rather than a confederation. But second, the very definition of a federation has varied over time. Dimitrios Karmis and Wayne Norman point out that until the twentieth century, the terms "federation" and "confederation" were typically used interchangeably.[24] Today, different writers emphasize different attributes in distinguishing federations from confederations. Under one definition, a federation is a model in which "two or more self-governing communities share the same political space."[25] Some will use the term "confederation" if the constituent units can veto constitutional changes or leave the union unilaterally or "if they are the primary locus of their citizens' identity and political loyalty."[26] For Ronald Watts, the key ingredient of a confederation is that the common government consists of delegates from the constituent units.[27]

Under these definitions, the US system, despite being generally perceived as a federation, has elements of both models. On the one hand, there are the trappings of a confederation. Any constitutional amendment requires (among other things) the ratifications of three-fourths of the state legislatures. The national Senate consists of delegates of the fifty states. And the President is elected by an Electoral College whose members are selected by the individual states. On the other hand, there are attributes of a federation. There is no constitutional provision that authorizes states to secede, and the one serious attempt of the southern states to leave the union

---

[23] The Tenth Amendment reads: "The powers not delegated to the United States by the Constitution, nor prohibited by it to the States, are reserved to the States respectively, or to the people."

[24] Dimitrios Karmis & Wayne Norman (eds.), Theories of Federalism – A Reader 5 (2005); accord, Robert A. Dahl, How Democratic Is the American Constitution? 180 (2nd ed. 2003).

[25] Karmis & Norman, note 24, at 3.

[26] *Ibid.*, at 5.

[27] Ronald Watts, *Models of Federal Power Sharing*, 167 Int. Soc. Sci. J. 25 (2001).

ended in defeat after a bloody civil war. The US House of Representatives is elected by the people, not by states. And while I offer this only as an impression, not as empirical fact, it would seem that in the United States "the primary locus of [most] citizens' identity and political loyalty" would be the nation, not their states of residence. So under the criteria offered either by Karmis and Norman or by Watts, this country is a hybrid, with both federal and confederal elements.

The third point on the spectrum is what some writers call "decentralization."[28] The terminology is a bit misleading, because the first two models also entail decentralized power – in fact, even more so than this one. But when these writers refer to decentralization, they mean "mere" decentralization, that is, decentralization without federalism or confederalism. Under that model, the national government is not constitutionally required to cede any powers to the states at all, but it can do so voluntarily whenever it wishes. The national government becomes the supreme authority on all matters, and the states effectively become just subunits to which the national government may delegate whatever responsibilities it wishes. There are no subject areas in which the states have the last word. Edward Rubin and Malcolm Feeley, who favor this model, liken it to a management regime, in which the top executives decide which duties to assign to their subordinates.[29]

The fourth point, at the very bottom of this spectrum, would be the one favored in this book. State government would cease to exist entirely. As with decentralization, the national government would have power over all subject matters (as long as they complied with all the remaining constitutional constraints). The powers currently possessed by the states would be reallocated between the national government and the local governments as Congress sees fit.

At the Constitutional Convention, the whole notion of a unitary republic was a nonstarter. Robert Dahl observes that it was "simply out of the question."[30] That is not to say there were no outliers. As Dahl also notes, there was at least one delegate, George Read of Delaware, who saw the states as an "evil," the only "cure" for which was "doing away with States altogether and uniting them all into [one] great Society."[31]

What all four of these points on the spectrum have in common is that the national government has supreme (though in some cases delegable) authority over all the

[28] Edward L. Rubin & Malcolm Feeley, *Federalism: Some Notes on a National Neurosis*, 41 UCLA L. Rev. 903 (1994).

[29] *Ibid.*, at 910–14. A similar distinction between federalism and decentralization is drawn by Barry Friedman, *Valuing Federalism*, 82 Minn. L. Rev. 317, 380–81 (1997). ("Federalism is a system in which government units actually have autonomy in decision-making, while in a decentralized system of government ultimate authority rests at the top, or center, and the center makes the strategic decision to delegate decision-making authority or administration to the lower levels of government.")

[30] Dahl, note 24, at 12. In 1819, a unanimous Supreme Court was similarly dismissive. McCulloch v. Maryland, 17 U.S. (4 Wheat.) 316, 403 (1819) (opinion written by Chief Justice Marshall).

[31] *Ibid.*, at 196–97 n.7; Max Farrand (ed.), The Records of the Federal Convention of 1787, vol. I, at 202 (1966).

subjects it is permitted to regulate and that the states have supreme authority over whatever is left, if anything. The difference among these models lies in what those respective jurisdictions are in the first place. As one moves from confederation to federation to (mere) decentralization to no states at all, the powers of the national government increase from only a few specifically designated subjects to many such subjects and finally (under the last two models) to any subjects it wishes. Conversely, the exclusively state powers decrease from all but a few subjects, to only a few subjects, to no subjects at all – and ultimately to nonexistence.

It is common to invoke state sovereignty as a distinguishing factor, at least as between federations and mere decentralization. While there are varying definitions of sovereignty, my view is that the simplest and most comprehensive definition is the one synthesized by Heather Gerken from previous formulations: that which "formally guarantees a state's power to rule without interference over a policymaking domain of its own."[32] The powers that are within the state's own policymaking domain might relate to the structure of its government, the services it provides, its regulation of private conduct, or anything else. But whatever those powers are, they could be considered "sovereign" powers under Gerken's definition if the state is free to exercise them without interference.

The difficulty with even that straightforward definition is that, by its terms, a state would be considered a sovereign entity as long as there is at least one power, however trivial, that it is free to exercise without interference. Perhaps that definition could be jiggered to convert the word "sovereign" into an adjective that merely describes specific powers rather than entire states. But that modification would merely provide a convenient shorthand for powers over which states have sole dominion. And for that, we already have a useful word – autonomy.

Other writers offer more substantive definitions of sovereignty. Frank Michaelman, for example, defines sovereignty as "a state's interest in governing its own internal governmental arrangements and affairs."[33] But these and other substantive definitions[34] seem to me to reflect little more than the authors' own normative opinions concerning the powers they believe states ought to have.

For these reasons, I don't find the concept of state sovereignty particularly useful as a device for deciding how specific powers ought to be allocated between the federal government and the states.[35] Rather, with one possible qualification described

---

[32] Heather Gerken, *The Supreme Court, 2009 Term: Foreword, Federalism All the Way Down*, 124 Harv. L. Rev. 4, 11 (2010).

[33] Frank I. Michelman, *States' Rights and States' Roles: Permutations of "Sovereignty" in National League of Cities v. Usery*, 86 Yale L. J. 1165, 1192 (1977).

[34] For example, Lewis B. Kaden, *Politics, Money, and State Sovereignty: The Judicial Role*, 79 Colum. L. Rev. 847, 851 (1979).

[35] Accord, Andrzej Rapaczynski, *From Sovereignty to Process, The Jurisprudence of Federalism After Garcia*, 1985 Supreme Ct. Rev. 341, 346–59 (arguing that "sovereignty is of questionable value both as an analytical tool and as a norm defining a desirable feature of political organization").

later, sovereignty appears to be more a conclusory term that is used once one has independently determined that a particular power is constitutionally reserved for the states. And that, in turn, is the same as saying that the particular power is not one of those that the Constitution has enumerated for the central government. The Supreme Court has come close to acknowledging this. In *Bond v. United States*, it said "[A]ction that exceeds the National Government's enumerated powers undermines the sovereign interests of States."[36]

The one possible qualification concerns the "anti-commandeering" doctrine. A series of Supreme Court decisions struck down federal laws that had directed the states or state officials to aid in the disposal of radioactive waste,[37] to perform background checks in connection with particular kinds of firearms purchases,[38] and to prohibit sports gambling.[39] In each of those cases the Court reasoned that the framers had deliberately constructed a constitutional framework that recognized "dual [i.e., both federal and state] sovereignty." In the words of Justice Scalia in *Printz v. United States*, the Constitution gives Congress "the power to regulate individuals, not States."[40]

These cases arguably contradict my view that state sovereignty is just a conclusory label that one can attach to a determination of states' rights once that result is reached, rather than an independent reason to recognize states' rights in the first place. After all, activities like radioactive waste disposal, firearms purchases, and sports gambling have consequences that can, and typically do, reach across state lines. The federal laws in question would therefore seem to qualify as "necessary and proper" to the exercise of Congress's power to regulate interstate commerce.[41] Thus, for the Court to strike down each of those laws despite its apparent nexus to an enumerated power, there had to have been some independent reason. The Court located that reason in the notion of state sovereignty, a concept that in the Court's view prohibited one sovereign (the federal government) from telling another sovereign (the state) what to do.

---

[36] 564 U.S. 211, 225 (2011).
[37] New York v. United States, 505 U.S. 144 (1992).
[38] Printz v. United States, 521 U.S. 898 (1997).
[39] Murphy v. National Collegiate Athletic Assn., 138 S.Ct 1461 (2018).
[40] Printz v. United States, 521 U.S. 898, 920 (1997).
[41] In Murphy, 138 S.Ct at 1476, Justice Alito says the matter is quite simple, really: "[C]onspicuously absent from the list of powers given to Congress is the power to issue direct orders to the governments of the States. The anticommandeering doctrine simply represents the recognition of this limit on congressional authority." That reasoning is specious. The content of the laws passed by Congress in the exercise of its enumerated powers rarely find specific expression in the Constitution. When Congress passed Medicare, for example, no one seriously argued that the program was unconstitutional because Medicare is "conspicuously absent" from the list of enumerated powers. If Justice Alito believed that the case turned on whether the federal law fell within the scope of Congress's enumerated powers, then the proper inquiry should have been whether the cooperation of the states in regulating sports gambling was "necessary and proper" to the exercise of Congress's power to regulate interstate commerce – not whether the Constitution said anything about a specific congressional power to issue direct orders to the states.

On the fundamental question discussed in this book – whether state government should be abolished – I see little profit in getting bogged down debating whether the states should be seen as "sovereign" entities. In the domestic context, for purely descriptive purposes, the key variable that distinguishes the possible governmental models seems to be simply the range of specific subjects over which the national government and the constituent subunits have jurisdiction and the final say. And for normative purposes, I again see little gain in invoking or disparaging state "sovereignty" as an argument for or against a strong national government – much less as an argument for or against abolishing state government. It is not that those who invoke state sovereignty offer no other justifications for state government or for particular state powers; it is just that muttering the word "sovereignty" doesn't add anything to those arguments.

One last point on terminology: In the Federalist Papers, Madison takes pains to distinguish what he refers to as a "republic" (which he favors) from a "democracy" (which he doesn't). In Federalist 10, he defines a "pure democracy" as "a society consisting of a small number of citizens, who assemble and administer the government in person." In contrast, when Madison speaks of a "republic," he contemplates "the delegation of the government ... to a small number of citizens elected by the rest." He repeats that distinction in Federalist 14 and 39, adding in the latter Paper that the delegates are to be "persons holding their offices during pleasure, for a limited period, or during good behavior." In Federalist 39 he emphasizes that the government must "deriv[e] all its powers directly or indirectly from the great body of the people." And in all these Papers he explains why, in a large country, he prefers a republic to a democracy.

Today, what Madison called a "democracy" or a "pure democracy" (and rejects) would be called a "direct democracy." A modern American example of direct democracy would be local or statewide referenda and initiatives, where the people themselves make changes to the law. What Madison called a "republic" (and favors) would ordinarily be called a "representative democracy," the main form of government in the United States today. In this book I use the terms "republic" and "representative democracy" interchangeably in describing the United States. And I use terms like "democracy," "democratic," and "democratic norms" generically, to describe any system built upon popular sovereignty, majority rule (with exceptions), and political equality.[42]

With that background, we can return to the Federalist and Antifederalist Papers. These papers were in broad agreement that the Articles of Confederation had left the national government too weak to address the states' many common problems, particularly their inability to pay off their huge Revolutionary War debts. There

---

[42] See Jessica Bulman-Pozen & Miriam Seifter, *The Democracy Principle in State Constitutions*, 119 Mich. L. Rev. 859, 879–81 (2021) (synthesizing writings that define the essential elements of a democracy). For elaboration, see the text accompanying notes 4–6 of Chapter 2, below.

was a general consensus that a stronger national government was needed.[43] But the Antifederalists believed passionately that the proposed constitution overcorrected. They felt it made the national government too powerful and the states too weak. They cited the examples of Switzerland as a successful republic with a weak national government and, conversely, ancient Rome as a republic that had failed soon after expanding into what is now Italy.[44] They also saw the Articles of Confederation themselves as an example of a successful confederation with a weak national government, arguing that all the Articles really needed were a few patches.[45] The Federalists countered with historical examples of loose confederations that had failed, from ancient Greece to countries in eighteenth century Europe.[46]

Of special concern to the Antifederalists was the interaction of two provisions of the proposed Constitution. Article I, Section 8, contains a long list of the federal government's powers. At the end of that list appears one final power: "To make all Laws which shall be necessary and proper for carrying into Execution the foregoing Powers, and all other Powers vested by this Constitution in the Government of the United States, or in any Department or Officer Thereof ..." The Antifederalists worried that this "necessary and proper" clause would be interpreted so expansively that the federal government would be able to regulate almost any subject matter it wished. Worse still, in their eyes, was that Article VI, Clause 2, declares the Constitution and all federal laws and treaties made under it to be "the supreme Law of the Land," superseding any conflicting state laws. The Antifederalists feared the combination of these two provisions; they foresaw a virtually unlimited range of subjects on which the federal government could legislate and, whenever the federal government exercised that broad authority, the supremacy of the resulting federal law over state law. This, they worried, would render the states practically powerless.[47]

For their part, the Federalists defended the "necessary and proper" clause as simply a declaration of an obvious "truth" – that the power to do anything would be illusory without the means necessary to exercise that power.[48] Hamilton articulated the issue as one of responsibility without power: "A government ought to contain in itself every power requisite to the full accomplishment of the objects committed to its care."[49] Along similar lines, the Federalists stressed the need for the federal government to be able to enforce the laws (especially the tax laws) directly, rather than have to depend on the cooperation of state authorities.[50]

---

43 See, for example, Federalist 15–22; Antifederalist 21.
44 Antifederalist 18.
45 Antifederalist 2, 16.
46 Federalist 18–20.
47 Antifederalist 17, 32, 46.
48 Federalist 31, 33, 34.
49 Federalist 31.
50 Federalist 15, 16, 21.

The Antifederalists saw the absence of a Bill of Rights as yet another major obstacle to constraining the federal government. This was a deep and recurring concern.[51] All of those objections were to the lack of a Bill of Rights that would constrain federal government actions, not state actions. The objectors apparently felt that the various state constitutions already provided adequate protection against states' oppression of their citizens; they did not anticipate the rash of voter suppression measures for which so many of today's states have been responsible. Nor could they have foreseen the Fourteenth Amendment prohibition on states denying due process, much less that the Supreme Court would one day interpret the due process clause as incorporating almost all of the Bill of Rights provisions, thus making them binding on the states.[52]

Writing for the Federalists, Hamilton pushed back on the need for a bill of rights, though not very persuasively. He observed that the New York State Constitution similarly lacked a bill of rights, implying hypocrisy on the part of those New Yorkers who had criticized the proposed US Constitution for lacking one. He pointed out that various provisions of the Constitution already protect certain individual rights, including the right to trial by jury and the right to petition for habeas corpus. He mentioned that the Magna Carta and other bills of rights had typically been forced upon monarchs, not added to republican constitutions. On the whole, not a very convincing case.

All this begs the question: Assuming that the proposed Constitution did indeed bestow broad authority on the federal government, why, exactly, did the Antifederalists regard that as a problem?

There were several related reasons. The big one was that they simply found it antithetical to the concept of state sovereignty, which they valued. As they saw it, the states were willing to band together and create a central government to which they would delegate a few limited functions, ones that can best be performed collectively, like defense against foreign invasion. But their assumption was that the states would retain their separate sovereign statuses and the consequent authority over almost all other matters. In the words of Antifederalist 32, "The idea of a confederated government is that of a number of independent states entering into a compact, for the conducting certain general concerns, in which they have a common interest, leaving the management of their internal and local affairs to their separate

---

[51] For example, Antifederalist 13, 18, 45, 46, 54, 60, 84.

[52] The Bill of Rights applies directly only as a constraint on federal government action. But in *Gitlow v. New York*, 268 U.S. 652, 666 (1925), the Supreme Court assumed for the sake of argument that Fourteenth Amendment due process incorporates the First Amendment freedoms of speech and press, thus making them binding on the states as well. (In that case, the Court ultimately held that the challenged law did not violate either freedom of speech or freedom of the press.) Over the ensuing years, the Supreme Court read the Fourteenth Amendment due process clause as incorporating the vast majority of the other Bill of Rights protections. For a good catalog of those latter developments, see Cornell Law School Legal Information Institute, Incorporation Doctrine (Oct. 2022), www .law.cornell.edu/wex/incorporation_doctrine#:~:text=The%20incorporation%20doctrine%20is%20 a,applies%20both%20substantively%20and%20procedurally.

governments." If the Constitution were interpreted to allow federal control of practically everything, as they feared, the qualified autonomy of the various states – the essence of sovereignty – would cease to exist.

Madison understood this and went out of his way to assure the Antifederalists that state sovereignty would be preserved. In Federalist 39, he said:

> [O]n one hand, ... the Constitution is to be founded on the assent and ratification of the people of America, given by deputies elected for the special purpose; but, on the other, that this assent and ratification is to be given by the people, *not as individuals composing one entire nation, but as composing the distinct and independent States to which they respectively belong* [emphasis added].

Two centuries later, this passage would be cited in a dissenting opinion of Justice Clarence Thomas.[53] He saw further evidence of state sovereignty in Article VII of the Constitution, which provides that the Constitution would be binding only on those states that ratified it. Still, in Federalist 20, Madison and Hamilton did not try to hide their distaste for the concept of state sovereignty, conceding it only as an unavoidable political compromise.

Although there were also other concerns (discussed below), the multiple emphases on the erosion of the states' authority come very close to arguing that the preservation of the states as autonomous governing bodies is an end in itself. On this point, the language in the various Antifederalist Papers is explicit: "[O]ur sovereignty, as a state, [is] to vanish."[54] "It is agreed by most of the advocates of this new system, that the government which is proper for the United States should be a confederated one; that the respective states ought to retain a portion of their sovereignty ...," but the Necessary and Proper clause "would totally destroy all the powers of the individual states."[55] The federal taxing power alone will "swallow up all the power of the state governments."[56] The Constitution treats state governments "as mere dependencies, existing solely by its toleration."[57] A federal judiciary means that "the states will lose their rights, until they become so trifling and unimportant, as not to be worth having."[58] And

> I have ... endeavored to shew, that [the proposed Constitution] was calculated to abolish entirely the state governments, and to melt down the states into one entire government, for every purpose as well internal and local, as external and national. ... Perhaps nothing could have been better conceived to facilitate the abolition of the state governments than the constitution of the judicial.[59]

---

[53] Term Limits v. Thornton, 514 US 779, 846 (1995) (5-4 decision, with the majority holding that states cannot constitutionally put term limits on members of Congress).
[54] Antifederalist 30–31.
[55] Antifederalist 32.
[56] Antifederalist 33.
[57] Antifederalist 45.
[58] Antifederalist 81.
[59] Antifederalist 82.

One of the Antifederalist Papers asks rhetorically "[W]ho could imagine, that any man but a Virginian, were [excise taxes] found to be necessary, would ever have a voice towards enacting them? … And that, if ever it should be found necessary to curse this land with these hateful excisemen, any one, but a fellow citizen, should be entrusted with that office?"[60]

One of the several authors of Antifederalist 40, identified only as "a Farmer and Planter," phrases that central question in a different and revealing way: "Who authorized [the drafters of the Constitution] to speak the language of, We, the people, instead of, We, the states? States are the characteristics and the soul of a confederation. If the states be not the agents of this compact, it must be one great, consolidated, national government, of the people of all the states."

In my view, the answer to that central question should be clear. The delegates to the Convention were writing a constitution for a representative democracy. To be sure, the individual states intended to play a vital role in the resulting arrangement. But unless those member states are to be considered ends in themselves rather than instruments for promoting the welfare of the people, weren't the drafters right to center the Constitution on the interests of "we the people," not "we the states"?

As usual, Madison makes the point more eloquently than I have. In Federalist 45, he writes:

> Was, then, the American Revolution effected, was the American Confederacy formed, was the precious blood of thousands spilt, and the hard-earned substance of millions lavished, not that the people of America should enjoy peace, liberty, and safety, but that the government of the individual States, that particular municipal establishments, might enjoy a certain extent of power, and be arrayed with certain dignities and attributes of sovereignty? We have heard of the impious doctrine in the Old World, that the people were made for kings, not kings for the people. Is the same doctrine to be revived in the New, in another shape that the solid happiness of the people is to be sacrificed to the views of political institutions of a different form? It is too early for politicians to presume on our forgetting that the public good, the real welfare of the great body of the people, is the supreme object to be pursued; and that no form of government whatever has any other value than as it may be fitted for the attainment of this object. … [A]s far as the sovereignty of the States cannot be reconciled to the happiness of the people, the voice of every good citizen must be, "Let the former be sacrificed to the latter."

He reemphasizes this basic principle in Federalist 46, adding "The adversaries of the Constitution seem to have lost sight of the people altogether in their reasonings on this subject."

Together, Madison and Hamilton actually go a step further in Federalist 20. Rather than acknowledge state sovereignty and argue merely that it is less

[60] Antifederalist 30–31.

important than the welfare of the people, Federalist 20 would not recognize state sovereignty at all:

> [A] sovereignty over sovereigns, a government over governments, a legislation for communities, as contradistinguished from individuals, as it is a solecism in theory, so in practice, it is subversive of the order and ends of civil polity, by substituting VIOLENCE in place of LAW, or the destructive COERCION of the SWORD in place of the mild and salutary COERCION of the MAGISTRACY [emphasis in original].

To be fair, however, the Antifederalists' opposition to a strong federal government did not rest solely on their apparent view of state sovereignty as an end in itself. They also feared an undue concentration of power in a single national government. They saw the diffusion of power that would result from a true federal-state partnership as a safeguard against government oppression – an especially critical safeguard in a constitution that lacked a bill of rights. Oppression aside, Antifederalist 3 and 60 saw an undue concentration of power in the national government as a recipe for corruption. In defense, Madison, in Federalist 47, asserted separation of powers among the three branches of the federal government as a sufficient safeguard.

The Antifederalists perceived another problem with concentrating too much power in the national government. A country as large, as populous, and as diverse as the United States, they argued, cannot be governed effectively by a single republic – by which they meant a republic with an all-powerful national government. In contrast, they maintained, a confederation of separate, small republics – in this case, states – would be the better model for a country the size of ours.

Why was that so? The various Antifederalist Papers offered several reasons. The vast territories make travel to the seat of government nearly impossible for most people. In addition, the larger the area, and the larger and more diverse the population, the more variation there will be in the laws, climates, customs, opinions, and needs of the different regions; uniform regulation thus becomes both less feasible and less desirable.[61] One of the Antifederalist Papers additionally quotes Montesquieu, who had articulated some of these same concerns and had added one other: "[I]n a large republic there are men of large fortunes, and consequently of less moderation" who will oppress their fellow citizens.[62] (Who am I to question Montesquieu, but it's not clear why that problem would be confined to large republics. Perhaps his notion was not so much that a large republic expands the incentive for oppression, but that the power it adds makes it easier to act on that incentive.)

To the contrary, said the Federalists, it is precisely in large countries that republics work best. What the Antifederalists described as physically distant regions populated by citizens whose diverse needs and preferences merit narrowly tailored laws

---

[61] See Antifederalist 13, 14, 17, 18, 37, and 47.
[62] Antifederalist 17.

and policies, Federalist 10, for example, saw as warring factions that only a strong national government can control. Moreover, the same Paper argued, larger populations mean a greater number of qualified representatives to choose from and a larger electorate that is both less vulnerable to trickery or oppression and more diverse in its interests. Federalist 14 conceded that these particular arguments assume a federal authority that is limited to certain specific subjects and that the arguments would be weaker if the Constitution were proposing the abolition of state government. (I agree and in this book do not offer either of these arguments to support the abolition of state government.) Finally, as for the difficulty of travel to a distant seat of government, Federalist 14 notes that the problem would be serious if the Constitution were proposing direct citizen participation in the decisions of government; the representative model substantially reduces the number of individuals who would have to travel. Today one might add that physical travel is not only far easier, but in the digital age more frequently avoidable. Whether the states are essential to the optimal diffusion of power is discussed in detail in Chapter 5, Section A.

These broad differences played out in the debates over many of the specific constitutionally enumerated powers. Although there was a consensus that the national government was best situated to provide a defense against foreign invasion,[63] there was disagreement over whether to authorize it to maintain a standing army, especially in peacetime.[64] There was strenuous disagreement over the professed need for the national government to prevent hostilities among states or other internal violence.[65] The opposing parties also clashed over the scope of Congress's powers to tax citizens directly (as opposed to requisitioning the states), borrow, and spend[66]; to regulate interstate commerce[67]; to have the final say in regulating the times, places, and manner of congressional elections[68]; to set uniform rules for naturalization[69]; and to create a federal judiciary.[70]

In contrast, there were a few subjects that received surprisingly scant attention. Neither the Federalist Papers nor the Antifederalist Papers devoted much space to the question of slavery. That subject came up only briefly, in connection with two different constitutional provisions. First, Article I, Section 9, Clause 1 (which expired on its own terms after twenty years and at any rate was superseded by the Thirteenth Amendment,

---

[63] See Federalist 2–5. Although the consensus was fairly broad, at least one person – Patrick Henry – dissented. He argued that the states didn't need the protection of the national government; the state militias, he contended, could get the job done. See Antifederalist 4.

[64] Compare Federalist 16 and 22–28 with Antifederalist 15 and 23–29.

[65] Compare Federalist 6–10 with Antifederalist 6–7. In fact, the author of Antifederalist 7 (identified as "Philanthropos") contended that, if anything, a strong central government that imposes uniform national laws on the states will make civil war more likely, not less so.

[66] Compare Federalist 12, 15, 21, 23, 30, 32–34, and 43 with Antifederalist 29–35.

[67] Compare Federalist 11, 23, and 42 with Antifederalist 11.

[68] Compare Federalist 43 and 59–61 with Antifederalist 26, 36, 44, 52, 59, and 61.

[69] See Antifederalist 11.

[70] Compare Federalist 22 with Antifederalist 80–82.

which prohibits slavery), reads as follows: "The Migration or Importation of such Persons as any of the States now existing shall think proper to admit, shall not be prohibited by the Congress prior to the Year one thousand eight hundred and eight …" The framers could not bring themselves to include the words "slave" or "slavery" in the text of the Constitution, but the import of this provision was that the States were free to import slaves until 1808. After that, Congress *could* prohibit the practice.

The few Antifederalists who addressed the issue were divided. On the one hand, both Antifederalist 15 (anonymous) and Antifederalist 16 (by "Alfred") objected to allowing the importation of slaves at all. The former commended Rhode Island for being the only state that had refused to send delegates to the constitutional convention, in part because their leaders saw little chance that the Constitution would prohibit the importation of slaves. On the other hand, in Antifederalist 54, Rawlins Lowndes of South Carolina objected to allowing Congress to prohibit the importation of slaves after 1808. He remarked that slavery can be "justified on the principles of religion, humanity, and justice; for certainly to translate a set of human beings from a bad country to a better, was fulfilling every part of these principles."[71]

The middle ground, a political compromise, was staked out by Hamilton and Madison. In Federalist 8, Hamilton acknowledged that the Constitution wasn't perfect but argued that it was at least better than the Articles of Confederation that it would replace. In particular, he pointed out that the Articles of Confederation gave Congress no power ever to prohibit the importation of slaves, while the proposed Constitution at least would give Congress that power after 1808. In Federalist 42, Madison made a similar point, while calling slavery "barbarism" and expressing regret that slavery would continue for at least twenty years.

Second, Article I, Section 2, Clause 3, originally read: "Representatives and direct Taxes shall be apportioned among the several States which may be included within this Union, according to their respective Numbers, which shall be determined by adding to the whole Number of free Persons … three fifths of all other Persons." As with the 1808 clause, the framers were unwilling to debase the constitutional text with the words "slave" or "slavery." Translated, this provision meant that for purposes of the population estimates that would determine how many House members each state gets, a slave would count as 3/5 of a person.

In Antifederalist Paper 54, "Brutus" condemns the importation of slaves as "inhuman" and calls its proponents "barbarous." He argues that if the southern states are

---

[71] Campaigning for the presidency, Florida Governor Ron DeSantis in 2023 famously offered an analogous view, claiming that slavery had taught African Americans skills that would benefit them once they were freed. See Kevin Sullivan & Lori Rozsa, The Washington Post, DeSantis Doubles Down on Claim That Some Blacks Benefited from Slavery (July 22, 2023), www.washingtonpost.com/politics/2023/07/22/desantis-slavery-curriculum/. See also Antifederalist 11, where James Winthrop criticized Pennsylvania for contaminating America's "pure race" by admitting diverse foreigners to naturalization. In a veiled reference to Rhode Island's anti-slavery laws, he implied that only Rhode Island had worse policies than Pennsylvania.

going to treat slaves as property, then slaves should not be counted at all for purposes of those states' representation in Congress.

But Federalist 54, believed to have been authored by either Hamilton or Madison (the records are not clear), once again opts for compromise. While referring to the southern states' "barbarous policy of considering as property a part of their human brethren," this Paper takes the position that all the states in the union deserve to have their views reflected in the Constitution. It argues that, given the laws that prevail in the southern states, slaves are in fact *both* persons and property. Those two authors were therefore willing to accept the 3/5 clause as a compromise.

Similarly striking was the almost complete absence of any attempt to justify equal Senate representation for states of wildly differing populations. The Federalist writers were clearly not fans, though they accepted that principle too as a necessary political compromise.[72] That Federalists would begrudge the arrangement is not surprising. Their vision of the new republic was that of a national government whose mission is to directly serve the people, not the states. Granting residents of some states far greater per capita Senate representation than others would be inconsistent with that mission.

What might initially seem counter-instinctive is that the same criticisms were coming from several Antifederalist writers.[73] After all, their commitment to state sovereignty would seem consistent with the notion of giving each state, not each individual, equal Senate representation.

But it was the high-population states whose residents would suffer the greatest disadvantage under this scheme.[74] It was likely no coincidence, then, that both the Federalist and Antifederalist writers who condemned the principle of equal Senate representation were from high-population states. Federalist Papers 22, 37, 43, and 62, which criticized equal state suffrage, were all written by James Madison (from Virginia) or Alexander Hamilton (from New York). Antifederalist Papers 36, 47, and 54, which echoed the same criticisms, were written by Richard Henry Lee (from Virginia), Samuel Bryan (from Pennsylvania), and Robert Yates (from New York), respectively.

The only qualification to add is that Yates ended up striking a more ambivalent tone. In Antifederalist 54, he wrote

> On every principle of equity, and propriety, representation in a government should be in exact proportion to the numbers, or the aids afforded by the persons represented. How unreasonable, and unjust then is it that Delaware should have a representation in the senate, equal to Massachusetts, or Virginia? The latter of which

---

[72] See, for example, Federalist 22, 37, 43, and 62.
[73] See Antifederalist 36, 47, and 54.
[74] Steven Levitsky and Daniel Ziblatt attribute the zeal for equal Senate suffrage to both slave states and states with low populations. See Steven Levitsky & Daniel Ziblatt, Tyranny of the Minority 151–56 (2023).

contains ten times her numbers and is to contribute to the aid of the general government in that proportion?

But in Antifederalist 62, he seems to approve of the equal suffrage provision in principle for a confederation, by which he means a country in which the member states retain the bulk of their sovereign powers. The merits of giving each state equal Senate representation are discussed more fully in Chapter 2, Section A.

If the Federalist and Antifederalist Papers are a guide, the Electoral College system was also surprisingly noncontroversial. Federalist 68, authored by Hamilton, extolled the virtues of the people voting for electors rather than for the President directly. Antifederalist 72, authored by "Republicus," preferred direct election by the people. But those were the only mentions of the Electoral College that I could find in either set of papers, and neither paper addressed the risk of the Electoral College producing a President whom the people didn't want, an issue taken up in Chapter 2, Section B.

As these observations about the Federalist and Antifederalist Papers demonstrate, the various authors provided thoughtful and serious analyses on a range of issues raised by the proposed constitution. But they were also flesh and blood human beings, and no discussion of these Papers would be complete without additional reference to the emotions that jump off so many of their pages.

First, deep passions on both sides often led to overheated, ad hominem attacks. To put it bluntly, these battles appear to have reflected genuine animosities.

Hamilton especially did not mince words. In Federalist 8, he derides "the airy phantoms that flit before the distempered imaginations of some of [the Constitution's] adversaries." In Federalist 12 he accuses the objectors of "ill-informed jealousy." In Federalist 84 he dismisses an objection to the Constitution as "the offspring of extreme ignorance or extreme dishonesty." And in his concluding Federalist 85, he refers to "the insincerity and affectation of some of the zealous adversaries of the plan of the convention."

The Antifederalists, for their part, were at least as venomous and a tad more verbose. Antifederalist 1 depicts the Federalists as:

> violent partisans ... [who] consist generally, of the NOBLE order of Cincinnatus, holders of public securities, men of great wealth and expectations of public office, Bankers and Lawyers: these with their train of dependents form the Aristocratick combination. The Lawyers, in particular, keep up an incessant declamation for its adoption; like greedy gudgeons they long to satiate their voracious stomachs with the golden bait.

Several other Antifederalist Papers similarly portray the Federalists as aristocrats who look down upon the masses.[75]

---

[75] For example, Antifederalist 9, 26, and 27.

Other Antifederalist Papers paint the Federalists as either lunatics or tyrants. Antifederalist 6, for example, attacks one of the Federalists' positions as having "sprung from the deranged brain of Publius" [the pen name for the authors of the Federalist Papers]. Antifederalist 40 attacks the "despotic advocates" of the proposed Constitution: "Unparalleled duplicity! That men should oppose tyranny under a pretence of patriotism, that they might themselves become the tyrants. How does such villainy disgrace human nature!"

Apart from the personal insults, both sets of papers reveal profound distrust – of the federal government by the Antifederalists and of the state governments by the Federalists. In Antifederalist 1, an anonymous author sums up his feelings this way: "I had rather be a free citizen of the small republic of Massachusetts, than an oppressed subject of the great American empire." Antifederalist 3 argues that more centralized power means more power in the hands of a few, which in turn increases the potential for corruption. Antifederalist 9 satirizes the expected all-powerful tyrannical central government.

Conversely, Hamilton makes clear that he would not trust the states to attend to the needs of the people. In Federalist 30, he defends the federal taxing power as the only way the federal government can reliably sustain itself. The Articles of Confederation had obligated the states to fund the federal government through requisitions, but too often the states had failed to come through, and under the Articles of Confederation there was nothing the federal government could do about it. Distrust similarly compels Hamilton to defend the "necessary and proper" clause. In Federalist 33, he acknowledges that common sense should make that clause unnecessary but says "the danger which most threatens our political welfare is that the State governments will finally sap the foundations of the Union; and might therefore think it necessary, in so cardinal a point, to leave nothing to con-struction." And in Federalist 80, he expresses various concerns about state courts acting in the parochial interests of their own territories or citizens whenever the opposing parties are two states, one state and citizens of another state, or citizens of different states.

More generally, Hamilton says in Federalist 85 that the proposed constitution gives security to a republican form of government, liberty, and property

> chiefly in the restraints which the preservation of the Union will impose on local factions and insurrections, and on the ambition of powerful individuals in single States, who may acquire credit and influence enough, from leaders and favorites, to become the despots of the people; … and in the precautions against the repetition of those practices on the part of the State governments which have undermined the foundations of property and credit, have planted mutual distrust in the breasts of all classes of citizens, and have occasioned an almost universal prostration of morals.

Madison agrees, arguing in Federalist 45 that, if anything, the states are a greater threat to the federal government than vice versa.

While both the ad hominem rhetoric and expressions of distrust seem equally distributed between the Federalist and Antifederalist Papers, there was at least one kind of personal excess on which the Antifederalist Papers held a clear monopoly – hysteria. Their pages overflow with apocalyptic warnings of the horrors that the proposed constitution would bring. The following sample – only partial, but representative – imparts the flavor:

Antifederalist 26 (in Part I) informs that if you don't pay your federal excise taxes,

> [t]he excise officers have power to enter your houses at all times, by night or day, and if you refuse them entrance, they can, under pretense of searching for excisable goods, that the duty has not been paid on, break open your doors, chests, trunks, desks, boxes, and rummage your houses from bottom to top. Nay, they often search the clothes, petticoats, and pockets of ladies or gentlemen (particularly when they are coming from on board an East-India ship), and if they find any the least article that you cannot prove the duty to be paid on, seize it and carry it away with them; who are the very scum and refuse of mankind, who value not their oaths, and will break them for a shilling.

Moreover, if you

> refuse or delay to pay your taxes, or do anything that they shall think proper to order you to do, they can, and I have not a doubt but they will, send the militia of Pennsylvania, Boston, or any other state or place, to cut your throats, ravage and destroy your plantations, drive away your cattle and horses, abuse your wives, kill your infants, and ravish your daughters.

But that is not all "they" will do. Antifederalist 27 contains this passage:

> [A] standing army, composed of the purgings of the jails of Great Britain, Ireland and Germany, shall be employed in collecting the revenues of this our king and government ... And (which is not improbable) should any one of those soldiers when employed on duty in collecting the taxes, strike off the arm (with his sword) of one of our fellow slaves, we will conceive our case remarkably fortunate if he leaves the other arm on. And moreover, because we are aware that many of our fellow slaves shall be unable to pay their taxes, ... our federal judges ... shall have power, without jury or trial, to order the said miscreants for immediate execution; nor will we think their sentence severe unless after being hanged they are also to be both beheaded and quartered.

According to Antifederalist 29, in addition to the army, "the whole host of revenue officers, will swarm over the land, devouring the hard earnings of the industrious like the locusts of old, impoverishing and desolating all before them."

The power to tax, we are advised in Antifederalist 33,

> will introduce itself into every corner of the city, and country – It will wait upon the ladies at their toilett, and will not leave them in any of their domestic concerns; it will accompany them to the ball, the play, and the assembly; it will go with them

when they visit, and will, on all occasions, sit beside them in their carriages, nor will it desert them even at church; it will enter the house of every gentleman, watch over his cellar, wait upon his cook in the kitchen, follow the servants into the parlour, preside over the table, and note down all he eats or drinks; it will attend him to his bedchamber, and watch him while he sleeps; it will take cognizance of the professional man in his office, or his study; it will watch the merchant in the countinghouse, or in his store; it will follow the mechanic to his shop, and in his work, and will haunt him in his family, and in his bed; it will be a constant companion of the industrious farmer in all his labour, it will be with him in the house, and in the field, observe the toil of his hands, and the sweat of his brow; it will penetrate into the most obscure cottage; and finally, it will light upon the head of every person in the United States. To all these different classes of people, and in all these circumstances, in which it will attend them, the language in which it will address them, will be GIVE! GIVE!

And in Antifederalist 34, Patrick Henry sums it all up: "The federal sheriff may commit what oppression, make what distresses, he pleases, and ruin you with impunity; for how are you to tie his hands? Have you any sufficiently decided means of preventing him from sucking your blood by speculations, commissions, and fees?" (Give me liberty or give me blood?)

A fitting place to conclude this overview of US federalism's historical origins is with Thomas Paine's Introduction to *Common Sense*: "PERHAPS the sentiments contained in the following pages, are not *yet* sufficiently fashionable to procure them general favor; a long habit of not thinking a thing *wrong*, gives it a superficial appearance of being *right*, and raises at first a formidable outcry in defense of custom. But the tumult soon subsides. Time makes more converts than reason" [emphasis in original].[76]

Paine thus acknowledges that his reasoned arguments might not "yet" be received favorably, though history would later prove that he had vastly underestimated his powers of persuasion. His hope, quickly realized, was that the already long history of oppression by the English monarchy, together with time for the ideas in his pamphlet to percolate and to feel more comfortable, would spur people to accept his call for independence.

Might a similar hope be expressed that one day – admittedly, not soon – there will be popular sentiment for an America without state government? "Perhaps ... a long habit of not thinking [our current federal system] *wrong* gives it a superficial appearance of being *right*." And, perhaps, the passage of further time will gradually make the idea of a two-level, national/local, unitary system more palatable.[77]

---

[76] Project Gutenberg, note 12.
[77] No, I am not comparing myself to Thomas Paine. I'm just cannibalizing his idea.

2

Democracy

Structural Problems

In recent years, the literature has called particular, and much-needed, attention to the cracks in the democratic foundations of the United States.[1] Some of those cracks are structural, the product of a constitutional design that elevates states over the people they are supposed to serve. At the heart of all these structural sources of counter-majoritarianism is the central constitutional theory of dual (federal and state) sovereignty. On that subject, most of the writings have singled out equal Senate representation of the states, the Electoral College, or the constitutional amendment process.[2] Several authors have more comprehensively covered two or more of those constitutional blind spots.[3]

Other writers have focused on the purposeful counter-majoritarian actions of state legislators, other state officials, and their enablers in both the public and the private sectors. There are separate massive literatures, for example, on gerrymandering, on specific voter suppression strategies, and on other state-regulated election practices.

---

[1] Those works are cited, where relevant, throughout the pages that follow.

[2] Sanford Levinson, denouncing the antidemocratic elements of the constitutionally mandated legislative process, goes beyond the equal representation of states in the Senate. He calls out bicameralism itself, the presidential veto power, and the powers of a lame duck Congress. Sanford Levinson, Our Undemocratic Constitution: Where the Constitution Goes Wrong (And How We the People Can Correct It) 25–77 (2006).

[3] A small sample includes Jack M. Balkin, The Cycles of Constitutional Time (2020); Edwin Chemerensky, No Democracy Lasts Forever: How the Constitution Threatens the United States (2024); Robert A. Dahl, How Democratic Is the American Constitution? (2nd ed. 2003); Tom Ginsburg & Aziz Z. Huq, How to Save a Constitutional Democracy (2018); Mark A. Graber, Sanford Levinson & Mark Tushnet (eds.), Constitutional Democracy in Crisis? (2018); Samuel Issacharoff *et al.*, The Law of Democracy – Legal Structure of the Political Process (6th ed. 2022); Alexander Keyssar, The Right to Vote: The Contested History of Democracy in the United States (rev. ed. 2009); Levinson, note 2; Steven Levitsky & Daniel Ziblatt, Tyranny of the Minority (2023) (including abundant helpful comparisons to the ways in which other democracies have either risen to the challenge or failed to do so); Steven Levitsky & Daniel Ziblatt, How Democracies Die (2018); Nancy MacLean, Democracy in Chains: The Deep History of the Radical Right's Stealth Plan for America (2017); Jessica Bulman-Pozen & Miriam Seifter, *The Democracy Principle in State Constitutions*, 119 Mich. L. Rev. 859 (2021); Pamela S. Karlan, *The New Countermajoritarian Difficulty*, 109 Calif. L. Rev. 2323, Part II (2021).

Still other writers have maintained that, to the contrary, state government affirmatively advances democratic norms. Those arguments will be deferred to Chapter 5, which examines more generally the contention that the benefits of state government outweigh the many democracy-related and other harms described in this and the next two chapters.

Three preliminary comments are necessary: a definition, a point of emphasis, and an acknowledgment.

I'll start by defining my terms. What, exactly, does it take for a country to qualify as a democracy? Importantly too, what *isn't* required?

Although there is no universally accepted definition of democracy, I go here with the most commonly understood – and in my judgment the most helpful – definition: A democracy is a system that embodies popular sovereignty (rule by the people), majority rule (more on that in a moment), and political equality.[4]

The main difficulty in applying that definition of democracy is that the various elements can be either hard to enforce or even in conflict. What if a constitution, like that of the United States, systematically gives some voters drastically different per capita representation than others, in both the legislative and the executive branches of the national government? There might well be popular sovereignty, but no political equality and, from time to time, a loss of majority rule as well. What if the majority of the people's chosen representatives in a state legislature enact an election process that makes it disproportionately harder for members of a racial or partisan minority to vote? In that scenario, the appearance of majority rule comes at the expense of actual political equality. As one eminent scholar put it, "Two visions of political malfunction – one stressing fear of the many and the other stressing fear of the few – coexist in our traditional views of government."[5]

To insist on perfection would rule out calling any country a democracy. Some leeway is needed. But how much and what kind?

Whether democracy requires that judges be elected by the people, as they are under most US state constitutions, will be taken up in Chapter 6. Important as the issue is in debates over the meaning of democracy, I do not see the difference between the various methods of selecting judges as a factor favoring either the retention or the abolition of state government. Any of those selection methods would be possible in either a federation or a unitary republic. So I will put off that debate for now. Rather, the focus in this and Chapter 3 will be on the officially political

---

[4] See, for example, Bulman-Pozen & Seifter, note 3, at 864 (citing copious scholarly commentary that defines "democracy" as requiring those same three elements). The authors' main thesis – convincingly demonstrated – is that state constitutions promote majoritarianism and political equality more explicitly and more effectively than the US Constitution does. As a potential benefit of state government, that feature is taken up in Chapter 5, Section G.

[5] Neil K. Komesar, *A Job for the Judges: The Judiciary and the Constitution in a Massive and Complex Society*, 86 Mich. L. Rev. 657, 668 (1988). See also Levitsky & Ziblatt, Tyranny, note 3 (calling out many of the ways in which US law consistently privileges a partisan minority).

branches – the applicable constitutional parameters and the practices of state officials that deviate from the principle of majority rule.

My view, as noted in the Introduction, is that departures from the strict requirement of majority rule are consistent with democratic theory only when they are
necessary to protect one of the other two elements of democracy itself – popular sovereignty or political equality – or are otherwise critical to the protection of any other
rights that are fundamental in a democracy or to the basic institutions of government.[6] As will be seen, the various constitutional departures from pure majoritarian
rule that are discussed in this chapter were not designed for the benign purposes of
safeguarding popular sovereignty, political equality, fundamental rights, or essential
government institutions. They were simply unavoidable concessions to state sovereignty. Similarly, abusive state actions in the contexts of districting maps, voter
qualifications, and election processes are not aimed at, and are often deliberately
intended to subvert, political equality.

The world's democracies come in all shapes and sizes. Among the modern variations, the broadest distinction is probably between what Robert Dixon and others[7] have described as majoritarian democracy and consensus democracy. In their
starkest forms, majoritarian democracies allow majorities to govern without regard
to minority representation. Consensus democracies also allow majorities to govern,
but in ways that simultaneously assure meaningful representation of significant
racial, political, or other minorities.

In most discussions of either democratic theory or electoral reform, that distinction is essential. But for present purposes, a different point is more crucial:
Whichever of these broad political philosophies one favors, neither of them contemplates what we see all too often in the United States – a systematic bias in favor
of governance by a partisan *minority*.

Nor is majority rule the only democratic casualty of the constitutional flaws and
state actions that are the subject of this book. Political equality has also fallen prey.
Indeed, the two fault lines are causally related, for it is political inequality that has
bred minority rule. Only by awarding some citizens more say in the electoral process than others has it been possible to achieve minority rule on so regular a basis.

From this discussion, I draw two conclusions: First, these sorts of deviations from
both majority rule and political equality are both serious and inconsistent with any
credible definition of democracy. Second, most of those deviations – again, not

---

6   For an overlapping formulation, see Levitsky & Ziblatt, Tyranny, note 3, at 137–43 (agreeing that
    supermajority requirements are necessary to protect certain basic civil liberties and to preserve the
    rules of democracy itself, but insisting that the majority prevail over the minority in electing leaders
    and that those leaders, once elected, be allowed to govern).

7   See, for example, Robert G. Dixon, Jr., Democratic Representation: Reapportionment in Law and
    Politics 10 (1968); Arend Lijphart, Democracies: Patterns of Majoritarian and Consensus Government
    in Twenty-One Countries (1984); Arend Lijphart & Bernard Grofman (eds.), Choosing an Electoral
    System: Issues and Alternatives (1984).

all – are ones that would not occur but for either the constitutionally assigned powers of states or the ways in which state legislatures or individual state officials have exercised those powers.

Next, a point of emphasis: As laid out in the Introduction, I am proposing here a true unitary republic that retains ample space for decentralized decision-making – *not* the wholesale transfer of all, or even most, state power to an ever-expanding national government. But instead of decentralization occurring through a combination of state action and whatever powers each state chooses to delegate to its local political subdivisions, decentralized power would be exercised by the local political subdivisions directly. They could act on their own or in partnership with either the national government or other local governments. Either way, they would no longer need the permission of their state governments, because the latter would no longer exist. Their only legal constraints would be the US Constitution and other sources of national law.

In this respect, my prescription differs from that of the several other writers who have similarly embraced expansion of local government powers. Their models all contemplate the retention of state government.[8] In an especially thoughtful article, Heather Gerken takes the expansion of local government power a step further. She argues that even those scholars who have encouraged greater devolutions of power from state governments to local governments have been remiss to stop with cities and towns. She advocates "federalism all the way down."[9] By this, Gerken means to include all the governmental "special purpose institutions" that, like cities and towns, lack sovereignty – for example, "juries, zoning commissions, local school boards, locally elected prosecutors' offices, state administrative agencies, and the like."[10] She makes a strong case. But if, as I propose, state government were abolished and the bulk of its current functions transferred to local governments, I would

---

[8] For example, David L. Shapiro, Federalism: A Dialogue 91–94 (1995); Nestor M. Davidson, *Cooperative Localism: Federal-Local Collaboration in an Era of State Sovereignty*, 93 Virginia L. Rev. 959 (2007); Barry Friedman, *Valuing Federalism*, 82 Minnesota L. Rev. 317, 389–91 (1997); Heather Gerken, The Supreme Court, 2009 Term: Foreword, *Federalism All the Way Down*, 124 Harvard L. Rev. 4 (2010); Deborah Jones Merritt, *The Guarantee Clause and State Autonomy: Federalism for a Third Century*, 88 Columbia L. Rev. 1, 7–8 (1988).

[9] Gerken, note 8; see also Roderick M. Hills, Jr., *The Constitutional Rights of Private Governments*, 78 NYU L. Rev. 144 (2003) (extending federalist principles even further, to "private governments" such as homeowners' associations, universities, corporations, and other institutions that govern individuals). Notably, Gerken does not specifically list counties (which are not "special purpose institutions" anyway) among her examples of entities to which broader powers should be devolved. Typically, but not always, municipalities are subordinate to their county governments. See generally Wikipedia, *Local Government in the United States*, https://en.wikipedia.org/wiki/Local_government_in_the_United_States. In this book I am agnostic with respect to (a) whether counties should continue to exist in the absence of states, and (b) if so, what their powers and roles should be vis-a-vis their constituent municipalities, special purpose institutions, and/or unincorporated areas. See Chapter 6, Section A.

[10] Gerken, note 8, at 8.

leave it to those local governments themselves to decide how best to utilize these special purpose institutions.

The final preliminary note is an acknowledgment. State government is not all that ails our democracy. As the Introduction concedes,[11] there are multiple other causes: single-member districts for the US House; the Senate's manipulation of the judicial appointment process; the weakening of traditional separation of powers constraints by modern political parties; racial, social, and economic inequalities that skew the political process; the roles of money and lobbying in exacerbating those inequalities; unprincipled elected officers; and, today, the threats of mob violence by the losers of elections.

Fine. Not *all* the threats to our democracy are the fault of the states. But most of them are. As the following discussion will show, the overwhelming majority of the problems that imperil our democracy can be traced, in most cases directly and in some cases indirectly, to either the states' constitutionally hardwired powers (this chapter) or the behaviors of state legislatures or state executive branch officials (Chapter 3).

So let's start with those counter-majoritarian attributes of states that are baked into the Constitution. This chapter identifies five of them. Unlike the examples considered in Chapter 3 (behaviors of state legislatures), these are examples to which one might respond as follows:

> Yes, these constitutional features are counter-majoritarian, but you don't have to abolish states in order to purge the counter-majoritarianism. That's overkill. If you want to fix the problem of small and large states getting the same number of Senators, for example, you could keep states and just apportion US Senate districts by population, as we do with House districts.[12] Sure, maybe that solution would introduce other sources of counter-majoritarian outcomes, like urban versus rural residential patterns and single-member legislative districts,[13] as is the case with House elections. But even without states that would be equally true, because the senators would still be elected from subdivisions of some kind.[14]

Similarly, one might observe, you don't have to get rid of states just to replace the Electoral College with a national popular vote or to reduce the dominant role of states in the counter-majoritarian constitutional amendment process. And so on.

Those responses would be fair. You don't *have to* abolish state government to neutralize their constitutionally enshrined counter-majoritarian effects. But it's also

---

[11] See Introduction, text accompanying notes 16–20.

[12] Put aside for the moment the potential problem posed by Art. V of the Constitution, which appears to bar any amendment of the Constitution's guarantee of equal state suffrage in the Senate. This issue is considered in Sections A and E.

[13] See Chapter 3, Section A.

[14] Unless, perhaps, a system of proportional representation were adopted. That too has pros and cons. See Chapter 6, Section B.

true that state government is a but for cause of those effects; without it, none of those particular counter-majoritarian effects could occur. Moreover, while there exist less drastic alternative solutions to the constitutionally enshrined counter-majoritarian effects discussed in this chapter, abolition of state government is the only way to excise some of the counter-majoritarian state legislative behaviors taken up in Chapter 3. Abolition is also the only way to eliminate the fiscal waste discussed in Chapter 4 of this book. And as Chapter 5 illustrates, the countervailing affirmative benefits claimed for state government turn out to be minimal, if any. So, why not kill two birds with one stone?

Abraham Lincoln asked us to resolve "that government of the people, by the people, for the people, shall not perish from the earth."[5] From Lincoln's simple statement of popular sovereignty, it is but a short step to two other guiding principles: Every citizen should have an equal voice in the selection of the country's leaders. And, subject only to the exceptions described above, the majority should be able to get elected and then to govern.

Thus, the criticisms in this and Chapter 3 deserve to resonate with everyone who believes in representative democracy. In his book advocating abolition of the Electoral College, Jesse Wegman hit the nail on the head when he implored the reader to "approach [his] book not as a liberal or a conservative, not as a Republican or a Democrat, not as a Texan or a Californian or a Kansan or a New Yorker, but as an American."[16] I humbly offer the same plea here.

With that, it's time to consider the major constitutional barriers to majority rule:

A TWO SENATORS PER STATE

Article I, Section 3, Clause 1 of the US Constitution reads: "The Senate of the United States shall be composed of two Senators from each State …"[17] Article V, which lays out the procedure for amending the Constitution, contains an exception to that process: "[N]o State, without its Consent, shall be deprived of its equal Suffrage in the Senate." As discussed in Section D, a literal reading of this exception would make it impossible ever to amend the equal Senate suffrage provision.

Neither the principle of equal state suffrage in the Senate nor the decision to preserve that principle for eternity was an accident. The Constitutional Convention was marked by a fierce battle between those who wanted every *citizen's* vote to count equally in electing members of Congress and those who wanted the *states* to be counted equally. As noted in Chapter 1, the low-population states (along

---

[5] Abraham Lincoln, Gettysburg Address (Nov. 19, 1863), reproduced in Abraham Lincoln Online, Gettysburg Address, www.abrahamlincolnonline.org/lincoln/speeches/gettysburg.htm.

[16] Jesse Wegman, Let the People Pick the President: The Case for Abolishing the Electoral College 34 (2020).

[17] This clause goes on to say that US senators are to be chosen by the state legislatures, but the Seventeenth Amendment, ratified in 1913, now provides for their direct election by the people.

with the slave states, large and small) generally feared that, under a one-person-one-vote system, their influence would be overwhelmed by the larger delegations from the high-population states. Leaders of the high-population states believed that, in the democracy that they were proposing to create, each of their citizens should enjoy the same voting power and the same per capita representation as everyone else (as long as they were white male landowners).

In his landmark treatment of the equal representation principle, Robert Dixon distinguished two ways of viewing the right that is at stake. It can be seen as the individual right of each voter to have the same say as voters in other districts. Or (in the context of legislative elections), it can be viewed as the collective right of the people in a given district to equal representation in the legislature.[18]

With the impasse threatening to undo the Convention, Benjamin Franklin urged both sides to seek middle ground. A majority of the delegates ultimately voted for the "Great Compromise," a proposal that had long been advanced by Roger Sherman of Connecticut. The compromise was a bicameral national legislature. Each state would have two senators, but in the House of Representatives the size of each state's delegation would be proportional to its population.[19]

If they wanted the Constitution to become a reality, those who believed in the principle of one-person-one-vote had no choice but to capitulate. But they were not happy about it. In Federalist 37, Madison observed that the interests of large states and small states diverged. He lamented that, as a result, the delegates to the constitutional convention were "compelled to sacrifice theoretical propriety to the force of extraneous considerations."

As Robert Dahl points out, several others among the most distinguished framers of the Constitution were also "bitterly opposed" to the counter-majoritarian concept of equal representation of states in the Senate. In Hamilton's words,

> As states are a collection of individual men, which ought we to respect most, the rights of the people composing them, or the artificial beings resulting from the composition? Nothing could be more preposterous or absurd than to sacrifice the former to the latter. It has been sd. that if the smaller States renounce *equality*, they renounce at the same their *liberty*. The truth is it is a contest for power, not for liberty [punctuation added].[20]

James Wilson, speaking at the Constitutional Convention, put the point concisely: "Can we forget for whom we are forming a government? Is it for *men*, or for the imaginary beings called *States*?"[21]

---

[18] Dixon, note 7.
[19] *Wesberry v. Sanders*, 376 U.S. 1, 9–14 (1964). That description is subject to the infamous proviso for counting three-fifths of the slave populations. See the discussion in the text accompanying note 117.
[20] Dahl, note 3, at 13–14, quoting Hamilton (emphasis and punctuation in original).
[21] *Ibid.*, at 52.

I have previously written that "countries don't immigrate; people do."[22] By way of analogy, and in keeping with the emphases of Hamilton and Wilson on states as "artificial" or "imaginary" creations, I would add here: "States don't have interests; people do." And from that, it seems a short step to "States shouldn't vote; people should."

Montesquieu would almost certainly have echoed similar sentiments. Though more frequently cited for his insights on separation of powers, he also had a great deal to say about what today would be called federalism. In particular, he would not have been a fan of the US Senate. In one essay, speaking about federations generally, he said this:

> It is difficult for the united states to be all of equal power and extent. The Lycian republic[23] was an association of twenty-three towns; the large ones had three votes in the common council, the middling ones two, and the small towns one. The Dutch republic consists of seven provinces of different extent of territory, which have each one voice. [He then offers additional examples of power exercised proportionately in the Lycian system but not in the Netherlands.] Were I to give a model of an excellent confederate republic, I should pitch upon that of Lycia.[24]

In *Wesberry* v. *Sanders*[25] and *Reynolds* v. *Sims*,[26] the Supreme Court proclaimed the one-person-one-vote principle for elections to the US House and for elections to both houses of state legislatures, respectively. Requiring roughly equal per capita representation in those legislative bodies, the majority opinion in *Reynolds*, an 8-1 decision, contains eloquent language from Chief Justice Earl Warren:

> Legislatures represent people, not trees or acres. Legislators are elected by voters, not farms or cities or economic interests. … [I]f a State should provide that the votes of citizens in one part of the State should be given two times, or five times, or 10 times the weight of votes of citizens in another part of the State, it could hardly be contended that the right to vote of those residing in the disfavored areas had not been effectively diluted. It would appear extraordinary to suggest that a State could be constitutionally permitted to enact a law providing that certain of the State's voters could vote two, five, or 10 times for their legislative representatives, while voters living elsewhere could vote only once. … Of course, the effect of state legislative districting schemes which give the same number of representatives to unequal numbers of constituents is identical. … Weighting the votes of citizens differently, by any method or means, merely because of where they happen to reside, hardly

---

[22] Stephen H. Legomsky, *Immigration, Equality, and Diversity*, 31 Columbia J. Transnat'l L. 319, 334 (1993).

[23] Located in what is now southwest Turkey, the Lycian Republic flourished for roughly a millennium, beginning in the fifteenth century BC. See https://en.wikipedia.org/wiki/Lycia.

[24] Montesquieu, *Combining the Advantages of Small and Large States*, in Dimitrios Karmis & Wayne Norman (eds.), Theories of Federalism – A Reader (2005), at 55–57.

[25] 376 U.S. 1 (1964).

[26] 377 U.S. 533 (1964).

seems justifiable. … Since legislators are responsible for enacting laws by which all citizens are to be governed, they should be bodies which are collectively responsive to the popular will.[27]

Precisely. And from the standpoint of democratic theory, every one of those normative statements applies with the same logical force to the United States Senate. That point was not lost on the defendant states. Their response to the Court, an attempt to justify unequal representation, boiled down to "Then how come the US Senate gets to do it?"

The Court gave them the only answer it could. Translated into lay English, it was "Because the Constitution says so." And the only reason the Constitution says so is that, more than 200 years ago, the counter-majoritarian Senate was the price the large sovereign states had to pay the small sovereign states to get them to vote for ratification.[28]

As a legal justification, the Court's answer was bulletproof. The Constitution is clear. As an account of the Constitution's political history, it was also dead on. But as to the normative question whether the US Senate, like all the other legislative chambers of a democracy, should be built on a foundation of one-person-one-vote, the Court's answer amounted to nothing more than "Sorry, this is just the hand we've been dealt." This book suggests that the same answer could be given to "Why do we have state government at all?"

The consequences of this unequal representation scheme have been dramatic from the start. In 1790, four states comprised a majority of the national population but held only eight of the Senate's then twenty-six seats, that is, 31 percent of the Senate.[29] And "the most populous State (Virginia) had 12.6 times the population of the least populous (Delaware)."[30]

The imbalance has only grown worse – in fact, much worse. In part that is because, in the years leading up to the Civil War, the original constitutional compromise was followed by a series of additional compromises. When it came to new admissions, one slave state would be paired with one free state – often with very different population sizes.[31] Since then, states have continued to be admitted with only minimal regard for their sizes. As per the most recent decennial Census in 2020, the 576,851 residents of Wyoming receive the same Senate representation as the 39,538,223 residents of California. Each Wyoming resident thus enjoys more than sixty-nine times as much Senate representation as each California resident. The nine most populous

---

[27] *Ibid.*, at 562–65. Among the many thoughtful writings decrying the unequal representation in the US Senate, see especially Dahl, note 3, at 46–54; Levinson, note 2, at 49–62; Levitsky & Ziblatt, Tyranny, note 3, at 175–78, 233–34.

[28] 377 U.S. at 571–77.

[29] Issacharoff *et al.*, note 3, at 365; Karlan, note 3, at 2336 & n.88.

[30] Issacharoff *et al.*, note 3, at 365.

[31] *Ibid.*, at 366–67; Karlan, note 3, at 2336.

states together comprise a majority of the US population but receive only 18% of the Senate's seats; that is, a minority of the US population receives 82% of the Senate's seats. The five least populated states collectively comprise only 1% of the country but receive 10% of the Senators – an overrepresentation of 10 to 1. And the ten least populated states account for only 2.83% of the national population, but their residents get 20% of the Senators.[32]

The inequities are likely to persist. As Pamela Karlan notes, "[B]y 2040, 70 percent of Americans will live in the fifteen largest states. So 70 percent of the population will elect only thirty senators, leaving less than a third of the population to control the selection of nearly three-quarters of the Senate."[33]

The Australian Senate follows the US model. It consists of twelve members from each state, regardless of population.[34] Rodney Hall, in his book advocating the abolition of the Australian states, pointed out that under that system "a Tasmanian vote [at the time was] ten times as valuable as a Victorian vote."[35] Hall's book was written in 1998. As in the United States, that imbalance has only grown worse. As of June 2022, Australia's most populous state, New South Wales (which is home to Sydney), had 8,153,600 residents; Tasmania had 571,500.[36] This gives Tasmanians more than 14 times as much per capita Senate representation as residents of New South Wales. For perspective, even that extreme disparity pales in comparison to the 69-1 advantage given to Wyoming residents over Californians.

As a result, it is not unusual for the party that controls the US Senate to represent significantly fewer Americans than the Senate's minority party. In the three Congresses that convened during the period 2015–21, the Republicans controlled the Senate despite representing states that collectively contained only 46.9%, 44.8%, and 46.8% of the national population, respectively.[37]

---

[32] My calculations in this paragraph are based on the population percentages displayed in Infoplease, *State Population by Rank (Update for 2023!)*, www.infoplease.com/us/states/state-population-by-rank.

[33] Karlan, note 3, at 2338.

[34] Parliament of Australia, Commonwealth of Australia Constitution Act § 7 n.8, www.aph.gov.au/constitution.

[35] Rodney Hall, Abolish the States – Australia's Future and a $30 Billion Answer to our Tax Problems 9 (1998). Otherwise, Hall's book focuses on the fiscal waste in funding three levels of government – national, state, and local. His observations on that subject are discussed in Chapter 4, Section A of the present book.

[36] Australian Bureau of Statistics, www.abs.gov.au/statistics/people/population/national-state-and-territory-population/latest-release#:~:text=Key%20statistics,-Statistics%20in%20this&text=Australia's%20population%20was%2025%2C978%2C935%20people,was%2088%2C200%20people%20(0.3%25).

[37] For these calculations I relied on the state population percentages in the 2020 US decennial census. They appear at Infoplease, *State Population*, note 32. The interstate population shifts from 2015 to 2020 did not significantly change those percentages. For states with only one Republican senator, I assigned one-half of the state's percentage of the national population. The lists of senators in the 114th, 115th, and 116th Congresses were taken, respectively, from Wikipedia, *114th United States Congress*, https://en.wikipedia.org/wiki/114th_United_States_Congress#Senate_3; Wikipedia, *115th United States Congress*, https://en.wikipedia.org/wiki/115th_United_States_Congress#Senate_3; and Wikipedia, *116th United States Congress*, https://en.wikipedia.org/wiki/116th_United_States_Congress#Senate_4.

Today, these patterns systematically benefit one political party – Republicans. Four of the five least populated states (Wyoming, Alaska, North Dakota, and South Dakota) are reliably red. Among the five, only Vermont is reliably blue.

It was not always this way. As Pamela Karlan observes, "For most of American history, while large-population and small-population states might have had distinctive interests, their differences did not map onto a *partisan* divide." During the twentieth century, small states were diverse in "their interests and political alignments. ... Overall, sparsely populated, low-population states now tilt decisively toward the Republican Party [emphasis in original]."[38]

If the correlation between state populations and Senate representation seems out of whack, actual voting in senatorial elections reflects similar inequities. In 2016, Democratic Senate candidates nationwide received 53% of the total Senate ballots cast, to Republicans' 42%. Yet, of the Senate seats that were filled in that election, Republican candidates came away with twenty-two, Democrats with only twelve.[39]

Those 2016 Senate elections illustrate how extreme the counter-majoritarian outcomes can be. Perhaps the most probative comparison of the disconnect between the national popular vote and the resulting composition of the Senate, however, would focus on the three most recent (at this writing) Senate election cycles – 2018, 2020, and 2022. Three consecutive cycles cover all 100 Senate seats. And this particular sequence of election cycles has the additional advantage of rough partisan symmetry, since it includes a midterm with a Republican President, a Presidential election year, and a midterm with a Democratic President.

As Table 2.1 demonstrates, in each of those three election years the party for whom the greater number of Americans voted in senatorial elections did indeed win a greater number of those races – unlike in 2016. But there the symmetry ends. For the three cycles combined, people voted for Democratic Senate candidates over Republicans by a sizeable margin – 53.2%–46.8%. Yet the number of Senate seats the parties ended up with was virtually identical.[40]

---

[38] Karlan, note 3, at 2333–34; accord, Levitsky & Ziblatt, Tyranny, note 3, at 169.

[39] Wikipedia, 2016 *United States Senate Elections*, https://en.wikipedia.org/wiki/2016_United_States_Senate_elections.

[40] Pamela Karlan observes that in 2018, despite getting absolutely clobbered by their Democratic Senate opponents in the aggregate national popular vote, Republicans ended up gaining two seats in the Senate. Karlan, note 3, at 2338–39. But I can't fairly add that striking result to the evidence of counter-majoritarian Senate outcomes. In 2018, the Democrats' lopsided majority in the national popular vote for the Senate did in fact translate into their winning two-thirds of that year's Senate races. Wikipedia, 2018 *United States Senate Elections*, https://en.wikipedia.org/wiki/2018_United_States_Senate_elections. How many seats a party gains or loses in a particular Senate election ultimately depends not just on the vote totals and how they are distributed nationally that year, but also on how the numbers and distribution of opposing votes in that election cycle compare to those of the election cycle six years earlier, when those same seats were up for election.

TABLE 2.1 *National popular vote versus Senate outcomes*[41]

Year	Votes		Senate seats won	
	Democrats	Republicans	Democrats	Republicans
2018	52,224,867	34,687,875	22	11
	58.2%	38.7%		
2020	38,011,916	39,834,647	15	20
	47.0%	49.3%		
2022	39,802,675	39,876,285	15	20
	49.0%	49.1%		
Total	130,039,458	114,398,807	52	51
	53.2%	46.8%		

Sources: Wikipedia, 2018 *United States Senate Elections,* https://en.wikipedia.org/
wiki/2018_United_States_Senate_elections; Wikipedia, 2020 *United States Senate
Elections,* https://en.wikipedia.org/wiki/2020_United_States_Senate_elections;
Wikipedia, 2022 *United States Senate Elections,* https://en.wikipedia.org/
wiki/2022_United_States_Senate_elections.

In the modern era, that cycle is not an outlier. Steven Levitsky and Daniel Ziblatt demonstrate that "the Democrats have won an overall popular majority for the Senate in *every six-year cycle since 1996–2002.* And yet the Republicans controlled the Senate for most of this period" [emphasis in original].[42]

As if the composition of the Senate didn't provide a large enough unfair advantage to the minority over the majority, the Senate's filibuster rule makes the inequities worse. It takes sixty senators to overcome a Senate filibuster and bring a bill to a vote ("cloture"). Thus, forty-one senators can thwart the combined votes of their fifty-nine Senate colleagues and the 435 House members, all of them elected by their respective constituents.

Moreover, the whole is worse than the sum of its parts. It is not just that a minority of states wield disproportionate power. The filibuster rule gives citizens of the low-population states yet another advantage, since senators who represent only a small number of people can obstruct legislation favored by far greater numbers. The combination of the Senate's counter-majoritarian makeup and the filibuster enables senators from states that comprise only 13% of the national population to thwart the will of those who represent the other 87%.[43]

---

[41] The reason the totals add up to 103 Senators rather than 100 is that, during this period, there were three special Senate elections for seats that would not otherwise have been up for election in those years (two in 2020 and one in 2022).

[42] Levitsky & Ziblatt, Tyranny, note 3, at 175.

[43] Issacharoff *et al.,* note 3, at 367, citing Gregory J. Wawro & Eric Schickler, Filibuster: Obstruction and Lawmaking in the U.S. Senate (2004). By 2023, the 13% figure had dropped to 11%. Levitsky & Ziblatt, Tyranny, note 3, at 175.

The filibuster rule is the product of the US Senate itself rather than an action by the states. At least in theory, the Senate might have created, and can preserve, the filibuster with or without states. But given the smaller states' incentive – and their disproportionate power – to create and maintain the filibuster, abolishing state government and replacing the states' equal Senate representation with a direct vote of the people would at least diminish the life prospects of this counter-majoritarian add-on to an already counter-majoritarian chamber.

These inequalities are not merely a theoretical problem. Sanford Levinson summarizes some of their more pernicious effects: systematic net movement of taxpayer funds from the residents of large states to the residents of small states, without regard to their respective poverty levels; a disproportionate adverse impact on minority representation; and disproportionate say of small-state senators in the composition of the federal Judiciary.[44]

The same inequalities have another source – the nearly total disenfranchisement of US citizens who live in the District of Columbia. Like their fellow citizens who live in the fifty states, they are subject to all federal taxes.[45] As of 2021, in fact, they "pay the highest per capita income tax rate in the nation."[46] Yet they are denied any representation in the US Senate and have only a nonvoting representative in the US House.[47] (The Twenty-third Amendment now awards the District the minimum three electoral votes in presidential elections.)[48] Congress has broad authority over the DC budget and absolute authority to nullify any legislation passed by the local DC government.[49]

The Constitution authorizes Congress to admit new states to the union,[50] but to date, Congress has declined to grant statehood to DC. Although some have argued that various provisions of the Constitution preclude DC statehood,[51] that uncertainty is not the main roadblock today. Until recently a relatively nonpartisan issue, the principal barrier to DC statehood today is rock-solid Republican opposition. The political math is straightforward: DC residents vote overwhelmingly for Democrats. In 2020 and again in 2021 the House voted to grant statehood to DC (with every House Republican voting no), but in both instances the bill failed to pass

---

[44] See Levinson, note 2, at 54–58. See also Levitsky & Ziblatt, Tyranny, note 3, at 158–64.

[45] Residents of the other US territories pay a variety of federal taxes, but DC is the only territory whose residents are subject to federal income tax. Rock the Vote, Medium, *An Explainer on Washington, D.C., Puerto Rico, and the U.S. Territories* (Feb. 16, 2021), https://rockthevote.medium.com/an-explainer-on-washington-d-c-puerto-rico-and-the-u-s-territories-3465c23a641d.

[46] *Ibid.*

[47] *Ibid.*

[48] *Ibid.*

[49] Maya Efrati, Brennan Center for Justice, *DC Statehood Explained* (Mar. 18, 2022), www.brennancenter.org/our-work/research-reports/dc-statehood-explained.

[50] U.S. Const. Art. IV, § 3, Cl. 1.

[51] For the opposing constitutional arguments, compare, for example, Efrati, note 49 (arguing DC statehood would be constitutional) with R. Hewitt Pate, Heritage Foundation, *DC Statehood: Not Without a Constitutional Amendment* (Aug. 27, 1993), www.heritage.org/political-process/report/dc-statehood-not-without-constitutional-amendment (arguing it would not).

the Senate.[52] The systematic advantage that the two-senators-per-state rule gives the Republican party, aggravated by the filibuster, makes Senate passage of a DC statehood bill a near impossibility for the foreseeable future. Abolishing states would put DC residents on an equal footing with other US citizens in voting for the president and for members of both houses of Congress.

The discussion in this section hopefully conveys the major counter-majoritarian effects of the two-senators-per-state principle. This book does not propose eliminating the Senate. But in the stateless unitary republic posited here, the Senate, like the House, would consist of members elected from equipopulous districts (fewer in number than the House districts) throughout the country. The details appear in Chapter 6, Section B.

B THE ELECTORAL COLLEGE SYSTEM

Hundreds of books and articles have provided histories, descriptions, or critiques of the Electoral College.[53] It is another of those many impediments to democratic rule that can fairly be laid squarely at the feet of the states. This section assembles and responds to all the arguments that have been made in its defense. But first, a few words on how it works and how it started.

The president of the United States is not chosen directly by the people. Instead, the people vote for "electors" who in turn choose the president. This is by constitutional design: "[E]ach State shall appoint, in such Manner as the Legislature thereof may direct, a Number of Electors, equal to the whole Number of Senators and Representatives to which the State may be entitled in the Congress ..."[54] Exercising that power, every state legislature today has directed that the electors of that state be chosen by a vote of its people.[55] Each candidate will have named

---

[52] Efrati, note 49.

[53] Defenses of the Electoral College include Robert M. Hardaway, The Electoral College and the Constitution: The Case for Preserving Federalism (1994); Michael C. Maibach, A *Defense of the Electoral College* (Nov. 14, 2016), https://edsitement.neh.gov/closer-readings/defense-electoral-college; and Tara Ross, Enlightened Democracy: The Case for the Electoral College (2004). Opposition writings include Dahl, note 3, at 73–89; George C. Edwards III, Why the Electoral College is Bad for America (3rd ed. 2019); Levinson, note 2, at 82–97; and Wegman, Let the People Pick, note 15. The most authoritative treatments of the origins of the Electoral College and the history of reform efforts are James W. Ceaser, Presidential Selection: Theory and Development (1979); and Alexander Keyssar, Why Do We Still Have the Electoral College? (2020). Other excellent historical treatments include Dahl, note 3at 73–89; and Neal Peirce & Lawrence Longley, The People's President: The Electoral College in American History and the Direct Vote Alternative (rev. ed. 1981) (also providing extensive elections data).

[54] U.S. Const. Art. II, § 1, Cl. 3. That the state legislatures decide the manner of choosing presidential electors raises issues discussed in Chapter 3, Section C.

[55] This has been true for more than 150 years. See Thomas H. Neale, Congressional Research Service, *The Electoral College: How It Works in Contemporary Presidential Elections* (May 15, 2017), https://sgp.fas.org/crs/misc/RL32611.pdf.

a slate of electors, publicly pledged to him or her, for whom the people cast their votes.[56]

As this provision says, the number of electors for a given state equals the number of its US House representatives plus its two Senators. (The District of Columbia, as just noted, is also awarded three electors.)[57] In every state except Nebraska and Maine, the presidential candidate who wins a plurality of the statewide vote receives all of that state's electoral votes – or, technically, the entire slate of the electors who are pledged to that candidate. Nebraska and Maine each award one electoral vote to the plurality winner of each of the state's congressional districts and two additional electoral votes to the candidate who wins a statewide plurality.[58]

That brings the total number of electors to 538-435 based on the number of House members, 100 based on the number of Senators, and 3 for DC Together, the 538 electors are commonly referred to as the Electoral College. The Electoral College members meet in their respective states and cast their votes. Those votes are then officially tallied by the vice president, in his or her capacity as president of the Senate, in a joint session of Congress.[59] To win a presidential election, a candidate must receive an outright majority of the Electoral College. If no candidate wins such a majority, the House of Representatives chooses the president from among the three candidates with the highest numbers of Electoral College votes, as discussed in Section C. In that event, each state delegation – large or small – gets one vote. To win the presidency in such a House election, a candidate needs the votes of a majority of the state delegations, today twenty-six states.[60]

Robert Dahl has described the unimpressive origins of the Electoral College. As he shows, the framers settled on the idea of the Electoral College out of a combination of weariness, desperation, and dissatisfaction with every alternative they could think of.[61]

---

[56] Occasionally there are so-called "faithless electors," also known as "rogue electors." These are electors who renege on their pledges and vote for candidates other than those to whom they are pledged. "Altogether, 23,507 electoral votes have been counted across 58 presidential elections. Only 90 electors have cast 'deviant' votes. … More than two-thirds of deviant votes (63) were due to the death of the party's nominee." Fair Vote, *Presidential Elections*, https://fairvote.org/resources/presidential-elections/. Faithless electors have never changed the outcome of a presidential election. *Ibid.* See also text accompanying notes 93–94.

[57] U.S. Const. Amend. 23. This amendment provides that DC gets as many electors as it would receive if it were a state, except that it may not end up with more electors than those of the least populous state. Each of the least populous states currently gets three electors (one for its single House member plus two for its Senators). So unless all of the least populous states grow dramatically, DC will always end up with exactly three electors whether its own population grows or shrinks.

[58] National Archives, *What is the Electoral College?* www.archives.gov/electoral-college/about.

[59] The counting of the votes in Congress was generally a noncontroversial part of the process until the 2020 election, when Republican members of both Houses lodged objections to the electors from several states and the vice president's role also became a live issue. These complications and the resulting mob violence are discussed in notes 97–105 and accompanying text.

[60] U.S. Const. Amend. 12.

[61] Dahl, note 3, at 74–76.

Although the question of how to elect the president generated considerable anguish at the Constitutional Convention,[62] the Federalist and Antifederalist Papers devote surprisingly little space to the subject. Two papers do address it head-on.

In Federalist 68, Hamilton thought it "desirable that the sense of the people should operate in the choice of the [president]," but not directly. They should instead vote for electors who "possess the information and discernment requisite to such complicated investigations." James Ceaser expands on that theme. He argues that the framers' dominant concern was that the president be a statesman – someone who would govern based on the best interests of the nation rather than a person who, out of personal ambition, would seek to curry favor with the masses. The framers wanted a strong leader rather than a follower. For that purpose, they did not trust popular sentiment. They feared it would be too easily swayed by either personal charisma or demagogic appeals on the issues.[63]

Hamilton in Federalist 68 saw additional advantages. Voting for electors avoids "tumult and disorder," for two reasons. First, he argued, the people will be voting for many electors, not just one president. Today, of course, electors are pledged to specific candidates, so as a practical matter people are still voting, albeit indirectly, for one candidate. Second, he wrote, the electors will be assembling in several places, not just one central location; thus, there is less likelihood of "heats and ferments."

He also maintained that this system will guard against corruption, "chiefly from the desire in foreign powers to gain an improper ascendant in our councils," because a foreign power won't know who the electors are until after the election. Modern readers of this Federalist paper will note the irony. Compelling evidence of successful and unsuccessful Russian influence on US elections arose in 2016 and 2020, respectively. And, if anything, it is much easier for someone to corrupt a handful of electors and swing a state in a close national election than to corrupt millions of individual voters.

Finally, and certain to induce derision in modern-day Americans, is this passage, also from Federalist 68:

> The [Electoral College system] affords a moral certainty, that the office of President will never fall to the lot of any man who is not in an eminent degree endowed with the requisite qualifications. ... It will not be too strong to say, that there will be a constant probability of seeing the station filled by characters preeminent for ability and virtue.

At a time when George Washington was the consensus choice as the first president, that assumption might well have seemed reasonable. But in 2016 the Electoral College system awarded the presidency to Donald Trump, a man whom few would describe as "pre-eminent for ability and virtue"; the national popular vote would have prevented that result.

---

[62] *Ibid.*, at 73–74; Ceaser, note 53.
[63] Ceaser, note 53, at 41–87.

At any rate, all of these arguments were merely for the proposition that the people should vote for "wise" electors who in turn would select the president, rather than vote for the president directly. Even if one subscribes to that viewpoint – highly unlikely in modern times – the specific counter-majoritarian effects built into the design of today's Electoral College, discussed below, raise different questions.

One paper did object strongly to the whole concept of indirect voting through electors. In Antifederalist 72, "Republicus" offered these comments: "Is it necessary, is it rational, that the sacred rights of mankind should thus dwindle down to Electors of electors, and those again electors of other electors?"[64] Rather, he points out, "To conclude, I can think of but one source of right to government, or any branch of it – and that is THE PEOPLE. They, and only they, have a right to determine whether they will make laws, or execute them, or do both in a collective body, or by a delegated authority [emphasis in original]."[65]

I note that that paper was published in the Kentucky Gazette. On the likely assumption that its anonymous author was from Kentucky, his preference for direct popular election of the president over the proposed Electoral College takes on extra moral force. The Electoral College system, in which every state receives the same two electoral votes from its senatorial representation, benefits small states like Kentucky by giving them a voice disproportionate to their populations. Yet he opposed it.

Importantly, however, even that writer's objection to the Electoral College system was rooted solely in his concern for popular sovereignty – indeed, one of the three essential elements of a democracy. Missing from his argument was any reference to either of the other two elements – majority rule and political equality. It is those latter elements that lie at the core of the modern objections to the Electoral College.

All of this matters. At least five US presidents have been elected despite finishing second in the national popular vote.[66] The first case is distinctive. In a multicandidate race in 1824, Andrew Jackson won a plurality, but not a majority, of both the national popular vote[67] and the Electoral College. Yet, the House of Representatives,

---

[64] That last phrase might be a reference to the fact that the presidential electors were originally chosen by the state legislatures rather than by the people directly. Under that system, the people voted for state legislatures that in turn voted for electors, who in turn voted for the presidential candidates. Thus, the people were electors of electors of electors.

[65] Antifederalist 72.

[66] President Kennedy is possibly a sixth example. In 1960, running against Richard Nixon, Kennedy handily won a majority of the Electoral College. But some distinctive features in Alabama's 1960 presidential ballots generated multiple possible methods for tabulating the popular vote in that state. Under some of those methods, Nixon won a slim plurality of the national popular vote. Wikipedia, *List of United States Presidential Elections in which the Winner Lost the Popular Vote*, https://en.wikipedia.org/wiki/List_of_United_States_presidential_elections_in_which_the_winner_lost_the_popular_vote.

[67] In that year, the "national" popular vote was really only *mostly* national. In six of the then twenty-four states, the electors were still chosen by the state legislatures rather than the people. Of the five

voting by individual state delegation as required by the Twelfth Amendment and discussed below, selected John Quincy Adams, who had finished second to Jackson in both the popular vote and the Electoral College.

In each of the last four of those instances, the winning candidate garnered an outright majority of the Electoral College despite losing the national popular vote. In 1876, Samuel Tilden won the national popular vote but lost to Rutherford B. Hayes by one vote in the Electoral College. In 1888 the Electoral College selected Benjamin Harrison, who had lost the popular vote to Grover Cleveland. In 2000, Al Gore won the popular vote but, after the Supreme Court's controversial 5-4 decision in *Bush* v. *Gore* halting the Florida recount,[68] narrowly lost the State of Florida; that result enabled George W. Bush to win the Electoral College with 271 electoral votes – just one more than the required majority.[69] And in 2016, the people chose Hillary Clinton over Donald Trump by a margin of almost three million votes, but Trump prevailed in the Electoral College.[70]

Those are the actual misses – where the American people chose candidate A over candidate B, but the Electoral College nonetheless delivered the presidency to candidate B. There have also been near misses – lots of them. These are cases in which the same candidate wins both the national popular vote and the Electoral College (so that the system didn't do any harm), but where a switch of just a tiny number of popular votes, either nationally or in one or more close states, would have produced an actual miss. There are two kinds of near misses: In one scenario, a candidate wins the national popular vote but barely wins the Electoral College. A shift of a small number of popular votes, in close elections in states with enough combined electoral votes, would have awarded the Presidency to the candidate who lost the national popular vote. In the second scenario, the near mismatch is reversed. A candidate wins the Electoral College but barely wins the national popular vote. A shift of a minute percentage of the popular votes nationwide would have resulted in that candidate losing the national popular vote but still winning the Electoral College and therefore the presidency.

There are several modern examples of the first scenario. In 1976, Georgia Governor Jimmy Carter won the popular vote by almost 1.7 million votes, but "a switch of fewer than 4,000 votes in Hawaii and 6,000 in Ohio would have given [incumbent] President Gerald Ford an Electoral College victory."[71]

In 2004, George W. Bush defeated John Kerry by more than three million popular votes. But Bush eked out a much narrower victory in the Electoral College, 286 electoral votes to 251, with 270 needed for a majority. (One faithless elector from

---

examples cited here, this was the only one that took place at a time when some state legislatures chose the electors. *Ibid.*

[68] 531 U.S. 98 (2000).

[69] Infoplease, *Presidential Election of 2000, Electoral and Popular Vote Summary*, www.infoplease.com/us/government/elections/presidential-election-of-2000-electoral-and-popular-vote-summary.

[70] Wikipedia, *List*, note 66.

[71] Keyssar, Electoral College, note 53, at 263.

Minnesota, a state that Kerry won, voted for Kerry's running mate, John Edwards). So Bush made it through by just sixteen electoral votes. In three of the states that Bush won – Iowa, Nevada, and New Mexico – his combined popular vote margin was only 37,547 votes – approximately 1.2 percent of the total votes in those states, or fewer than one in 83 voters.[72] So those states could easily have gone the other way. If they had, their seventeen combined electoral votes would have swung the election for Kerry, despite Bush's decisive national popular vote margin.

More dramatic still was a near miss in 2020. In that election, Joe Biden defeated Donald Trump by more than 7 million popular votes but won the Electoral College with only 306 electoral votes – 36 more than he needed. In three of the states that Biden won – Arizona, Georgia, and Wisconsin – his combined popular vote margin was only 42,918 votes – approximately 0.37 percent of the total vote in those three states. Thus, if 21,459 of those who voted for Biden in those states – that is, just one out of every 269 of Biden's 5,776,642 voters – had instead voted for Trump (and of course assuming they were distributed among the three states in the way most favorable to Trump), those states could easily have gone the other way. If they had, their thirty-seven combined electoral votes would have swung the election for Trump, despite Biden's overwhelming national popular vote margin.[73]

An example of the second kind of near miss occurred in 1968. Richard Nixon handily won the Electoral College over Hubert Humphrey. But his victory margin over Humphrey in the national popular vote was slim. Nixon garnered 31,783,783 votes to Humphrey's 31,271,839, a difference of only 511,944 votes (0.7 percent of the total).[74] Therefore, if 255,972 of those who voted for Nixon (a large-sounding number but only one out of every 125 of his voters) had instead voted for Humphrey, the latter would have won the national popular vote but Nixon would still have been awarded the presidency.

These are just some of the modern examples of near misses. The aggregate probabilities illustrate that those elections were not quirks. One mathematically sophisticated paper finds that "[i]n elections within a one percentage point margin – about 1.3 million votes, based on 2016 turnout – the probability of [the winner of the popular vote losing the election] is around 40 percent. In historical fact, six presidential elections of the 46[75] since 1836 have yielded a popular vote margin within one percentage point."[76]

---

72 Wikipedia, *2004 United States Presidential Election*, https://en.wikipedia.org/wiki/2004_United_States_presidential_election.

73 Wikipedia, *2020 United States Presidential Election*, https://en.wikipedia.org/wiki/2020_United_States_presidential_election.

74 Wikipedia, *1968 United States Presidential Election*, https://en.wikipedia.org/wiki/1968_United_States_presidential_election. Segregationist George Wallace ran as a third-party candidate. He received almost ten million popular votes, and he won five southern states and forty-six electoral votes. *Ibid.*

75 Now 47. The cited paper was written before the 2020 election.

76 Michael Geruso *et al.*, *Inversions in US Presidential Elections: 1836–2016*, Nat'l Bureau of Economic Research Working Paper No. 26247, at 17 (Sept. 2019), www.nber.org/papers/w26247.

Jesse Wegman sums it up nicely:

[W]hat's remarkable is not that a split between the Electoral College and the popular vote has happened twice in the past two decades, it's that it hasn't happened far more often. In sixteen other elections, a shift of 75,000 votes or fewer in key states ... would have made the popular vote loser president. Six times, a shift of fewer than 10,000 votes would have done the trick.[77]

Frequent future recurrences, in other words, are a statistical certainty.

What is it about the Electoral College that has produced these counter-majoritarian outcomes? Two of its features are to blame.

The principal culprit is the winner-take-all element. As noted earlier, except in Nebraska and Maine, whoever wins a plurality of the statewide popular vote receives all of that state's electoral votes. It doesn't matter how close the popular vote in that state was.

By way of illustration, in 2000 George W. Bush won the State of Colorado over Al Gore with only 51 percent of the popular vote. But his prize was all eight of Colorado's electoral votes. Had Gore received a share of those electoral votes proportionate to his popular vote within the state – even just three of those votes, rounded down – he would have become president.[78] Attempts to save the Electoral College have in fact included proposals to mandate precisely such a proportional allocation system in every state. That idea is discussed below, though for the reasons given, it would be an incomplete solution and at any rate inapplicable to the stateless country imagined in this book.

Furthermore, the disconnect between how people vote and how the Electoral College votes is asymmetrical. Today, the likelihood of a Democrat winning the national popular vote but losing the Electoral College is much greater than vice versa.[79] That's because, "in the Modern period, Democrats have tended to win large states by large margins and lose them by small margins."[80] For example,

in 2016, Hillary Clinton won the electoral votes of three of the ten largest states – by 30 percentage points in California, 22.5 percentage points in New York, and 16.8 percentage points in Illinois. But in the seven large states that Donald Trump won, his largest margin of victory was 9 percentage points (in Texas), and in three states (Florida, Michigan, and Pennsylvania), his margin of victory was less than 1.3 percent. Overall, in the ten largest states, Hillary Clinton received 36,440,207 votes and Donald Trump received 31,295,308. But because of how their supporters were geographically distributed, Clinton garnered only 98 of that group of states' electoral votes, while Trump garnered 138. These large states accounted for the majority of Trump's electoral vote victory margin.[81]

---

[77] Wegman, Let the People Pick, note 16, at 28.
[78] Keyssar, Electoral College, note 53, at 334.
[79] Geruso *et al.*, note 76, at 3 & 23.
[80] *Ibid.*, at 23.
[81] Karlan, note 3, at 2340; see also Geruso *et al.*, note 76, at 23.

There is a second source of the Electoral College's counter-majoritarian out-comes. Every state (and DC) receives one electoral vote for every member of its US House delegation, plus two additional electoral votes for its two Senators. The size of each state's House delegation is proportional to its population, but its Senate representation is not. As discussed in Section A, Wyoming gets two Senators, as does California. Those two electoral votes per state are freebies. They bear no relation to the size of the state's population.

Several writers have suggested that, contrary to conventional wisdom, the two-extra-vote feature of the Electoral College system doesn't really produce a net ben-efit for citizens of the small states. These writers acknowledge that citizens of small states receive a slight bump by getting the same two extra electoral votes as the large states. But, they point out, that advantage is far less mathematically significant than what the winner-take-all rule provides voters in large swing states. The latter have the potential to produce a much greater net electoral vote gain for their preferred candidates than their counterparts in small swing states have for theirs.[82]

These writers' comparative point is clearly correct, and it can help to explain why the various states' stances on Electoral College reform have not correlated especially well with population size. But that doesn't mean (and they don't imply) that the two extra votes are fair. It merely means that *both* the winner-take-all feature and the two-extra-votes feature are counter-majoritarian. Neither the fact that the two effects work in opposite directions (with respect to the balance between large states and small states) nor the fact that one effect is usually greater than the other changes that inescapable bottom line.

Of more practical importance, while a disconnect between the popular vote win-ner and the Electoral College winner is *more* likely to result from the winner-take-all rule than from the two-extra-vote feature, the latter is still consequential. For one thing, it systematically tilts the playing field in favor of one major political party – Republicans, since they command clear majorities among the populations of the smaller states.[83] Given the impact that the choice of US President has on both the nation and the world, the two-vote bump would have enormous consequences if it were to make the difference in even one presidential election.

As it turns out, it already has. Those two "free" votes per state changed the out-come in 2000. Even after the Supreme Court awarded Florida to Bush, he ended up with only 271 electoral votes to Gore's 266. (One elector, from DC and therefore pledged to Gore, abstained.) Bush won thirty states; Gore won twenty states plus DC.[84] If the two free electoral votes per state (and DC) were subtracted from each candidate's total, Bush would have ended up with 60 fewer electoral votes, for a total

[82] Wegman, Let the People Pick, note 16, at 173–79; Karlan, note 3, at 2340.
[83] Geruso *et al.*, note 76, at 23.
[84] 270 to Win, 2000 *Presidential Election*, www.270towin.com/2000_Election/; Infoplease Presidential Election of 2000, note 69.

of 211. Gore would have ended up with 42 fewer electoral votes, for a total of 224. Gore would thus have won the presidency by thirteen electoral votes.

We will never know how different the course of history would have been. It seems a safe bet that the United States would have pursued a more forceful climate change policy and that doing so would have spurred other world powers to agree to do the same. Perhaps the Iraq War would have been avoided. Whatever one's views on those and other issues, the two extra votes changed the world.

Except for "state sovereignty is an end in itself" and "the framers were smart people who knew what they were doing," are there today good reasons to use this complicated, counter-majoritarian institution to choose our presidents? To address that question, it is necessary to add "Compared to what?" To reframe the issue slightly, is there a better way to choose our presidents?

There has been no shortage of ideas. Two recurring proposals would eliminate actual human "electors" and therefore the Electoral College, but preserve electoral votes and the requirement of a majority of those electoral votes to win the presidency. More substantively, these proposals would abolish the winner-take-all feature as it now stands. As the preceding discussion shows, it is that feature, after all, that accounts for the lion's share of the Electoral College's counter-majoritarian effects.

One of those proposals is for a constitutional amendment that mandates the Nebraska/Maine model for every state. Two electoral votes would still be awarded to the candidate who wins a statewide plurality, but the rest of the state's electoral votes would be allocated to the plurality winners of each of the state's congressional districts. One variant of this proposal would be to allow each state legislature to create "presidential districts" in place of congressional districts for this purpose. A subvariant of the latter proposal would be to fold the two senatorial electoral votes into these presidential districts.[85]

On its face, any of these district system variants might look like improvements, since they make it possible for a candidate who falls short of a statewide plurality to pick up at least some of the state's electoral votes. In the end, however, each of these variants would still be a winner-take-all system. It's just that the winner-take-all rule would be applied to each district rather than to each state. In the view of many, in fact, a district system of any kind would be even worse than the present system, because the combination of residential patterns, gerrymandering, and the retention of the single-member district feature makes the congressional districts poor proxies for proportional allocation of the electoral votes.[86] A district system, therefore, doesn't eliminate the risk of the popular vote loser winning a majority of the Electoral College. In some elections, it might even increase that risk. By way of

---

[85] Congressional Research Service, *Electoral College Reform: 110th Congress Proposals, the National Popular Vote Campaign, and Other Alternative Developments* (Feb. 9, 2009), at 25 & 26 n.86, https://crsreports.congress.gov/product/pdf/RL/RL34604/7.

[86] See Chapter 3, Section A.

illustration, Jesse Wegman points out that "[i]f the district system had been in use nationwide in 2012, Mitt Romney would have become president, despite losing to Barack Obama by about five million votes."[87]

A second reform proposal would distribute each state's electoral votes among the candidates in proportion to their popular votes in that state.[88] This proposal would be a clear improvement over the district proposal. It avoids not only the winner-take-all feature, but also the counter-majoritarian effects of intrastate residential patterns and gerrymandering, thus greatly reducing the chances of the popular vote loser becoming the electoral vote winner.

Still, while it would reduce those chances, in a reasonably close election it won't always prevent the popular vote loser from walking away with the presidency. Moreover, as Wegman observes, it could result in no one getting a majority, since third-party and independent candidates could get significant numbers of votes in one or more states. In fact, that would have been the case in 2016. Hillary Clinton won the popular vote, but with a proportional allocation system the election would have been thrown into the House.[89] Anyway, if the goal of such a reform is to bring the electoral vote into close proximity to the popular vote, wouldn't a direct national popular vote serve that purpose both more simply and more reliably? Why settle for an approximation when we could have the real thing? Put another way, why settle for "hopefully" when we could have "definitely"?

So neither of these reform proposals, in any of their variants, eliminates the counter-majoritarian effects of relying on electoral votes. That is reason enough to look for an alternative. Moreover, if state governments were abolished entirely, as this book recommends, there would be no practical way to implement an electoral vote system anyway, unless some kind of regional allocation of electoral votes were to replace the state-based system. And that would simply recreate the same counter-majoritarian problem. Thus, if we are to rid ourselves of the whole concept of electoral votes, the question is what would replace it. The most obvious alternative is a direct national popular vote. The next step, therefore, is to compare that to the status quo.

As the preceding discussion suggests, the major criticism of the Electoral College system, throughout its history, has been its counter-majoritarian structure and effects. Robert Hardaway, one of its leading defenders, mocks the many studies "devoted to proving by complex mathematical equations and formulae that voters in different states do not have *precisely* [my emphasis] the same voting power in electing a President."[90] The implication is that the only problem with the Electoral College is that the outcomes don't match the popular vote with scientific exactitude. With respect, no one has criticized the Electoral College system for not providing

[87] Wegman, Let the People Pick, note 16, at 183.
[88] Congressional Research Service, *Electoral College Reform*, note 85, at 26–27.
[89] Wegman, Let the People Pick, note 16, at 187–88.
[90] Hardaway, note 53, at 6.

"precisely the same voting power." Put aside the two free electoral votes that each of the fifty states receives just for being a state – whether it's California or Wyoming, with the previously mentioned population ratio of approximately 69-1. The winner-take-all feature of the Electoral College system gives the voter in a swing state infinitely – not just slightly – more power than the voter in a safe state.

Hardaway's ultimate response to demonstrations of unequal voting power is to point out that both the requirement of equal Senate representation (discussed in Section A) and the constitutional amendment process (discussed in Section E) could similarly be faulted for depriving citizens of equal voting parity.[91] Michael Maibach offers the same argument: "The Electoral College is no more 'undemocratic' than is the Senate or the Supreme Court."[92]

Indeed. Those who believe that equality demands a national popular vote for the presidency should also object to the makeup of the Senate and the states' roles in the constitutional amendment process – as I do. But simply pointing out that other features of the Constitution are similarly flawed isn't much of a defense.

Maibach acknowledges that the Electoral College system wastes votes because each state-by-state winner takes all the electors from that state. His response is that awarding the presidency to whoever wins the national popular vote would also be a winner-take-all system in which the votes for the losing candidate would be wasted.

That response misconceives the objection. The problem with the present system is not simply that it contains a winner-take-all feature. It is that it contains fifty different winner-take-all pieces and then adds them together without regard to the victory margins in each of those fifty pieces.

Faithless electors only amplify the counter-majoritarian essence of the Electoral College. These are electors who renege on their pledge to vote for a particular candidate. As of 2020, thirty-two states had laws that require the state's electors to vote for the candidate who won a plurality of the popular vote in their respective states.[93] But the other eighteen states do not. In those states, a faithless elector may substitute his or her preferred candidate for the one chosen by the people. And even in the thirty-two states that require fidelity, there are often minimal consequences for those who stray.

To date, faithless electors have not altered the outcome of any US presidential election. But the potential is real. "[I]n 2016, 10 of the 538 electors cast ballots for someone other than their state's popular vote winner, an unusually high number that could have changed the outcome of five of the previous 58 previous US presidential elections."[94]

[91] *Ibid.*, at 7.
[92] Maibach, note 53. The Supreme Court comparison raises different issues; the accepted decisional independence of federal courts is considered in Chapter 6, Section C.
[93] *Chiafalo* v. *Washington*, 140 S.Ct. 2316, 2321 (2020).
[94] Andrew Chung & Lawrence Hurley, Reuters, *U.S. Supreme Court curbs "faithless electors" in Presidential Voting* (July 20, 2020), www.reuters.com/article/us-usa-court-electoral/u-s-supreme-court-curbs-faithless-electors-in-presidential-voting-idUSKBN2471TI.

Even after all the popular votes have been tabulated and the totals certified by the relevant officials in each state, the Electoral College system leaves several hurdles to clear. As will be seen, these additional steps create the potential – recently diminished but not eliminated – for still more counter-majoritarian effects. Each state's governor (unless the state's law designates another official for this purpose) officially submits a list of his or her state's electors to Congress. Days later, the Electoral College formally votes. The vice president, presiding over a joint session of Congress, counts the electoral votes and announces the totals. Members of both Houses have an opportunity to object to the appointments of particular electors or to the votes those electors cast. To be sustained, an objection requires majority votes in both Houses of Congress. At the conclusion of the debate, both Houses vote on whether to certify the Electoral College results. Upon certification, the winner[95] of the election is sworn in as the president.[96]

Until the 2020 presidential election, this part of the process was rarely controversial. But that year, President Trump ran for reelection against Democratic nominee Joe Biden. Even before the Electoral College returned a majority for Biden, Trump and many of his fellow Republicans had claimed repeatedly that Biden's reported victories in several states were the product of widespread voter fraud. There was never even a kernel of truth to those claims, as detailed below,[97] but the Trump campaign tried nonetheless to persuade state election officials to revise the vote totals. Failing that, the campaign argued, Vice President Mike Pence (himself running for reelection as Trump's running mate) legally could, and should, use his role as electoral vote-counter to refuse to declare Biden the winner. Pence, to his credit, made clear that he did not have that power. Nonetheless, all these claims aired nonstop on Fox News and other television and social media outlets favorable to Trump. Wild conspiracy theories flourished. In one December 2020 survey, "over 75% of Republican voters found merit in claims that millions of fraudulent ballots were cast, voting machines were manipulated, and thousands of votes were recorded for dead people."[98]

The ensuing hysteria triggered several events in rapid succession. First, approximately 14 Senate Republicans and 140 House Republicans announced their

---

[95] This description assumes that a candidate has won a majority of the Electoral College. If there is no majority, then under the Twelfth Amendment the House of Representatives chooses the president via the process described in Section C.

[96] See, for example, 3 U.S.C. § 15; Protect Democracy, *Understanding the Electoral Count Reform Act of 2022* (Dec. 23, 2022), https://protectdemocracy.org/wp-content/uploads/2022/12/UPDATED-Protect-Democracy-ECRA-Explainer-12.23-1.pdf; Democracy Docket, *After Election Day: The Basics of Election Certification* (Nov. 29, 2021), www.democracydocket.com/analysis/after-election-day-the-basics-of-election-certification/; Wikipedia, *Electoral Count Act*, https://en.wikipedia.org/wiki/Electoral_Count_Act.

[97] See Chapter 3, Section B.

[98] Andrew C. Eggers *et al.*, PNAS, *No Evidence For Systematic Voter Fraud: A Guide To Statistical Claims about the 2020 Election*, www.pnas.org/doi/10.1073/pnas.2103619118.

intentions to object, when the time came, to the certifications of Arizona's or Pennsylvania's electoral outcomes, or both.[99]

On January 6, 2021, the time came. This was the appointed date for Congress to certify the final electoral vote. But before Congress could finish doing so, the false claims of election fraud spawned a second event – the storming of the Capitol building by heavily armed Trump supporters who had been led to believe that the Democrats had stolen the election. Amidst cries of "Hang Mike Pence," the mob breached the Capitol walls, looted and ransacked the building, assaulted more than 100 Capitol police officers, and roamed the halls in search of terrified members of Congress hiding in bunkers and locked offices for several hours. The insurrection was eventually put down, but it delayed the required congressional certification until the wee hours of the following morning.[100]

Even after all the violence (which included four deaths) and the toll it had taken on the members of Congress, police and other staff, the Capitol building, and democracy itself, and even as the nation watched the attack replayed on TV with a mixture of revulsion and horror, a third event occurred. When the police finally cleared the building and Congress belatedly reconvened, 6 Republican senators and 121 House members carried out their threats to object to Arizona's electoral outcome; 7 Republican senators and 138 Republican House members voted to object to Pennsylvania's. Some House Republicans, but no Senate Republicans, also objected to the results in Georgia, Michigan, and Nevada.[101] Among those who earlier had pledged to object, only a handful changed their minds in light of the onslaught they had just experienced.[102]

On December 29, 2022, President Biden signed into law the Electoral Count Reform and Presidential Transition Improvement Act (ECRA).[103] This statute amended the Electoral Count Act, which had governed the Electoral College and congressional certification processes since 1887. Among other things, the new law

---

[99] Vox, *147 Republican Lawmakers Still Objected to the Election Results after the Capitol Attack* (Jan. 7, 2021), www.vox.com/2021/1/6/22218058/republicans-objections-election-results.

[100] The events are recounted in thousands of media sources. See, for example, History Channel, *U.S. Capitol Riot*, www.history.com/this-day-in-history/january-6-capitol-riot.

[101] NPR, *Here Are the Republicans Who Objected to the Electoral College Count* (Jan. 7, 2021), www.npr.org/sections/insurrection-at-the-capitol/2021/01/07/954380156/here-are-the-republicans-who-objected-to-the-electoral-college-count.

[102] Vox, note 99. A chillingly similar series of events took place in Paris in February 1934. A mob of several thousand right-wing extremists, driven by a baseless belief in a left wing conspiracy to steal the national elections and aided in that belief by right-wing members of the parliament, stormed the Chamber of Deputies in an attempt to prevent recognition of the duly elected government. Fourteen of the rioters and one police officer were killed, and thousands of others were injured. After the attack, mainstream conservative politicians not only refused to chastise the insurrectionists, but ultimately even portrayed them as heroes and martyrs. The episode is vividly recounted in John Ganz, Unpopular Front, *Feb 6 1934/Jan 6 2021* (July 15, 2021), https://johnganz.substack.com/p/feb-6-1934jan-6-2021. See also the Brazilian events in 2022, described in Chapter 6, Section B.

[103] Pub. L. 117–328 (Dec. 29, 2022).

preserved the power of individual members of Congress to lodge objections but made it harder, in ways discussed below, for a small handful of such individuals to sabotage or delay the process. It also made explicit the existing understanding, which had been expressed only vaguely in the original law, that the vice president's role in the counting of the electoral votes is purely ministerial. ECRA is in effect for the 2024 election.

ECRA, therefore, will now make it harder for congressional objectors to disrupt the timely selection of the President. Harder, but not impossible. Before ECRA, a single member of either House could object to the certification of a state's electoral votes, thereby triggering debate and delay.[104] Under ECRA, an objection will now require a 20 percent vote in both Houses of Congress. And upon such a vote, it still takes majorities of both Houses to sustain the objection.

The 20 percent rule is a clear improvement. But if the 2020 election is a guide, the numbers related earlier show that even the new threshold is surmountable. Twenty percent means twenty Senators and eighty-seven Representatives. As noted, on January 6, 2021, even after the violent mob attack on the Capitol just hours earlier, 121 Representatives supported objections to Arizona's slate of Biden electors and 138 supported objections to Pennsylvania's – in both cases far in excess of the new 20 percent threshold. The Senate would have fallen short of the current threshold, as only six Senators supported objections to Arizona's electors, seven to Pennsylvania's. All those numbers, however, would surely have been greater but for some Members' change of heart upon the violent attack that had interrupted their certification process and threatened their lives. The fourteen senators who before the insurrection had threatened to object got uncomfortably close to the current threshold of twenty, and the House objectors easily cleared the threshold.[105]

So it is not hard to imagine a future scenario in which even ECRA's 20 percent hurdle is cleared and the congressional certification delayed. Admittedly, there is one crucial safeguard: it will still take a majority vote in both Houses to ultimately reject a slate of electors. But even that check is less than ironclad in an age when those who fail to toe the party line face likely recriminations in the next round of their party's primaries.

The antics of the congressional objectors in 2020 cannot be blamed – at least not directly – on the states. They did nothing wrong. But the existence of states is essential in multiple ways to the process that permits those congressional obstructions to occur. First, take away the states and there is no Electoral College system to begin with. Second, the congressional objectors themselves are elected through counter-majoritarian voting systems that account for at least some of the members of both chambers – in the House, because of intrastate residential patterns, single-member districts, gerrymandering, and voter suppression strategies (discussed in Sections A

---

[104] See Protect Democracy, note 96.
[105] See Vox, note 99.

and B of Chapter 3), and in the Senate because of the equal state suffrage rule (discussed in Section A). Third, the congressional objections were only to the vote counts in selected states where the victory margins were relatively small, not to the national popular vote that Biden won handily.

Furthermore, the January 6, 2021 insurrection that Trump's enraged followers staged, and the killings and destruction left in its wake, while still possible under a national popular vote system, would have been appreciably less likely. Since President Biden won the national popular vote by over seven million votes, getting people to swallow the myth of voter fraud on a scale that massive would have been a tougher sell. The events of 2020 thus provide a vivid illustration of the potential harms that could be avoided in a unitary republic, cleansed of state government, in which a majority of the voters choose the President through a process that is simpler, fairer, and more direct.

Of course, even with a national popular vote, the final tally would still have to be certified by somebody. That responsibility *could* be left with Congress and the vice president. For reasons considered in Chapter 6, however, this book instead proposes that the entire presidential election system be administered, and the votes ultimately certified, by a nonpartisan commission located within the national judicial branch, as is done with great success in Brazil.

Alexander Keyssar notes other, less publicized, features of the Electoral College system that have drawn criticism over the years. He points out that state legislatures could change the methodology from one election cycle to another whenever doing so achieves a partisan advantage.[106] As he also observes, the Constitution leaves the method for choosing the electors up to each state legislature. They arguably could, and in the early years of the republic did, choose the electors themselves rather than allow the people to do so.[107]

In the current, radically polarized political climate, that scenario is not far-fetched. The recent attempts to resurrect the Independent State Legislature Theory (the "ISLT"), discussed in Chapter 3, Section C, make this danger quite real. The Supreme Court in 2023 rejected only the most extreme version of that theory, and only as it applied to congressional elections. But in the same case the Court opened the door wide for what I term "ISLT-lite," and at any rate, the Court had no occasion to address its applicability to presidential elections at all. As a result, one cannot dismiss the real possibility of legislatures, particularly when the combination of counter-majoritarian forces discussed in this and Chapter 3 produces a Republican majority in a state where the voters lean Democratic, reclaiming a right to select their own presidential electors rather than leave the decision to the people.[108]

---

[106] Keyssar, Electoral College, note 53, at 4.
[107] *Ibid.*
[108] The case is *Moore v. Harper*, 143 S.Ct. 2065, § I.A (2023). See Chapter 3, Section C.

An affirmative benefit of the Electoral College system, Maibach earnestly contends, is that it requires that "the winner build support across the nation, not in just a handful of large urban areas." Hardaway similarly equates winning the Electoral College system with "winning the support of the people in States across the nation."[109] In contrast, defenders of the Electoral College system contend, in a national popular vote a few big cities would control the election.[110]

To begin with, once a majority of the voters nationwide have made their choice known, it shouldn't matter where in the country those who voted for or against particular candidates live. In a democracy, every person's vote should count the same, whether they live in cities, small towns, or anywhere else. Yes, the aggregate vote totals in a big city will have a greater impact than the aggregate vote totals in a small town. And they should. More people live there.

At any rate, the Electoral College hardly requires the winner to "build support across the nation." The winner need only build support in states that collectively comprise a majority of the Electoral College. Those states might well be concentrated in one or two specific regions, such as the west coast, the northeast, the south, or the midwest. As discussed below,[111] in today's America very few states are competitive. Presidential elections are decided in a handful of swing states. Certain regions have become predictable. At this writing, the Northeast and the West Coast for the most part are solidly blue; the Deep South and the Central Midwest states are reliably red. Over time, that might well change. For the moment, though, whether our presidents are chosen by the Electoral College or a direct national vote, winning support "across the nation" is, sadly, a rarity.

Moreover, the idea that a few big cities will dominate the electorate isn't even factually true. As Jesse Wegman points out, the fifty largest cities in the country together comprise only about 15 percent of the nation's population – roughly the same population percentage as those who live in the rural areas. As he also notes, the aggregate vote split is about 60-40 for Democrats in those cities and about 60-40 for Republicans in the rural areas.[112] The feared urban domination of the national popular vote is as factually inaccurate as it is democratically irrelevant.

Related to the claim that urban voters would dominate the election is Maibach's assertion, made by others as well, that in a direct popular election candidates would campaign only in densely populated urban areas. But where do they think the presidential candidates campaign now? Again, the vast majority of the states today are either solid red or solid blue. There is little incentive to spend precious campaign time and resources on those states. In practical terms, candidates today do almost

---

[109] Hardaway, note 53, at 29.
[110] Jesse Wegman notes this argument and refutes it empirically. See Wegman, Let the People Pick, note 16, at 223–25.
[111] Chapter 3, Section A.
[112] Wegman, Let the People Pick, note 16, at 225.

all their campaigning in the few remaining battleground states. And if the worry is about rural voters being ignored in a national popular vote, does anyone imagine that in the present system the major party presidential nominees are spending their limited time giving speeches to small crowds in sparsely populated rural areas?

The actual numbers are jarring. During the 2020 general presidential election campaign, 96 percent of the campaign events (204 of 212) by the Democratic and Republican presidential and vice presidential nominees were confined to twelve states. One hundred percent of the events were in seventeen states. Neither of the two major party presidential nominees or their vice presidential running mates held a single campaign event in any of the other thirty-three states (or the District of Columbia). Two states – Pennsylvania and Florida – together received three-eighths of the nation's campaign events for the major parties' presidential and vice presidential nominees.[113]

That election was not an anomaly. Similar numbers describe the 2012 and 2016 general presidential election campaigns. In 2016, twelve states drew 94 percent of the events; six of those states drew two-thirds of them. And in 2012, 100 percent of the events were in only twelve states; four of those states received two-thirds of the nation's total.[114]

Nor is it just a matter of in-person candidate appearances. As of October 13, 2020 (exactly three weeks before Election Day), almost 90 percent of all the money that the presidential campaigns had spent on TV advertisements nationwide had been channeled into six of the fifty states.[115]

Modern writers are not the first to object to a national popular vote on the ground that it would deprive some individuals of their disproportionate influence over the selection of the president. Alexander Keyssar highlights several early examples. Senator Robert Goodloe Harper, an influential US senator from Maryland, was a strong opponent of a constitutional amendment, introduced in 1816, that would have replaced the Electoral College with a national popular vote. He argued that the latter would violate the role of state sovereignty in the election of the president, thus obliterating the compromises that had been built into the Constitution. It would "destroy" the influence of the smaller states, he explained, because they

---

[113] National Popular Vote, *Map of General-Election Campaign Events and TV Ad Spending by 2020 Presidential Candidates*, www.nationalpopularvote.com/map-general-election-campaign-events-and-tv-ad-spending-2020-presidential-candidates. This trend has accelerated. In 2020, the states in which presidential candidates made appearances accounted for only 25 percent of the population. This compares to 75 percent in the years 1952 through 1980. Michael Scherer et al., Washington Post, 2024 *Vote Could Bring Electoral College Distortions to the Forefront* (Dec. 8, 2023), www.washingtonpost.com/nation/2023/12/08/electoral-college-votes-swing-states-decline/?utm_campaign=wp_post_most&utm_medium=email&utm_source=newsletter&wpisrc=nl_most.

[114] See Scherer *et al.*, note 113.

[115] NPR, *Presidential Campaign TV Ad Spending Crosses $1 Billion Mark in Key States* (Oct. 13, 2020), www.npr.org/2020/10/13/923427969/presidential-campaign-tv-ad-spending-crosses-1-billion-mark-in-key-states.

would each lose the two electoral votes they receive just for being states. By way of example, he pointed out that Louisiana would lose disproportionately more than a large state like New York.[116]

Indeed it would. And it should. All Louisiana would be losing is the extra advantage the Electoral College gives it – an advantage that in a representative democracy it does not, and never did, deserve to have. In contrast, the national popular vote would give each citizen of Louisiana exactly the same influence that each citizen of New York and every other state has – namely, one vote. In the end, Harper's arguments boiled down to nothing more than (i) state sovereignty is an end in itself; and (ii) we shouldn't change the bargain that the framers had to strike to get nine ratifications.

Another Senator, William Wyatt Bibb of Georgia, shared Harper's sovereignty concerns and added a new objection. The slave states, he lamented, would lose a constitutional advantage they then had. In tabulating the number of US House members the various states receive, and therefore their relative strength in the Electoral College, the slave states were allowed to count three-fifths of their slave populations even though they barred slaves from voting.[117] Apart from both the obscenity of slavery itself and the compound injury of artificially granting the slave states both more representation in Congress and more Electoral College votes than their free populations would merit, the abolition of slavery mooted that specific argument.

Even still, none of the post-Civil War amendments have put African American voters on the same footing as white voters. As discussed below,[118] the southern states in particular, and a broader range of Republican-controlled states today, have adopted increasingly sophisticated measures to depress the African American vote. Having done so, some of those states have nonetheless argued with a straight face that these very voting restrictions would unfairly disadvantage their residents in a national popular vote. Why? Because those voting restrictions would cause their citizens' percentage of the national turnout to be lower than the state's percentage of the national population, which in turn determines the size of their congressional delegation and therefore their percentage of the Electoral College vote. Now that is chutzpah! And it continues to play a prominent role in the Deep South's opposition to a national popular vote.[119]

In the early twentieth century, the issue of women suffrage triggered a somewhat parallel objection. For a period of time leading up to the Nineteenth Amendment in 1919, some states allowed women to vote and others didn't. That differential, the argument went, would give the states in which women could vote an unfair advantage in a national popular vote.[120] The obvious remedy – granting women the vote – apparently

---

[116] Keyssar, Electoral College, note 53, at 175.
[117] *Ibid.*, at 176.
[118] Chapter 3, Sections A and B.
[119] Keyssar, Electoral College, note 53, at 189–94.
[120] *Ibid.*, at 189.

was not an acceptable option. At any rate, their argument was just as vulnerable as the earlier argument made by the slave states. Apart from the injustice of disenfranchising women in the first place, these states sought to have it both ways: They wanted to deny the vote to half the adults in their states, but still count disenfranchised women for purposes of maximizing the sizes of their states' congressional delegations and, therefore, the amount of say they got in choosing the president.

Perhaps the most substantial defense of the Electoral College system is that, as Maibach argues, it almost always yields an outright majority. In fact, only twice in our history has the Electoral College failed to do so.[121] That is because it is rare, at least today, for a third-party or independent candidate to win a plurality in a single state.[122] The winner-take-all rule thus virtually ensures that all the electoral votes will go to the two major party candidates. In contrast, it is not at all unusual for independent or third-party candidates to prevent any one person from winning an outright majority of the national popular vote.

This is a fair concern. But I take exception to his fix. He says "The Electoral College creates a national majority for new presidents regardless of the popular vote margin. Reflecting the will of majorities in the fifty states, the College *legitimizes the result*"[123] [my emphasis].

It does no such thing, because the Electoral College is an artificial construct. The winner-take-all rule in forty-eight of the fifty states means that the majority Maibach extolls is a fiction, unless one believes that the president should be chosen not by the people collectively but by states – which, to add yet another layer of abstraction, are themselves creations aptly described by Hamilton as "artificial beings" and by Wilson as "imaginary." Dressing up a mere plurality of the voters as a majority of politically constructed electoral votes doesn't add any legitimacy to the process. Put another way, the Electoral College system does not salvage majority rule; it just masks its absence. Whatever the fiction, the bottom line remains: one can become president even when the majority of the voters choose other candidates.

That said, adoption of a national popular vote admittedly would require a decision as to what happens when no candidate wins a nationwide majority. One option, included in many of the constitutional amendments introduced in Congress in recent years,[124] would be simply to settle for presidents who win only pluralities of

---

[121] Those were the 1800 and 1824 elections. As provided by the Constitution, the House of Representatives, voting by state delegations, chose the president. See Section C.

[122] It hasn't happened since 1968, when George Wallace, a segregationist running as a third-party "states' rights" candidate, won pluralities, and therefore electoral votes, in five southern states. In that election, Richard Nixon nonetheless won a majority of the electoral votes, defeating Hubert Humphrey. Wikipedia, *1968 United States Presidential Election*, https://en.wikipedia.org/wiki/1968_United_States_presidential_election.

[123] Maibach, note 53.

[124] See Congressional Research Service, *The Electoral College: Reform Proposals in the 114th and 115th Congress* (Aug. 24, 2017), at 6–12, file:///C:/Users/legomsky/Downloads/R44928.pdf.

the national popular vote. In reality, we do this now, as just discussed. In fact, under the Electoral College system, we do this on the statewide level as well, because in every state except Nebraska and Maine, a plurality – not a majority – is all a candidate needs to win all the electoral votes of the state. In gubernatorial and other statewide elections as well, a plurality is typically all that is needed. Typically too, election to both houses of the US Congress and to both chambers of the various state legislatures requires only a plurality of the relevant popular vote.

But if the notion of a plurality president suddenly becomes unacceptable, a majority of the national popular vote could still be required. Options for accomplishing this include (i) a ranked-choice voting system; or (ii) a runoff election between the top two vote-getters when no majority emerges in the first round. The pros and cons of these options – not just for presidential elections, but in general – are discussed in Chapter 6.[125]

A related defense of the Electoral College system is that it forces the voters to confine their focus to two candidates. Maibach's argument here is that, as a practical matter, third-party or independent candidates have little to no chance of winning entire states. The winner-take-all feature of the Electoral College system therefore discourages them from running. In turn, any rule that discourages third-party and independent candidates from running increases the likelihood that some candidate will achieve an outright majority of the Electoral College. Maibach's additional point here, though, is that discouraging third-party and independent candidates also helps avoid the often messy and unstable coalition governments that dominate many other western democracies.

But even assuming *arguendo* that limiting the voters to the choice between two political parties' nominees is a good thing, the Electoral College system does not achieve that goal. People still run as third-party or independent candidates. Perhaps more would do so under a national popular vote system. Again, however, if it were decided that plurality presidents are no longer acceptable, either ranked-choice voting or a runoff election would solve the problem.

Hardaway also credits the Electoral College's track record: It "has functioned far more successfully than was ever envisioned by the constitutional framers, and has, over the past 100 years, consistently produced clear-cut winners, all of whom received more popular votes than their opponents."[126] Having published the book in 1994, Hardaway could not have anticipated that in two of the next six presidential elections, the Electoral College would hand the presidency to the candidate who lost the national popular vote. Still, his rosy assessment is surprising in the light of the many near misses that the country had already experienced.

---

[125] See Keyssar, Electoral College, note 53, at 277–78. Other writers favoring adoption of a national popular vote advocate a runoff election between the top two vote-getters when no candidate wins a majority in the first round. For example, Dahl, note 3, at 205 n.20; Levinson, note 2, at 214 n.35.

[126] Hardaway, note 53, at 5.

Another claimed benefit of the Electoral College is what Hardaway calls the "immediate and decisive effect" of its "verdict." As he puts it, "Amazingly, … advocates of direct election have chosen to find fault even with this undeniable feature of the Electoral College."[127] Well, that feature, too, turns out not to be as "undeniable" as he thought. The ink was barely dry on his confident indictment of the critics when Al Gore in 2000 indisputably won the national popular vote, besting George W. Bush by more than half-a-million votes.[128] Had a national popular vote system been in effect, the outcome would have been clear and promptly known.[129] Instead, the Electoral College system triggered a weeks-long saga that ended only when the Supreme Court's 5-4 decision halted the Florida recount and thereby decided the election.[130] The Court reasoned that a fair recount would not have been possible within the deadlines embedded in the Electoral College process.[131] I am not suggesting either that a national popular vote will always yield clear and immediate results or that the Electoral College system never will. The point is that, in any given presidential election, either system could succeed or fail on that score. That is the reality in a nation as closely divided as ours.

During the early twentieth century, another objection to a national popular vote arose: If there were a national popular vote, the objectors said, elections would have to be managed by federal officials rather than state officials.[132] Why that was a bad thing was never really explained, and Chapter 4, Section C.3 of this book considers the question of which level of government is best situated to manage federal elections. But even assuming *arguendo* that federal administration of presidential elections is an inherent evil, the argument is a non sequitur. Nothing about switching from the Electoral College to a national popular vote would prevent state officials from continuing to administer elections within the boundaries of their own states, just as they do now. For that matter, such a change doesn't even have to alter the mechanics of the voting process. Of course, my view that state government should be abolished would make the question moot.

As with most defenses of the Electoral College system, Hardaway's argument ultimately rests, more than anything else, on his deep-seated belief – reflected in the title of his book – in the value of American federalism and the Electoral College's

---

[127] *Ibid.*, at 28.
[128] Infoplease, Presidential Election of 2000, note 69.
[129] Gore's popular vote victory was a plurality, not a majority. *Ibid.* So in my assertion that under a national popular vote system the result would have been known promptly, I am assuming that either (i) a plurality of the popular vote would still be sufficient to win the presidency, as it is now; or (ii) a majority is required but ranked-choice voting has been adopted. If instead the system were to provide for a runoff election, then of course the result, though ultimately clear, would not have been immediate. Even then, however, it would at least have been free of the legal uncertainties and the ensuing (and in my opinion self-inflicted) damage to the nonpartisan reputation of the Supreme Court.
[130] *Bush v. Gore*, 531 U.S. 98 (2000).
[131] *Ibid.*, at 121–22.
[132] Keyssar, Electoral College, note 53, at 188.

federalist roots. Maibach too defends the Electoral College as a necessary political compromise struck more than 200 years ago. It is, he says, just "part of American federalism."

That observation is merely a description of its historical origins, not a normative justification on the merits – and certainly not a refutation of its antidemocratic effects. When the dust settles, it is hard for me to see any substance in the federalist defense of the Electoral College beyond "we've always done it this way" and "this and similar compromises accommodate the twin goals of popular democracy and state sovereignty" (my paraphrasing). Unless state sovereignty is seen – and somehow defended – as an end in itself, these arguments add no normative value.

Not surprisingly, public opinion surveys taken from the inception of scientific polling in the 1940s to the present day (with short-lived blips immediately following President Trump's Electoral College win in 2016) have consistently demonstrated public discontent with the current system. Respondents in almost every poll have not only favored distributing electoral votes proportionally to the popular votes within each state (versus winner-take-all), but also abolishing the Electoral College entirely in favor of a national popular vote. And they have expressed both of those preferences by lopsided margins.[133]

Despite the flimsiness of these defenses of the Electoral College, despite the longstanding and numerically overwhelming public preference for abolishing it, despite both the older and the more recent recurrences of its counter-majoritarian outcomes, despite the statistical certainty of many more to come, and despite the fact that "every other presidential democracy in the world did away with indirect elections during the twentieth century,"[134] the Electoral College has survived for more than 200 years. What is keeping it afloat?

Alexander Keyssar has written a (brilliant) 531-page book devoted to that one question. As he shows, two of the obstacles are fundamental and permanent. One of them, discussed in some detail in Section D, is that in general, the US Constitution is excruciatingly difficult to amend. The clash of diverse interests has impeded the degree of political consensus the amendment process requires. The other problem, already discussed, is states. Eliminating any state power is never easy, for states guard their authority jealously. Taking away the particular power, currently assigned to the state legislatures, to decide how to choose their presidential electors, is especially fraught.[135]

The other main obstacles identified by Keyssar are more transient. They fluctuate with various states' perceptions of whether abolition of the Electoral College would work to the short-term benefit or detriment of their specific partisan or other interests. As the preceding discussion suggested, at various times in our history states that

---

[133] *Ibid.*, App. A, at 383–87.
[134] Levitsky & Ziblatt, Tyranny, note 3, at 215, 217.
[135] Keyssar, Electoral College, note 53, at 8–9.

believed rightly or wrongly that the Electoral College worked in their favor have included small states, slave states, and states that didn't allow women to vote before the Nineteenth Amendment.[136] Today, states controlled by Republicans similarly tend to perceive that their partisan advantage is best served by keeping the Electoral College just as it is.

Given these difficulties, proponents of a national popular vote have turned to a clever alternative strategy. It is called the National Popular Vote Interstate Compact[137] (NPVIC). The idea is for individual states to enact legislation that awards all of their electoral votes to whichever presidential candidate wins a plurality of the national popular vote. Importantly, each such law will operate only in a year when the same law is in effect in states that collectively possess a majority of the electoral votes.[138] If enough such states pass this law, the winner of the national popular vote would gain a majority of the Electoral College and become president.

As of January 2024, the NPVIC has been enacted into law in sixteen states and the District of Columbia. Together they possess 205 electoral votes – 65 short of the 270 required for an Electoral College majority.[139]

Getting to 270 will not be easy. As Wegman points out, "To date, all the states that have passed the compact did so under a Democratic-led [i.e., Democratic control of both houses] legislature and, with the exception of Hawaii, a Democratic governor."[140] As a result of the 2022 midterm elections, Michigan now has a Democratic governor and Democratic majorities in both houses of the legislature. Still, even its additional sixteen electoral votes would leave the compact forty-nine electoral votes shy.

In addition, any interstate compact – especially one like this, which hinges on adoption and retention by states that together possess 270 electoral votes – is more fragile than a constitutional amendment that would enshrine a national popular vote permanently. Any state could withdraw from the compact, and, depending on the numbers, withdrawal by even a single state could take down the whole system. That risk will always be real, especially in battleground states, if a Republican Party trifecta suddenly displaces a Democratic Party trifecta.

---

[136] *Ibid.*, at 9–10, 175–89.
[137] The National Center for Interstate Compacts defines an interstate compact as "A Legally Binding Agreement between Two or More States." *Frequently Asked Questions*, https://compacts.csg.org/faq/. See also Ballotpedia, *Interstate Compact*, https://ballotpedia.org/Interstate_compact.
[138] The same provisions apply to the election of the vice president. The text of the NPVIC can be found at National Popular Vote, *Text of the National Popular Vote Compact Bill*, www.nationalpopularvote .com/bill-text. The most comprehensive, and the most authoritative, book on the NPVIC is John R. Koza *et al.*, Every Vote Equal: A State-Based Plan for Electing the President by National Popular Vote (4th ed. 2013). See also Keyssar, Electoral College, note 53, at 341–47; Wegman, Let the People Pick, note 16, chap. 7, at 190–218.
[139] Wikipedia, *National Popular Vote Interstate Compact*, https://en.wikipedia.org/wiki/National_ Popular_Vote_Interstate_Compact. See also Keyssar, Electoral College, note 53, at 345–46, Table 7.1.
[140] Wegman, Let the People Pick, note 16, at 195.

Finally, there are constitutional concerns. First, there is always a danger that the Supreme Court will strike down the compact as an impermissible end run around the Constitution's Electoral College provision. Second, the Constitution says "No State shall, without the Consent of Congress, … enter into any Agreement or Compact with another State."[141] Congressional approval will be highly unlikely unless and until the Democratic Party controls the White House and both Houses of Congress; even then, Senate approval will be a challenge unless the filibuster rule is repealed.

But as others have explained, the Supreme Court has rejected a literal reading of the congressional approval requirement. The National Center for Interstate Compacts, an entity established by the Council of State Governments, describes the Court's case law as requiring congressional approval only when a compact "would increase state political power in a manner that would encroach upon federal authority." It observes that only "[a]pproximately 40% of existing compacts required federal consent."[142] The Sightline Institute agrees, citing several Supreme Court decisions from 1893 to 1978. It goes on to point out that the Constitution requires each state to appoint electors "in such Manner as the Legislature thereof may direct."[143] Thus, they conclude, the NPVIC does not encroach on any federal authority and therefore does not require congressional approval.[144] Others disagree,[145] and there is no certainty as to how the current Supreme Court would rule.

C HOUSE'S STATE DELEGATIONS CHOOSING THE PRESIDENT

The same inequality of voting power is reflected in the Twelfth Amendment. If no presidential candidate gains a majority in the Electoral College, the House of Representatives chooses the president. Even if that were all there were to it, and even taking as a given both the Electoral College itself and the requirement of a majority of its electors, this wouldn't be the best way to select the President when no candidate wins an outright Electoral College majority. As described in greater detail later,[146] the combination of intrastate residential patterns, single-member districts, and widespread gerrymandering makes the House anything but representative.

---

[141] U.S. Const. Art. I, § 10, Cl. 3.

[142] National Center for Interstate Compacts, *Frequently Asked Questions*, https://compacts.csg.org/faq/ (under link to "Where do states obtain legal authority to enter compacts?").

[143] U.S. Const. Art. II, § 1, Cl. 2.

[144] Sightline Institute, *The National Popular Vote Interstate Compact Requires No Congressional Approval*, www.sightline.org/2021/01/19/the-national-popular-vote-interstate-compact-requires-no-congressional-approval/.

[145] See the analysis of the competing constitutional arguments in Wikipedia, *National Popular Vote Interstate Compact*, note 139.

[146] Chapter 3, Section A.

But it gets worse. When the election goes to the House, the president is chosen not by a majority of the House Members, but by a majority of state delegations. Those delegations that represent tens of millions of residents get no more say than those that represent only a small fraction of that number.

As Jesse Wegman has noted, several of the founders expected House selection of the president to become the norm. George Mason, in fact, predicted that nineteen out of every twenty presidential elections would be decided by the House.[147] Thankfully, as noted earlier, this process has been necessary only twice. In the 1800 presidential election, the Democratic-Republican Party ran Thomas Jefferson for president and Aaron Burr for vice president, against incumbent president John Adams and his vice presidential running mate, Charles Pinckney, both Federalists. The Jefferson–Burr ticket won just over 60 percent of the national popular vote. At the time, however, each elector cast two votes, with no distinction as to which vote was for president and which was for vice president. The result was that Jefferson and Burr ended up each receiving seventy-three electoral votes for president, to Adams's sixty-five. Because no one candidate had a majority of the Electoral College, it fell to the House of Representatives, voting by state delegation, to choose the president. The contest came down to a battle between the two Democratic-Republican candidates, Jefferson and Burr. Jefferson was elected on the thirty-sixth ballot.[148] Amidst the political fireworks, at least on that occasion the outcome reasonably reflected the wishes of the majority of the voters.[149]

Not so in 1824. That election featured four candidates, all members of the same Democratic-Republican Party. Andrew Jackson won 41 percent of the national popular vote. John Quincy Adams finished second with 31 percent. Henry Clay and William Crawford garnered 13% and 11%, respectively.[150]

Jackson also won a plurality of the Electoral College with ninety-nine electoral votes to eighty-four for Adams.[151] But when the election got to the House, Clay threw his support to Adams, whom the House, voting by individual state delegation as

---

[147] Jesse Wegman, The New York Times, *The Real Danger in Robert F. Kennedy Jr.'s Independent Run* (Oct. 14, 2023), www.nytimes.com/2023/10/14/opinion/the-real-danger-in-robert-f-kennedy-jrs-independent-run.html?action=click&module=RelatedLinks&pgtype=Article.

[148] Wikipedia, *1800 United States Presidential Election*, https://en.wikipedia.org/wiki/1800_United_States_presidential_election.

[149] Bruce Ackerman provides a spellbinding account of the background behind the 1800 presidential election and its (temporary) role in conforming the presidential election system to the will of the people. Bruce Ackerman, The Failure of the Founding Fathers: Jefferson, Marshall, and the Rise of Presidential Democracy (2005). The book also highlights the framers' failure to foresee the dominant role of political parties. See Chapter 5 of the present book, note 15.

[150] John Woolley and Gerhard Peters, *The American Presidency Project*, www.presidency.ucsb.edu/statistics/elections/1824. Here I need to repeat a caveat. In 1824, a popular vote was actually held in only eighteen of the then twenty-four states; in the other six, the state legislatures chose the electors. Wikipedia, *List*, note 66.

[151] Woolley & Peters, note 150.

constitutionally required, ultimately selected. Adams ended up winning thirteen of the twenty-four state delegations; Jackson won seven and Crawford four.[152]

To be fair, the final outcome in 1824 would have been no different had the House voted by membership rather than by state delegation. The results would have been closer, but either way, Adams would have won the election in the House, albeit just narrowly. He received the votes of 109 House members (51%) to Jackson's 104 (49%).[153] But the basic takeaways remain the same: First, Jackson won a plurality of the national popular vote by a healthy margin over Adams; yet Adams won the presidency. And second, even if selection by the House were otherwise a fair way to resolve the lack of an Electoral College majority, the tightness of the House membership vote illustrates how close we came to the presidency, already having been tarnished once by the counter-majoritarian Electoral College, being tarnished again by the additional counter-majoritarian principle of one vote per House state delegation. And, of course, as public dissatisfaction with both of today's major political parties grows, one cannot dismiss the possibility of a future third-party candidate winning a plurality of the popular votes in one or more states, thereby preventing an Electoral College majority.

D THE JUDICIAL APPOINTMENT PROCESS

The appointment of a federal judge is a two-step process – nomination by the president and confirmation by the Senate.[154] To be clear, my counter-majoritarian objection to this process is *not* that federal judges are not elected by the people. As explained in Chapter 6, I wouldn't want them to be.

Rather, as this section will illustrate, both steps in the process – nomination and confirmation – have been hijacked by counter-majoritarian forces that would not exist without the constitutionally assigned roles of the states. The first step becomes counter-majoritarian when the judge is nominated by a president whom the American people rejected but whom the state-centered Electoral College installed in the White House. The second step becomes counter-majoritarian when the Senate is under the control of a political party that the voters repudiated nationwide and that Senate, in turn, either votes to confirm the nominee of a popularly rejected president or, conversely, votes to block or delay the confirmation of a candidate nominated by a popularly elected president.

The impact of counter-majoritarian judicial partisanship has been the most visible at the Supreme Court level. At this writing (2024), conservative Justices appointed

---

[152] U.S. House of Representatives, History, Art and Archives, https://history.house.gov/Historical-Highlights/1800-1850/The-House-of-Representatives-elected-John-Quincy-Adams-as-President/.
[153] Wikipedia, *1824–25 United States House of Representatives elections*, https://en.wikipedia.org/wiki/1824%E2%80%9325_United_States_House_of_Representatives_elections.
[154] U.S. Const. Art. II, § 2, Cl. 2.

by Republican presidents hold six of the nine Supreme Court seats. Three of those Justices – Gorsuch, Kavanaugh, and Barrett – were appointed by President Trump,[155] who as noted earlier had lost the national popular vote to Hillary Clinton by a margin of almost three million. Had Clinton become president (and had the Republican Senate functioned in a majoritarian manner), it is a safe bet that it is Democratic appointees who would be holding a 6-3 majority.

That example illustrates the counter-majoritarian effect of the nomination component alone. The same three appointments reveal the additional counter-majoritarianism of the Senate confirmation process. President Obama, who had won both election and reelection by winning outright majorities of both the national popular vote and the Electoral College,[156] nominated Judge Merrick Garland for the Supreme Court. The nomination was made in March 2016, with approximately ten months remaining in his term. The Republicans, then in control of the Senate despite still collectively representing only a minority of the US population,[157] refused even to hold a hearing on Garland's nomination.[158] Their stated reason was that the appointment was too close to the upcoming November election. It was necessary to see how the people would vote, they argued. Yet, when President Trump later nominated Amy Coney Barrett to the Court, the Republican-controlled Senate (with the Republicans still collectively representing only a minority of the US population) had no trouble confirming her only *one week* before Election Day and after tens of millions of Americans had already cast early ballots. The candidate who should have received a hearing did not; the candidate whose nomination truly was so close to the election that the Senate should have waited was rushed through.

Then-Senate majority leader Mitch McConnell's defense was that "Americans re-elected our [Senate Republican] majority in 2016 and expanded it in 2018."[159] As Pamela Karlan rightly points out, "a majority of Americans did no such thing."[160] Per her cited sources, the Senate's Republican majority that confirmed Justice Barrett represented only a minority of the US population.[161] Population aside, as

[155] Supreme Court of the United States, Current Members, www.supremecourt.gov/about/biographies.aspx.

[156] See Wikipedia, 2008 *Presidential Election*, https://en.wikipedia.org/wiki/2008_United_States_presidential_election and Wikipedia, 2012 *Presidential Election*, https://en.wikipedia.org/wiki/2012_United_States_presidential_election.

[157] See the calculation for the 114th Congress (Jan. 2015 to Jan. 2017), described in note 36.

[158] Wikipedia, *Merrick Garland*, https://en.wikipedia.org/wiki/Merrick_Garland.

[159] Carl Hulse, The New York *Times*, *For McConnell, Ginsburg's Death Prompts Stark Turnabout from 2016 Stance* (Sept. 18, 2020), www.nytimes.com/2020/09/18/us/mitch-mcconnell-rbg-trump.html.

[160] Karlan, note 3, at 2339.

[161] Balkin, note 3, at 141 (pointing out that Justices Thomas, Alito, Gorsuch, and Kavanaugh were all confirmed by senators who represented only a minority of the then-US population); Camille Caldera, USA Today, *Fact Check: "Living Under Minority Rule" Post Contains 6 True Facts on Trump, Barrett* (Oct. 21, 2020), www.usatoday.com/story/news/factcheck/2020/10/21/fact-check-minority-rule-post-has-6-true-facts-trump-barrett/3669988001/ (agreeing that Barrett was confirmed on a party-line vote and that "Republicans in the Senate represent 14.3 million fewer Americans than Senate Democrats").

detailed earlier,[162] Americans voted overwhelmingly in favor of Democratic senatorial candidates in both of the years that McConnell cited.

Justice Kavanaugh, meanwhile, after being nominated by a president who had lost the national popular vote, was confirmed by a Senate whose Republican majority not only collectively represented just a minority of the US population,[163] but had soundly lost the national senatorial popular vote in the then-most recent election, 53% to 42%, only to be rewarded with twenty-two of the thirty-four Senate seats up for election that year.[164] Had the Democrats come away from that election with even an equal split of the Senate seats that had been voted on – let alone a share proportionate to the votes of the people – they would have controlled the Senate by a comfortable margin.[165]

It is not only the Trump nominees who owe their Supreme Court appointments to counter-majoritarianism. As Jack Balkin has observed, a majority of the current Supreme Court Justices – Justices Thomas, Alito, Gorsuch, Kavanaugh, and Barrett – were all confirmed by senators who collectively represented only a minority of the then-existing US populations.[166] Moreover, for them as well, it wasn't just population. Democratic presidential nominees have won the national popular vote in a majority of the last fourteen elections (8-6). Yet, during the presidential terms resulting from those elections (1968–2024),[167] Republican Supreme Court appointments have outnumbered those by Democratic presidents 15 to 5.[168]

That's just the Supreme Court. During that same period, again despite losing the presidential popular vote in a majority of the elections, Republican presidents were able to appoint approximately 1,482 lower court judges; Democratic presidents managed only approximately 1,082.[169] That disparity can be traced to the hundreds

---

[162] See Section A.

[163] Justice Kavanaugh took his Supreme Court seat in October 2018. At that time, Republicans represented only about 44.8 percent of the national population. See the calculations in note 37.

[164] Wikipedia, *2016 United States Senate Elections*, https://en.wikipedia.org/wiki/2016_United_States_Senate_elections.

[165] Even after being awarded twenty-two of the thirty-four Senate seats up for election in 2016 despite the Democrats' solid majority of the Senate votes cast nationwide, the Republicans held only fifty-two seats overall. *Ibid.* If the Democrats had received even one-half of the Senate seats decided in that election – that is, seventeen instead of twelve, the Republicans would have ended up with only forty-seven Senate seats in total.

[166] Balkin, note 3, at 141.

[167] U.S. House of Representatives, History, Art, note 152.

[168] Supreme Court of the United States, *Justices 1789 to present*, www.supremecourt.gov/about/members_text.aspx; United States Courts, *Judgeship Appointments by President*, www.uscourts.gov/sites/default/files/apptsbypres.pdf. The Supreme Court website shows three Chief Justice appointments and eighteen Associate Justice appointments, but the name of Chief Justice Rehnquist is listed twice (once under each category). So the total number of Justices appointed during this time span is twenty, consistent with the US Courts website.

[169] United States Courts, note 168. I tabulated these figures by adding the numbers displayed for each of the Republican presidents and those for each of the Democratic presidents. The figures include appointments to all the federal courts – the Supreme Court, the courts of appeals, the district courts,

of appointees by national popular vote losers President George W. Bush (in his first term) and President Trump.[170] In addition, however, the Republican-controlled Senate (whose members represented only a minority of the country's people, in case I haven't reminded you of this often enough), blocked and delayed the nominations of popular vote winner President Obama (during the last six years of his eight-year tenure) and then expedited the nominations of popular vote loser President Trump. As a result, President Obama was limited to an average of only forty-two federal judges per year[171] – the lowest annual average of any President during this period (except for President Ford, a caretaker President who served the final two years of President Nixon's second term after Nixon's resignation). In contrast, the Senate's actions enabled President Trump to average sixty-one appointments per year,[172] by far the highest annual average of any president during this period (except for the special circumstance of President Carter, who benefitted from Congress's huge expansion of the federal judiciary).[173]

If both the composition of the US Senate and its actual practice (discussed below) make the judicial confirmation process counter-majoritarian, the Senate "blue slip" tradition adds insult to injury. A "blue slip" is the paper that any member of the Senate may submit to the chair of the Judiciary Committee to support a judicial nominee who would "represent" that Senator's home state – meaning the nomination is for a district judgeship located in that state or for a court of appeals seat for which the particular state is regarded as deserving a "turn." Depending on the policy of the Judiciary Committee chair, withholding a blue slip either automatically kills the nomination without so much as a committee hearing or implies that the

---

and (in much smaller numbers) the territorial courts and the Court of International Trade. I say "approximately" because a handful of judges were counted twice, having been appointed to one federal court and then promoted to another. The figures are as of December 31, 2022; thus, they cover only the first two years of the Biden Administration.

[170] The table does not distinguish between the numbers appointed by President Bush in his first term, following his loss in the national popular vote, and those he appointed during his second term, for which he won the national popular vote. On the assumption that his appointments were split roughly equally between the two terms, the numbers of judicial appointees during his first term and President Trump's term were approximately ½ of 340 (Bush) plus 245 (Trump), for a total of 415. Had those appointments been made by the candidates who had won the popular vote but lost the Electoral College vote (Al Gore and Hillary Clinton), Democratic presidents would have appointed 1,497 judges and Republican presidents 1,067, figures more closely tracking the percentage of elections during this period in which the respective parties had won the national popular vote.

[171] President Obama appointed 334 judges over 8 years, for an annual average of 42. United States Courts, note 168.

[172] President Trump appointed 245 judges over 4 years, *ibid.*, for an annual average of 61.

[173] The Omnibus Judge Act of 1978 added 117 federal district court judgeships and 35 court of appeals judgeships. Jimmy Carter, The American Presidency Project, *Statement on Signing H.R. 7483 into Law: Appointments of Additional District and Circuit Judges* (Oct. 20, 1978), www.presidency.ucsb.edu/documents/statement-signing-hr-7843-into-law-appointments-additional-district-and-circuit-judges.

nomination should be blocked as a matter of "Senate courtesy." No reason for with-holding a blue slip need be given.[174]

As of this writing (2024), Senator Dick Durbin (D-Ill) chairs the Judiciary Committee. He has said he will follow the precedents established by his two imme-diate predecessors, Senators Charles Grassley (R-Iowa) and Lindsay Graham (R-So. Car.). Under that policy, a positive blue slip from the home state senator is required for district court nominees but not for court of appeals nominees.

The blue slip process is rife with partisan counter-majoritarian abuse. First, empowering a single senator to stop the appointment of a federal judge is inherently counter-majoritarian. Even lower federal court decisions frequently have interstate and even nationwide impact. As noted below, recent years have witnessed a spate of federal district courts entering nationwide injunctions that prohibit the federal gov-ernment from carrying out its announced policies. And the precedential decisions of the US courts of appeals (except for the DC Circuit and the specialized "Federal Circuit") always have at least multistate, and often nationwide, effects. As a matter of principle, the notion that a single state – much less, just one of the state's two sen-ators – deserves a veto power over the President's selection of a federal judge should be a nonstarter for that reason alone.

Actual experience, especially in recent years, attests to the partisan abuse that the blue slip process invites. Senator Pat Toomey (R-Pa.) withheld his blue slip for President Biden's nomination of Arianna Freeman for a seat on the US Court of Appeals for the Third Circuit because her area of practice was a "niche" area.[175] She was a public defender. I could find no record of his having withheld blue slips for nominees who were criminal prosecutors. When President Biden nominated Andre Mathis to a seat on the US Court of Appeals for the Sixth Circuit, Senator Marsha Blackburn (R-Tenn.) withheld her blue slip, describing as a "rap sheet" what the President of the NAACP described as "less than a handful of speeding tickets."[176]

Does this really matter much? Oh my, yes, as the following discussion will show. By shaping the composition of the federal courts, these powerful counter-majoritarian structures have fundamentally transformed US law. The impact has been especially pronounced in the election law cases themselves. Here is just a sample of the affected outcomes:[177]

---

[174] Ballotpedia, *Blue Slip (federal judicial nominations)*, https://ballotpedia.org/Blue_slip_(federal_judicial_nominations).

[175] *Ibid.*

[176] *Ibid.*

[177] The bare-bones descriptions of these cases in this section, with emphasis on how the various Justices voted, are designed only to illustrate the impact of the counter-majoritarian judicial appointment process on actual case outcomes. The substantive aspects of these election law cases are revisited in various parts of Chapter 3, Sections A and B, as they relate to gerrymandering and voter suppression, respectively.

In 1986, a six-Justice majority of the Supreme Court in *Davis* v. *Bandemer*[178] had held that federal courts could review claims of partisan gerrymandering of state legislative districts. In 2004 the Court returned to the issue in *Vieth* v. *Jubelirer*,[179] this time in the context of alleged partisan gerrymandering of congressional districts. By then the composition of the Court had become decidedly more conservative. Four Justices concluded that such claims were nonjusticiable and wanted to overrule *Bandemer*; the other five disagreed (one of them holding out the possibility that the Court might one day declare them nonjusticiable if a manageable standard could not be agreed on). But by 2019 new appointments had moved the Court even further to the right. In its decision that year in *Rucho* v. *Common Cause*,[180] the Court overruled *Bandemer*, holding that partisan gerrymandering claims (in that case, relating to congressional districts) were nonjusticiable. Even in the face of what the Court admitted were "blatant examples of partisanship driving districting decisions,"[181] the Court held that partisan gerrymandering claims present political questions beyond the reach of the federal courts.[182] Essential to that 5-4 decision were Justices Gorsuch and Kavanaugh. Both had been nominated by President Trump, who had lost the national popular vote, and then confirmed by Senators who together had represented only a minority of the national population.

In *Abbott* v. *Perez*,[183] the issue was whether Texas maps updating both congressional and state legislative districts had been drawn with a racially (not just partisan) discriminatory intent, in violation of Section 2 of the Voting Rights Act. Again the Justices divided along party lines. The five Republican appointees held that the challengers had failed to prove a racially discriminatory intent; the four Democratic appointees felt otherwise and dissented. Justice Gorsuch, filling a spot that as noted earlier should have been filled by President Obama (and, failing that, would have been filled by Hillary Clinton had the national popular vote been honored), voted with the majority. As in *Rucho*, his vote made the difference.

In *Husted* v. *A. Philip Randolph Institute*,[184] the Supreme Court upheld an Ohio law that required the purging of eligible voters' names from the registration lists for having failed to vote in recent prior elections. This was another 5-4 decision in which the Justices divided along partisan lines. And, again, the vote of Justice Gorsuch was essential to the outcome.

---

[178] 478 U.S. 109 (1986). In that case, there was no majority as to the applicable standard and the challenged plan was ultimately upheld.

[179] 541 U.S. 267 (2004). Again, the majority could not agree on a specific standard, and the challenged districting plan was upheld.

[180] 139 S.Ct. 2484 (2019).

[181] *Ibid.*, at 2505.

[182] *Ibid.*, at 2506–507.

[183] 138 S.Ct. 2305 (2018).

[184] 138 S.Ct. 1833 (2018).

In *Brnovich* v. *Democratic National Committee*,[185] the Supreme Court addressed two of Arizona's voting restriction laws. One of those laws required election officials to throw out any votes cast on election day unless they were cast in the precinct in which the voter lived. The other challenged law made it a criminal offense for anyone other than the voter or his or her family member, household member, or caregiver, or a postal worker or elections official, to collect or return the person's ballot – practices that no one denied were most prevalent in African American communities. The question was whether either of these laws violated the race discrimination provisions of the Voting Rights Act.

Splitting 6-3, once again along strictly partisan lines, the Court upheld both Arizona laws. The three Trump appointees – Justices Gorsuch, Kavanaugh, and Barrett – all voted with the majority. As noted earlier, the Gorsuch spot should have been President Obama's to fill. And if majoritarian principles had been followed, the Kavanaugh and Barrett spots would have been filled by national popular vote winner Hillary Clinton – or, in the case of Justice Barrett, arguably held over for President Biden. As in the preceding cases, counter-majoritarian judicial appointments made the difference.

Those are just the election law cases. They barely scratch the surface, as there are countless other subject areas in which counter-majoritarian Supreme Court appointees have made the difference in cases of huge national import. In 2022 alone, the votes of one or more of the three Trump appointees were frequently outcome-determinative. The blockbuster, of course, was *Dobbs* v. *Jackson Women's Health Organization*,[186] where a 5-4 majority that included all three Trump appointees overruled the Court's landmark decision in *Roe* v. *Wade*[187] and its constitutional protection of abortion rights.

There were so many more. In that same year, the Court declared a Second Amendment right to carry handguns outside the home for self-defense; banned the EPA from regulating the carbon emissions of existing power plants; prohibited the federal government from mandating that large employers require their employees to either vaccinate or self-test for COVID; barred states from selectively denying public grants to religious schools; and allowed the football coach of a public high school to lead prayer sessions on the fifty-yard line of the school's field.[188] In 2023, in *Sackett* v. *EPA*,[189] the Court voted 5-4 to strip the EPA of its power to regulate huge areas of wetlands and other waterways, jeopardizing important sources of clean water. And on the last two days of June 2023, the Supreme Court, by identical 6-3

[185] 141 S.Ct. 2321 (2021).
[186] 142 S.Ct 2228 (2022).
[187] 410 U.S. 113 (1973).
[188] These and other 2022 Supreme Court decisions are collected in Ann E. Marimow, Aadit Tambe, and Adrian Blanco, Washington Post, *How the Supreme Court Ruled in the Major Cases of 2022*, www .washingtonpost.com/politics/interactive/2022/significant-supreme-court-decisions-2022/.
[189] 143 S.Ct. 1322 (2023).

votes, struck down colleges' race-based affirmative action programs[190] and the Biden Administration's student loan forgiveness program.[191] In every one of those cases, Justices appointed by President Trump, whom voters nationwide had rejected, made the difference on matters of huge public importance.

Nor is it just the Supreme Court. In recent years, the ideological and partisan preferences of federal lower court judges have assumed increased importance. That, of course, means that the selections of both the Presidents who nominated them and the Senates that confirmed them – and therefore the methods by which those presidents and senators are elected – have taken on greater significance as well.

One empirical study, analyzing 650,000 US Court of Appeals cases, found that judges' political affiliations help predict the outcomes in categories of cases that represent 90 percent of all court of appeals decisions. In particular, this study demonstrated, judges appointed by Democratic presidents are significantly more likely than those appointed by Republican presidents to rule in favor of the less powerful party.[192]

Two particular features of the US legal system, acting in concert, are especially notable at the district court level. One feature is that, since actions of the federal government ordinarily apply nationwide, lawsuits challenging the legality of those actions may usually be filed in any federal district court in the country. That fact gives the challenging parties considerable leeway to choose the forum they believe will be most favorable to their positions. Often they can find a judicial district in which there is only one active judge, whose views are known or easily discerned to favor the challengers' positions. Second, the judges they select have shown not only a marked tendency to issue injunctions blocking the government's actions – not surprising, since that's why the challengers chose those judges in the first place – but also a sharply increased willingness to extend those injunctions nationwide rather than confine them to the territory covered by the particular district court or the state in which the challengers reside.

These realities have armed state politicians with a powerful weapon that they have begun to use to shut down federal executive actions to which they object on either policy or purely political grounds. The resulting power that these developments offer to each individual state would be of concern in almost any political era. But the present era is one in which three trends have combined to form a now-familiar sequence. First, extreme polarization and the US model of divided government virtually paralyze Congress. Second, the executive branch steps in to fill the void, addressing urgent national issues through major policy initiatives of its own. And third, the willingness and the ease with which state officials can now use their favored judges to frustrate the Administration's policy decisions does more than create a vacuum in which pressing problems go unaddressed; they also enable officials

---

[190] *Students for Fair Admissions* v. *President and Fellows of Harvard College*, 143 S.Ct. 2121 (2023).

[191] *Biden* v. *Nebraska*, 143 S.Ct. 2355 (2023).

[192] Alma Cohen, Harvard Law and Economics Discussion Paper No. 1109, Harvard Public Law Working Paper 24-01, *The Pervasive Influence of Political Composition on Circuit Court Decisions* (Aug. 3, 2023).

who at best reflect the view of their local constituents to thwart the policy decisions of nationally elected presidents and their chosen appointees.

So investing a single state with these powers has unusually far-reaching effects. Whichever political party controls the executive branch of the US government, there will always be at least one state with the incentive – borne of either sincere policy concerns or crass political advantage – to use its newfound power to cancel controversial federal policies.

There have always been examples of these judicial interventions, but state lawsuits against the federal government began popping up with dizzying regularity during the Obama years. Texas has been an especially zealous plaintiff, having frequently teamed up with other Republican-controlled states to challenge actions of the Obama Administration and more recently the Biden Administration. States controlled by Democrats returned the favor during the Trump Administration.

Many of the lawsuits took aim at a series of President Obama's executive decisions on immigration. Those policy decisions had offered a form of temporary relief, called "deferred action," to undocumented immigrants who met certain specific criteria and were found to merit the favorable exercise of prosecutorial discretion. One such policy, relating to certain individuals who had been brought to the United States as children and had lived here continuously ever since arrival and ever since specified past dates, was "Deferred Action for Childhood Arrivals," better known by its acronym, DACA.[193] The other, relating to certain parents of US citizens and certain parents of lawful permanent residents, was "Deferred Action for Parents of Americans" (DAPA).[194]

Shortly after the 2014 announcement of DAPA, a group of twenty-six states led by Texas and represented by Republican governors or attorneys general brought a lawsuit seeking to block it. Although one might have expected the Texas attorneys to file the lawsuit in the state capital of Austin, where the state's legal operations were based, they elected instead to file it in the federal district court some 351 miles away in Brownsville, Texas. At the time, the only active judge in that courthouse was Andrew Hanen, who was already on record as a staunch critic of President Obama's immigration policies, particularly on matters of prosecutorial discretion. As other legal scholars have noted, this judge in several previous cases had excoriated President Obama's immigration policies in vitriolic, emotional, ad hominem language rarely seen in judicial opinions.[195]

---

[193] Memorandum from Janet Napolitano, Secretary of Homeland Security, *Exercising Prosecutorial Discretion with Respect to Individuals Who Came to the United States as Children* (June 15, 2012).

[194] Memorandum from Jeh Charles Johnson, Secretary of Homeland Security, *Exercising Prosecutorial Discretion with Respect to Individuals Who Came to the United States as Children and with Respect to Certain Individuals Who Are the Parents of U.S. Citizens or Permanent Residents* (Nov. 20, 2014).

[195] *See*, for example, *United States v. Cabrera*, 711 F.Supp.2d 736, 738–39 (S.D. Tex. 2010); *United States v. Nava-Martinez*, No. B-13-441-1, at 1, 2013 WL 8844097 (S.D. Tex., Dec. 13, 2013). For detailed accounts of those opinions and their relationship to Judge Hanen's opinion in *United States v. Texas*, see Anil Kalhan, *Deferred Action, Supervised Enforcement Discretion, and the Rule of Law Basis for Executive Action on Immigration*, 63 UCLA L. Rev. Discourse 58, 78–84 (2015).

The judge did not disappoint. In an opinion that this writer would respectfully describe as long in words but embarrassingly weak in legal reasoning, the judge issued a preliminary injunction prohibiting the Administration from implementing the challenged policies anywhere in the country.[196] Relevant here, Judge Hanen was a first-term appointee of President George W. Bush,[197] who as noted earlier had lost the national popular vote.

Although the Texas litigation and the history of the particular judge furnish an admittedly extreme example, there were many similar episodes during the same period. Several of them involved related immigration issues,[198] but President Obama's executive actions in other subject areas also fell prey to lawsuits brought by Texas and other adversary states.

In a case similarly named *Texas* v. *United States*,[199] a group of thirteen states, again led by Texas, went to court to enjoin an Obama Administration interpretation of the federal civil rights laws. The federal interpretation required schools to grant transgendered individuals equal access to restrooms and similar facilities based on their gender identity rather than on the gender assigned at birth. Once again Texas's attorneys found an exceptionally conservative judge, who promptly issued a preliminary injunction nullifying the federal government's interpretation. And once again, the judge elected to extend the injunction nationwide. In another case, also decided by a federal district judge in Texas,[200] twenty-one states sued to prevent the Obama Administration from implementing a Labor Department regulation that would have expanded the number of employees who qualify for overtime pay. The judge granted the injunction and applied it nationwide. In none of these cases was there any convincing explanation of how a narrower injunction limited to the plaintiff states would have failed to serve their interests. Nor could these judges explain how the broader injunction could avoid burdening the federal government or the other twenty-nine states (who opposed it) more than was necessary to protect the interests of the plaintiff states.

In 2017 Donald Trump became president. He immediately rescinded DACA and issued a long series of other executive actions on immigration and other subjects. Suddenly the tables were turned. Now it was Democratic-controlled states (and private plaintiffs) doing their own forum-shopping and obtaining nationwide injunctions in the vast majority of the cases.[201]

---

[196] *State of Texas* v. *United States*, 86 F.Supp.3d 591 (S.D. Tex. 2015).

[197] Wikipedia, *Andrew Hanen*, https://en.wikipedia.org/wiki/Andrew_Hanen.

[198] See generally Congressional Research Service, *The Legality of DACA: Recent Litigation Developments* (periodically updated, as of Oct. 7, 2022 at this 2023 writing), https://crsreports.congress.gov/product/pdf/LSB/LSB10625.

[199] Civ. No. 7:16-cv-00054-O (N.D. Tex., order filed 21 Aug. 2016).

[200] *Nevada* v. *United States Dept. of Labor*, 275 F. Supp. 3d 795, 798 (E.D. Texas 2017).

[201] See, for example, *NAACP* v. *Trump*, No. 17-CV-01907 (D.D.C. Apr. 24, 2018); *New York* v. *Trump*, No. 17-CV-5228 (E.D.N.Y. Feb. 13, 2018); *Regents of the University of California* v. *DHS*, No. 17-cv-02942-RWT (N.D. Calif. Jan. 9, 2018).

Upon the election of President Biden, the tables turned yet again. As a partial response to the limited capacity of US detention facilities, the Biden Administration adopted a policy of using supervisory alternatives to the detention of some asylum seekers. In *Florida* v. *United States*,[202] the State of Florida sued to shut down that policy. Florida might have been expected to file the lawsuit in the state capital of Tallahassee, where its legal operations were based. Instead, their lawyers chose to file it 196 miles away in Pensacola, where all four active judges had been appointed by Republican presidents.[203] They landed a judge appointed by President Trump,[204] and the judge accommodated the state's request to terminate the Biden Administration's policy nationwide.

Trump-appointed District Judge Drew Tipton is the only active federal judge in Victoria, Texas. He had already blocked two of President Biden's immigration policies. In one of those cases, he had ruled not only that states had standing to challenge the federal government's immigration enforcement priorities, but also that those priorities were illegal.[205] That ruling was in such clear violation of established Supreme Court precedent that even the current Supreme Court had to reject it by a vote of 8-1 (Justice Alito being the lone dissenter).[206] So Texas filed a lawsuit in his court challenging yet another Biden Administration immigration policy. That policy had allowed limited numbers of nationals of a few specified countries that are in turmoil to apply for a statutory remedy called "parole," which authorizes the Secretary of Homeland Security to permit temporary entry into the United States. Calling out Texas's forum-shopping, and observing that the case had no connection to Victoria, the Administration asked Judge Tipton to transfer the case to either the state capital or DC. He refused. The Administration had previously filed similar requests, also in vain, to other Trump-appointed judges in small-city courthouses with only one active judge and no apparent connection to their respective cases.[207]

As the only active judge in the Lubbock Division of the Northern District of Texas, Trump-appointed District Judge James Wesley Hendrix[208] is assigned two-thirds of the civil cases filed in that court.[209] He too has a history of blocking President Biden's

[202] Case No. 3:21-cv-1066-TKW-ZCB (N.D. Fla. Mar. 8, 2023).

[203] United States District Court, Northern District of Florida, *Pensacola*, www.flnd.uscourts.gov/pensacola.

[204] United States District Court, Northern District of Florida, *T. Kent Wetherell*, II, www.flnd.uscourts.gov/judge/us-district-judge-t-kent-wetherell-ii.

[205] *Texas* v. *United States*, 606 F. Supp. 3d 437 (S.D. Tex. 2022).

[206] *United States* v. *Texas*, 143 S.Ct. 1964 (2023).

[207] Daniel Wiessner, Reuters, *Trump-appointed Judge Rejects Request to Give Up Biden Immigration Case* (Mar. 10, 2023), www.reuters.com/legal/government/trump-appointed-judge-rejects-request-give-up-biden-immigration-case-2023-03-10/.

[208] Wikipedia, James Wesley Hendrix, https://en.wikipedia.org/wiki/James_Wesley_Hendrix.

[209] At this writing, the other civil cases are all assigned to senior judge Sam Cummings, appointed by President Reagan. United States District Court, Northern District of Texas, *Senior District Judge Sam R. Cummings*, www.txnd.uscourts.gov/judge/senior-district-judge-sam-cummings.

policies. Not surprisingly, therefore, Lubbock is where the Texas state lawyers elected to file their lawsuit challenging Congress's Biden-supported 1.7 trillion dollar government spending plan for fiscal year 2023.[210] In 2024, he held that Congress's enactment of that law had been unconstitutional because members had been allowed to vote by proxy under COVID-era rules. In particular, he struck down the challenged provision that had strengthened workplace protections for pregnant women.[211]

Another Trump appointee is Chief Judge Terry A. Doughty of the Western District of Louisiana. (Unlike the others discussed here, Judge Doughty is not the only available judge in his division.) At the height of the COVID pandemic, President Biden had required COVID vaccinations for workers in the federal Head Start program. Judge Doughty issued a twenty-four-state injunction blocking President Biden's order. His opinion has been sharply criticized for its series of false statements about vaccinations – including a bizarre declaration that these vaccines are useless because boosters would eventually be required.[212] In a subsequent case, Judge Doughty entered an injunction prohibiting the Biden Administration from asking (not requiring, since the federal government doesn't have that power) social media companies to remove misinformation endangering public health.[213] The same judge has also enjoined the Biden Administration's ban on new leases of federal land for oil and gas drilling.[214]

Yet another Trump appointee, District Judge Matthew Kacsmaryk in Amarillo, Texas, is well-known as "a favorite judge for litigants opposing Biden administration

---

[210] Nate Raymond, Reuters, *Biden Administration Accuses Texas of "Judge-Shopping" Spending Law Case* (Feb. 28, 2023), www.reuters.com/legal/government/biden-administration-accuses-texas-judge-shopping-spending-law-case-2023-02-28/.

[211] Reuters, *Federal Judge in Texas Rules Congressional Passage of 2022 Spending Bill Unconstitutional* (Feb. 27, 2024), www.nbcnews.com/politics/politics-news/federal-judge-texas-rules-congressional-passage-2022-spending-bill-unc-rcna140829?taid=65df3c6de6aea1000198beae&utm_campaign=trueanthem&utm_medium=social&utm_source=twitter.

[212] Wikipedia, *Terry A. Doughty*, https://en.wikipedia.org/wiki/Terry_A._Doughty.

[213] *Ibid.*; see also Steven Lee Myers & David McCabe, The New York Times, *Federal Judge Limits Biden Officials' Contacts with Social Media Sites* (July 4, 2023), www.nytimes.com/2023/07/04/business/federal-judge-biden-social-media.html?algo=editorial_importance_fy_email_news&block=4&campaign_id=142&emc=edit_fory_20230704&fellback=false&imp_id=140738542742571400&instance_id=96716&nl=for-you&nlid=76642304&pool=fye-top-news-ls&rank=2&regi_id=76642304&req_id=464510804541613000&segment_id=138368&surface=for-you-email-news&user_id=2785b718e28912cce3f4ef8d2794344a&variant=0_edimp_fye_news_dedupe.

[214] Myers & McCabe, note 213. Judge Doughty later enjoined a Biden Administration regulation that interprets the prohibition on sex discrimination (by schools that accepted federal funding) as including discrimination on the basis of sexual orientation and gender identity – even though the Supreme Court in *Bostock v. Clayton County*, 140 S.Ct. 1731 (2020), had rejected Judge Doughty's interpretation in the context of employment discrimination. See Laura Meckler, Washington Post, *Court Blocks Enforcement of Title IX Rules Protecting Transgender Students* (June 24, 2024), www.washingtonpost.com/education/2024/06/14/transgender-titleix-schools-federal-court/?utm_campaign=wp_post_most&utm_medium=email&utm_source=newsletter&wpisrc=nl_most&carta-url=https%3A%2F%2Fs2.washingtonpost.com%2Fcar-ln-tr%2F3dffda8%2F666c67794ca0ef3edc8e64 4b%2F5976f9099bbc0f6826be4986%2F10%2F50%2F666c67794ca0ef3edc8e644b.

policies."[215] He has been easy to access, especially since September 2022, when the District Court for the Northern District of Texas decided that "any civil case filed in Amarillo would be assigned to Judge Kacsmaryk."[216] As journalist Kate Riga notes, "Of the couple dozen lawsuits that Texas Attorney General Ken Paxton (R) has filed against the Biden administration, over a third have been funneled through the relatively small city [Amarillo], despite its distance [485 miles] from the state capital."[217]

In one case, Judge Kacsmaryk issued an injunction prohibiting President Biden from ending President Trump's "Remain in Mexico" policy. Under that policy, people applying for asylum at the southern border were required to wait in Mexico, under extremely dangerous conditions, during the months or years before hearings on their claims could be scheduled. Among other things, continuation of the policy would require the US government to enter into negotiations with the government of Mexico – and with all the leverage on Mexico's side. Even for the current Supreme Court, this was a bit much. Holding both that Judge Kacsmaryk had badly misread the relevant law and that at any rate a judge had no business effectively ordering the federal government to enter into negotiations with a foreign country, the Court sent the case back to Judge Kacsmaryk for a redo.[218] He promptly found another way to at least temporarily block the Biden Administration from rescinding Trump's Remain in Mexico policy.

Judge Kacsmaryk is best known for legal interpretations that appear to be driven by his publicly expressed, deeply held, personal religious beliefs. In one such case, despite a Supreme Court decision that had clearly held to the contrary, he interpreted the Affordable Care Act's prohibition on sex discrimination as not covering discrimination based on sexual orientation or gender identity. To distinguish a binding Supreme Court decision, he had to reason that "discrimination *because* of sex" is somehow different from "discrimination *based on* sex."[219] And in *Deanda* v. *Becerra*,[220] Judge Kacsmaryk was faced with a federal law that "encouraged" family participation in minors' family planning decisions but pointedly did not require

[215] Trish Garner, *The Fate of Mifepristone in Judge Kacsmaryk's Court* (Feb. 25, 2023), www.lwvor.org/post/o-what-a-tangled-web-we-weave-the-fate-of-mifepristone-in-judge-kacsmaryk-s-court.

[216] *Ibid.* See also Kate Riga, Talking Points Memo, Right-Wingers Have A New, Very Dependable Strategy To Game The Courts. Can It Be Stopped? (Mar. 8, 2023), https://talkingpointsmemo.com/news/judge-shopping-courts-texas.

[217] *Ibid.* In one case that is pending before Judge Kacsmaryk at this writing, Texas sued to block a Biden Administration Labor Department rule. The challenged rule, while requiring retirement plans to put financial considerations first, also allows them to consider environmental, social, and corporate governance (ESG) factors. Daniel Wiessner, Reuters, U.S. Republican States Move to Keep ESG Investing Lawsuit in Texas Court (Mar. 1, 2023), www.reuters.com/business/sustainable-business/us-republican-states-move-keep-esg-investing-lawsuit-texas-court-2023-03-01/.

[218] *Biden* v. *Texas*, 142 S.Ct. 2528 (2022).

[219] *Neese* v. *Becerra*, Case # 2:21-CV-163-Z (N.D. Tex. Apr. 26, 2022).

[220] No. 2:20-CV-092Z (N.D. Tex. Dec. 8, 2022).

parental consent. He nonetheless interpreted that law as allowing the State of Texas to require parental consent for minors who wish to obtain contraception.

But Judge Kaczmaryk's best-known ruling came in 2023, when he struck down the FDA's approval of mifepristone, an abortion medication that had been in use for twenty-four years. The judge rejected the longstanding findings of both the FDA and the health care profession that the drug is safe. Coming less than a year after the Supreme Court's overruling of *Roe* v. *Wade*, the litigation assumed outsized importance, because medication abortion then accounted for roughly one-half of all abortions in the country. Even the Republican-controlled US Court of Appeals for the Fifth Circuit reversed Kaczmaryk's ruling in part, but it let stand his injunction on obtaining mifepristone by mail.[221]

Judge Kacsmaryk and the other judges described here are just part of the bonanza for Texas Republicans. As journalist Kate Riga observes, "Texas works out particularly well for judge shoppers – they can get a case into Kacsmaryk's hands in Amarillo, or maybe into Reed O'Connor's in Wichita Falls or Drew Tipton's in Victoria – resting easy in the knowledge that the state is controlled by the ultraconservative Fifth Circuit Court of Appeals. That leaves as liberals' greatest hope for intervention … the Supreme Court."[222]

Riga was certainly right to describe the Fifth Circuit as "ultra-conservative." More to the point here, it is also one of the most grotesquely counter-majoritarian courts in the country. At the risk of overkill, I will note that, as of December 16, 2022, twelve of the sixteen active Fifth Circuit judges (there was one vacancy) were appointed by Republican presidents, including six by national popular vote loser President Trump. All of those judges were appointed between 1985 and 2022,[223] a period in which the Democratic presidential nominees had won the national popular vote in seven of the ten elections. In fact, fourteen of the sixteen judges were appointed between 1994 and 2022, during which period the Democratic presidential nominees had won the national popular vote in seven out of eight elections.[224] So when rogue federal district judges based anywhere in the states that the Fifth Circuit covers – Texas, Louisiana, and Mississippi – issue nationwide injunctions against policies of Democratic presidential administration, appellate remedies typically prove illusory.

---

[221] See, for example, Morgan Winsor, ABC News, *U.S. Appeals Court Partially Blocks Federal Judge's Ruling on Abortion Drug Mifepristone* (Apr. 13, 2023), https://abcnews.go.com/US/us-appeals-court-partially-blocks-federal-judges-ruling/story?id=98547745; Michael Cuviello, Amarillo Globe-News, *Women's Group Protests Amarillo Lawsuit, Judge in Medical Abortion Case* (Feb. 12, 2022), www.amarillo.com/story/news/2023/02/12/womens-group-protests-amarillo-judge-in-medical-abortion-case/69896275007/; Garner, note 215; Riga, *Right-Wingers*, note 216. Without opining on the merits, the Supreme Court ultimately ordered the lawsuit dismissed for lack of plaintiffs' standing to sue. *FDA v. Alliance for Hippocratic Medicine*, 602 S.Ct. 367 (2024).
[222] Riga, *Right-Wingers*, note 216.
[223] Wikipedia, *United States Court of Appeals for the Fifth Circuit*, https://en.wikipedia.org/wiki/United_States_Court_of_Appeals_for_the_Fifth_Circuit.
[224] U.S. House of Representatives, History, Art, note 152.

Some will applaud this state of affairs; others will bemoan it. But whatever one's normative views on the specific issues presented in those cases,[225] there should be deep concern. Individual states whose political predilections do not align with those of the national government have now amassed an unhealthy power to impose their political views on the entire country. That power has come at the expense of both individual states with contrary policy preferences and the nation as a whole.

My objections to the constitutional process for appointing federal judges, then, are twofold: First, because of the powers that the Constitution confers on the states in the first place – specifically concerning the Electoral College and the equal suffrage of states in the Senate – both the nomination and the confirmation of federal judges are by inherently counter-majoritarian actors. Second, I worry about the combination of (i) individual states' abilities to file their lawsuits with whichever judges they see as their ideological and political soulmates and (ii) politically radical judges who are all too happy to accommodate those states by shutting down actions of the federal government nationwide. That combination has been a gift to states, as well as to judges who either were nominated by a president whom the people had rejected or were confirmed by a nationally unrepresentative Senate (or both). Those state officials, and selected judges, now possess the frightening ability to impose their own policy preferences on the entire nation in place of the policy judgments of nationally elected presidents.

While court-shopping is not new, it has become more lethal in recent years in at least one way. Most federal district courts have multiple judges. This means would-be forum shoppers, at least in the past, could not guarantee getting the judge they wanted; they had to settle for playing the odds. But as Riga points out, today "the surgical specificity of targeting divisions of district courts overseen by one or two judges is newer."[226]

None of this should be surprising, except perhaps as to the increased brazenness of some of the legal contortions these judges have had to perform. At his Senate confirmation hearing, now-Chief Justice Roberts famously disclaimed the influence

---

[225] As for the immigration examples, full disclosure is required. U.S. Citizenship and Immigration Services (USCIS), in the Department of Homeland Security, is the agency charged with implementing both DACA and DAPA. I served as Chief Counsel of USCIS when the agency rolled out DACA in 2012. Several years later, as a private citizen testifying at hearings before both the Senate and the House Judiciary Committees, I conveyed my opinion that both DACA and DAPA were "well within" President Obama's legal authority. See Stephen H. Legomsky, Testimony before U.S. House of Representatives Committee on the Judiciary, Hearing on the Constitutional Issues Raised by President Obama's Executive Actions on Immigration (Feb. 25, 2015), https://docs.house.gov/meetings/JU/JU00/20150225/103010/HHRG-114-JU00-Wstate-LegomskyS-20150225.pdf; Stephen H. Legomsky, Testimony before U.S. Senate Committee on the Judiciary, Confirmation Hearing on Nomination of Loretta Lynch for Attorney General (Jan. 29, 2015), www.judiciary.senate.gov/imo/media/doc/01-29-15%20Legomsky%20Testimony.pdf. Finally, in the main litigation on DACA, I was called as an expert witness to defend its legality. See Declaration of Stephen H. Legomsky in *Texas v. United States*, Case No. 1:18-CV-68 (S.D. Tex. July 16, 2018).

[226] Riga, *Right-Wingers*, note 216.

of ideology on the decisions of judges; all he does, he testified, is "call balls and strikes."[227] Then-nominee Neil Gorsuch added a slightly different twist, looking the Senators in the eye as he told them that "[t]here's no such thing as a Republican judge or a Democratic judge."[228]

I don't blame them for saying those things. No one who is nominated for a federal judgeship and who wants the job would dare acknowledge candidly, before the US Senate, that they intend to decide cases based on their personal policy preferences, their religious views, or their perceptions of the best electoral interests of the Republican Party. But both of these men had to know that what they were saying was not true. For decades, empirical studies have consistently exposed the extremely high positive correlations between judges' decisions and (i) their personal ideologies and (ii) in the case of federal judges, the political parties of the presidents who nominated them.[229]

If there has been a shift – and I believe there has – it has been in the subtle transformation from ideologically driven judicial decisions to those driven by naked partisanship. The Supreme Court's decision in *Bush* v. *Gore*, discussed earlier for the light it sheds on other issues, seems a likely foundation for this evolution as well.

In that case, the American people in 2000 chose Democratic nominee Al Gore over Republican nominee George W. Bush. But in the Electoral College, the outcome hinged on the electoral votes of one state – Florida. The voting machine tabulations in that state showed Bush holding a razor-thin lead. But there were widespread mechanical problems with the paper ballots in several counties with Democratic-leaning populations. Chief among the problems were the famous "hanging chads" and "dimples." On those ballots, the voter had punched an indentation or hole for a particular candidate, but not all the way through, with the result that the machines did not record their votes. Florida law required every ballot to be counted as long as

---

[227] U.S. Senate Comm. on the Judiciary, Confirmation Hearing on the Nomination of John G. Roberts, Jr. to Be Chief Justice of the United States, 109th Cong. (2005), at 56.

[228] See E. J. Dionne Jr., Washington Post, *Gorsuch's Big Fat Lie* (Mar. 22, 2017), www.washington post.com/opinions/gorsuchs-big-fat-lie/2017/03/22/7828ae5c-0f3e-11e7-9b0d-d27c98455440_story .html?utm_term=.a048761d2b3a. To Justice Gorsuch's credit, he recently expressed frustration over the practice of plaintiffs shopping for judges who will enter nationwide injunctions against policies they dislike. During oral argument in a case challenging President Biden's student debt relief plan, Justice Gorsuch let loose: "Talk about ways in which courts can interfere with the processes of government. ... Two individuals in one state who don't like the program seek and obtain universal relief, barring it for anybody anywhere." Riga, *Right-Wingers*, note 216.

[229] Amidst the wealth of literature on this subject, see especially the careful empirical studies by Neal Devins & Lawrence Baum, Split Definitive: How Party Polarization Turned the Supreme Court into a Partisan Court (2017); Lee Epstein *et al.*, The Behavior of Federal Judges: A Theoretical and Empirical Study of Rational Choice (2013) (acknowledging that judges are not driven *solely* by ideology, and also suggesting that the role of ideology is greatest at the highest level of court). See generally Jeffrey A. Segal, *Ideology and Partisanship*, in Lee Epstein & Stefanie A. Lindquist (eds.), The Oxford Handbook of U.S. Judicial Behavior, chapter 16, at 303–16 (2017). For a useful compilation of older studies, see S.S. Nagel, *Multiple Correlation of Judicial Backgrounds and Decisions*, 2 Fla. State Univ. L. Rev. 258, 266–69 & especially 268–69 n.37 (1974).

the intent of the voter could be ascertained. So the Florida Supreme Court, interpreting the Florida election laws, ordered a manual recount. But different counties
employed different standards in judging the voters' intentions. On that basis, a US
Supreme Court majority of five Republican Justices rejected the Florida Supreme
Court's interpretation of Florida's election law, found a likely denial of equal protection, and therefore temporarily halted the ongoing recount.

When the Court returned to the case for a final decision, the same majority
decided that equal protection did indeed require the same evidentiary standard
in every county. As the four dissenters pointed out, even then the Court could
have given the Florida election officials a chance to restart the recount using the
required uniform standard. By then, however, it was getting close to what the
majority regarded as a firm deadline for Florida to submit its slate of electors to
Congress. The majority thus decided on its own that the Florida election officials
would not be able to get the job done in time. So the recount was permanently
enjoined. With Bush holding a lead of just 537 votes out of more than 100 million cast, he was declared the winner of Florida's electoral votes and therefore the
presidency.[230]

The majority had to dodge several bullets to reach that result. These *federal*
Justices – all five of them states' rights conservatives – had to overturn a state court's
interpretation of the state's own law. They also had to hold that equal protection
required all the counties in the state to employ the same criteria when assessing the
intent of the voter in cases where the machines do not record the votes. And once it
did that, the Court weeks later had to deny the Florida election officials any opportunity to try to complete the recount in the required manner before a deadline that
the dissenters pointed out was not inflexible anyway.

For me, the most interesting part of the obstacle course that the majority was willing to run involved the equal protection issue. Five conservative Republican Justices
who until this case had barely noticed the equal protection clause suddenly not only
discovered it, but, having done so, placed on it an interpretation far more expansive
than what any of their more progressive colleagues could ever have dreamed of. And
that epiphany just happened to occur in a case where their robust interpretation of
the equal protection clause enabled Republican nominee George W. Bush to win
the presidency over his Democratic rival.

Without entirely dismissing the possibility of mere coincidence, one cannot help
but be struck by the typical lineups in the election law cases in particular – both
those just discussed in this section and the many others that will be discussed in
Chapter 3. Time and again, it is Democratic-appointed judges who vote to rein
in both gerrymandering efforts and voter suppression strategies. It is Republican-
appointed judges who strain to uphold them.

---

[230] Infoplease, Presidential Election of 2000, note 69.

The New York Times editorial board did not mince words: "Over the past several years, the court has been transformed into a judicial arm of the Republican Party. ... In cases involving money in politics, partisan gerrymandering, and multiple suits challenging the Voting Rights Act, the court has ruled in ways that make it easier for Republicans and harder for Democrats to win elections."[231]

The public has also noticed. In the same editorial, the Times said this:

> In a Gallup poll taken in June, [even] *before* [my emphasis] the court overturned *Roe v. Wade* with *Dobbs v. Jackson Women's Health Organization*, only 25 percent of respondents said they had a high degree of confidence in the institution. That number is down from 50 percent in 2001 – just months after the court's [already] hugely controversial 5-4 ruling in *Bush v. Gore*, in which a majority consisting only of Republican appointees effectively decided the result of the 2000 election in favor of the Republicans.[232]

The Presidential Commission on the Supreme Court of the United States, in a passage relating the arguments in favor of Supreme Court expansion, said:

> [C]ritics maintain that the Supreme Court has been complicit in and partially responsible for the "degradation of American democracy" writ large. On this view, the Court has whittled away the Voting Rights Act and other cornerstones of democracy, and affirmed state laws and practices that restrict voting and dis-enfranchise certain constituencies, such as people of color, the poor, and the young. This has contributed to circumstances that threaten to give outsized power over the future of the presidency and therefore the Court to entrench that power.[233]

In addition, the report might have added, the nation suffers when the vast majority of its citizens lose faith in the basic institutions of government.

All this is disturbing enough. But as this section has sought to illustrate, so many of the most egregious abuses of judicial power have been by judges who would not even have been on the bench but for a federal judicial appointment process riddled with systematic counter-majoritarian biases. At multiple levels, those biases, in turn, would not exist but for the constitutionally entrenched roles of the states.

---

[231] The New York Times, Editorial, *The Supreme Court Isn't Listening, and It's No Secret Why* (Oct. 1, 2022), www.nytimes.com/2022/10/01/opinion/supreme-court-legitimacy.html. See also Jesse Wegman, The New York Times, *The Crisis in Teaching Constitutional Law* (Feb. 26, 2024), www.nytimes .com/2024/02/26/opinion/constitutional-law-crisis-supreme-court.html (observing that, on today's Supreme Court, "the result virtually always aligns with the policy priorities of the modern Republican Party.")

[232] *Ibid.*

[233] Presidential Commission on the Supreme Court of the United States, Final Report (Dec. 2021), https://constitutional-governance.law.columbia.edu/sites/default/files/content/docs/SCOTUS-Report-Final-12.8.21-1.pdf.

E THE CONSTITUTIONAL AMENDMENT PROCESS

The process for amending the US Constitution is yet another example of elevating the equality of the states over the equality of the citizens. And this one takes counter-majoritarianism to an extreme. Article V of the Constitution reads:

> The Congress, whenever two thirds of both Houses shall deem it necessary, shall propose Amendments to this Constitution, or, on the Application of the Legislatures of two thirds of the several States, shall call a Convention for proposing Amendments, which, in either Case, shall be valid to all Intents and Purposes, as Part of this Constitution, when ratified by the Legislatures of three fourths of the several States, or by Conventions in three fourths thereof, as the one or the other Mode of Ratification may be proposed by the Congress …

As the text indicates, there are two ways to *begin* the process of amending the Constitution. Two-thirds of the House membership, already distorted by the residential patterns, single-member districts, and gerrymandering and voter suppression practices discussed below,[234] together with two-thirds of the Senate, in which the citizens of high-population states are grossly underrepresented, may propose a constitutional amendment. Alternatively, two-thirds of the state legislatures – similarly both individually unrepresentative of their respective citizens' voting preferences[235] and representing dramatically different state populations to start with – may file an "application" for a constitutional convention that could then propose amendments. Thus, even the origination of a constitutional amendment is layered with counter-majoritarian hurdles.

Once that first set of hurdles has been cleared, additional supermajority requirements govern ratification. Three-fourths of the state legislatures – *not* states that collectively represent three-fourths of the American people, but three-fourths of the state legislatures, no matter how large or small the populations of the states they represent might be – must ratify the proposed amendment. And since the state legislatures themselves are counter-majoritarian for all the reasons just mentioned, one might think of this step in the process as a counter-majoritarian trifecta: Amending the Constitution requires ratification by (i) three fourths (ii) of already counter-majoritarian state legislatures (iii) that represent states of any population size. And all this is *after* a 2/3 majority vote by both of the counter-majoritarian chambers of the United States Congress. One book advocates eliminating the need for ratification entirely,[236] and this book considers the alternative option of ratification by nationwide referendum.[237]

---

[234] Chapter 3, Sections A and B.
[235] *Ibid.*
[236] Levitsky & Ziblatt, Tyranny, note 3, at 235.
[237] Chapter 6, Section D.

As many others have observed, this process makes the US Constitution painfully hard to amend. Donald Lutz, in his thorough 1995 comparative study, found the US Constitution to be the hardest to amend of any constitution in the world.[238]

To Madison, that was a good thing.[239] To Jefferson, it was a problem. He felt that new generations should be able to alter the US Constitution far more easily.[240] State constitutions, in contrast, are quite easy to amend. Typically, all they require is a simple majority vote of the people[241] – by definition, pure majoritarianism.

The resulting data are not surprising. The US Constitution has been amended only twenty-seven times – and only seventeen times since the final ratification of the Bill of Rights in 1791. In contrast, the average state constitution has been amended 150 times,[242] even though 37 of the 50 states have been around for far fewer years than the US Constitution.

I won't wade deeply into that part of the debate. I do not object to the requirement of a supermajority for amendment of the Constitution. Our supreme law, which guarantees fundamental rights and protects other essential institutions, requires some measure of durability. Too easy an amendment process would leave the Constitution, and especially unpopular minorities, dangerously vulnerable to rapidly shifting political winds. But if the state constitutions are too fluid to rely on, the US Constitution seems to me to veer too far in the opposite direction.

The question being one of degree, my objection is to the endless layers of supermajoritarian requirements piled on top of one another. So much of that (not all) traces back to the outsized roles assigned to the states. The requirement of a 2/3 vote in the Senate accentuates the small-state favoritism already built into that chamber, and the requirement of subsequent ratification by three-fourths of the states (small versus large doesn't matter) adds another dose of double counter-majoritarianism – a triple dose, actually, when one considers the counter-majoritarian problems that afflict so many state legislatures to start with. As in other places, the Constitution sacrifices the equality of citizens for the equality of states.

The supermajority requirements matter. Take the case of the Equal Rights Amendment. Proposed by the requisite two-thirds of both Houses of Congress, it provided, in Section 1, that "Equality of rights under the law shall not be denied or abridged by the United States or by any State on account of sex." By the 1979 expiration date specified in Congress's proposal, the amendment had garnered the ratifications

---

[238] Donald Lutz, *Toward a Formal Theory of Constitutional Amendment*, in Sanford Levinson (ed.), Responding to Imperfection: The Theory and Practice of Constitutional Amendment, at 237, 261 (1995). See also Levinson, note 2, at 159–66; Levitsky & Ziblatt, Tyranny, note 3, at 217.

[239] See Federalist 49.

[240] Jeffrey S. Sutton, Who Decides? States as Laboratories of Constitutional Experimentation 331–32 (2022), citing Jefferson's letter to Thomas Kercheval (July 12, 1816), in Thomas Jefferson, Writings 1402 (1984).

[241] Sutton, note 240, at 343.

[242] *Ibid.*, at 332.

of thirty-five states, falling just short of the required thirty-eight. In six additional states, one of the two Houses of the state legislature had voted to ratify, but the other had not. To estimate the percentage of the US population represented by the opposing groups of legislatures, I added the populations of the ratifying states to one-half of the populations of the six states where half the legislature had voted to ratify. (I did not add in the populations of three other states that voted to ratify the amendment after the congressional deadline had passed.) Under those assumptions, pro-ratification legislatures accounted for 78.4 percent of the national population. Legislatures that declined to ratify, even in combination with those legislatures that ratified it too late, accounted for only 21.6 percent of the national population. Despite the lopsided score, the latter won out.[243]

Apparently feeling that the dizzying array of counter-majoritarian requirements did not erect a high enough hurdle, the framers attempted to make one provision of the Constitution unamendable entirely. The last line of the amendment provision creates the following exception: "No State, without its Consent, shall be deprived of its equal Suffrage in the Senate."[244] This insistence on not only constitutionalizing the principle of equal Senate suffrage, but then taking the further step of insulating that principle from the already backbreaking constitutional amendment process, showcases how zealous the Antifederalists were about state sovereignty. Madison understood this. In Federalist 43, he explains this exception by saying that it "was probably insisted on by the States particularly attached to that equality." It was, in other words, just a concession necessary to get all the states' agreement, not a normative argument for the equal suffrage provision – much less an argument for perpetuating it.

This Senate exception to the amendment process does present an interesting, if inconsequential, conundrum. If it had been a freestanding provision, rather than a proviso to the amendment process, it might be easier to change. If there were enough support for making each state's Senate representation proportional to its population, an amendment would have been able to simply do that. Even an amendment abolishing states could either expressly delete the requirement of equal state Senate suffrage or simply ignore that requirement, as the issue would become moot. There simply wouldn't be any states with unequal Senate suffrage, because there wouldn't be any states at all.

---

[243] Sources: The list of non-ratifying states was taken from ERA, *Ratification Info State by State*, www .equalrightsamendment.org/era-ratification-map. The state populations were taken from US 1970 Census Data, per Wikipedia, *List of U.S. States and Territories by Historical Population*, https:// en.wikipedia.org/wiki/List_of_U.S._states_and_territories_by_historical_population. Five of the ratifying states later attempted to revoke their ratifications, but the legal effect of those efforts remains doubtful. Compare, for example, Travis Crum, *The Lawfulness of the Fifteenth Amendment*, 97 Notre Dame L. Rev. 1543, 1601–603 (2022) (arguing that states are not permitted to rescind their ratifications) with Akhil Reed Amar, *America's Constitution: A Biography* 456 (2005) (arguing that rescissions are valid when passed before three-fourths of the states have ratified).

[244] Unlike the language that precedes it, this constraint does not appear to be limited to actions taken before 1808.

But the provision is not freestanding. It is cast as an exception to the constitutional amendment process itself. How could the Constitution be amended to eliminate equal state Senate suffrage when the very process that would have to be followed to amend the Constitution contains an express prohibition on the elimination of equal Senate suffrage?

One possible way around the exception is to argue that no legal document, and no provision of any legal document, should ever be interpreted to permanently prohibit the parties from agreeing to any future changes. The counterargument would be that, while such a principle makes sense when there is some elasticity in the relevant text, this language is crystal clear. It expressly prohibits depriving a state of its equal suffrage in the Senate without its consent. Besides, if this exception were interpreted as merely a statement that states must have equal state suffrage in the Senate, and not as a bar on using the constitutional amendment process to end that practice, the provision would be superfluous. The principle of equal state suffrage in the Senate is already guaranteed elsewhere in the Constitution.[245]

Alternatively, perhaps one could argue that a constitutional amendment abolishing states would not violate the equal suffrage requirement. If there were no states, then there would be no unequal state Senate suffrage. Or if, as proposed here, states remain as geographic areas and as sources of identity, affiliation, and pride, and state *government* is all that is eliminated, then it would seem that the states' suffrage in the Senate would remain equal: Every state would have zero senators.

Perhaps the most clearly valid solution – assuming for the sake of discussion that there were the political will to abolish state government in the first place – would be to proceed sequentially. First, amend Article V itself, deleting the Senate proviso. That amendment would not violate the exception because it would not eliminate equal state suffrage; it would merely eliminate the exception to the constitutional amendment process. Then, once that amendment has been ratified, add a second amendment, either to make Senate districts equipopulous or to abolish states entirely. Perhaps even a single constitutional amendment with two clauses, rather than a sequence of two amendments, could effect both changes. As long as the clause abolishing states takes effect only after the clause that deletes the exception to the amendment process – and perhaps even if they take effect simultaneously – the amendment should be valid.

At any rate, the Senate suffrage exception to the amendment process, whether or not interpreted literally, is also one illustration of how counter-majoritarianism feeds on itself. The states, whose counter-majoritarian impact on our democracy has manifested itself in the many ways described in this chapter, insisted on that exception. By doing so, they have at least attempted, very possibly successfully, to inoculate themselves from termination even by a supermajority, thus preserving themselves for all eternity. As will be discussed in Chapter 3, Section A, state legislatures have achieved an analogous self-reinforcing effect through partisan gerrymandering.

[245] U.S. Const. Art. I, § 3, Cl. 1.

3

Democracy

State Behavior Problems

Chapter 2 described the main structural barriers to democracy in the United States. All of those flow, directly or indirectly, from the constitutionally enshrined roles and powers of the states. This chapter turns to the many ways in which state legislatures and state executive branch officials have filled those roles and deployed those powers. As will be seen, their actions have further eroded the same two core elements of democratic governance – political equality and majority rule.

A GERRYMANDERS

Under the United States Constitution, "[t]he Times, Places and Manner of holding Elections for [United States] Senators and Representatives, shall be prescribed in each State by the Legislature thereof; but the Congress may at any time by Law make or alter such Regulations, except as to the Places of chusing Senators."[1] This provision gives the state legislatures the first crack at deciding the times, places, and manner of congressional elections, but it allows Congress to supersede those decisions. Congress has exercised that power on several occasions. Among other examples,[2] it has required states to use single-member districts (as opposed to multimember at large districts) to elect US House members.[3] The 1965 Voting Rights Act (VRA) bars racially discriminatory state voting laws.[4] And the National Voter

---

[1] U.S. Const. Art. I, § 4. The exception for "chusing Senators" reflects the fact that US senators were originally chosen by the state legislatures. U.S. Const. Art. I, § 3, Cl. 1. Thus, there was no reason to specify the "place" of choosing them. The Seventeenth Amendment, ratified in 1913, transferred this power to the people of each state.

[2] See Library of Congress, *Constitution Annotated*, *ArtI.S.4.C1.3, Congress and Elections Clause*, https://constitution.congress.gov/browse/essay/artI-S4-C1-3/ALDE_00013640/ (citing congressional regulation of the "contiguity, compactness, and substantial equality of population to districting requirements").

[3] Pub. L. 90–196, 81 Stat. 581 (Dec. 14, 1967).

[4] The VRA is discussed in some detail in Section B.

Registration Act (NVRA) of 1993[5] requires states to offer several specified options for registering to vote.

In contrast, the Constitution doesn't specifically speak to states' authority to decide the times, places, and manner of elections for their own legislatures. Unlike the federal government, states are not confined to powers affirmatively enumerated in the Constitution. So they can make these sorts of decisions as they wish, subject only to any independent constitutional constraints. One important such constraint is the equal protection clause,[6] which among other things binds states to the principle of one-person-one-vote and, therefore, roughly equipopulous districts.[7] States must also maintain a "republican form of government,"[8] and various constitutional amendments specifically prohibit states from denying the vote on account of "race, color, or previous condition of servitude,"[9] sex,[10] "failure to pay a poll tax or other tax,"[11] or age (if over eighteen).[12]

That brings us to gerrymandering. A good definition of this term is that gerrymandering occurs "when elected or appointed officials in charge of redistricting reconfigure districts to favor a political party, incumbent, or candidate."[13] The practice has been with us since the founding of the Republic.[14] It has its roots in England, but it got its name some time later from a plan drawn up by then-Massachusetts Governor (and future Vice President) Eldridge Gerry for the Commonwealth Senate before the 1812 elections. One of the districts he devised had such a strange shape that a cartoonist at the Boston Gazette drew up a caricature of Gerry's map and coined the term "gerrymander," apparently a contraction of "Gerry" and "salamander."[15]

There has long been a giant-sized disconnect, detailed shortly, between the people's votes for both Congress and the state legislatures, on the one hand, and the resulting overall compositions of those legislative bodies, on the other. In a democracy, these frequent counter-majoritarian outcomes should set off alarm bells.

---

[5] Pub. L. 103–31, 107 Stat. 77, as amended, 42 U.S.C. §1973gg *et seq.* (May 20, 1993). See especially *Arizona v. Inter Tribal Council of Arizona [ITCA]*, 570 U.S. 1 (2013), discussed in Section B.1.

[6] U.S. Const. Amend. 14, § 1.

[7] *Reynolds v. Sims*, 377 U.S. 533 (1964). In the same year, the Court decided *Wesberry v. Sanders*, 376 U.S. 1 (1964), which announced a similar principle for the drawing of US House districts.

[8] U.S. Const. Art. IV, § 4.

[9] U.S. Const. Amend. 15, § 1.

[10] U.S. Const. Amend. 19.

[11] U.S. Const. Amend. 24, § 1.

[12] U.S. Const. Amend. 26, § 1. Two thoughtful books focusing on some of the electoral abuses of state legislatures are J. Morgan Kousser, The Shaping of Southern Politics: Suffrage Restrictions and the Establishment of the One-Party South, 1880–1910 (1974); and David Pepper, Laboratories of Autocracy: A Wake-Up Call from Behind the Lines (2021) (focusing mainly on Ohio).

[13] Common Cause, *Redistricting and Gerrymandering*, www.commoncause.org/oregon/our-work/gerrymandering-and-representation/gerrymandering-and-redistricting-2/.

[14] Samuel Issacharoff *et al.*, The Law of Democracy – Legal Structure of the Political Process 717 (6th ed. 2022).

[15] *Ibid.*, at 716–17. See also *Rucho v. Common Cause*, 139 S.Ct 2484, 2494–95 (2019).

As Miriam Seifter explains, state legislatures have been afflicted by two separate kinds of counter-majoritarian takeovers:

> State legislatures are typically a state's least majoritarian branch. Often they are out-right countermajoritarian institutions. Across the nation, the vast majority of states in recent memory have had legislatures controlled by either a clear or probable minor-ity party. Even where state legislatures do cross the majority threshold, ... a majority [vote can translate into a veto-proof supermajority outcome] and the potential for incumbent entrenchment.[16]

In his superb book, "Why Cities Lose," Jonathan Rodden offers some striking examples:

> Consider the state of Michigan, where it has become commonplace for the Democrats to win the statewide popular vote without winning a majority of seats in either chamber of the Michigan legislature. In 2012, for instance, the Democrats received around 54 percent of the total votes cast in elections for both state legisla-tive chambers in Michigan, but they came away with only 45 percent of the seats in the Michigan House of Representatives, and 42 percent of the seats in the state Senate. This has been happening over the last decade in the other states of the industrialized Midwest as well, including Minnesota, Missouri, Ohio, Wisconsin, and Pennsylvania. Most recently, it happened in Virginia in 2017, and once again in Michigan, Ohio, Wisconsin, and Pennsylvania in 2018. Remarkably, as of 2019, the Republican Party has controlled the Pennsylvania Senate for almost forty con-secutive years, even while losing the statewide popular vote around half of the time. The Republicans have controlled the Ohio Senate for thirty-five years, dur-ing which time Democrats won half of the state's US Senate elections and around one-third of the gubernatorial elections.[17]

Seifter's compilation further highlights how extreme the counter-majoritarianism in state legislatures has become:

> The most obvious marker of a manufactured majority is when "a party with less than half of the statewide votes ... receive[s] more than half of the seats" – a pattern that "happens routinely in U.S. state legislatures." The vast majority of states have crossed this threshold in elections since 1960; some have done so in election after election. States in this group in recent memory include Florida, Indiana, Iowa, Michigan, Minnesota, New Jersey, North Carolina, New Hampshire, New York, Ohio, Pennsylvania, Virginia, and Wisconsin.
>
> There is more. ... Between 1968 and 2016, thirty-eight states experienced at least one manufactured majority as a result of a general election in their state

---

[16] Miriam Seifter, *Countermajoritarian State Legislatures*, 121 Colum. L. Rev. 1733, 1735 (2021).

[17] Jonathan Rodden, Why Cities Lose: The Deep Roots of the Urban-Rural Political Divide 1–2 (2019). See also *Common Cause* v. *Lewis*, No. 18-CVS-014001, 2019 WL 4569584 (N.C. Super. Ct. Sept. 3, 2019) (holding the Republicans' extreme gerrymandering of North Carolina's state legislative districts violated the "free elections" clause of the state constitution).

senate, while ten states did not. Similarly, forty states experienced at least one manufactured-majority election in their state house, while eight states did not.[18]

As Seifter rightly acknowledges, both split ticket voting and the large numbers of uncontested legislative seats might be distorting the mismatch between statewide popular votes and resulting legislative outcomes. It is possible, therefore, that the problem is less severe than it might first appear. For the reasons she elaborates, however, those distortions most likely explain away only a small percentage of the disparity.[19]

One's first instinct might be to blame the disconnect on gerrymandering and, therefore, states. But despite the focus of this section, gerrymandering admittedly is not the *principal* cause of these counter-majoritarian legislative outcomes. Two of the factors that would exist with or without states have such a dominant joint impact on both US House and state legislative elections that fairness prevents me from relegating them to a footnote. The first factor is residential patterns, particularly urban/rural divides. The second is single-member district elections. As noted earlier, Congress has mandated single-member US House districts,[20] and all but eight of the fifty state legislatures are elected from single-member districts as well.[21] Rodden demonstrates convincingly that that interaction is responsible for the bulk of the counter-majoritarian outcomes.[22]

More specifically, Democratic voters are heavily concentrated in cities and their inner suburbs, where they win huge majorities, but they lose by smaller margins in the more numerous rural and exurban districts.[23] Indeed, "[b]y the beginning of this century, the Democrats had become an almost exclusively urban political party."[24] Today, Pamela Karlan notes, "[t]here is virtually a straight-line relationship between population density and the Democratic share of the presidential vote."[25]

Rodden further notes that "the Democrats suffer in the transformation of votes to seats most clearly in states that are hotly contested, like Pennsylvania, as well as

---

[18] Seifter, note 16, at 1762–64.
[19] *Ibid.*, at 1765–66. See also Michael Scherer *et al.*, Washington Post, *2024 Vote Could Bring Electoral College Distortions to the Forefront* (Dec. 8, 2023), www.washingtonpost.com/nation/2023/12/08/electoral-college-votes-swing-states-decline/?utm_campaign=wp_post_most&utm_medium=email&utm_source=newsletter&wpisrc=nl_most (observing that "in 7 of 8 major battleground states [n]o more than 3 percent of voters in the 2020 presidential election split their tickets" and that "[i]n Nevada, the share was just 0.1 percent."
[20] Pub. L. 90–196, 81 Stat. 581 (Dec. 14, 1967).
[21] Ann O'M. Bowman *et al.*, State and Local Government 149 (11th ed. 2022).
[22] Rodden, note 17.
[23] *Ibid.*, at 3–5. See also Steven Levitsky & Daniel Ziblatt, Tyranny of the Minority 177–79 (2023); Pamela S. Karlan, *The New Countermajoritarian Difficulty*, 109 Calif. L. Rev. 2323, 2331–35 (2021); Seifter, note 16, at 1735.
[24] Rodden, note 17, at 5.
[25] Karlan, note 23, at 2331.

in states where they typically expect to win majorities, like New York."[26] Ironically, "urban clustering actually helps the Democrats in the state legislatures of a handful of Republican-dominated states."[27] By way of example, "the geographic clustering of Democrats in Nashville and Memphis is not necessarily a bad thing for the Democrats in Tennessee. With a statewide vote share that is typically around 40 percent, Democrats are able to win two congressional seats. If their support were more dispersed across smaller cities – as in West Virginia – they would perhaps not win any."[28]

Rodden is certainly right, but that last point must be put in perspective. Yes, Tennessee Democrats do better than they would if they were more dispersed. Even with the benefit of urban concentration in that state, however, they still end up with only half the representation that their statewide voting strength merits. Tennessee has nine congressional districts,[29] so if outcomes were proportional to voting strength Democrats would average four House seats rather than two. Put another way, they have 40% of the votes but get only 22% of the House seats. At any rate, as Rodden points out, "on the whole, the representational cost of urban concentration far outweighs its occasional benefit for the Democrats."[30]

Analogous patterns have emerged in other countries in which legislators are elected from single districts, including the UK, Canada, Australia, and, until very recently, New Zealand. In those countries the national and, if applicable, state or provincial, legislative district maps are drawn by independent commissions rather than by partisan legislatures. Thus, those patterns do not result from gerrymandering.[31]

All that said, gerrymandering has made the problem much more acute. And that, unlike residential patterns and single-member district elections, falls squarely on the states.

In *Rucho*, noted earlier as an example of a Supreme Court decision in which two Justices appointed by a popularly rejected president made the difference,[32] the dissenting opinion of Justice Kagan described just a few of the extreme counter-majoritarian consequences of gerrymandering. While denouncing the grotesquely disproportionate effects of gerrymandered US House districts in North Carolina and Maryland that were at issue in that case, she adds:

---

[26] Rodden, note 17, at 166.
[27] *Ibid.* For the statistical modeling, see *ibid.*, at 175–88.
[28] *Ibid.*, at 174.
[29] Tennessee Comptroller of the Treasury, *U.S. District Maps*, https://comptroller.tn.gov/maps/u-s–congress-districts.html (based on the 2020 decennial census).
[30] Rodden, note 17, at 166.
[31] *Ibid.*, at 5–7. See also Nicholas O. Stephanopoulos, *Our Electoral Exceptionalism*, 80 U. Chi. L. Rev. 769, 781 (2013) (describing how rare it is for liberal democracies to assign the redistricting functions to the legislators themselves); Seifter, note 16, at 1761 (describing "how the unusual American approach of putting political officials in charge of districting has the potential to substantially distort representation").
[32] See Chapter 2, Section D.

But the voters in those States were not the only ones to fall prey to such districting perversions. Take Pennsylvania. In the three congressional elections occurring under the State's original districting plan (before the State Supreme Court struck it down), Democrats received between 45% and 51% of the statewide vote, but won only 5 of 18 House seats. Or go next door to Ohio. There, in four congressional elections, Democrats tallied between 39% and 47% of the statewide vote, but never won more than 4 of 16 House seats.[33]

Rucho was decided in 2019. Very soon thereafter, the politics in North Carolina became darker still. As a result of the 2020 decennial census, the Republican-controlled legislature had to draw up new districts for the US House and for both chambers of the state legislature. The trial court found that all three plans had been intentionally manipulated to reflect "extreme" partisan gerrymandering. In a state closely divided between Democratic and Republican voters, the legislature's plan "all but guaranteed Republicans" ten of the fourteen US House seats and similarly inflated Republican control of both houses of the state legislature.[34] The words of the Republican cochair of the General Assembly's redistricting committee, Representative David Lewis, were revealing: "I think electing Republicans is better than electing Democrats. So I drew this map to help foster what I think is better for the country."[35]

The North Carolina Supreme Court concluded that the US House redistricting plan violated several provisions of the state constitution. After the legislature's second attempt was found equally wanting, the trial judge supervised the drawing of a remedial plan free of partisan gerrymandering.[36]

So far, so good. But then 2022 happened. The midterm elections transformed the North Carolina Supreme Court from a 4-3 Democratic majority to a 5-2 Republican majority.[37] Just three months after the second North Carolina Supreme Court decision invalidating the gerrymandered US House map, the newly constituted Republican court majority overruled its decision. Neither the facts nor the law were any different from three months earlier; only the partisan composition of the Court had changed. The five Republican judges reinterpreted the state constitution as

---

[33] *Rucho v. Common Cause*, 139 S.Ct. 2484, 2513 (2019). Another example is the congressional map drawn up by the New York state legislature and struck down by the state's highest court in *Matter of Harkenrider v. Hochul*, 38 N.Y.3d 494 (NY 2022).

[34] *Harper v. Hall*, 886 S.E.2d 393, 451 (N.C. 2023) (Justice Earls, dissenting).

[35] *Ibid.*, at 449, citing *Rucho*, 139 S.Ct. at 2491.

[36] *Moore v. Harper*, 143 S.Ct. 2065 (2023).

[37] Michael Wines, The New York Times, *North Carolina Gerrymander Ruling Reflects Politicization of Judiciary Nationally* (May 2, 2023), www.nytimes.com/2023/04/28/us/north-carolina-supreme-court-gerrymander.html?campaign_id=60&emc=edit_na_20230428&instance_id=0&nl=breaking-news&ref=cta&regi_id=13788254&segment_id=131629&user_id=e16deb82e8516f294a4077a86c02f5c2; Democracy Docket, North Carolina Supreme Court Will Rehear Two Voting Rights Cases with New GOP Majority (Feb. 3, 2023), www.democracydocket.com/news-alerts/north-carolina-supreme-court-will-rehear-two-voting-rights-cases-with-new-gop-majority/.

barring state courts from reviewing claims of impermissible partisan gerrymandering.[38] And since the US Supreme Court had earlier declared such claims to be similarly unreviewable in federal court, the combined effect was to invest the North Carolina state legislature with seemingly unfettered power to engage in partisan gerrymandering to its heart's content. The US Supreme Court ultimately affirmed the North Carolina Supreme Court's initial decision (invalidating the state legislature's original districting map),[39] but the Court's ruling creates major uncertainties that will be discussed in Section C.

The actions of the North Carolina Supreme Court's Republican members triggered an angry dissent from that court's two surviving Democratic members. Writing for both of them, Justice Earls lashed out at the Republican majority in ad hominem language not often seen in a judicial opinion:

> [T]he majority abolishes the fundamental right to vote on equal terms regardless of political party through a process driven by partisan influence and greed for power. Let there be no illusions about what motivates the majority's decision to rewrite this Court's precedent. Today's result was preordained on 8 November 2022, when two new members of this Court were elected to establish this Court's conservative majority. To the Court's new majority, … [t]he merits of Plaintiffs' arguments do not matter. For at stake in this case is the majority's own political agenda. …
>
> To be clear, this is not a situation in which a Democrat-controlled Court preferred Democrat-leaning districts and a Republican-controlled Court now prefers Republican-leaning districts. Here, a Democratic-controlled Court carried out its sworn duty to uphold the state constitution's guarantee of free elections, fair to all voters of both parties. This decision is now vacated by a Republican-controlled Court seeking to ensure that extreme partisan gerrymanders favoring Republicans are established.[40]

Justice Earls wasn't finished. In concluding his dissent, he wrote:

> [A]n injustice that is so glaring, so lawless, and such a betrayal to the democratic values upon which our constitution is based will not stand forever. As *Harper II* explained, the rights that prohibit partisan gerrymandering in this state "are … the enduring bedrock of our sacred system of democratic governance, and may be neither subordinated nor subverted for the sake of passing political expediency."
>
> I dissent from this Court's majority opinion and its shameful manipulation of fundamental principles of our democracy and the rule of law. I look forward to the day when commitment to the constitutional principles of free elections and equal protection of the laws are upheld and the abuses committed by the majority are recognized for what they are, permanently relegating them to the annals of this Court's darkest moments. I have no doubt that day will come.[41]

---

[38] *Harper v. Hall*, 886 S.E.2d 393 (N.C. 2023).
[39] *Moore v. Harper*, 143 S.Ct. 2065 (2023).
[40] *Harper v. Hall*, 886 S.E.2d 393, 450 (N.C. 2023) (Justice Earls, dissenting).
[41] *Ibid.*, at 477–78.

The combined effects of residential patterns, single-member district elections, and extreme partisan gerrymandering have not been limited to the specific states where these patterns have played out. The impact is nationwide. In US House elections in 2012, Democratic candidates nationwide beat Republican candidates by a margin of 1.4 million votes but ended up with only 45 percent of the House members. And in 1996, they also won the nationwide popular vote, only for the Republicans to gain control of the House nonetheless.[42]

Despite its long lineage, today's gerrymanders, in the words of Justice Kagan, "are not your grandfather's – let alone the Framers' – gerrymanders." She explains:

> [B]ig data and modern technology ... make today's gerrymandering altogether different from the crude linedrawing of the past. ... Mapmakers now have access to more granular data about party preference and voting behavior than ever before. County-level voting data has given way to precinct-level or city-block-level data; and increasingly, mapmakers avail themselves of data sets providing wide-ranging information about even individual voters. Just as important, advancements in computing technology have enabled mapmakers to put that information to use with unprecedented efficiency and precision. While bygone mapmakers may have drafted three or four alternative districting plans, today's mapmakers can generate thousands of possibilities at the touch of a key – and then choose the one giving their party maximum advantage (usually while still meeting traditional districting requirements). The effect is to make gerrymanders far more effective and durable than before, insulating politicians against all but the most titanic shifts in the political tides.[43]

The most obvious cost of these disconnects is the damage they do to what should be a majoritarian system for electing the people's representatives. In *Rucho*, the Court candidly acknowledged that the two challenged congressional districting maps were "blatant examples of partisanship driving districting decisions."[44] In turn, the Court recognized that "[e]xcessive partisanship in districting leads to results that reasonably seem unjust" and "that such gerrymandering is incompatible with democratic principles."[45] But it disclaimed any federal judicial role in the solution, holding that claims of partisan gerrymandering are not justiciable in federal courts.

Justice Kagan, writing for the four dissenters, aptly quotes the compelling language of an earlier Supreme Court decision: "The 'core principle of republican government,' this Court has recognized, is 'that the voters should choose their representatives, not the other way around.' Partisan gerrymandering turns it the other way around."[46]

---

[42] Rodden, note 17, at 1.
[43] Rucho, 139 S.Ct. at 2512.
[44] *Ibid.*, at 2505.
[45] *Ibid.*, at 2506.
[46] *Ibid.*, at 2512, citing *Arizona State Legislature v. Arizona Independent Redistricting Comm'n*, 576 U.S. 787, 824 (2015).

There are several other costs as well. Unquestionably, partisan gerrymandering usually dilutes the voting power of people of color.[47] In the modern era, although both major political parties engage in partisan gerrymandering when they can, the overall net advantage lies systematically with one party – Republicans.[48] Moreover, when drawing their own state legislative districts, legislators have an inherent incentive to favor themselves as incumbents. That requires maximizing the number of safe districts.[49] The conflict of interest is obvious.

There are additional ways in which gerrymandering of state legislative districts is worse than gerrymandering of congressional districts. First, the latter damage is at least limited to selected US House delegations (though, as seen, those effects can be enough to alter the balance of power in the House); in contrast, the former changes the composition of the entire legislature.[50]

Second, gerrymanders of state legislative districts tend to be self-perpetuating. When state legislators gerrymander their own districts, they make it easier for the gerrymandering party to win a majority of the seats in the particular election that follows the next decennial census. In turn, that means the same party will likely draw the next redistricting map as well. Remaining in control, they can continue to pass and expand gerrymandering, voter suppression, and other counter-majoritarian laws. This further helps their party inoculate itself from termination by popular majorities. They can remain in power and pass still more of these counter-majoritarian voting measures.

For these reasons, counter-majoritarian state legislatures are very difficult to dislodge, even when a new decennial census intervenes. The cycle is hard to break, as voting them out often effectively requires a supermajority of the state's population – a daunting challenge in the many states where the same partisan gerrymandering, combined with residential patterns and single-member district elections, have already stacked the deck. In this way, the counter-majoritarianism that gerrymandering produces feeds on itself. Of course, it also enables gerrymandered state legislatures to pass unrelated laws that a majority of the voters do not favor.

The 1965 VRA (discussed more fully in Section B below) took dead aim at racial discrimination in voting. Section 2 (since amended) now prohibits states and their political subdivisions from adopting any voting practice "which *results* in a denial or abridgement of the right of any citizen of the United States to vote on account of race or color …" [emphasis added]. This means that the political process must be "equally open to participation" by citizens of every race and color and that all citizens, regardless of race or color, must have equal opportunity "to elect representatives

---

[47] See especially Jessica Bulman-Pozen & Miriam Seifter, *The Democracy Principle in State Constitutions*, 119 Mich. L. Rev. 859, 862 (2021).

[48] Rodden, note 17, at 166–67.

[49] See, for example, the multiple sources cited in Issacharoff *et al.*, note 14, at 715.

[50] See Adam B. Cox, *Partisan Gerrymandering and Disaggregated Redistricting*, 2005 Sup. Ct. Rev. 409, (2005).

of their choice."[51] There are similar protections from discrimination based on one's membership of a language minority group.[52] Importantly, the "results" language eliminates the need to prove an easily concealed intent to discriminate.

As originally enacted, Section 5 of the VRA required certain states with particularly egregious histories of discriminating against racial minorities to obtain US Justice Department approval (called "pre-clearance") for any changes in their voting laws. To obtain such preclearance, the affected states often had to devise districting plans that assured the creation of at least one, and occasionally more than one, district in which a racial minority comprised a majority of the population. These are the so-called "majority-minority" districts.

But by the 1990s, conservative Republican appointees had attained a majority on the Supreme Court. Having held (with narrow exceptions) that race cannot constitutionally be the "predominant" factor in drawing congressional district maps, the Court began applying that prohibition *against* the interests of racial minorities rather than *for* them. In at least two cases, the Court struck down the creation of majority–minority districts upon finding that race had been a predominant factor in creating them.[53] In another case, the Supreme Court held the district court was right *not* to create more than one majority African American district despite African Americans' much larger statewide population percentage.[54] And when the Supreme Court in 2013 gutted Section 5 of the VRA,[55] the states that had been creating majority–minority districts in order to gain Justice Department approval simply stopped doing so.

The VRA (and the Constitution) still prohibit racial discrimination in voting laws and practices, but the law does not require that members of any class of people be "elected in numbers equal to their proportion in the population."[56] And the Court has not made it easy to prove intentional discrimination *against* racial minorities.[57]

That said, the Supreme Court's 5-4 decision in *Allen* v. *Milligan*[58] in 2023 leaves a ray of hope for those challenging racial gerrymandering. The Court issued a preliminary injunction against an Alabama congressional districting plan that had resulted in only one black majority district out of seven in a state where African Americans comprised 26 percent of the population. An alternative plan presented by the challengers would have generated two such districts. Crucial to the Court's decision were that Alabama had a well-documented history of racial discrimination in voting; that the black and white populations of the state formed their own solid

---

[51] 52 U.S.C. § 10301(b).

[52] 52 U.S.C. § 10303(f)(2).

[53] *Bush* v. *Vera*, 517 U.S. 952 (1996); *Shaw* v. *Hunt*, 517 U.S. 899 (1996).

[54] *Abrams* v. *Johnson*, 521 U.S. 74 (1997).

[55] *Shelby County* v. *Holder*, 570 U.S. 529 (2013). This case is discussed in greater detail in Section B.

[56] 42 U.S.C. § 1973(b).

[57] *Abbott* v. *Perez*, 138 S.Ct. 2305 (2018).

[58] 143 S.Ct. 1487 (2023).

voting blocs; and that the alternative plan followed conventional criteria by creating compact, reasonably configured districts. That combination of facts meant that Alabama had effectively denied African American voters the equal opportunity to elect their preferred candidates, in likely violation of Section 2 of the VRA. Still, absent the combination of facts present in *Milligan*, racial gerrymandering remains difficult to prove in court.

Partisan gerrymandering is another matter, but distinguishing it from racial gerrymandering is often difficult. For one thing, racial gerrymandering can be disguised as merely partisan gerrymandering. For another, even if the gerrymandering reflects only the legislative majority's desire to maximize the strength of its party, and not the purpose of diluting the votes of racial minorities, the reality is that African American voters tend to reside disproportionately in urban centers and to vote overwhelmingly for Democrats over Republicans. Thus, diminishing the impact of urban voters can be a highly effective electoral strategy for Republicans. The VRA does not cover partisan gerrymandering, no matter how extreme its counter-majoritarian effects. The equal protection clause of the US Constitution might well prohibit it, but as noted earlier,[59] the Court has now foreclosed federal court review of challenges to partisan gerrymandering.

That leaves the states as the last bulwark against partisan gerrymandering. To be sure, several states have passed statutes or amended their constitutions to prohibit or restrict partisan gerrymandering.[60] And in *Rucho* the Court added that state courts have the power to review districting plans for compliance with those state laws.[61]

Indeed, several state courts have done just that, striking down partisan gerrymandering schemes held to violate their states' election laws or constitutions.[62] Those courts had no trouble finding administrable standards to guide those determinations, in contrast to the US Supreme Court's professed inability to do so in *Rucho*. For the Pennsylvania Supreme Court, it was enough that expert analysts were able to produce computer-generated maps accommodating all the relevant requirements.[63]

But danger continues to loom, in the form of what has been called the independent state legislature theory. An important 2023 Supreme Court decision, *Moore v. Harper*,[64] has reduced the threat posed by this theory but has not eradicated it

---

[59] See the discussion of *Rucho* v. *Common Cause* in Chapter 2, Section D.

[60] *Rucho* v. *Common Cause*, 139 S.Ct. 2484, 2507–508 (2019) (citing Florida, Missouri, Iowa, and Delaware as examples).

[61] *Ibid.*, at 2507.

[62] See Bulman-Pozen & Seifter, note 47, at 910 ns. 297 & 298 (citing court decisions in Pennsylvania and North Carolina, respectively). See also *In re 2021 Redistricting Cases Matanuska-Susitna Borough*, S.Ct. Nos. 18332–419 (Consolidated) No. 7646, 2023 Alas. Lexis 33 (Alaska Apr. 21, 2023) (holding Alaska's partisan gerrymandering of state legislative districts violated state constitution); *Matter of Harkenrider* v. *Hochul*, 38 N.Y.3d 494 (NY 2022); Brennan Center, *Redistricting Litigation Roundup* (Dec. 20, 2021), www.brennancenter.org/our-work/research-reports/redistricting-litigation-roundup-0.

[63] *League of Women Voters of Pennsylvania* v. *Commonwealth*, 178 A.3d 737 (Penn. 2018).

[64] 143 S.Ct. 2065 (2023).

entirely, as Section C will explain. The upshot is that, at this writing, the power of state courts to review claims of partisan gerrymandering of congressional districts is uncertain.

There are ways to ameliorate these various counter-majoritarian effects. Proportional representation, the preferred system in almost all the countries of the European continent (though not the UK and most of its former colonies) would solve much of the problem. Alternatively, if single-member district elections are retained, the district boundaries could be set by bipartisan – or, preferably, nonpartisan – redistricting commissions. Some US states,[65] as well as many other countries,[66] employ those commissions, with the result that overt partisan gerrymandering is rare outside the United States.[67] Both systems are discussed in Chapter 6, Section B.2.

Either proportional representation or nonpartisan districting commissions could be established without abolishing state government entirely. But the abolition of state government would pave the way for the adoption of these beneficial processes while simultaneously promoting all the other democratic and efficiency-related goals considered in this book.

B VOTER SUPPRESSION LAWS

In the aftermath of the Civil War, three important amendments were added to the US Constitution.[68] One of them, the Fifteenth Amendment, was ratified in 1870. It prohibited both the federal and the state governments from denying the vote to any US citizen on account of "race, color, or previous condition of servitude," and it empowered Congress to enforce that prohibition through "appropriate legislation."[69]

But this amendment, standing alone, did little to prevent states from deploying racially discriminatory voting practices. In Alexander Keyssar's comprehensive legal and political history of suffrage in the United States, one concise paragraph summarizes the major American voting restrictions from the founding of the Republic until passage of the 1965 VRA:

> Until the 1960s most African Americans could not vote in the South. Women were barred from voting in a majority of jurisdictions until 1920. For many years Asian immigrants were disenfranchised because they could not become citizens, and

[65] *Rucho*, 139 S.Ct. at 2307–308; Issacharoff *et al.*, note 14, at 741–43.
[66] Rodden, note 17, at 5–7; Wikipedia, *Apportionment by Country*, https://en.wikipedia.org/wiki/Apportionment_by_country#:~:text=The%20apportionment%20of%20seats%20in,is%20specified%20by%20negotiated%20treaty.
[67] Rodden, note 17, at 5.
[68] U.S. Const. amends. XIII, XIV, and XV.
[69] For a detailed, comprehensive history of both the congressional approval and the states' ratifications of the Fifteenth Amendment, see Travis Crum, *The Unabridged Fifteenth Amendment*, 133 Yale L. J. (Mar. 2024).

Native Americans lacked the right to vote far more often than they possessed it. In the early nineteenth century, moreover, states generally granted the franchise only to property owners, and well into the twentieth century paupers often were prohibited from voting. The list could [and] does go on: for much of American history, the right to vote has been far from universal.[70]

The Carnegie Corporation of New York adds a further example to that list: "Some states also employed religious tests to ensure that only Christian men could vote."[71]

To circumvent the Fifteenth Amendment ban on race discrimination in voting, states quickly enacted a variety of measures. Two of the most common were poll taxes and literacy tests. Poll taxes began popping up in the late nineteenth century, and by 1904 every former confederate state had adopted them.[72] The motivation to depress the African American vote turnout was often explicit,[73] and on that score the poll tax was highly effective.[74] But the Twenty-fourth Amendment, ratified in 1964, prohibited poll taxes in federal elections, and the 1965 Voting Rights Act (the VRA), discussed below, extended the prohibition to state elections.[75] The following year, the Supreme Court declared poll taxes (and property or wealth taxes) unconstitutional, as a denial of equal protection.[76] Ironically, one of the Antifederalists' great fears had been that *the federal government* would impose a poll tax *against* the will of the states.[77]

Literacy tests ultimately met a similar fate. The Supreme Court upheld their use in 1959,[78] but the 1965 VRA all but eliminated them.[79] In 1970, Congress, finding that they had been used to disenfranchise minority groups, temporarily suspended

---

[70] Alexander Keyssar, The Right to Vote: The Contested History of Democracy in the United States, at xx (rev. ed. 2009). See also *South Carolina v. Katzenbach*, 383 U.S. 301, 310–12 (1966) (laying out the evidence of purposeful – in many cases brazenly acknowledged – racial discrimination by states and counties in implementing their voting restrictions); National Geographic, Voting Rights in United States History, https://education.nationalgeographic.org/resource/voting-rights-throughout-history (describing history of state voter exclusions based on race, gender, and land ownership); Bulman-Pozen and Seifter, note 47, at 891.

[71] Carnegie Corp. of New York, *Voting Rights: A Short History* (Nov. 18, 2019), www.carnegie.org/our-work/article/voting-rights-timeline/.

[72] Issacharoff *et al.*, note 14, at 105.

[73] *Ibid.*, citing the examples quoted in *Harman v. Forssenius*, 380 U.S. 528 (1965) and *United States v. Louisiana*, 225 F. Supp. 353 (E.D. Louisiana), aff'd, 380 U.S. 145 (1965).

[74] Kousser, note 12.

[75] Pub. L. 89–110, 79 Stat. 437 (Aug. 6, 1965), § 10.

[76] *Harper v. Virginia State Board of Elections*, 383 U.S. 663 (1966).

[77] See Antifederalist Papers 26, 32, and especially 54 (Cato fearing that Congress will impose "an odious poll-tax – the offspring of despotic governments"). These fears might have been fed inadvertently by none other than leading Federalist Alexander Hamilton. In Federalist 36, while expressing "disapprobation" of poll taxes, Hamilton had nonetheless favored giving both the federal and state governments the power to impose them when necessary.

[78] *Lassiter v. Northampton County Board of Elections*, 360 U.S. 45 (1959).

[79] Pub. L. 89–110, 79 Stat. 437 (Aug. 6, 1965), § 4(c).

literacy tests nationwide, a prohibition upheld by the Supreme Court the same year.[80] In 1975, Congress finished them off for good.[81]

The Republican-controlled Rhode Island legislature had already passed a law designed specifically to suppress the votes of Irish Americans, who tended to vote for Democrats by wide margins. Rhode Island accomplished this by prohibiting its naturalized citizens – the vast majority of whom were Irish Americans – from voting unless they met specified property ownership requirements. US-born citizens were exempt from that requirement. The (intended) effect was to disenfranchise approximately 90 percent of Rhode Island's naturalized citizens.[82]

Despite the Fifteenth Amendment, in the interval between its ratification and the passage of the VRA, states that were intent on suppressing or diluting the votes of people of color found plentiful ways to do it. These included extreme gerrymandering, registration and voting restrictions, and other well-documented strategies.[83]

Travis Crum challenges the conventional wisdom that the Fifteenth Amendment was not meant to constrain these or other racial proxies. He relies, persuasively, on a combination of the amendment's literal language (in particular the words "abridge" and "race") and the framers' understanding that voting rights include a group element. Crum concludes that the prevailing intention of the Fifteenth Amendment's drafters was to prohibit racially motivated proxies, no matter how cleverly masked in facially nondiscriminatory language.[84]

During the brief liberal renaissance of the mid-1960s, Congress and President Lyndon Johnson transformed American life. The years 1964 and 1965 alone saw the enactment of such landmark legislation as the Civil Rights Act,[85] the abolition of national origin discrimination in immigration quotas,[86] Medicare, and Medicaid.[87]

---

[80] *Oregon v. Mitchell*, 400 U.S. 112 (1970).

[81] 52 U.S.C. § 10501.

[82] See Crum, note 69, at 24, 31–32; Patrick T. Conley, *No Landless Irish Need Apply: Rhode Island's Role in the Framing and Fate of the Fifteenth Amendment*, 68 Rhode Island History 79, 79 (2010).

[83] See, for example, *Johnson v. De Grandy*, 512 U.S. 997, 1018 (1994) (noting "the demonstrated ingenuity of state and local governments in hobbling minority voting power" as "jurisdictions have substantially moved from direct, overt impediments to the right to vote to more sophisticated devices that dilute minority voting strength"); *South Carolina v. Katzenbach*, 383 U.S. 301, 311–12 (1966) (describing both the history of such discrimination and the federal government's inability to curb it); *N.C. State Conference of the NAACP v. McCrory*, 831 F.3d 204, 215 (4th Cir. 2016) ("state legislatures have too often found facially race-neutral ways to deny African Americans access to the franchise"); Carnegie Corp. of New York, note 71; National Geographic, note 70; Issacharoff et al., note 14, at 233–34.

[84] See Crum, note 69, at 3, 42–43, 54, 79. As Crum also points out, Senator William Stewart (R.-Nev.), the author of the Fifteenth Amendment, stated on the record that the Amendment was meant to prohibit racial proxies targeting protected classes. *Ibid.*, at 54.

[85] Civil Rights Act of 1964, 88 Pub. L. 352, 78 Stat. 241 (July 2, 1964).

[86] Immigration and Nationality Act of 1965, Pub. L. 89–236, 79 Stat. 911 (Oct. 3, 1965).

[87] See National Archives, *Medicare and Medicaid Act* (1965), www.archives.gov/milestone-documents/medicare-and-medicaid-act.

It was in this political environment that Congress was finally able to meaningfully address the problem of racial discrimination in voting. The VRA[88] made it much harder for states to engage in racially discriminatory voting practices. Two of its most important provisions are also the ones most relevant here.

Section 2, discussed earlier in connection with gerrymandering,[89] prohibits racial discrimination in voting. But the heart of the VRA was Section 5, which imposed a "pre-clearance" requirement on states (or their political subdivisions) with recent histories of racial discrimination. For this purpose, racial discrimination was evidenced by the state or subdivision having conditioned voting eligibility on literacy tests, educational levels, "good moral character," or vouchers by other individuals.[90] Several southern states, and a few miscellaneous counties elsewhere in the US, fell within those categories. The affected states and political subdivisions had to preclear any changes in their voting practices with either the Department of Justice or a three-judge panel of the US District Court for the District of Columbia. To obtain preclearance, they had to show that the new practice "neither has the purpose nor will have the effect of denying or abridging the right to vote on account of race or color … [or diminishing citizens' ability] to elect their preferred candidates of choice."[91]

In 1966, the Supreme Court upheld the constitutionality of the VRA in *South Carolina v. Katzenbach*.[92] Chief Justice Earl Warren, writing for the Court's 8-1 majority,[93] laid out the evidence of purposeful – in many cases explicitly acknowledged – racial discrimination by the affected states and counties in the implementation of their voting laws. He also described the unsuccessful attempts by the federal government to curb those abuses and the consequent need for the preclearance requirements.[94] On those bases the Court overwhelmingly ruled that the preclearance requirement was a valid exercise of Congress's power to enforce the Fifteenth Amendment prohibition of racial discrimination.

Mainly through its preclearance requirement, the VRA produced immediate, dramatic results. In the words of others, "In the five years after the Act was passed, more black citizens registered to vote in six of the southern states than had registered in

---

[88] Pub. L. No. 89-110, 79 Stat. 437 (Aug. 6, 1965).

[89] See Section A of this chapter.

[90] Section 5, which describes the preclearance process, is now codified as 52 U.S.C. § 10304. Section 4, which lays out the criteria for identifying the states and political subdivisions that will be subject to the preclearance requirement, has now been codified as 52 U.S.C. § 10303. In addition to the use of the suspect voting restrictions, states and political subdivisions had to have had low voter registration rates or low voter turnout rates in order to be subject to the preclearance requirement.

[91] 52 U.S.C. § 10304(a,b).

[92] 383 U.S. 301 (1966).

[93] The lone dissenter was Justice Black, who objected to the preclearance requirement on grounds of state sovereignty.

[94] *Katzenbach*, 383 U.S. at 311–12.

the entire century since the Fifteenth Amendment had been ratified."[95] The gains
continued for almost half a century. In its 2013 decision in *Shelby County* v.
Holder, discussed below, the Supreme Court emphasized that, in the states and counties
to which the preclearance requirement applied, "[v]oter turnout and registration
rates now approach parity. Blatantly discriminatory evasions of federal decrees are
rare. And minority candidates hold office at unprecedented levels."[96] The dissent
agreed,[97] calling the VRA "one of the most consequential, efficacious, and amply
justified exercises of federal legislative power in our Nation's history."[98]

In recent years, however, two developments have conspired to reverse those
decades of progress. First, Republicans achieved stunning successes in capturing
control of state legislatures in 2010. As Steven Levitsky and Daniel Ziblatt point
out, it was then that voter ID laws and other voter suppression measures began their
resurgence.[99] These laws specifically targeted African American, Hispanic, and poor
voters.[100]

On the heels of the 2010 elections came the second, even more crushing, blow
to voting rights – the Supreme Court's 2013 decision in *Shelby County* v. *Holder*.[101]
Congress has periodically extended and amended the preclearance and other provisions of the VRA. In 2006, Congress extended the preclearance requirement for
twenty-five years. But it did not update the formula, which relied on decades-old
data, for identifying which states and counties would be subject to the preclearance
requirement.[102]

That failure proved fatal. In *Shelby County*, the Court struck down the formula
for determining which states and counties would be subject to the preclearance
requirement. There was no possibility that Republicans in Congress would agree
to update the formula, since the minority populations whom the VRA was meant
to protect tend to vote overwhelmingly for Democrats. The practical effect of the
Court's decision, therefore, was to wipe the Section 5 preclearance requirement
off the books entirely, thus gutting by far the most successful provision of the VRA.

---

[95] Issacharoff *et al.*, note 14, at 477, citing Chandler Davidson, *The Voting Rights Act: A Brief History*, in
Bernard Grofman & Chandler Davidson (eds.), Controversies in Minority Voting 7, 21 (1992).
[96] *Shelby County* v. *Holder*, 570 U.S. 529, 547 (2013), quoting *Northwest Austin Municipal Utilities
District Number One* v. *Holder*, 557 U.S. 193, 202 (2009).
[97] *Shelby County*, 570 U.S. at 562 (citing Congress's findings that the improvements were directly attributable to the VRA). See also *N.C. State Conference of the NAACP* v. *McCrory*, 831 F.3d 204, 215 (4th
Cir. 2016) (statistically demonstrating dramatic improvement in African American registration rates
and turnout).
[98] *Shelby County*, 570 U.S. at 562. See also Keyssar, Right to Vote, note 70, at 233–38 (summarizing preclearance developments up to publication of his book in 2009).
[99] Levitsky & Ziblatt, Tyranny, note 23, at 108–109.
[100] *Ibid.*, at 109–11. See also Ari Berman, *Give Us the Ballot: The Modern Struggle for Voting Rights in
America* (2016).
[101] 570 U.S. 529 (2013).
[102] For a detailed chronology, see Issacharoff *et al.*, note 14, at 180–89.

The five Republican appointees on the Court comprised the majority; the four Democratic appointees all dissented. Two of the Justices essential to the Court's 5-4 majority had been confirmed by senators who represented only a minority of the US population.[103] Writing the majority opinion, Chief Justice John Roberts acknowledged (how could he not?) that "voting discrimination still exists; no one doubts that." Referring to the huge gains in minority voter registration since the enactment of the VRA, he added "There is no doubt that these improvements are in large part *because of* the Voting Rights Act [emphasis in original]. The Act has proved immensely successful at redressing racial discrimination and integrating the voting process."[104]

The problem, in the majority's mind, came back once again to federalism. "Not only do the States retain sovereignty under the Constitution," he said, "there is also a 'fundamental principle of *equal* sovereignty' among the States."[105] The unstated premise was that the equality of the states trumped the racial equality of their citizens. The same principle that gave states with wildly different populations equal representation in the Senate apparently compelled Congress to provide the same treatment to states with vastly different histories of racial discrimination in voting. The other premise, stated explicitly, was that the very success of the preclearance requirement in the covered states was reason enough to render the formula for identifying those states obsolete; there was no evidence, the court said, that it was still necessary in those states.

Justice Ginsburg's powerful dissent, joined by three other Justices, blasted the very notion that the Constitution required Congress to treat all the states the same. She cited numerous examples of federal laws that singled out particular states either favorably or unfavorably.[106] The dissent also pointed out that racial discrimination in the covered states still exists, as evidenced by those states' disproportionately high rate of successful lawsuits for racial discrimination in voting.[107] The dissenters argued that preserving the preclearance formula, therefore, remained essential, both to solidify the gains it had already produced and to prevent backsliding.[108] Without this vital tool, the dissenters feared, states with a history of racial discrimination would resume that pattern. Indeed, they pointed out, there had already been an "evolution of voting discrimination into more subtle second-generation barriers."[109]

They were right. To the surprise of almost no one (except, apparently, the Court's partisan majority), the ink was barely dry on the *Shelby County* opinion when states

---

[103] 570 U.S. 529 (2013). The two Justices were Thomas and Alito. See Jack Balkin, The Cycles of Constitutional Time 141 (2020).

[104] 570 U.S. at 548.

[105] *Ibid.*, at 544.

[106] *Ibid.*, at 587–89.

[107] *Ibid.*, at 577–85. See also V*easey* v. *Abbott*, 830 F.3d 216 (5th Cir. 2016)(describing Texas's very restrictive 2011 voter-ID law and significant evidence that the legislature had specifically targeted minority voters). See generally Keyssar, Right to Vote, note 70, at 277–87 (summarizing voting barriers enacted from 2000 to 2009).

[108] 570 U.S. at 576–77.

[109] *Ibid.*, at 593.

all over the country – not just the states that the Court had freed from the preclearance requirement – began passing the avalanche of voter suppression laws that will be described in the pages that follow.

One study found that "[a] whopping 23 states created new obstacles to voting in the decade leading up to the 2018 elections."[110] On the very first day after the *Shelby County* decision, the Republican Chair of the North Carolina Senate rules committee announced that the legislature would take up a new omnibus elections law. The legislature quickly gathered data on the use of particular registration and voting practices in African American communities. It took less than seven weeks for the legislature to analyze those data and enact a sweeping law that, in the words of the US Court of Appeals for the Fourth Circuit, "target[ed] African Americans with almost surgical precision."[111]

The one constant in all these post-VRA examples has been state-level partisanship. More specifically, as Samuel Issacharoff has observed, "the single predictor necessary to determine whether a state will impose voter-access restrictions is whether Republicans control the [state's] ballot-access process."[112] Most of the techniques have involved putting roadblocks in the way of either registration drives or voting procedures, particularly in the predominantly Democratic-leaning African American communities.[113] The common, barely concealed strategic assumptions are simple: First, the more time, energy, hassle, and expense that voting requires, the higher will be the percentage of eligible voters who sit it out. And second, as the data described in connection with the various suppression techniques discussed below bear out, the burdens fall disproportionately on the poor and on African American and other minority voters – not coincidentally, populations that tend to vote for Democratic candidates by large margins.

Travis Crum, in a 2010 student Note,[114] correctly anticipated the Supreme Court's decision in *Shelby County* and identified ways in which another provision of the VRA could mitigate the damage. Section 3(c) of that Act[115] contains what has commonly

---

[110] Carnegie, Voting Rights, note 71, citing the nonpartisan organization, *Election Protection, Upcoming Elections in Your State*, https://866ourvote.org/; see also Brennan Center for Justice, *New Voting Restrictions in America* (2019), www.brennancenter.org/sites/default/files/2019-11/New%20Voting%20 Restrictions.pdf.

[111] *North Carolina State Conference of the NAACP v. McCrory*, 831 F.3d 204, 214 (2016). The bill was signed into law on August 12, 2013. *Ibid.*, at 218. The *Shelby County* decision had been handed down on June 25, 2013. See also *Brnovich v. Democratic National Committee*, 141 S.Ct. 2321 (2021) (upholding Arizona's 2016 law that criminalized the types of early ballot collection assistance prevalent in African American communities).

[112] Samuel Issacharoff, *Ballot Bedlam*, 64 Duke L. J. 1363, 1370 (2015). Accord, Keyssar, Right to Vote, note 70, at 153; Michael Wines, The New York Times, *After Record Turnout, Republicans Are Trying to Make It Harder to Vote* (Jan. 30, 2021), www.nytimes.com/2021/01/30/us/republicans-voting-georgia-arizona.html?searchResultPosition=1.

[113] See Keyssar, Right to Vote, note 70, at 277–87.

[114] Travis Crum, Note, *The Voting Rights Act's Secret Weapon: Pocket Trigger Litigation and Dynamic Preclearance*, 119 Yale L. J. 1992 (2010).

[115] 52 U.S.C. § 10302.

been referred to as its "bail-in mechanism" or its "pocket trigger." Under that section, if a court finds that voting rights violations of either the 14th Amendment or the 15th Amendment "have occurred" in a particular state or political subdivision, the court may require the jurisdiction to obtain preclearance of future changes to its voting laws. In such a case, the jurisdiction must convince the court that the change in its law did not have the purpose, and will not have the effect, of denying the right to vote based on race or on membership in a language minority group. Alternatively, the jurisdiction may submit the change to the US Department of Justice; if the Department doesn't object within sixty days, the change will go into effect.

Crum highlights the many advantages of this strategy. It meets the Court's concerns over differential treatment of the states and the Court's view that the Section 4 formula is outdated. In addition, courts have the discretion to limit both the duration of the preclearance requirement and the types of voting law changes to which the requirement applies. In these ways, they can more precisely tailor the remedies to the violations.

At the same time, Section 3(c) doesn't apply at all until the triggering constitutional violation has been found. This is a problem, because the Supreme Court has been hesitant to find such violations without a showing of (easily concealed) discriminatory intent. Crum therefore recommends amending Section 3(c) to make discriminatory *effect* an alternative trigger.[116]

The claimed justification for almost all the voter suppression measures that will be discussed in this Section has been "election integrity." Republicans have insisted that widespread voter fraud has altered the outcomes of recent elections. That assertion has been thoroughly debunked by countless others. Here is a brief summary:

Claims of widespread voter fraud didn't originate with Donald Trump. Keyssar, writing in 2009, showed that most of the Republicans' post-*Bush* v. *Gore* voter suppression measures were presented as essential to preventing widespread voter fraud.[117] Just a year earlier, the Supreme Court in *Crawford* v. *Marion County Election Board* had cited the prevention of voter fraud as a legitimate state interest justifying Indiana's photo ID law.[118] Since then, accusations of widespread voter fraud have only increased. In 2021, the Supreme Court in *Brnovich* v. *Democratic National Committee*[119] cited voter fraud (and the related notion of "pressure and intimidation)" in upholding Arizona's ban on third-party ballot collection. Similar assertions of voter fraud and related claims are now made routinely by losing candidates.[120]

---

[116] Crum, *The Voting Rights Act's Secret Weapon*, note 114, at 2036–37.
[117] Keyssar, Right to Vote, note 70, at 277–87.
[118] 553 U.S. 181, 194–97 (2008).
[119] 141 S.Ct. 2321, 2340, 2348 (2021).
[120] PBS News Hour, *Exhaustive Fact Check Finds Little Evidence of Voter Fraud, But 2020's "Big Lie" Lives On* (Dec. 17, 2021), www.pbs.org/newshour/show/exhaustive-fact-check-finds-little-evidence-of-voter-fraud-but-2020s-big-lie-lives-on; see also all the sources cited in note 122 below (describing the lack of evidence of widespread voter fraud).

But here's the thing: Study after study has shown beyond any doubt that, with just one recent localized exception related to just one specific voting method,[121] widespread voter fraud – much less, voter fraud so widespread as to justify laws that disproportionately (and often deliberately) burden minority voters – simply does not exist in the United States.[122] In a voting population of millions, the incidence of voter fraud will never be zero. Anecdotes will always be available. But voter fraud on a level that is even remotely likely to alter the outcome of an election is exceedingly rare.

Republican-appointed Supreme Court Justices have stretched to find contrary evidence. In the *Crawford* case, upholding an Indiana law that required a photo ID for in-person voting, these Justices had to acknowledge that "[t]he record contains no evidence of any such fraud actually occurring in Indiana at any time in its history."[123] But these Justices went on to say that "flagrant examples of such fraud in other parts of the country have been documented throughout this Nation's history by respected historians and journalists [and] that occasional examples have surfaced in recent years." The Court's examples? One was a nineteenth century New York City mayoral election during the infamous Tammany Hall era.[124] Their only examples of data purportedly showing in-person voter fraud from "recent years" turned out to be badly flawed. The Justices relegated to a footnote their acknowledgment that the amicus brief submitted by the Brennan Center for Justice had shown those

---

[121] In Bridgeport, Connecticut, a court recently found clear evidence of prohibited ballot collection by third parties and ordered a new election. See Amelia Nierenberg, The New York Times, *Election Fraud Is Rare. Except, Maybe, in Bridgeport, Conn.* (Jan. 21, 2024), www.nytimes .com/2024/01/21/nyregion/joe-ganim-john-gomes-bridgeport-mayor-election.html?campaign_ id=9&emc=edit_nn_20240121&instance_id=113082&nl=the-morning&regi_id=76642304&segment_ id=155912&te=1&user_id=2785b718e28912cce3f4ef8d2794344a.

[122] Brennan Center for Justice, *Debunking the Voter Fraud Myth*, www.brennancenter.org/sites/default/ files/analysis/Briefing_Memo_Debunking_Voter_Fraud_Myth.pdf (citing numerous studies by researchers, government agencies, and courts all finding zero evidence of significant voter fraud); Philip Bump, Washington Post, *There Have Been Just Four Documented Cases of Voter Fraud in the 2016 Election*, www.washingtonpost.com/news/the-fix/wp/2016/12/01/0-000002-percent-of-all-the- ballots-cast-in-the-2016-election-were-fraudulent/ (finding 4 documented cases of voter fraud out of more than 135 million ballots cast in the 2016 election); Andrew C. Eggers et al., PNAS, *No Evidence For Systematic Voter Fraud: A Guide to Statistical Claims about the 2020 Election*, www.pnas.org/ doi/10.1073/pnas.2103619118; Issacharoff et al., note 14, at 151 (citing studies that "consistently show virtually no meaningful levels of in-person voter fraud"); Keyssar, Right to Vote, note 70, at 264, 281–82 (showing that Republicans' numerous post-*Bush* v. *Gore* efforts to produce evidence of significant voter fraud came up empty, and that all indications were that the incidence of voter fraud was miniscule); PBS News Hour, note 120; Levitsky & Ziblatt, note 23, at 28–29; Zach Schonfeld, *Conservative Group Finds "Absolutely No Evidence of Widespread Fraud" in 2020 Election* (July 14, 2022), https:// thehill.com/homenews/campaign/3559758-conservative-group-finds-absolutely-no-evidence-of- widespread-fraud-in-2020-election/. See also Justin Jouvenal, The Washing Post, *GOP Voter-Fraud Crackdown Overwhelmingly Targets Minorities, Democrats* (Dec. 20, 2023), www.washingtonpost .com/dc-md-va/2023/12/20/voter-fraud-prosecutions-2020/?utm_campaign=wp_post_most&utm_ medium=email&utm_source=newsletter&wpisrc=nl_most (describing the ways in which the voter fraud argument has purposely targeted African American and other minorities).

[123] *Crawford* v. *Marion County Election Bd.*, 553 U.S. 181, 194 (2008).

[124] *Ibid.*, at 195 n.11.

data to be vastly overstated. There had in fact been only "scattered instances of in-person voter fraud." In one of the cited examples, a gubernatorial election in the State of Washington, investigation revealed a grand total of one person in the state who had cast one ballot in the name of a dead person.[125]

The Court's Republican appointees performed similar acrobatics in *Brnovich* v. *Democratic National Committee*.[126] There, the Supreme Court majority likewise had to acknowledge that Arizona (the state whose voting restrictions were at issue) could find not a single instance of voter fraud in its state's history. Still, the majority insisted, "election fraud has had serious consequences in other States."[127] The Court's example was the North Carolina Board of Elections' decision to invalidate the results of a 2018 race in one state legislative district because of evidence that a Republican Party operative had generated fraudulent mail-in ballots. As pointed out by the newspaper article that the Court cited, however, "officials never proved that Mr. Dowless's group touched enough ballots in and around Bladen County to account for the entirety of Mr. Harris's 905-vote edge, …"[128] So even in the one example that those Justices were able to dig up, there was no evidence that the alleged fraud had been great enough to affect the outcome.

Commenting specifically on mail-in voting, and despite the lack of evidence of widespread voter fraud in Arizona or anywhere else, the Court in *Brnovich* explained:

> [A] State may take action to prevent election fraud without waiting for it to occur and be detected within its own borders. [The law] surely does not demand that "a State's political system sustain some level of damage before the legislature [can] take corrective action." Fraud is a real risk that accompanies mail-in voting even if Arizona had the good fortune to avoid it. [The Court here cites the North Carolina example noted earlier.] The Arizona Legislature was not obligated to wait for something similar to happen closer to home.[129]

Thus, the fact that Arizona had never had any serious voter fraud problem did not matter; for the Court's majority Justices, it was enough that one day it possibly could.

Perhaps recognizing the hazards of relying solely on nonexistent evidence of actual widespread voter fraud, the Supreme Court in both *Crawford* and *Brnovich* added a related argument: "[P]ublic confidence in the integrity of the electoral process has independent significance, because it encourages citizen participation

---

[125] *Ibid.*, at 195 n.12. The Court cited one other example, a mayoral election in which one candidate had hired people to encourage voters to vote absentee and then assist them in filling out their ballots. The example did not involve in-person voter fraud, and at any rate there was no indication that those ballots had affected the final outcome. *Ibid.*, at 195–96 n.13.

[126] 141 S.Ct. 2321 (2021).

[127] *Ibid.*, at 2348.

[128] See Alan Blinder, The New York *Times*, *Election Fraud in North Carolina Leads to New Charges for Republican Operative* (July 30, 2019), www.nytimes.com/2019/07/30/us/mccrae-dowless-indictment .html, cited in *Brnovich* at 2348 n.20.

[129] *Brnovich*, 141 S.Ct. at 2348.

in the democratic process."[130] That explanation is, to be kind, ironic. Far from suppressing the vote, the Court tells us in effect, voter ID laws actually "encourage" voting. To the African American and other Democratic-leaning voters who had found the ID requirement unduly burdensome, the Court's observation must have come as quite a surprise. Not at all surprising, however, was the Court's failure to cite any empirical evidence to support this counter-instinctive assumption.

Besides, election integrity entails more than keeping ineligible individuals from voting; in a democracy, election integrity should also facilitate eligible individuals voting. As detailed below,[131] almost all other democracies either *require* all adult citizens to vote, or make registration automatic when citizens reach voting age, or proactively assist registration. At the least, the law should not erect unnecessary obstacles that affirmatively – and selectively – discourage minorities from voting.

The same point goes for the "public confidence" argument: Citizens of course deserve to have confidence that the system is screening out ineligible voters. But surely they also deserve to be confident that the laws are not making it disproportionately hard for African American and other minorities to vote. And if the miniscule frequency of actual voter fraud were really enough to discourage people from voting, one can only imagine the deterrent effects that the prolific false claims of voter fraud and system failure have on turnout.

I don't want to leave the impression that the recent election laws have *all* been one-sided. As the Introduction to this book acknowledges, there are "good" states as well as "bad" ones; which are which depends, of course, on one's point of view. More specifically, at least as of May 2023, "there [we]re more newly enacted laws that improve voter access or election administration than restrict it," although "restrictive laws represent[ed] a higher proportion of laws enacted in 2023 than in either 2022 or 2021."[132] At any rate, arguing that only about half the states are purposely trying to discourage certain demographic groups from voting is not the strongest endorsement of state government. And so, in order not to lose the forest for the trees, let us return once more to the central theme of this discussion: *All* of the voter suppression measures described in this section are the conscious creations of individual states. Every single one. The following is a sample:

1 *Making Voter Registration Harder*

One of the post-VRA strategies by which many states reduce African American voter turnout is making the registration process as hard as possible.[133] Responding,

---

[130] *Crawford*, 553 U.S. at 197; *Brnovich*, 141 S.Ct. at 2340 ("Fraud can also undermine public confidence in the fairness of elections and the perceived legitimacy of the announced outcome.")

[131] See notes 153–54 below and accompanying text.

[132] Voting Rights Lab, *Another Change-Making Year* (May 2023), https://votingrightslab.org/wp-content/uploads/2023/05/VRL-2023_YOYT-Report.pdf.

[133] See, for example, the sources cited in Bulman-Pozen & Seifter, note 47, at 891 n.187 (2021).

Congress in 1993 passed the National Voter Registration Act (the NVRA).[134] Among other things, that Act requires every state to offer its citizens three ways to register to vote in federal elections: simultaneously with an application for a driver's license; by mail; and in person at designated federal, state, or nongovernmental offices.[135] (States are free to offer additional options as well). Although the NVRA governs only federal elections, states typically conduct federal and state elections at the same time. As a practical matter, therefore, a single registration usually qualifies the person to vote in elections for both federal and state offices.

A second important provision of the NVRA requires states to "accept and use" (for federal elections) the standardized voter registration application form prescribed by a federal agency called the Election Assistance Commission (the EAC).[136] This application is commonly referred to as the "Federal Form."[137] Although the Federal Form contains uniform, nationwide content, it also includes any necessary state-specific content – most importantly, the address for mail-in registrations and the state's voter eligibility and registration criteria.[138] All state-specific information requires EAC approval.[139] If the EAC denies a state's request to add particular content to its registration form, the state has the right to challenge the EAC's decision in court.[140]

On the issue of citizenship, all the Federal Form requires is that the applicant attest under penalty of perjury that he or she is a US citizen. Undeterred by the NVRA, the State of Arizona adopted, by popular initiative in 2004, a law that required something additional before one could register to vote – furnishing documentary proof of US citizenship. That is often more easily said than done. Birth certificates and passports – the most common ways in which those who were born in the US can prove their citizenship – are often harder for the poor to access. In *Arizona* v. *Inter Tribal Council of Arizona* [ITCA], the US Supreme Court held that states may not require the applicant "to submit information beyond that required by the [Federal Form]."[141] By insisting on further proof of citizenship in the form of documents, the state was therefore in violation of the NVRA.

At the same time, the Court reaffirmed the distinction between the "times, places, and manner" of federal elections – a decision on which the Constitution

---

[134] Pub. L. 103–31, 107 Stat. 77 (May 20, 1993), codified at 52 U.S.C. §§ 20501–11.

[135] 52 U.S.C. § 20503.

[136] 52 U.S.C. § 20505(a)(1). Originally, the relevant agency was the Federal Election Commission.

[137] The Federal Form is available at US Election Assistance Commission, *Register To Vote In Your State by Using This Postcard and Guide*, www.eac.gov/sites/default/files/eac_assets/1/6/Federal_Voter_Registration_ENG.pdf and at US Election Assistance Commission, *National Mail Voter Registration Form*, www.eac.gov/voters/national-mail-voter-registration-form. Although Section 20507 generally deals with mail-in registration, the instructions on the Federal Form make clear that its use is mandatory for all registrations, whether mailed or submitted in person. *Ibid.*

[138] 11 C.F.R. § 9428.3.

[139] *Arizona* v. *Inter Tribal Council of Arizona [ITCA]*, 570 U.S. 1, 6 (2013).

[140] *Ibid.*, at 19.

[141] *Ibid.*, at 20.

gives Congress the last word – and the substantive voter *eligibility* requirements – which the state has the sole power to decide[142] (subject to any specific constitutional constraints). Thus, a state may, and every state does, require US citizenship as a condition for voting in federal elections. But it may not insist on more proof of US citizenship than what the Federal Form regards as sufficient. Arizona's only recourse, the Court said, was to request the EAC's permission to add documentary proof of citizenship to the state-specific information on its version of the Federal Form and, if denied, to seek review in court.[143] The Court's decision is comforting, but as explained in Section B.4 below, there are reasons to fear successful future state efforts to condition voting on documentary proof of US citizenship.

Arizona, joined by Kansas, took up that suggestion. Both requested the EAC's permission to add documentary proof of citizenship to the state-specific instructions to their respective versions of the Federal Form. The EAC denied both requests, and both states sought judicial review. The federal district court granted relief, holding that the EAC has a "non-discretionary" duty to approve those states' requests, but in *Kobach v. U.S. Election Assistance Commission*,[144] the US Court of Appeals for the Tenth Circuit reversed. The EAC decision was discretionary, the court held, and it found no basis for second-guessing the Commission's call. The Tenth Circuit reached the same result in a 2020 case, adding that requiring documentary proof of citizenship also violated the Constitution's equal protection clause. In the past nineteen years, the requirement had caused the cancellation or suspension of more than 30,000 voter registrations of US citizens in Kansas, compared to those of only thirty-nine non-US citizens who had managed to register to vote.[145] The combination of a miniscule "citizenship fraud" problem and a massive disenfranchisement solution was held to violate the constitutional requirement of equal protection.

But there were (and are) still other ways to make voter registration harder. Earlier discussion highlighted the actions taken by North Carolina, starting one day after the Supreme Court had gutted the VRA in the 2013 *Shelby County* case.[146] The package of five voter restriction laws passed by the North Carolina state legislature in the wake of *Shelby County* included two that specifically targeted the registration process. The US Court of Appeals for the Fourth Circuit, in *N.C. State Conference of the NAACP*

---

[142] U.S. Const. Art. I, § 4 and U.S. Const. Amend. XVII.

[143] 570 U.S. at 20. Arizona had already made that request, which the EAC had denied on a deadlocked 2-2 vote of its members. The Court invited Arizona to try again.

[144] 772 F.3d 1183 (10th Cir. 2014).

[145] *Fish v. Schwab*, 957 F.3d 1105 (10th Cir. 2020).

[146] See text accompanying note 111. Several Republican-controlled states have recently passed laws that make organized voter registration drives risky or impractical. A Florida law, for example, makes it a criminal offense for a group to collect registration forms and submit them to election officials if any of the forms contain mistakes. See Michael Wines, N.Y. Times, *How Some States Are Making It Harder to Register Voters* (July 26, 2024), www.nytimes.com/2024/07/26/us/voter-registration-drive-restrictions.html.

v. McCrory,[147] ultimately struck down all five restrictions on equal protection grounds. As noted earlier, the court found overwhelming evidence of a specific intent to discriminate against African American voters with "almost surgical precision."[148]

One of the two registration-related laws was a repeal of preregistration. This was a process that had allowed sixteen- and seventeen-year-olds to preregister to vote when obtaining driver's licenses or attending mandatory high school registration drives. The process had been highly successful, enabling elections officials to verify eligibility in advance and register eligible voters once they reached age eighteen. It had increased turnout among young voters.[149]

The other law relevant here was a repeal of same-day registration. That procedure had been especially valuable to several groups – those who had not been able to register earlier, those who had been shunted into the "incomplete registration queue" after previous unsuccessful attempts to register, those who moved frequently, and those who needed personal assistance from poll workers.[150]

These two laws had two common denominators. For multiple reasons laid out by the court, they had a disproportionate adverse impact on African American turnout. And both laws had been passed only after the legislature had sought and obtained data demonstrating those disproportionate adverse effects.[151] The evidence of discriminatory intent was unmistakable.

It shouldn't have to be this hard. As Issacharoff et *al.* point out, one state (North Dakota) has decided that no voter registration at all is necessary. You just show up and vote. Twenty others allow same-day registration.[152] The United States, as the same authors observe, "is distinctive among western democracies in that the government takes virtually no affirmative responsibility for registering citizens [to vote]." In almost all other democracies, registration is either automatic when citizens reach voting age[153] or proactively assisted by the national government – typically without requiring identification or allowing non-photo identification. And some countries, including Argentina, Australia, and Brazil, make voting mandatory.[154]

2 *Purging Voter Rolls*

Getting your name onto the voter registration list is one thing. Making sure it stays there is another.

---

[147] 831 F.3d 204 (4th Cir. 2016).
[148] *Ibid.*, at 214.
[149] *Ibid.*, at 217–18.
[150] *Ibid.*, at 217.
[151] *Ibid.*, at 217–18.
[152] Issacharoff et *al.*, note 14, at 149.
[153] For one example of advocacy of automatic voter registration at age 18, see Levitsky & Ziblatt, *Tyranny*, note 23, at 232.
[154] *Ibid.*, at 228–29 (Argentina and Australia); Wikipedia, *Elections in Brazil*, https://en.wikipedia.org/wiki/Elections_in_Brazil#Electoral_systems (Brazil).

From time to time, states cull names from their voter rolls. They have legitimate reasons to do so. Voters die, move out of their districts, or become ineligible to vote because of felony convictions. Updating the list helps prevent people from either impersonating dead voters or voting in multiple districts in the same election, rare as voter fraud is in reality.[155] It also aids states in keeping their registration lists at a manageable length. The NVRA in fact requires states to make a "reasonable" effort to remove the names of voters who have died or moved out of their voting districts.[156]

At the same time, administrative errors in maintaining voter registration lists are not uncommon; voters should not be disenfranchised because of those errors. Beyond that concern, an unbridled power of state election officials to purge voters on change of residence grounds would allow election officials of one particular political party to deliberately target population areas that tend to vote for the opposing party. Examples of precisely such practices, typically aimed at minority populations, are endemic and are highlighted below. Until passage of the NVRA in 1993, in fact, some states would purge people from the voting rolls without any notice and therefore without any opportunity to confirm their continued residence within the district.[157]

A word on terminology: As explained by Ballotpedia, "Voter *caging* [by either public or private actors] is the practice of sending mail to registered voters and challenging their eligibility to vote if the mail is returned as undeliverable." The Ballotpedia article offers several modern examples of voter caging, all by either the national or state Republican Parties. The next step, "[v]oter *purging*, is the practice of removing names from the voter rolls ..."[158]

As discussed earlier, the Supreme Court's 2013 decision in *Shelby County v. Holder*[159] cut out the heart of the 1965 VRA by effectively nullifying Section 5 of that Act. This was the provision that required states and counties with histories of racial discrimination in voting, as measured by specified metrics, to obtain advance Justice Department clearance for any proposed changes to their election laws. As the earlier discussion illustrated, once freed from that requirement, the states and counties that had been subject to it wasted no time in adopting or accelerating a range of strategies to suppress African American and other minority votes.

Voter purging is one of the many suppression strategies that has proliferated in the wake of *Shelby County*. A Brennan Center study found that, in the five years immediately following *Shelby County* (2013–18), four states actually carried out, and four others adopted rules that would permit, illegal purges. Those eight states together account for one-fourth of the nation's registered voters.[160]

---

[155] See the discussion of voter fraud in notes 117–31 and accompanying text.
[156] 52 U.S.C. § 20507(a)(4).
[157] *Husted v. A. Philip Randolph Institute*, 138 S.Ct. 1833, 1838 (2018).
[158] Ballotpedia, *Voter Caging and Purging*, https://ballotpedia.org/Voter_caging_and_purging.
[159] 570 U.S. 529 (2013).
[160] Jonathan Brater *et al.*, Brennan Center for Justice, *Purges: A Growing Threat to the Right to Vote* (2018), at 1–2, file:///C:/Users/legomsky/Downloads/Report_Purges_Growing_Threat%20(1).pdf.

After *Shelby County*, actual voter purging escalated dramatically in the counties that the Court had freed from the preclearance requirement. The Brennan Center report doesn't assess how many of those purges were improper, but the circumstantial evidence is strong. Using data compiled by the US Election Assistance Commission (the EAC), the Brennan Center spotted two empirical patterns. First, the purge rates of counties whose histories of racial discrimination had subjected them to the VRA's preclearance requirement had been at roughly the national average while the preclearance requirement was keeping them in check. As soon as the Supreme Court lifted that requirement, their purge rates increased instantly and sharply. Second, their post-*Shelby County* purge rates were significantly higher than those for counties that had not been subject to preclearance.[161] So much higher, in fact, that if the former preclearance states had purged only at the lower rate prevailing in the other states, two million fewer voters would have been purged during the interval between the 2012 and 2016 elections.[162]

The numbers are significant. The same Brennan Center study compared the national voter purge figures for the 2006–2008 period (when preclearance was still in force) to the 2014–16 period (just after *Shelby County*). From the former period to the latter, the number of voters purged from the rolls increased by one-third – and by an even higher percentage in the former preclearance states and counties.[163]

Wrongful purges haven't been confined to any one geographic region of the country. Thousands of eligible voters were erroneously purged in Virginia in 2013 and in both New York and Arkansas in 2016.[164] Wisconsin experienced a near miss. In 2019, a Wisconsin state court judge ordered the purge of 200,000 voters, a majority of whom lived in Democratic Party strongholds. His order was reversed by both the state court of appeals and the state's Supreme Court.[165] And "Georgia purged twice as many voters – 1.5 million – between the 2012 and 2016 elections [*i.e.*, mainly after *Shelby County*] as it did between 2008 and 2012 [*i.e.*, before *Shelby County*]."[166]

But the mother of all voter purges – in terms of both numbers and audacity – has to be Georgia's subsequent 2017 purge of 560,000 voters, just in time for the 2018 gubernatorial election. These individuals were purged for having failed to vote often enough in recent elections. What makes that purge particularly noteworthy is that it was ordered by Georgia's then-secretary of state, Brian Kemp, himself a candidate for governor. A Republican, he was opposed in the general election by Democrat

---

[161] *Ibid.*, at 1; Kevin Morris, *Brennan Center for Justice, Voter Purge Rates Remain High, Analysis Finds* (Aug. 21, 2019), www.brennancenter.org/our-work/analysis-opinion/voter-purge-rates-remain-high-analysis-finds.

[162] Brater *et al.*, note 160, at 1.

[163] *Ibid.*

[164] *Ibid.*

[165] See *State ex rel. Zignego* v. *Wisconsin Election Commission*, 396 Wis.2d 391, 957 N.W.2d 208 (2021); see also Wikipedia, *Paul V. Malloy*, https://en.wikipedia.org/wiki/Paul_V._Malloy.

[166] Brater *et al.*, note 160, at 1.

Stacey Abrams, an African American with strong support in the very places that the purge disproportionately singled out. The tactic was successful; Kemp won the election by fewer than 55,000 votes out of almost 4 million votes cast.[167] An investigation revealed that approximately 107,000 of the purged voters would have been eligible to vote; 70,000 of them, in fact, reregistered to vote after the election.[168]

In theory, the NVRA should constrain manipulative voter purges. For purposes of federal elections, it prohibits states from removing a voter's name "by reason of the person's failure to vote."[169] But there are loopholes. The Help America Vote Act (HAVA), passed in 2002, contains a similar provision but with the addition of a keyword: It says only that the person's name may not be removed "solely" for failure to vote.[170] That language permits consideration of failure to vote when it is coupled with other factors. In addition, the NVRA provision expressly allows the state to remove a voter's name for presumed change of residence in two (though only in two) circumstances. It may do so if the person confirms in writing that he or she has moved out of the district. And it may do so if the elections officials mail the person a preaddressed, postage-prepaid card requesting confirmation that the voter is still at the same address and the person does not reply – and then fails to vote in at least one of the next two general federal elections.[171] Moreover, as noted earlier, the NVRA affirmatively requires states to make a "reasonable" effort to remove the names of people who have either died or left their districts.[172]

But here's the question: To whom may a state send these confirmation requests in the first place? Limitations are obviously essential. Unfettered, a state could send the confirmation notices selectively to voters or population centers that are known to support one particular political party, with the result that some percentage of the addressees will fail to return the cards and thereby disqualify themselves from voting. The NVRA allows states to send those requests to people who have submitted change-of-address information to the US Postal Service,[173] but it says nothing about whether the cards may be sent under any other circumstances. In particular, may the state choose to send the notices only to those who have failed to vote recently enough or often enough?

This is where Ohio and the US Supreme Court come in. Under Ohio law, the state automatically sends confirmation requests to anyone who hasn't voted (or registered to vote or signed a petition or updated a voting address) in the past two years. If

---

[167] Wikipedia, *2018 Georgia Gubernatorial Election*, https://en.wikipedia.org/wiki/2018_Georgia_guber natorial_election.

[168] Angela Caputo et al., APM Reports, *After the Purge* (Oct. 29, 2019), www.apmreports.org/story/2019/10/29/georgia-voting-registration-records-removed.

[169] 52 U.S.C. § 20507(b)(2).

[170] 52 U.S.C. § 21083(a)(4)(A).

[171] 52 U.S.C. § 20507(d)(1), d(2)(A).

[172] 52 U.S.C. § 20507(a)(4).

[173] 52 U.S.C. § 20507(c)(1).

the person doesn't respond and doesn't vote in the next four years (including two general federal elections), that person's name is then removed from the registration list.

In *Husted* v. A. *Philip Randolph Institute*,[174] the Supreme Court split along partisan lines in upholding the Ohio law. The five Republican Justices interpreted the NVRA to mean that the person's failure to vote can still be a factor in its decision to remove the person's name – just not the sole factor. Because Ohio doesn't remove people for failure to vote unless they also failed to return their confirmation cards, the Court held that Ohio's practice was lawful – even though the *sole* reason for sending the cards to those particular individuals in the first place had been their failure to vote in the past two years.

Justice Sotomayor, joining the principal dissent and adding her own, is explicit in highlighting *which* of these voters are most likely to be erroneously disenfranchised. Calling out the elephant in the room, she observes that "Congress enacted the NVRA against the backdrop of substantial efforts of States to disenfranchise low-income and minority voters, *including programs that purged eligible voters from registration lists because they failed to vote in prior elections*" [emphasis added]. She cited an additional study documenting various states' registration practices that "sharply reduced turnout, particularly among blacks and immigrants."[175] The American Bar Association agrees, observing that "[f]ailure to vote regularly correlates with lower socioeconomic status and, at least in some places, with being a member of a racial minority."[176]

Justice Breyer, writing for the four dissenters and citing the House committee report on the bill that would become the NVRA, similarly points out a history of "selective purges" in the late nineteenth and early twentieth centuries. These, the report emphasized, were designed "to keep certain groups of citizens from voting" and were among the very reasons Congress passed the NVRA.[177]

Because the negotiations and strategy sessions that precede the adoption of purging policies are ordinarily hidden from view, there is no way to know how much of the disparate impact on minority voters is intentional and how much is the product of either a "let the chips fall where they may" decision or innocent error. One Brennan Center study attributes some of the problems to a combination of faulty data and faulty methodologies.[178] Another Brennan Center study pinpoints errors involving voters with the same names and dates of birth, especially in large states.

---

[174] 138 S.Ct. 1833 (2018).
[175] *Ibid.*, at 1863.
[176] Paul M. Smith, American Bar Association, *"Use It or Lose It": The Problem of Purges from the Registration Rolls of Voters Who Don't Vote Regularly* (Feb. 9, 2020), www.americanbar.org/groups/crsj/publications/human_rights_magazine_home/voting-rights/-use-it-or-lose-it---the-problem-of-purges-from-the-registration0/?login. Accord, Rock the Vote, *Voter Rolls and Voter Purging*, www.rockthevote.org/explainers/voter-rolls-and-voter-purging-an-explainer/.
[177] 138 S.Ct. at 1850.
[178] Brater *et al.*, note 160.

That study points out that identical names are particularly common in minority communities.[179] One organization capsulizes these multiple problems in one succinct sentence: Voter purging can be "shrouded in secrecy, prone to error and vulnerable to manipulation."[180]

Apart from the disparate impact of these practices, failure to vote in recent elections is a highly inaccurate proxy for likelihood of death or change of residence. More than one-third of all eligible voters nationwide sit out even the high turnout presidential elections.[181] Far fewer than that number die or move out of their districts within those same narrow time periods. Singling out that population for the required return of confirmation notices thus does not make even statistical sense.

A use-it-or-lose-it policy also doesn't make legal sense. In the United States, eligible voters are never obligated to vote. You have the right to sit out an election without risking the forfeiture of your right to vote in future elections.

If failure to vote in recent elections is a weak proxy for death or change of residence, failure to reply to a card received in the mail is, if anything, an even weaker proxy. As Justice Breyer's dissent observes, Ohio sent cards to 20 percent of the state's registered voters. About two-thirds of the recipients – that is, roughly 13 percent of the state's registered voters – failed to return the cards. Yet, only about 4 percent of Americans move from their counties each year. And there is no reason to think Ohioans move across county lines three times as often as other Americans. The much more obvious explanation is "the human tendency not to send back cards received in the mail." It is clear that Ohio removes far more eligible voters than ineligible voters.[182]

Finally, reliance on such poor proxies for voter ineligibility is entirely unnecessary. If the goal really were simply to cull the names of voters who have died or moved out of the district, or who otherwise had managed to double register, there are simpler and far more reliable methods. The American Bar Association explains:

> Most of the states have found they can do that job just fine by relying on indicators like the National Change of Address system maintained by the U.S. Postal Service and, in recent years, data generated by the Electronic Registration Information Center (ERIC). The latter ... identifies out-of-date voter records by comparing the voting rolls of the member states to each other and to each state's motor vehicle records. Using this system, states can identify registrants who moved away and got a driver's license and/or registered to vote in their new location.[183]

---

[179] Morris, note 161.
[180] Ballotpedia, *Voter Caging*, note 158.
[181] Wikipedia, *Voter Turnout in United States Presidential Elections*, https://en.wikipedia.org/wiki/Voter_turnout_in_United_States_presidential_elections.
[182] 138 S.Ct. at 1856–57. Accord, Smith, note 176.
[183] Smith, note 176.

ERIC began in 2012.[184] At its peak, it had 32 member states.[185] By any objective measure, it has been a stunning success. Jesse Wegman describes why:

> ERIC has succeeded by devoting the time, money and expertise necessary to build a comprehensive, secure and useful database of voter information. That information – drawn from voter rolls, department of motor vehicle records, Social Security death records and change-of-address data – gets analyzed, matched and compiled into reports that are provided to the states to help them clean up their rolls.

He continues:

> The work has paid off: Through April 2023, ERIC has identified nearly 12 million voters who moved across state lines, more than 24 million whose in-state registrations required updates, more than one million in-state duplicates and nearly 600,000 dead people who had not been removed from the rolls. In addition, ERIC requires that member states reach out to eligible but unregistered voters …[186]

Republican and Democratic officials alike offered "glowing" reviews.[187]

Then something happened. In January 2022, the far-right website "Gateway Pundit" made the puzzling announcement that ERIC was "essentially a left-wing voter registration drive disguised as voter roll cleanup." Former President Trump piled on two months later, claiming falsely that ERIC "pumps the rolls" for Democrats. Predictably, Republican-controlled states began bailing out. In the eighteen months following the Gateway Pundit posting, at least eight states, all Republican-controlled, left ERIC. More are expected to follow.[188] Their departures will make it politically easier to substitute far less accurate purging methods that target unfavorable voting populations in the partisan ways previously discussed.

Provisional voting has mitigated some of the harmful effects of voter purging. The 2002 Help America Vote Act (HAVA), mentioned earlier, gives voters the right to cast provisional ballots. They may do so when an election official tells them their name doesn't appear on the registration list and the person then declares in writing that he or she is a registered voter who is eligible to vote in the particular jurisdiction. If the election officials later verify that the person was indeed eligible to vote in that jurisdiction, the provisional ballot is counted.[189]

---

[184] Jesse Wegman, N.Y. Times, *Republicans Are No Longer Calling This Election Program a "Godsend"* (June 6, 2023), www.nytimes.com/2023/06/06/opinion/republican-voter-fraud-eric .html?campaign_id=39&emc=edit_ty_20230606&instance_id=94328&nl=opinion-today&regi_ id=13788254&segment_id=134801&te=1&user_id=e16deb82e8516f294a4077a86c02f5c2.

[185] Josh Kovensky, Talking Points Memo, *Texas Sets Off Right-Wing Bidding War With ERIC Departure* (June 2, 2023), https://talkingpointsmemo.com/news/texas-sets-off-right-wing-bidding-war-with-eric-departure.

[186] Wegman, N.Y. Times, note 184.

[187] *Ibid.*

[188] *Ibid.*

[189] 42 U.S.C. § 15482.

That is a welcome development. Surely, however, it would be better to address the problem of wrongful purging than to rely on after-the-fact, case by case, mitigation. Not every voter will be willing to go through the written declaration process. Voters who learn in advance that their names have been purged might also have less incentive to stand in long voting lines with the prospect of then being turned away. At any rate, the need to verify the provisional ballots adds further delay to a vote-counting process that too often is already needlessly prolonged. More effective would be to prohibit the practice of states requiring the return of confirmation notices solely for those who have not voted recently enough – the step the five Republican Supreme Court Justices were unwilling to take in *Husted*.

A final note: Apart from purging the names of voters, can a state constitutionally purge members of Congress? In 1973 Arkansas, by voter initiative, amended its constitution to prohibit anyone who had already served three terms in the US House or two terms in the US Senate from appearing on the ballot for another term.[190] At the time, whether coincidentally or not, three of the state's four US House representatives were Democrats (Reps. Alexander, Thornton, and Anthony), as were both of its US Senators (Pryor and Bumpers).[191] In *Term Limits* v. *Thornton*,[192] the Supreme Court struck down the amendment, holding that the Constitution lays out the exclusive requirements for serving in Congress and that the states' power to decide the "manner" of congressional elections did not authorize them to superimpose additional qualifications.

3 Requiring Photo IDs

In 1950, South Carolina passed the nation's first voter ID law. Since then, these laws have proliferated.[193] By March 29, 2023, some 36 states were requiring specified types of identification documents for in-person voting. The remaining states and DC verify the voter's identity in other ways, usually by comparing the voter's signature against signatures that are already on file.[194]

One state's experience bears special mention. As noted earlier, the North Carolina Republican-controlled legislature's all-out assault on voting rights began literally 24 hours after the Supreme Court in *Shelby County* had cut out the heart of the preclearance requirement for states (including North Carolina) with histories of racial discrimination in voting. The legislature commissioned various studies of the impact that certain changes in the election laws would have on African American turnout. It then used those data to pass a series of measures to depress

---

[190] *Term Limits* v. *Thornton*, 514 US 779 (1995).
[191] See Wikipedia, *United States Congressional Delegations from Arkansas*, https://en.wikipedia.org/wiki/United_States_congressional_delegations_from_Arkansas#1963%E2%80%93present:_4_seats.
[192] 514 U.S. 779 (1995).
[193] Issacharoff *et al.*, note 14, at 147.
[194] National Council of State Legislatures, *Voter ID Laws* (Mar. 29, 2023), www.ncsl.org/elections-and-campaigns/voter-id.

African American votes with what the US Court of Appeals for the Fourth Circuit in the *McCrory* case called "almost surgical precision."[195]

One of those strategies was to require voters to present one of several specified photo ID documents (including driver's licenses) that the legislature's data showed to be disproportionately lacking among African American voters. It simultaneously excluded alternative documents that African Americans were disproportionately likely to possess.[196] The Fourth Circuit in *McCrory* had little difficulty in striking down this entire bundle of restrictions.

In *Crawford v. Marion County Election Bd.*,[197] the Supreme Court upheld Indiana's voter ID law, mainly on the now familiar theory that it helps prevent voter fraud. But the only type of voter fraud that voter ID laws even ostensibly prevent is impersonation of eligible voters.[198] ID documents establish, at most, that the people who present themselves at polling stations are who they say they are. They don't prove US citizenship or other voter eligibility requirements such as noncriminal backgrounds. Some of the acceptable ID documents display a residential address, but even these don't prove that the address is still current. Nor do IDs prevent double voting.

This limited purpose is worth keeping in mind, because, rare as voter fraud is in general,[199] voter impersonation fraud is rarer still. In his *Crawford* dissent, Justice Souter says this:

> [T]he State has not come across a single instance of in-person voter impersonation fraud in all of Indiana's history. Neither the District Court nor the Indiana General Assembly that passed the Voter ID Law was given any evidence whatsoever of in-person voter impersonation fraud in the State. This absence of support is consistent with the experience of several veteran poll watchers in Indiana, each of whom submitted testimony in the District Court that he had never witnessed an instance of attempted voter impersonation fraud at the polls. It is also consistent with the dearth of evidence of in-person voter impersonation in any other part of the country. [Even the lead opinion concedes] that there are at most "scattered instances of in-person voter fraud."[200]

The Brennan Center for Justice agrees, adding "Our research has established that impersonation fraud rarely occurs. Indeed, more Americans are struck by lightning each year."[201]

---

[195] See N.C. *State Conference of the NAACP v. McCrory*, 831 F.3d 204, 214 (4th Cir. 2016), and the discussion in notes 111 and 146–51 and accompanying text.

[196] *Ibid.*, at 216.

[197] 553 U.S. 181 (2008).

[198] *Ibid.*, at 194 (lead opinion), 225–26 (Souter, dissenting); Nhu-Y Ngo, Brennan Center for Justice, *Voter ID a Misguided Effort* (Dec. 14, 2010), www.brennancenter.org/our-work/analysis-opinion/voter-id-misguided-effort.

[199] See notes 117–31 and accompanying text.

[200] 553 U.S. at 226 (Souter J. dissenting).

[201] Ngo, note 198.

Those results should not be surprising. An individual would rarely find voter impersonation to be worth the risk. There's almost no chance that a single vote will alter the outcome of an election and, for anyone caught, the criminal penalties would be severe.[202]

Against these minimal or nonexistent benefits, there are huge costs. They disproportionately hamper the poor, racial minorities, and the elderly.[203] That is both because those groups are less likely than the general population to have qualifying IDs and because the "free" ID cards that voter ID states provide for voters who need them are seldom actually cost-free. The two principal costs relate to travel and documentation.

As for travel, a Brennan Center study by Keesha Gaskins & Sundeep Iyar sums up the practicalities:

> The 11 percent of eligible voters who lack the required photo ID must travel to a designated government office to obtain one. Yet many citizens will have trouble making this trip. In the [then] 10 states with restrictive voter ID laws: • Nearly 500,000 eligible voters do not have access to a vehicle and live more than 10 miles from the nearest state ID-issuing office open more than two days a week. Many of them live in rural areas with dwindling public transportation options. • More than 10 million eligible voters live more than 10 miles from their nearest state ID-issuing office open more than two days a week. • 1.2 million eligible black voters and 500,000 eligible Hispanic voters live more than 10 miles from their nearest ID-issuing office open more than two days a week. People of color are more likely to be disenfranchised by these laws since they are less likely to have photo ID than the general population. • Many ID-issuing offices maintain limited business hours. For example, the office in Sauk City, Wisconsin is open only on the fifth Wednesday of any month. But only four months in 2012 – February, May, August, and October – have five Wednesdays. In other states – Alabama, Georgia, Mississippi, and Texas – many part-time ID-issuing offices are in the rural regions with the highest concentrations of people of color and people in poverty. More than 1 million eligible voters in these states fall below the federal poverty line and live more than 10 miles from their nearest ID-issuing office open more than two days a week.[204]

Apart from travel costs, applicants need certain primary documents in order to acquire the acceptable IDs. Those primary documents can themselves place travel, time, and financial burdens on poor citizens. Again, Gaskins and Iyar explain:

> Birth certificates can cost between $8 and $25. Marriage licenses, required for married women whose birth certificates include a maiden name, can cost between $8

---

[202] 553 U.S. at 227–28 (Souter J. dissenting).
[203] Ngo, note 198.
[204] Keesha Gaskins & Sundeep Iyar, *Brennan Center for Justice, The Challenge of Obtaining Voter Identification*, at 1 (July 29, 2012), file:///C:/Users/legomsky/Downloads/Report_Challenge_of_Obtaining_Voter_ID.pdf.

and $20. By comparison, the notorious poll tax – outlawed during the civil rights era – cost $10.64 in current dollars. The result is plain: Voter ID laws will make it harder for hundreds of thousands of poor Americans to vote.[205]

As of 2012, this combination of factors had left 10 percent of voting-age US citizens without unexpired government-issued IDs. For African Americans, Hispanics, and those over age sixty-five, the percentages in 2012 were higher still – 25%, 16%, and 18%, respectively.[206] Justice Souter's powerful dissent in *Crawford* supplies further documentation of these same problems. He points out that, for thousands of the state's residents, the travel required to obtain a qualifying ID would be burdensome, and the costs of both the travel itself and the procurement of the documents needed to obtain the required ID significant.[207] The studies he cites show how disproportionately the ID requirements burden the poor and African Americans especially.[208]

The particulars of many of the voter ID laws – not all – specifically disadvantage college and university students as well. Those effects require special discussion and are considered below.

Given the flimsy character of voter ID laws' claimed benefits and their immense toll on whole swaths of the voter-eligible population, it is fair to ask why these laws have become so popular. There is only one credible answer – crass partisanship by state legislatures and governors.

How do we know? Occasionally, Republican Party operatives have let their guard down either orally or in writing, saying the quiet part out loud. A staffer for a Wisconsin Republican state legislator quit his job and left the party before writing "I was in the closed Senate Republican Caucus when the final round of multiple Voter ID bills were being discussed. A handful of the GOP Senators were giddy about the ramifications and literally singled out the prospects of suppressing minority and college voters." Both the former Republican Party Chair and the former Republican governor of Florida similarly admitted that their state's "voter ID law was designed to suppress Democratic votes."[209]

Today, of course, most key operatives are savvy enough to whisper their partisan motives behind closed doors. But the circumstantial evidence is hard to dismiss. First, as the foregoing discussion demonstrates, the chasm between the minimal-to-nonexistent policy benefits claimed for voter ID laws and their conclusively proven harms belies any suggestion that the decisions to pass these laws were based on

---

[205] *Ibid.*

[206] *Ibid.*, at 2.

[207] 553 U.S. at 211–16.

[208] *Ibid.*, at 221 & n.25.

[209] For these and additional examples, see, for example, Michael Wines, The New York Times, *Some Republicans Acknowledge Leveraging Voter ID Laws for Political Gain* (Sept. 16, 2016), www.nytimes.com/2016/09/17/us/some-republicans-acknowledge-leveraging-voter-id-laws-for-political-gain.html; Head Count, *GOP Pol Says Voter ID Laws Will Help Romney Win* (2016), www.headcount.org/politics-and-elections/telling-gaffe-gop-pol-says-voter-id-laws-will-help-romney-win/.

the merits. Second, there is a clear correlation between strict voting laws (including voter ID laws) and Republican control of the legislative process.[210] Even the Supreme Court in *Crawford* acknowledged that, since every Republican legislator had voted in favor of the ID requirement and every Democrat had voted against it, "it is fair to infer that partisan considerations may have played a significant role in the decision to enact" the law.[211]

Third, those groups that are disproportionately hampered by voter ID laws tend overwhelmingly to vote for Democrats. To be fair, this is not universally the case. Two of the groups especially likely to feel the burden of voter ID requirements are rural voters and elderly voters. Rural voters can be affected mainly because of difficulties in getting transportation to the government offices that issue free IDs. As noted earlier, these voters tend to skew Republican.[212] And the elderly can be affected for the same reason and for lack of current driver's licenses, although any Republican losses attributable to the effects of voter ID laws on elderly voters are likely minimal. That is because, despite voter ID laws, seniors already have very high turnout rates. Moreover, their voting preferences fluctuate and, in times when they favor Republicans, they typically do so only by narrow margins.[213]

But three other groups – all of them heavily Democrat-leaning – bear by far the greatest brunt of the voter ID laws: the poor, racial minorities, and students. In *Veasey v. Abbott*, for example,[214] a federal district judge had found that the Texas voter ID law was passed with the specific intent to discriminate against African American and Hispanic voters and that it would in fact produce discriminatory results, both in violation of the VRA. Even the ultraconservative US Court of Appeals for the Fifth Circuit agreed with the judge's finding of discriminatory results. It also found ample evidence of discriminatory intent, though it ordered the judge to reconsider that finding because some of the evidence the judge had relied on was in its view not probative enough.

Perhaps the strongest evidence of ulterior partisan motives can be found in the lists of the specific documents that will satisfy particular states' voter ID laws. As of March 2023, at least seven states prohibit the use of college and university IDs entirely.[215] At least two others allow them only if the college or university is located

---

[210] See Issacharoff *et al.*, note 14, at 153.

[211] 553 U.S. at 203.

[212] See, for example, Rodden, note 17; Karlan, note 23, at 2332–34.

[213] Joy Intriago, *Older Americans and Their Voting Patterns* (May 4, 2021), www.seasons.com/older-americans-voting-patterns/2492286/ ("Over the years, [older voters] have gone back and forth, but always within the moderate ranges of the parties.")

[214] 830 F.3d 216, 234–42 (5th Cir. 2016).

[215] A website maintained by the National Council of State Legislatures, *Voter ID Laws*, Table 2, State-by-State Details of In-Effect Voter Identification Requirements (Mar. 9, 2023), www.ncsl.org/elections-and-campaigns/voter-id#toggleContent-15991, provides a state-by-state listing of the acceptable documents. For four of those states – Arkansas, Tennessee, Texas, and Utah – college and university IDs are not listed among the documents that will satisfy the ID requirement. *The New York Times*

within the particular state.[216] And at least one other state (Georgia) allows only those IDs that are issued by public institutions, thus ruling out student IDs issued by the historically black private colleges and universities.[217]

Gun licenses are another story. Among the states that prohibit the use of student IDs or confine their acceptability to IDs from public educational institutions or to institutions located within the state, at least six take precisely the opposite approach with gun licenses. These states explicitly include them in the list of acceptable IDs, regardless of whether they were issued within the particular state.[218]

That contrast between accepting gun licenses and rejecting university IDs lends strong support to suspicions of partisan motives for voter ID laws. Young Americans – and especially college students – tend to vote overwhelmingly for Democratic candidates and progressive initiatives, and in recent years their turnout rates have increased rapidly.[219] Republicans' desires to minimize student turnout have been well publicized and manifest themselves in suppression strategies that go beyond voter ID laws.[220] In sharp contrast, as of December 2022, some 48% of Republicans reported that they owned at least one gun, compared to only 20% for Democrats. And 66% of Republicans reported living in a household in which there was at least one gun, compared to 31% for Democrats. Republicans, in other words, were more than twice as likely as Democrats to own at least one

---

article lists six such states – Idaho, North Dakota, Ohio, South Carolina, Tennessee, and Texas. Neil Vigdor, The New York Times, *Republicans Face Setbacks in Push to Tighten Voting Laws on College Campuses* (Mar. 29, 2023), www.nytimes.com/2023/03/29/us/politics/republicans-young-voters-college.html. That article's reference to North Dakota conflicts with the National Council's compilation, which shows North Dakota as accepting an "authorized university document for voters using a student photo ID card."

[216] NCSL, Voter ID Laws, (Mar. 9, 2023), note 215 (Kansas and West Virginia). See also Meryl Kornfield, *"Clear as Mud": Ohio's New Voting Restrictions from GOP Raise Alarm* (Jan. 19, 2023), www .washingtonpost.com/politics/2023/01/19/ohio-strict-voter-id-law/?utm_campaign=wp_post_most&utm_ medium=email&utm_source=newsletter&wpisrc=nl_most&carta-url=https%3A%2F%2Fs2.washington post.com%2Fcar-ln-tr%2F38e6b62%2F63cad02aef9bf67b23680e61%2F5976f9099bbc0f6826be4986%2F42 %2F72%2F63cad02aef9bf67b23680e61&wp_cu=46ff53dcffa9ac52f667b1c4cc42a07c%7C476A9E88348030 8EE0530100007FF804.

[217] Vigdor, note 215; accord, Fredreka Schouten & Shania Shelton, CNN, *Republican-Controlled States Target College Students' Voting Power Ahead of High-stakes 2024 Elections* (May 2, 2023), www.cnn .com/2023/05/02/politics/gop-targets-student-voting/index.html.

[218] NCSL, *Voter ID Laws* (Mar. 9, 2023), note 211 (Arkansas, Kansas, Tennessee, Texas, Utah, and West Virginia).

[219] See, for example, Vigdor, note 215; Schouten & Shelton, note 217.

[220] Josh Dawsey & Amy Gardner, The Washington Post, *Top GOP Lawyer Decries Ease of Campus Voting in Private Pitch to RNC* (Apr. 20, 2023), www.washingtonpost.com/nation/2023/04/20/cleta-mitchell-voting-college-students/?utm_campaign=wp_post_most&utm_medium=email&utm_ source=newsletter&wpisrc=nl_most&carta-url=https%3A%2F%2Fs2.washingtonpost.com%2Fcar-ln-tr%2F39c6882%2F64416907afd891675414cbcb%2F5976f9099bbc0f6826be4986%2F28%2F72%2F644 16907afd891675414cbcb&wp_cu=46ff53dcffa9ac52f667b1c4cc42a07c%7C476A9E883480308EE0530 100007FF804 (Republican officials arguing against campus polling places, allowing university ID cards to satisfy voter ID requirements, early voting, and mail-in voting).

gun and more than twice as likely to live in a household where there was at least one gun.[221]

Despite the conclusive empirical refutations of claims of widespread voter fraud generally and impersonation of eligible voters in particular, despite voter ID laws' serious and discriminatory impediments to voting, and despite strong evidence of inappropriate partisan motives, the Supreme Court in *Crawford* approved photo ID laws. Why?

The Court in *Crawford* identified three state interests that photo IDs are claimed to serve: verifying the person's legal eligibility to vote; preventing voter fraud; and promoting citizens' confidence in the integrity of the election process.[222] All three interests are indisputably valid, but their connections to photo ID laws are embarrassingly thin. As noted earlier, and despite the Court's statement to the contrary, photo IDs do not verify one's eligibility to vote; at most, they verify the voter's identity, a check that many other states find other secure ways to accomplish.[223] As for voter fraud, the Court acknowledges that the state failed to identify a single instance of it,[224] and as discussed earlier voter impersonation is truly rare. And while the Court extolls the state interest in citizen confidence in the integrity of the voting system, it never considers the effects on public confidence of the partisan manipulation of the voting laws that it candidly acknowledges.[225] Moreover, when there arises the very reasonable perception that laws making it as hard to vote as possible are deliberately designed to minimize turnout by citizens of color, one can safely assume that the threats to public confidence in the integrity of the electoral system become greater still.

The Court concludes nonetheless that the law is "nondiscriminatory" and "supported by valid neutral justifications."[226] But in describing the law as "nondiscriminatory," the Court is content to ask only whether the law is neutral *on its face* and whether it serves any *theoretically* plausible benefits. That is all it was willing to require.

Having stopped at that point, the Court never considers either the actual disproportionate impact on racial minorities or the state legislature's motives in passing this law. After acknowledging the fair inference that partisan considerations might have played a significant role, the Court never asks the logical follow-up question: Why would the legislature's partisan majority think photo ID's serve the party's interests? By failing to ask that question, the Court is able to avoid the answer that is

[221] Statista, *Percentage of Population in the United States Owning at Least One Gun in 2022, by Political Party Affiliation* (Dec. 7, 2022), www.statista.com/statistics/249775/percentage-of-population-in-the-us-owning-a-gun-by-party-affiliation/.

[222] 553 U.S. at 191–97.

[223] NCSL, *Voter ID Laws*, note 215.

[224] 553 U.S. at 194–95.

[225] *Ibid.*, at 203.

[226] *Ibid.*, at 204.

obvious to everyone with a pulse: Because the Republicans know full well that people of color vote overwhelmingly for Democrats and that this is the voting bloc most adversely affected by restrictive voting requirements. (Republican politicians have protested that the reason photo ID laws benefit their party is that they help prevent voter fraud by Democrats; again, however, significant voter fraud has been shown to be nonexistent, and at any rate, there is no evidence to suggest that Democrats are more likely than Republicans to engage in it.)

Legislatures today are quite sophisticated in concealing impermissible motives. When the two opposing parties divide so sharply on this and practically every other voting issue, the Court needs to be willing to examine the magnitudes of both the benefits and the harms far more closely, and with its eyes more open to the realities on the ground, than it did in the *Crawford* case.

Justice Scalia's concurring opinion, joined by Justices Thomas and Alito, goes even further. Those Justices find it "irrelevant" whether a voter ID law imposes a "special burden on some voters."[227] As with so many of the other issues discussed in this book, state sovereignty was paramount. "That sort of detailed judicial supervision of the election process would flout the Constitution's express commitment of the task to the States," the three concurring Justices explained.[228] Once more, state sovereignty took precedence over political equality.

4 Requiring Documentary Proof of US Citizenship

Some states have attempted to go beyond voter ID requirements, additionally insisting on documentary proof that the voter is a US citizen. But in 2013 the Supreme Court in *Arizona* v. *Inter Tribal Council of Arizona* [*ITCA*][229] substantially restricted (though it didn't entirely foreclose) such efforts.

The *ITCA* case, discussed in Section B.1 above for its general role in the voter registration process, focuses on the effects of the "Federal Form" that the EAC requires for registering to vote in federal elections. That form reminds the voter, in distinctive red letters at the top of the form, that only US citizens may vote. To that end, the form requires the registrant to attest under penalty of perjury that he or she is a US citizen.[230] It does not require that the oath be supported by written documentation proving one's citizenship; the declaration under oath is enough. Arizona, by statewide initiative in 2004, nonetheless passed a law that requires such documentary proof. The Supreme Court interpreted the relevant provision of the NVRA as establishing the exclusive requirements for voter registration; states could not insist on more documentation than the Federal Form requires. And the Constitution's

---

[227] *Ibid.*
[228] *Ibid.*, at 208, citing U.S. Const. Art. I, § 4.
[229] 570 U.S. 1 (2013).
[230] The text of the Federal Form appears in both of the websites described in note 137.

elections clause,[231] the Court held, gives Congress the last word when it comes to the times, places, and manner of congressional elections.

But the Court left a potentially wide opening for proof of citizenship laws. As noted earlier, the "times, places, and manner" of congressional elections are not the same as voter qualifications, which are left to the states.[232] Thus, Arizona can require US citizenship for voter registration; in fact, every state does, for all state and federal elections. And it can enforce that requirement. It's just that if it wants to enforce it by requiring information beyond that required by the Federal Form, it has to follow the procedure specified by Congress. Under that procedure, the state must request the approval of the EAC. If the EAC denies the state's request, the state may appeal the decision to the federal courts. So Arizona, joined by Kansas, requested EAC approval for adding documentary proof of US citizenship to their state-specific versions of the Federal Form. The EAC denied those requests, and in *Kobach v. U.S. Election Assistance Commission*,[233] the US Court of Appeals for the Tenth Circuit upheld the denials on the grounds that the proposed restrictions would violate both the NVRA and the Constitution's equal protection clause.

In 2016, after *ITCA* and *Kobach*, three states – Alabama, Georgia, and (again) Kansas – all requested permission to amend the Federal Form to require documentary proof of citizenship for voting in their respective states. This time the EAC granted their requests, but in *League of Women Voters* v. *Harrington*,[234] the federal District Court for the District of Columbia struck down the EAC's approvals. Under a provision of the Help America Vote Act (HAVA), the court noted, the Federal Form may contain only whatever information is "necessary" for election officials to assess voter eligibility or administer the election.[235] In this case, the EAC had approved the requests without even considering whether the states had made the required necessity showing. Indeed, one of the commissioners had inexplicably stated that proof of necessity was "irrelevant."

This line of cases is a welcome development, but the danger posed by proof of citizenship laws has not passed. As the Supreme Court made clear, states may still request permission from the EAC to require documentary proof of citizenship. A federal Administration sympathetic to such a requirement, or to voting restrictions generally, might well grant such a request; as noted, the EAC granted three states' requests, only to be reversed in the *Harrington* case. And even if the EAC were to deny the request, a sympathetic federal court could reverse the denial on appeal. Given the ease, described earlier, with which states can choose the specific federal forum – and in many cases even the specific judge – this is always a live possibility.

---

[231] U.S. Const. Art. I, § 4.
[232] U.S. Const. Art. I, § 2, Cl.1 & Amend. 17.
[233] 772 F.3d 1183 (10th Cir. 2014), *cert.* denied, 576 U.S. 1055 (2015).
[234] Civ. Case No. 16-00236 (RJL) (D.D.C. Sept. 16, 2021).
[235] 52 U.S.C. § 20508(b)(1).

Moreover, the NVRA applies only to federal elections. States always have the option of declining to use the Federal Form for elections to state legislative and other state offices, though their usual preference for conducting federal and state elections on the same days would make such a practice inefficient.

Indeed, despite the Supreme Court's decision in *ITCA* and the subsequent lower court decisions in the *Kobach* and *Harrington* cases, Arizona in 2022 passed another law requiring documentary proof of US citizenship.[236] Its apparent hope is that the current Supreme Court will reverse course and approve the legislation. And as of May 15, 2023, bills to require documentary proof of citizenship were under active consideration in at least ten states.[237]

In practice, laws that require documentary proof of US citizenship put voting beyond the reach of millions of eligible voters. A 2006 survey found that up to 7 percent of all US citizens lack ready access to documents that would prove their citizenship.[238] Between 2013 and 2016, the Kansas law that the court ultimately struck down had blocked approximately one out of every seven new voters (more than 14 percent) from registering or voting. Almost half of the disenfranchised voters were under age thirty,[239] a voting bloc that as noted earlier skews heavily Democratic.[240]

But if you have to be a US citizen in order to vote, one might ask, what's wrong with requiring you to prove it? And what is so hard about it, anyway?

For people born in the United States, by far the two most common documents for proving US citizenship are their birth certificates or, if they have them, passports. For obvious reasons, the poor are disproportionately unlikely to be able to afford either passports or the international travel that necessitates them. As of 2024, passports alone cost $165.[241] They also take a lot of time. As of March 24, 2023, the average processing time was 10–13 weeks, plus several additional weeks for mailing the applications, having them accepted for processing, and mailing the passports.[242]

---

[236] Liz Avore, Voting Rights Lab, *Unconstitutional and on the Rise: Proof of Citizenship Requirements in 2022* (June 27, 2022), https://votingrightslab.org/unconstitutional-and-on-the-rise-proof-of-citizenship-requirements-in-2022/. As this book was going to press, a 5-4 all-Republican Supreme Court majority handed down an emergency order that allowed the State of Arizona to enforce its proof of citizenship requirement for those who register via the state (though not the federal) voter registration form. The Court did not acknowledge the ITCA precedent or offer any explanation for its decision. Republican National Committee v. Mi Familia Vota, No. 24A164 (S.Ct. Aug. 22, 2024).

[237] Voting Rights Lab, *Bill Search*, https://tracker.votingrightslab.org/pending/search?number= 6366901584738999.

[238] Avore, note 236.

[239] Amrit Cheng, ACLU, *Kobach's Documentary Proof-of-Citizenship Law Heads to Trial* (Mar. 1, 2018), www.aclu.org/news/voting-rights/kobachs-documentary-proof-citizenship-law-heads-trial.

[240] See notes 215–17 and 308–309 below and accompanying text.

[241] U.S. Dept. of State, *Passport Fees*, https://travel.state.gov/content/travel/en/passports/how-apply/fees .html.

[242] U.S. Dept. of State, Processing Times, https://travel.state.gov/content/travel/en/passports/how-apply/ processing-times.html.

In addition, those who want passports in order to prove US citizenship are caught in a catch-22: You need proof of US citizenship to get the passport.

Birth certificates, fortunately, are a more widely available option. But they too are costly and typically take a long time to acquire, depending on one's state of birth. The costs generally range between $20 and $55 and they require an average of 4–8 weeks to process.[243] Apart from the required expense, time, and energy involved, many Americans are unable to obtain birth certificates for the same reasons that they were born without them in the first place. Alfred Lubrano explains:

> [Lack of a birth certificate is] surprisingly common among poor African Americans born in the South in the mid-twentieth century. ...
>
> For decades, many low-income African American women in the South gave birth in family homes instead of hospitals, aided by midwives. ... The births often went unrecorded.
>
> Tens of thousands of babies were born off the grid, real people with the status of ghosts.
>
> Quite often, the white establishment running records offices in the Jim Crow South weren't all that eager to record the births anyway.
>
> And, in some cases, pregnant black women were denied entrance to hospitals, historians have written. ...
>
> And people with low incomes are more than twice as likely to lack documentation such as a birth certificate that proves their citizenship. ...
>
> That's partly because of the Southern midwife problem. But even for people who can access their birth certificates, it costs money to secure documents, and poor people preoccupied with food, rent, and heat rarely have the cash to get their papers in order ...[244]

Married women who changed their surnames have an additional problem. For them, the original birth certificate will not be enough. Additional documentation to prove that the would-be voter is the same person described in the birth certificate will be required.

There is yet another effect of making documentary proof of US citizenship a requirement for voter registration. Organized voter registration drives are typically held in parks, shopping malls, athletic events, concerts, and political demonstrations

---

[243] Vital Records Online, *How Long Does It Take to Get a Birth Certificate*, www.vitalrecordsonline .com/faqs/birth-certificates/how-long-does-it-take-to-get-a-birth-certificate#:~:text=It%20typically%20 takes%204%20to,within%202%2D3%20business%20days.

[244] Alfred Lubrano, Face to Face, *For Many Americans Obtaining a Birth Certificate Proves Challenging*, https://facetofacegermantown.org/many-americans-obtaining-birth-certificate-proves-challenging-alfred-lubrano-inquirer-staff-writer/. See also Brennan Center for Justice, *Proof of Citizenship* (Sept. 2006), www.brennancenter.org/sites/default/files/analysis/Proof%20of%20Citizenship.pdf (outlining, pre-ITCA, many of the practical ways in which such laws disenfranchised huge numbers of voters, especially African Americans).

sites, among other venues. People don't ordinarily bring their passports or their birth certificates with them when they visit those places.

All these harms might at least be understandable, if not acceptable, were there important reasons for requiring that citizenship be proved through written documentation rather than by declarations under penalty of perjury. But the only justification offered by supporters of these laws tends to be the elimination of voter fraud. Previous discussions have documented the rarity of voter fraud generally and impersonation of eligible voters in particular.

Citizenship fraud in voting is rarer still,[245] and for obvious reasons. First, noncitizen voting in a federal election is (with limited exceptions) a federal crime punishable by fines and imprisonment for up to a year.[246] Also, since the Federal Form requires voters to attest under oath that they are US citizens, one who knowingly makes such a false claim is additionally guilty of perjury, a federal felony punishable by a fine and imprisonment of up to five years.[247] On top of that, both false claims of citizenship[248] and unlawful voting[249] are independent grounds on which non-US citizens can be deported from the United States. Who would do this? The probability that one vote will change an electoral outcome is minute. For any noncitizen to take so huge a risk for so miniscule a potential gain would be beyond irrational.

5 Severely Curtailing Early and Mail Voting

Upon the founding of the American Republic, all voting in both federal and state elections took place in person on election day. Since then, the ways in which Americans vote have evolved steadily.[250] Today, two particular adaptations have taken root in a big way and are the subject of the present subsection – early voting and mail voting.

The terminology varies and can be confusing. This book uses the term "early voting" to mean any voting in which ballots are cast before election day. The voter might send the completed ballot by mail or deliver it in person at an officially designated polling place or drop box. As of March 23, 2023, the National Conference of State Legislatures reports that forty-six states (and DC, Puerto Rico, Guam, and the US Virgin Islands) offer early in-person voting to all eligible voters. Many of those states also allow early voting by mail, eight of them (and DC) conducting elections almost

---

[245] See, for example, Brennan Center for Justice, *Beyond Voter ID* (Apr. 13, 2009), www.brennancenter
    .org/our-work/analysis-opinion/beyond-voter-id.
[246] 18 U.S.C. § 611.
[247] 18 U.S.C. § 1621.
[248] 8 U.S.C. § 1227(a)(3)(D).
[249] 8 U.S.C. § 1229(a)(6).
[250] National Conference of State Legislatures, *Voting Outside the Polling Place: Absentee, All-Mail, and
    Other Voting at Home Options* (July 12, 2022), www.ncsl.org/elections-and-campaigns/voting-outside-
    the-polling-place.

entirely by mail.[251] The early voting periods vary, with an average starting date of twenty-seven days before Election Day and an average duration of twenty days.

"Mail voting," as the term is used in this book, describes what many people think of as absentee voting. Elections officials mail the blank ballot to the voter, who then returns it either in person or by putting it in a mailbox or drop box. As of July 12, 2022, thirty-five states and DC allow any eligible voter to vote absentee. The other states offer that option only to those with specified excuses, and the list of qualifying excuses varies from state to state. In eight of the no-excuse-needed states, absentee ballots are automatically mailed to all registered voters; in the others, absentee ballots must be requested individually.[252]

Regrettably, both compilations of state practices and statistical analyses of partisan voting patterns often lump these two voting methods together. But they are apples and oranges. What distinguishes early voting is simply the timing; what distinguishes absentee voting is the way the voter *receives* the blank ballot – by mail, as opposed to in person at the polling station.

The partisan effects of early voting and mail voting are not the same either. In recent elections, when early in-person votes and early mail votes are combined, early Democratic voters have consistently outnumbered early Republican voters. That was especially true for the 2018, 2020, and 2022 November elections.[253] In 2022, when early voting (driven mainly by COVID) accounted for approximately 45% of the total national vote,[254] the nonprofit organization TargetEarly estimated that among early voters Democrats outnumbered Republicans 51%–38%.[255]

As elections expert Michael McDonald pointed out, it was not always that way. At one time, Republicans were more likely than Democrats to vote early; the pattern reversed only when President Trump warned his supporters not to trust early voting, urging them to cast their ballots on election day.[256]

Again, however, these numbers fail to disaggregate early in-person voting from early mail voting. The partisan divide in mail voting is more extreme. As anyone who has stayed awake at night watching election returns is well aware, Democrats today are far more likely than Republicans to vote by mail. In 2020, when the pandemic prompted states to greatly expand opportunities for mail ballots, Biden

---

[251] National Conference of State Legislatures, *Early In-Person Voting* (Mar. 23, 2023), www.ncsl.org/elections-and-campaigns/early-in-person-voting.

[252] NCSL, *Voting Outside the Polling Place*, note 250 (also laying out the pros and cons of mail voting).

[253] TargetEarly, *National 2022 Early & Absentee Vote Report* (May 16, 2023), https://targetearly.targetsmart.com/g2022.

[254] Matt Grossmann Interview of Michael McDonald, Niskanen Center, *How Early Voting is Changing American Elections* (Nov. 30, 2022), www.niskanencenter.org/how-early-voting-is-changing-american-elections/.

[255] TargetEarly, note 253. See also Aaron Blake, Washington Post, *What the 2022 Early Vote Data Says about Democrats' Prospects* (Nov. 7, 2022), www.washingtonpost.com/politics/2022/11/07/2022-early-vote-data-democrats/.

[256] Grossmann, note 254.

supporters chose that option at twice the rate of Trump supporters. In some states, the ratios were even more dramatic – for example, 3-1 in North Carolina and almost 4-1 in Pennsylvania. Republicans, in contrast, are far more likely to vote in person, whether early or on election day.[257]

To be clear, these percentages alone don't necessarily prove that either generous early voting rules or generous mail voting rules favor Democrats. It might be that the number of early or mail-voting Democrats who would not have voted on Election Day if that had been their only option is no greater than the number of early or mail-voting Republicans for whom the same can be said. McDonald posits that early voting "activates people who are already high propensity voters. And so who are the high propensity voters? Well, by and large they tend to be more Republican than Democratic."[258]

Whether the first part of McDonald's premise is correct is not clear. It might instead be the case that, all else equal, it is precisely the low-propensity voters for whom the ease of voting is more likely to be the decisive factor. Perhaps, in other words, the high-propensity voters would have been the more determined to find their way to the polls on Election Day if that had been their only option.

Regardless, as long as Republican strategists *perceive* that early and/or mail voting generally benefits Democrats, that belief can be a powerful incentive to pass laws that restrict those voting methods and other turnout-boosting measures, with the specific aim of making voting as hard as possible. In recent years, that perception has been evident. In 2013, for example, North Carolina's Republican legislature requested and obtained data showing that in both 2008 and 2012 African American voters, who skew heavily Democratic, were far more prone to vote early than were white voters – especially during the first week of the early voting period. Immediately upon receiving those data, the legislature eliminated that first week, shortening the early voting period from seventeen days to seven.[259] In 2014, the Wisconsin legislature cut back the hours for early voting on weekdays and eliminated all early voting on weekends.[260] In 2023, Arkansas's Republican legislature made it a criminal offense for election workers to send ballot *applications* – not even actual absentee ballots – to voters who had not requested them.[261] And on the national level, the

[257] Miles Parks, NPR, 2020 *Changed How America Votes. The Question Now is Whether Those Changes Stick* (Oct. 28, 2022), www.npr.org/2022/10/28/1128695831/united-states-2022-patterns-mail-early-voting.

[258] Grossmann, note 254.

[259] *N.C. State Conference of the NAACP v. McCrory*, 831 F.3d 204, 216 (4th Cir. 2016).

[260] Brennan Center for Justice, *New Voting Restrictions in America* (Nov. 18, 2019), www.brennancenter .org/sites/default/files/2019-11/New%20Voting%20Restrictions.pdf.

[261] Matthew Brown, Washington Post, *Ahead of 2024 Election, Several States Overhauled Voting Laws* (May 15, 2023), www.washingtonpost.com/politics/2023/05/15/2024-state-voting-laws/?utm_ campaign=wp_post_most&utm_medium=email&utm_source=newsletter&wpisrc=nl_most&carta- url=https%3A%2F%2Fs2.washingtonpost.com%2Fcar-ln-tr%2F3a04d29%2F646255335dfb5222c4ba80 9d%2F5976f9099bbc0f6826be4986%2F23%2F72%2F646255335dfb5222c4ba809d.

same Republican strategists who were campaigning to suppress voting by college students were strenuously advocating against early voting and mail voting.[262]

One specific early voting issue – weekend voting – requires special mention. As of April 2023, twenty states offered Saturday voting, and seven others gave local election officials the discretion to do so. Eight states offered Sunday voting, and eight others gave local election officials the discretion to offer it.[263]

Sunday voting is the real issue, as it holds both symbolic meaning and exceptional practical importance for African American communities. Part of a tradition that dates back to Reconstruction and Jim Crow, Sunday voting has continued through the modern civil rights era.[264] Known as "Souls to the Polls," it remains a critical tool with which African Americans try to overcome voter suppression. In the words of Bishop Reginald Jackson of the African Methodist Episcopal Church, "[w]e gather in our churches on Sunday morning, you have morning worship and then after the service you get on the church buses, church vans, get in cars and people go to vote."[265] Church official Christy Jackson adds that "[i]t became something that gave us comfort, to go in a group with our church group during those times to go and vote" and that "[c]hurches are especially important for mobilizing African Americans in rural counties," because "[t]here are some polling locations, voting locations that are 10, 15, 20 miles from where a person lives. And so these central[ly] located churches, for example, then become what we call neighborhood hubs."[266]

Preparing for the 2012 elections, several Republican state legislatures and local elections officials restricted early voting periods, including targeting Sunday voting.[267] In 2013, North Carolina's string of voter suppression measures included the elimination of one of the state's two Sunday voting days.[268]

Some of the more blatant actions took place in Georgia, again during the governorship of Brian Kemp. In February 2021, the Republican-controlled state House of Representatives passed a bill that would have eliminated Sunday voting entirely. Amidst a public outcry, the Republicans backed down, opting instead for a law that gives local elections officials the discretion whether to allow Sunday voting – but in no event more than two Sundays.

Even that action was just one element in a larger plan. "The GOP-led legislature also handed control of more election board appointments to conservative local judges

---

[262] Dawsey & Gardner, note 220.

[263] NCSL, *Early In-Person Voting*, note 251.

[264] See, for example, James Doubek & Steve Inskeep, NPR, *Black Church Leaders in Georgia on the Importance of "Souls to the Polls"* (Mar. 22, 2021), www.npr.org/2021/03/22/977929338/black-church-leaders-in-georgia-on-the-importance-of-souls-to-the-polls; Aaron Morrison, AP, *Black Churches Mobilizing Voters Despite Virus Challenges* (Oct. 12, 2020), https://apnews.com/article/election-2020-virus-outbreak-race-and-ethnicity-new-york-voting-c8f6ec1b9eb46c6e49340747d781bb11.

[265] Doubek & Inskeep, note 264.

[266] *Ibid.*

[267] Morrison, note 264.

[268] *N.C. State Conference of the NAACP v. McCrory*, 831 F.3d 204, 217 (4th Cir. 2016).

or GOP-controlled county commissions in at least five counties." This was a critical move, because in Georgia "local boards of elections oversee voter registration lists and certifications of elections and decide when voting can take place." Exercising their newfound powers, election officials in at least seven Georgia counties eliminated Sunday voting in advance of the 2022 midterm elections. For further context, this occurred during the same election cycle in which Georgia's Republican legislature "created new voter identification requirements for absentee ballots, empowered state officials to take over local elections boards, limited the use of ballot drop boxes and made it a crime to approach voters in line to give them food or water."[269]

It is hard to construct even a theoretical defense for these actions. Of course, any day in which staff must be available for early in-person voting entails some public expense, but the costs need not be any greater for Sunday voting than for weekday voting, except perhaps when there is a small add-on for overtime pay. Nor have opponents of Sunday voting even attempted to play the fraud card, as there is simply no reason to associate Sunday voting with fraud. About the most they have been able to come up with is that "Black church leaders influence their members on how to vote."[270] But even assuming for the sake of argument that that is true,[271] there is a name for that kind of influence: free speech. If church leaders or anyone else want to advocate for their beliefs, that is their right. And if congregants or anyone else want to hear those opinions, and choose to find them persuasive, that is their right.

The real purpose of laws and policies eliminating or restricting Sunday voting, often part of a broader package of voting restrictions, is surely more cynical. In the words of historian Rebecca Brenner Graham, "Bills aiming to eliminate Sunday voting have a transparent purpose: countering [Souls to the Polls] because African Americans vote overwhelmingly Democratic."[272]

One antidote – not a form of early voting, but a step that would at least mitigate the effects of restrictions on Sunday and other early voting – would be to make Election Day a national holiday.[273] As others have pointed out, this would enable people to vote without taking time off from work.[274] From time to time, bills have

---

[269] Simone Pathe & Kelly Mena, CNN, *Black Faith Leaders Push Back after Elimination Of Sunday Voting in One Georgia County* (May 21, 2023), www.cnn.com/2022/05/21/politics/voting-2022-primary-georgia/index.html. See also Doubek & Inskeep, note 264.

[270] See Doubek & Inskeep, note 264.

[271] Bishop Jackson emphasizes that "You don't tell them how to vote, but we are encouraging them to vote," acknowledging that he will advise people if he is asked, just as happens routinely "in white, heavily Republican, evangelical churches." *Ibid.*

[272] Rebecca Brenner Graham, The Washington Post, *Attacking Sunday Voting is a Part of a Long Tradition of Controlling Black Americans* (Mar. 4, 2021), www.washingtonpost.com/outlook/2021/03/04/attacking-sunday-voting-is-part-long-tradition-controlling-black-americans/.

[273] See, for example, Levitsky & Ziblatt, Tyranny, note 23, at 232 (advocating making election day either a Sunday or a national holiday); William G. Gale & Darrell M. West, Brookings Institution, *Make Election Day a National Holiday* (June 23, 2021), www.brookings.edu/blog/fixgov/2021/06/23/make-election-day-a-national-holiday/.

[274] Gale & West, note 273.

been introduced in Congress to do precisely that. One such bill, introduced on January 6, 2021 (Insurrection Day), would have made Election Day, in November of every even-numbered year, a national holiday for purpose of federal employment. The same bill would also have encouraged private employers to give their employees the day off.[275] But there were not enough Democratic votes to overcome staunch Republican opposition. Like its predecessors, the bill died.

6 Closing and Strategically Locating Election Day Polling Places

Several states have been closing polling places, in carefully selected locations, with lightning speed. Like so many of the other voter suppression strategies described in this section, the modern explosion of polling place closures traces back to the 2013 decision of the Supreme Court in *Shelby County* v. *Holder*.[276] As previously noted, that decision gutted the heart of the 1965 VRA, leaving the states and counties with histories of racial discrimination far freer to suppress the votes of racial minorities without the need for Justice Department preclearance. By far the most detailed, carefully documented, and comprehensive study of the link between *Shelby County* and polling place closures is a 2019 report by the Leadership Conference Education Fund (LCEF).[277] In this subsection, I draw liberally from that report.

The LCEF's 2019 report, which updated and expanded on its analogous 2016 report,[278] studied polling place closures during the period 2014–18 by those states and counties that the *Shelby County* decision had freed from the VRA's preclearance requirements.[279] In total, it found a decrease of 1,173 polling places in those counties during this period "despite a significant increase in voter turnout."[280]

In absolute numbers, the top three offenders were Texas (by far), Arizona, and Georgia. What the report described as "quieter efforts" to close polling places "without clear notice or justification" took place in Louisiana, Mississippi, Alabama, North Carolina, and Alaska (in that order). South Carolina, constrained by some

---

[275] Congress.gov, *H.R.222 – Election Day Holiday Act of 2021*, www.congress.gov/bill/117th-congress/house-bill/222/text.

[276] 570 U.S. 529 (2013).

[277] Leadership Conference Education Fund, *Democracy Diverted: Polling Place Closures and the Right to Vote* (Sept. 2019), http://civilrightsdocs.info/pdf/reports/Democracy-Diverted.pdf. See also The Guardian, *More than 1000 US Polling Sites Closed Since Supreme Court Ruling, Report Finds* (Sept. 11, 2019), www.theguardian.com/us-news/2019/sep/11/us-polling-sites-closed-report-supreme-court-ruling (mainly describing the LCEF report); Hannah Klain *et al.*, Brennan Center for Justice, *Waiting to Vote: Racial Disparities in Election Day Experiences* (June 3, 2020), www.brennancenter.org/sites/default/files/2020-06/6_02_WaitingtoVote_FINAL.pdf.

[278] Leadership Conference Education Fund, *The Great Poll Closure* (Nov. 2016), http://civilrightsdocs.info/pdf/reports/2016/poll-closure-report-web.pdf.

[279] By way of exception, the Report had to exclude closings in Virginia and in three Texas counties for lack of reliable data. LCEF, *Democracy Diverted*, note 277, at 11.

[280] *Ibid.*, at 10.

specific state laws governing polling places, closed very few polling stations, relying instead on other post-*Shelby County* voter suppression strategies.[281]

Georgia once again deserves special mention. In terms of percentages of polling places closed, the top five counties in this study (having closed between 80% and 89% of their polling places), and seven of the top ten, were all in Georgia.[282] It was there, you might recall, that the state official in charge of elections – Republican Secretary of State Brian Kemp – was running for governor and purging the voter rolls disproportionately in minority communities.[283] Kemp sent a memo to local elections officials encouraging them to "consolidate" polling stations and reminding them that in light of the *Shelby County* decision they no longer had to worry about Justice Department preclearance or even notification. And in the lead-up to his 2018 gubernatorial contest, Kemp's recommended elections consultant, Mike Malone, "led an effort to close polling places in 10 counties with large Black populations. Malone told local boards of elections that Kemp had recommended polling place consolidation and sought [unsuccessfully] to close seven of nine polling places in Randolph County, which is 60 percent African American."[284] In 200-square-mile Lanier County, which is 24 percent African American, only one of the four polling stations survived, even though its population had recently almost doubled.[285] The report adds: "In addition to five-hour lines, voters in communities of color faced countless obstacles on Election Day, including delayed polling place openings and broken voting machines."[286]

Similar examples, not always quite as blatant, occurred throughout the other former preclearance states. In absolute numbers, the data from Texas are particularly striking:

> With 74 closures, Dallas County, which is 41 percent Latino and 22 percent African American, is the second largest closer of polling places, followed by Travis County, which is 34 percent Latino (−67), Harris County, which is 42 percent Latino and 19 percent African American (−52), and Brazoria County, which is 13 percent African American and 30 percent Latino (−37), tied with Nueces County, which is 63 percent Latino (−37).[287]

And then there is North Carolina. Elizabeth City is 52 percent African American but is situated in Pasquotank County, which is majority white. Citing cost concerns, the county closed four of the eight polling places in Elizabeth City – and none anywhere else in the county.[288]

[281] *Ibid.*, at 12.
[282] *Ibid.*, at 15.
[283] See *ibid.*, at 30; see also notes 167–68 and accompanying text.
[284] *Ibid.*, at 32–33.
[285] *Ibid.*, at 33.
[286] *Ibid.*
[287] *Ibid.*, at 17.
[288] *Ibid.*, at 21, 42.

The effects of these closures have been stark. The LCEF report summarizes some of them:

> Closing polling places has a cascading effect, leading to long lines at other polling places, transportation hurdles, denial of language assistance and other forms of in-person help, and mass confusion about where eligible voters may cast their ballot. For many people, and particularly for voters of color, older voters, rural voters, and voters with disabilities, these burdens make it harder – and sometimes impossible – to vote.[289]

As that summary explains, the mass closing of polling places does more than increase the time and cost of travel to the remaining stations. It also spells longer lines once you get there. Worse, those longer lines are not distributed equally. The data reveal a clear pattern of significantly longer waiting times for African American and Latino voters than for white voters. From a nationwide standpoint, part of that differential can be ascribed to the fact that African American population percentages happen to be especially high in the southeast, where the average wait times for all voters are generally higher than the national averages.[290] But even within the southeast, the wait time disparities can be huge, as the five-hour waits experienced by Georgia voters in communities of color illustrate. Closures in Arizona's Maricopa County, where 31 percent of the population is Latino, have similarly resulted in five-hour lines.[291]

Admittedly, waits of that length are the exception, even in minority communities. Still, the empirical evidence now confirms that the *average* wait times correlate strongly with the percentage of nonwhite voters in a given precinct. Nationwide, in precincts where more than 90 percent of the voters are white, the average wait time in the 2018 elections was only 5.1 minutes. In contrast, in precincts where over 90 percent of the voters are nonwhite, that wait time increased to 32.4 minutes.[292] The many additional studies cited by the Brennan Center for Justice have made similar findings.[293]

Consistently with those findings, the Bipartisan Policy Center reports that in 2018 "[r]esidents of the most densely populated neighborhoods waited 25% longer than residents of the least densely populated neighborhoods."[294] Recall that the most densely populated neighborhoods are those that tend to vote for Democrats by heavy margins.[295] Further, the average 2018 wait times in precincts in which the mean annual income was $40,000 or less was exactly twice the wait times in districts in which the

---

[289] *Ibid.*, at 8.

[290] Klain *et al.*, note 277, at 8.

[291] LCEF, Democracy Diverted, note 277, at 29–30.

[292] Matthew Weil et *al.*, Bipartisan Policy Center, *The 2018 Voting Experience: Polling Place Lines* (Nov. 2019) at 21, https://bipartisanpolicy.org/download/?file=/wp-content/uploads/2019/11/The-2018-Votin-Experience.pdf.

[293] Klain *et al.*, note 277, at 8.

[294] Weil, note 292, at 7.

[295] See notes 20–31 and accompanying text.

mean annual income exceeded that amount.[296] That is not surprising, given the high positive correlation between racial minorities and average annual incomes.[297]

All told, the Bipartisan Policy Center found, in 2018 "over 560,000 eligible voters failed to cast a ballot because of problems related to polling place management, including long lines."[298] As noted, it is the poor, the urban, and racial minorities – particularly African Americans and Latinos – who are disproportionately burdened.

To be clear, there can be legitimate reasons to reduce the number of polling stations. Populations can shift. Election officials might have reasons to expect lower turnout rates for particular elections; midterm elections, for example, almost always generate lower turnout rates than those in presidential election years. An increase in the use of early and mail voting might be expected to reduce the total in-person Election Day turnout. And some states, especially Texas and Arizona, have made ambitious use of "vote centers," where any eligible voters may cast their ballots regardless of which precincts they live in.

But there are far more closings, and far more *selective* closings, than these factors can explain. None of the examples noted earlier coincide with reductions in population. The lower turnout expectations for midterm elections are similarly a nonfactor. To the contrary, the LCEF Report, analyzing the data for the former preclearance states, found that 69 percent of the closures from 2012 to 2018 occurred only after the 2014 midterms.[299] Nor does the increased use of mail voting support the need to close polling places. As the Bipartisan Policy Center study shows, "Although the number of people voting by mail has been steadily increasing over the past two decades, 2018 also set a record for the number of votes cast in-person in a midterm election, 91.2 million. This was a 39 percent increase in the number of in-person ballots cast compared with the last midterm election in 2014."[300]

As for the vote centers in Texas and Arizona, the flexibility that they afford has been another stated justification for "massive reductions in polling places."[301] The LCEF reports:

> In 2014, Graham County, which is 33 percent Latino and 13 percent Native American, closed half of its polling places when it converted to vote centers. In 2012, Graham had 18 polling sites; today, it has half that – six vote centers and three precincts. Cochise County, which is 35 percent Latino, closed nearly two-thirds (65 percent) of its polling places when it converted to vote centers, falling from 49 in 2012 to 17 in 2018. Gila County, which is 16 percent Native American and 19 percent Latino, closed almost half of its polling places; it had 17 in 2018, down from 33 in 2012.[302]

---

[296] Weil, note 292, at 22.
[297] *Ibid.*, at 23–24.
[298] *Ibid.*, at 6.
[299] LCEF, Democracy Diverted, note 277, at 12.
[300] Weil, note 292, at 4.
[301] LCEF, Democracy Diverted, note 277, at 23. See also Klain, note 277, at 12.
[302] LCEF, Democracy Diverted, note 277, at 23.

Similarly, only 24 percent of Texas's counties participate in the state's vote center program but account for about two-thirds of the poll closings.[303]

One might well ask whether voters would prefer voting at an assigned polling place in their neighborhoods or the "flexibility" of finding transportation to a distant vote center. Moreover, many of the Texas counties that don't create vote centers have also closed the vast majority of their polling places. These include "Somervell (–80 percent), Loving (–75 percent), Stonewall (–75 percent), and Fisher (–60 percent) – all of which have large Latino populations."[304]

If none of these factors explains the massive number of polling station closures, then what does? There is ample room for cynicism here. As the foregoing data make clear, the closures were overwhelmingly in the states and counties that, by reason of their histories of racial discrimination in voting, had been subject to the VRA preclearance requirements. The numbers skyrocketed the moment the Supreme Court in *Shelby County* lifted that constraint. The cuts took place very disproportionately in heavily African American and Latino communities. And in several of those states – including Texas, Alabama, and North Carolina[305] – the severe reductions in polling stations coincided with a range of other measures clearly aimed at depressing turnout in minority communities.

For all these reasons, there can be little doubt that at least a significant chunk of the racial disparities in polling station closures is the product of conscious racial discrimination. Moreover, whatever the explanation for the disparities, the very fact that racial minorities must systematically endure longer voting lines than whites is unacceptable in a democracy that purports to embrace political equality.

A related strategy is to prohibit otherwise eligible voters from voting, even provisionally, at other than their assigned precincts. Such a rule might initially seem reasonable from a management standpoint, but it has a sinister side. The US Court of Appeals for the Fourth Circuit, reviewing a package of voter restriction laws enacted by the North Carolina state legislature immediately after the *Shelby County* decision, had this to say:

> Legislators additionally requested a racial breakdown of provisional voting, including out-of-precinct voting. Out-of-precinct voting required the Board of Elections in each county to count the provisional ballot of an Election Day voter who appeared at the wrong precinct, but in the correct county, for all of the ballot items for which the voter was eligible to vote. This provision assisted those who moved frequently, or who mistook a voting site as being in their correct precinct.
> ... [T]he General Assembly that had originally enacted the out-of-precinct voting legislation had specifically found that "of those registered voters who happened to vote provisional ballots outside their resident precincts" in 2004, "a

---

[303] *Ibid.*, at 24.
[304] *Ibid.*, at 27.
[305] *Ibid.*, at 26, 38, and 41, respectively.

disproportionately high percentage were African American." With [this law], the General Assembly altogether eliminated out-of-precinct voting.[306]

But five years later, the Supreme Court in *Brnovich* v. *Democratic National Committee*[307] saw things differently. The Arizona legislature had passed a law requiring election officials to reject any Election Day votes not cast in the precinct in which the voter lived. The evidence at trial had demonstrated that Arizona changed its polling places with uncommon frequency, that minority voters on average lived further from their precinct polling places than other voters, and that, as a result of the confusion and the distances, the votes that were thrown out were disproportionately those of minority voters.

None of that mattered. Splitting 6-3, once again along strictly partisan lines, the Court upheld the restriction. It did so despite the explicit provision in Section 2 of the VRA that discriminatory "results," occurring because members of a particular group lacked an equal "opportunity" to vote, would be a violation. In addition, the majority held, Arizona had a strong interest in preventing voter fraud. The fact that Arizona had not had any serious voter fraud problem also did not matter; for the majority Justices it was enough that, perhaps one day, such a problem might arise.

Polling place decisions have also targeted college students, another solidly Democratic voting bloc. In her speech at a Republican National Committee donor retreat in 2023, a top party strategist, Cleta Mitchell, called for Republicans to oppose locating polling stations on college campuses. She targeted campus voting sites in five states – Arizona, Georgia, Nevada, Virginia and Wisconsin. All have in common that they are swing states with huge public universities that enroll large in-state student populations.[308] And in Texas, a bill introduced in 2023 would prohibit all voting on college campuses.[309]

Ironically, in the lead-up to the ratification of the Constitution, the *antifederalists* had expressed repeated fears that *Congress* would limit the number of polling states in areas unfavorable to the majority party.[310] Once again, however, it is state legislatures – not the federal government – that are to blame.

7 *Limiting Ballot Drop Boxes*

Ballot drop boxes have become a popular alternative to both voting in person and mailing in a completed ballot. Voters may deposit their completed ballots in locked boxes, which are typically located in or outside city halls, public libraries, and/or

---

[306] N.C. *State Conference of the NAACP* v. *McCrory*, 831 F.3d 204, 217 (4th Cir. 2016).
[307] 141 S.Ct. 2321 (2021).
[308] Dawsey & Gardner, note 220.
[309] Schouten & Shelton, note 217.
[310] See Antifederalist 26, 36, 44, 52, 59, and 61.

various other state or local office buildings, including but not limited to elections board offices and polling places.[311]

These ballot drop boxes bring a range of benefits. On the eve of the 2020 elections, when huge numbers of voters wanted to avoid in-person voting because of the COVID-19 pandemic, ballot drop boxes became a safe way to vote without health risks to oneself and without further spreading of the disease.[312] Otherwise, in the words of one observer, voters "could be forced to choose between their vote and their health."[313] For elderly and disabled voters, those considerations take on additional importance.

Beyond their public health benefits, ballot drop boxes make voting more convenient for many. As Democracy Docket's Mac Brower points out, they "offer voters an accessible, 24/7 option for returning their ballot. Voting becomes as easy as filling out a ballot at home and depositing it in a secure box whenever the voter has time, a much more convenient process than going to a polling place or dropping it off at an election office during their limited hours of operation."[314]

He adds: "Drop boxes are more convenient for election officials too, as they allow election offices to collect ballots directly from voters. They don't need to worry about issues with the US Postal Service causing unforeseen delays in returning ballots."[315] Avoiding postal delays, it might be added, does more than help beleaguered elections officials; it reduces the burden on the US Postal Service as well.[316] For similar reasons, drop boxes eliminate voters' fears that the combination of strict absentee ballot deadlines and lengthy mail delivery times will prevent their ballots from arriving in time to be counted.[317] Prompt arrival of ballots also means that the elections officials can complete their tabulations, and the American people can thus learn the results of the election, that much sooner.

With all these benefits, one would expect ballot drop boxes to be a no-brainer. Yet, throughout the nation, Republican legislatures, executive officials, and judges have made it their mission to ban or restrict them whenever they can. In Brower's words, "What started as a Trump-led attack in 2020 has turned into an all-out Republican war on drop boxes, a cornerstone of their coordinated strategy to stop people from voting."[318]

---

[311] Rachel Epstein, Marie Claire, *Ballot Drop Boxes: A Guide to the 2022 Midterm Elections* (Nov. 8, 2022), www.marieclaire.com/politics/ballot-drop-boxes-guide/.

[312] See, for example, Kaanita Iyer, *Capital News Service, Some States Have Tried to Limit Ballot Drop-off Locations, But the Voters Keep Coming* (Oct. 22, 2020), https://cnsmaryland.org/2020/10/22/some-states-have-tried-to-limit-ballot-drop-off-locations-but-the-voters-keep-coming/; Epstein, note 311.

[313] Iyer, note 312.

[314] Mac Brower, Democracy Docket, *The Republican War on Drop Boxes* (Jan. 27, 2022), www.democracydocket.com/analysis/the-republican-war-on-drop-boxes/.

[315] *Ibid.*

[316] *Ibid.*

[317] Iyer, note 312.

[318] Brower, note 314.

The campaign against drop boxes began in earnest with a 2020 tweet from then-President Trump, running for reelection. He wrote: "So now the Democrats are using Mail Drop Boxes, which are a voter security disaster. Among other things, they make it possible for a person to vote multiple times. Also, who controls them, are they placed in Republican or Democrat areas? They are not COVID sanitized. A big fraud!"[319]

Although Trump's claims about drop boxes were false (as explained below) and in the pre-Elon Musk era Twitter flagged them as such, they remained on Twitter and became the gospel among many Republican voters and elected officials. In the run-up to the 2020 election, Ohio's Republican Secretary of State issued an order prohibiting all off-site ballot drop boxes and limiting each county, regardless of population, to one on-site drop-off location. The federal district judge, a Clinton appointee, had enjoined the order, finding that the latter limit had a "disproportionate effect on people of color" in the more populous counties and thus significantly burdened their right to vote.[320] In Ohio's Franklin County, where African Americans and Latinos together comprised 30% of the population, there was only one drop box for 1.3 million voters.[321] "While it maybe said that the 7,903 registered voters in Noble County may find a single drop box location sufficient, the record demonstrates that the 858,041 registered voters in Cuyahoga County will likely not," the district court wrote. But the all-Republican three-judge panel of the US Court of Appeals for the Sixth Circuit voted 2-1 to reverse the district court and uphold the restrictions.[322]

During the same period, Texas's Republican governor announced a similar plan to limit drop boxes to one per county, regardless of population differences. Harris County, with a population that was 64 percent African American and Latino, provided one drop box for its 4.7 million residents.[323] A three-judge panel of the US Court of Appeals for the Fifth Circuit – all three of them Trump appointees – upheld the governor's order.[324]

In some of the Republican-controlled[325] states, even one drop box per county was too much. At least three of those states (Mississippi, Tennessee, and Missouri) did

---

[319] The tweet is reproduced in Kim Lyons, The Verge, *Twitter Says President Trump's Tweet about Mail Drop Boxes Violated Its Rules But Will Stay Visible* (Aug. 23, 2020).

[320] Randy Ludlow, Columbus Dispatch, *Split Federal Appeals Court Blocks Multiple Ballot Drop Boxes in Ohio Counties* (Oct. 10, 2020), www.dispatch.com/story/news/2020/10/10/appeals-court-issues-stay-ballot-box-order/5951882002/.

[321] Iyer, note 312.

[322] Ludlow, note 320.

[323] Brower, note 314; Alison Durkee, Forbes, *1 Ballot Box for 4.7 Million People: Trump Judges Reinstate Texas Limit on Drop-Off Locations* (Oct. 13, 2020), www.forbes.com/sites/alisondurkee/2020/10/13/trump-judges-reinstate-texas-limit-on-ballot-drop-off-locations/?sh=54f9d3e46c68.

[324] Durkee, note 323.

[325] The solidly Democratic state of New York also decided not to install any ballot drop boxes. But as of September 2020, that state was offering the functional equivalent: absentee ballots could be

not allow ballots to be dropped off in person at all, even at county offices. North Carolina, also under Republican control, allowed drop-offs at a county's one elections office (which on average served 100,000 people) and was the only 2020 battleground state that provided no ballot drop boxes anywhere else. At least seven other Republican-controlled states similarly limited ballot drop-off locations to elections offices.[326]

After the 2020 elections, these efforts metastasized. As of March 2023, at least eleven states have adopted complete bans on drop boxes.[327] The bans are ordinarily passed in the normal course by state legislatures, but in Wisconsin the state supreme court used its conservative majority to ban them via judicial fiat – extending the ban even to those drop boxes that are located inside the official offices of the county election clerks.[328]

The stated justification for these bans is almost always that drop boxes are unacceptably vulnerable to fraud. President Trump's 2020 tweet to that effect has already been discussed. That tweet and its progeny have since been echoed repeatedly in state legislative chambers that are under Republican Party control.[329]

But the claims of widespread fraud in the use of drop boxes are just as empty as the claims of widespread fraud in the other voter suppression contexts. There are two points here: The security measures that attend the use of drop boxes make widespread fraud nearly impossible. And the evidence, as consistently reported by both nonpartisan elections officials and those with either Democratic or Republican Party affiliation, is that drop box fraud on a scale that remotely approaches what would be required to alter the outcome of an election simply has never occurred.

As to the security measures, ballot drop boxes are made of steel, bolted to the ground, often monitored by surveillance cameras or election workers, and often located in public buildings.[330] The Orange County [California] Registrar of Voters, described them this way: "They are very large, a thousand pounds, quarter-inch steel, sturdy boxes … They are designed with fire suppression systems as well

---

dropped off at any of 300 early voting sites, plus county election board offices, and, on election day, an additional 1,300 polling places. Carl Campanile, The New York Post, *Voters Can Deliver Ballots at Drop-off Boxes on Election Day* (Sept. 8, 2020), https://nypost.com/2020/09/08/voters-can-deliver-ballots-at-drop-off-boxes-during-nov-3-election/.

[326] Iyer, note 312.

[327] Stu Whitney, Dakota News Now, *Most South Dakota County Auditors Disagree with Election Drop Box Ban* (Apr. 15, 2023), www.dakotanewsnow.com/2023/04/15/most-south-dakota-county-auditors-disagree-with-election-drop-box-ban/.

[328] Epstein, note 311.

[329] See, for example, Brower, note 314; Anthony Izaguirre & Christina A. Cassidy, *No Major Problems with Ballot Drop Boxes in 2020, AP Finds* (July 17, 2022), https://apnews.com/article/voting-rights-2022-midterm-elections-covid-health-wisconsin-c61fa93a12a1a51d6d9f4e0a21fa3b75; Whitney, note 327.

[330] Epstein, note 311.

as liquid damage protection. And so I'll tell you what, they're a lot more secure than a mailbox."[331] Moreover, the ballot signatures are verified in the same way as those on other ballots, and they are closely tracked as they work their way through the process.[332]

The evidence confirms the absence of widespread voter fraud in the use of drop boxes. Brower describes their "proven track record in many states – including red ones."[333] The Associated Press surveyed elections officials in every state and received responses from all but five states. Those responses "revealed *no* cases of fraud, vandalism or theft that could have affected the results." ... And "*[n]one* of the election offices in states that allowed the use of drop boxes in 2020 reported *any* instances in which the boxes were connected to voter fraud or stolen ballots. Likewise, *none* reported incidents in which the boxes or ballots were damaged to the extent that election results would have been affected [emphasis added]."[334] In a similar survey of all South Dakota county auditors, to which almost all replied, a majority reported using drop boxes in 2020 and again in 2022. According to the county auditors, there was not a single recorded case of voter fraud related to ballot drop boxes in either 2020 or 2022.[335]

The real reason for banning or limiting ballot drop boxes, of course, is that Republican legislators and strategists believe – seemingly correctly – that Democratic voters are more likely than their Republican counterparts to use them. As the earlier discussion revealed, the impact of banning or restricting drop boxes falls particularly heavily on large African American, Latino, or other Democratic-leaning communities. In Texas, for example, where the one-box-per-county edict disproportionately harms voters in high-population counties, the burden falls especially heavily on voters in "Harris County (Houston), Travis County (Austin), [and] Fort Bend County (in suburban Houston), which are not only huge, they're also ... more diverse than the state ... and in reality, far more blue than the rest of the state."[336] The executive director of Common Cause Wisconsin explains the Republicans' similar strategy for that state: "[M]ore Democrats vote by absentee ballot overall than Republicans, so they view it in their interests to be able to restrict how absentee ballots are returned. By getting rid of all the drop boxes, their calculation is that this will help them."[337]

Again, this is state government at work. And it is anathema to small-d democratic rule.

---

[331] ABC7 Eyewitness News, *Election Officials Say Their Drop Boxes Are More Secure Than USPS Mailboxes* (Oct. 15, 2020), https://abc7.com/mail-in-ballots-official-ballot-boxes-election-2020-how-to-submit/7147152/.
[332] Whitney, note 327.
[333] Brower, note 314.
[334] Izaguirre & Cassidy, note 329.
[335] Whitney, note 327.
[336] Iyer, note 312.
[337] Epstein, note 311.

8 *Restricting Third-Party Collection of Absentee Ballots*

Collection and return of absentee ballots by individuals other than the voter has become another flash point in the running debate over how best to encourage voting without unduly sacrificing election integrity. Pejoratively called "ballot harvesting" by those who seek to cultivate an image of a practice riddled with fraud, third-party ballot collection is now the subject of sharp state-to-state variation.

As of March 2023, Ballotpedia reports that the states break down as follows: Twenty-four states and DC allow voters to entrust the delivery of their absentee ballots to anyone they choose. Fourteen states permit only specified individuals to return other voters' ballots; typically, the eligible group includes some combination of family members, other household members, and caregivers. One state (Alabama) prohibits all third-party absentee ballot deliveries. The laws of the remaining eleven states do not specify which third parties, if any, may return ballots.[338]

Some of the state laws restrict third-party absentee ballot delivery in other ways. In nine states, again as of March 2023, laws affirmatively prohibit certain specific individuals from returning other people's ballots; the more common examples include employers, union agents, and campaign staff (including candidates). Twelve states restrict the number of ballots that any third-party may return. In seven states, only voters with disabilities, emergency circumstances, or other specified circumstances may entrust their ballot returns to third parties.[339]

As with the other voter restriction measures discussed in this section, those who favor tight restrictions on third-party returns of absentee ballots invoke the specter of fraud and related misconduct. Unlike in those other contexts, however, these fears are not as easily dismissed. In the words of the Heritage Foundation:

> Allowing individuals other than the voter or his immediate family to handle absentee ballots is a recipe for mischief and wrongdoing. Neither voters nor election officials can verify that the secrecy of the ballot was not compromised or that the ballot submitted in the voter's name by a third-party accurately reflects the voter's choices and was not fraudulently changed by the vote harvester. And there is no guarantee that vote harvesters won't simply discard the ballots of voters whose political preferences for candidates of the opposition party are known.
>
> [Permitting third party collection and delivery of absentee ballots] also gives campaign and political party intermediaries the ability to influence voters while they are casting a ballot out of election officials' sight and without any supervision by them.
>
> Thus, there is no one present to ensure that voters are not being coerced, intimidated, threatened or paid for their vote.[340]

---

[338] Ballotpedia, *Ballot Harvesting (Ballot Collection) Laws by State* (Mar. 2023), https://ballotpedia.org/Ballot_harvesting_(ballot_collection)_laws_by_state.

[339] *Ibid.*

[340] Ballotpedia, *Arguments for and against Ballot Harvesting/Ballot Collection* (undated), https://ballotpedia.org/Arguments_for_and_against_ballot_harvesting/ballot_collection#Arguments_at_a_glance.

To show that these worries are more than hypothetical, the Heritage Foundation cites two examples. Both involve mayors who were seeking reelection. Both mayors were criminally convicted of coercing local citizens to vote for them and, in one case, actually filling out the voters' ballots.[341] A third example, not cited by the Heritage Foundation, would be the earlier-discussed episode in which a Republican operative had generated fraudulent absentee ballots in a state legislative race, although in that case there was no evidence that the numbers involved could have tipped the election.[342]

So the potential for abuse cannot be denied. Still, while the potential exists, examples of actual abuse remain rare.[343] Moreover, supporters argue, restricting ballot collection is ineffectual, because anyone intent on any of the feared violations – coercion, fraudulent tampering with the ballots, or discarding them – could avoid detection simply by depositing the ballots in a mailbox.[344]

But the principal cost of these restrictions is, again, their disproportionate adverse impact on several minority voting populations. They particularly burden "communities that have traditionally relied on ballot collection, such as the elderly, differently-abled, Native American, and Latino communities, by preventing them from casting a ballot in the manner that is easiest for them."[345] Increasingly, this method of voting is organized by black churches as well; African American churchgoers might either travel to post offices en masse to mail their ballots after Sunday services or allow church leaders to collect the ballots and mail them off in bulk.[346]

The impact on Native American communities requires elaboration. As the ACLU points out,

> In Montana, Election Day voting for voters on the Flathead Indian Reservation requires a three and one-half hour roundtrip drive from Dixon to the Sanders County courthouse. On the Duckwater reservation in Nye County, Nevada, the nearest in-person early voting and Election Day voting location is at least a five hour roundtrip drive because of the road conditions and mountainous regions. ... Home mail-service does not exist throughout Indian Country. ... [R]ural post offices are often 20 miles or more away from tribal communities. Roads within reservation communities can be difficult to navigate and dirt or

[341] *Ibid.*

[342] See note 128 and accompanying text.

[343] The Conversation, *Is Ballot Collection, or "Ballot Harvesting," Good for Democracy? We Asked 5 Experts* (Mar. 15, 2021), https://theconversation.com/is-ballot-collection-or-ballot-harvesting-good-for-democracy-we-asked-5-experts-156549 (comments of elections expert Nancy Martorano Miller). The one significant exception is the Bridgeport, Connecticut example described in note 121.

[344] Ballotpedia, *Arguments*, note 340.

[345] *Ibid.*

[346] Stephanie Russell-Kraft, The Nation, *Voting from the Pews* (Oct. 11, 2018), www.thenation.com/article/archive/voting-from-the-pews/.

gravel roads may be impassible during bad weather, especially during the winter election season of November.[347]

Additional restrictions on third-party collection and delivery of absentee ballots might well be on the horizon, because in 2021 the Supreme Court gave at least one state the green light. In *Brnovich* v. *Democratic National Committee*,[348] the Court addressed two of Arizona's voter restriction laws.[349] One of those laws makes it a criminal offense for anyone other than the voter or his or her family member, household member, or caregiver, or a postal worker or elections official, to collect or return the person's ballot.

Splitting 6-3 along strictly partisan lines, the Court upheld these restrictions. The Arizona legislature had been well aware that the practice of ballot collection by community volunteers was an important way to make voting easier and that it was utilized disproportionately in minority communities. Additionally, the court of appeals had held that the record at trial should have required a finding of discriminatory intent. But the Supreme Court's majority Justices disagreed. The majority also chose to give Section 2 of the VRA a narrow reading, despite the law's explicit command that discriminatory "results," occurring because members of a particular group lacked an equal "opportunity" to vote, would be a violation – whether or not there had been discriminatory intent. On its face the Arizona law applied equally to all voters, and for the Court's majority that was enough. Besides, the majority held, Arizona had a strong interest in preventing voter fraud. The fact that Arizona had not had any serious voter fraud problem – let alone voter fraud relating specifically to third-party collection or delivery of absentee ballots – did not matter; again, it was enough that the problem might conceivably arise one day.

The correlation between Republican Party control of a state's legislative process and the adoption of restrictions on third-party collection or delivery of absentee ballots is weaker than for many of the other voter restriction laws considered in this section. Some solid blue states – including California and Maryland – are also in the group that have restricted the practice.[350] Still, the vast majority of the restrictions are in solid red states,[351] a reflection of the Republicans' probably accurate perceptions that the minority populations most dependent on the assistance of third parties skew strongly Democratic. And again, in those states the mere possibility of a small number of fraudulent ballots has taken precedence over the far greater number of eligible minority voters effectively disenfranchised.

---

[347] Ballotpedia, *Arguments*, note 340. See also Sam Metz, The Washington Post, *Tribes See Ballot Collection as a Lifeline in Indian Country* (Sept. 27, 2020), www.washingtonpost.com/health/tribes-see-ballot-collection-as-a-lifeline-in-indian-country/2020/09/27/1cc1b04a-00d5-11eb-b92e-029676f9ebec_story.html.

[348] 141 S.Ct. 2321 (2021).

[349] One of those laws, the prohibition on voting out of precinct, was discussed in Section B.6.

[350] Ballotpedia, *Ballot Harvesting*, note 338.

[351] *Ibid.*

9 Disenfranchising Citizens Convicted of Crimes

Denying the vote to citizens who have been convicted of particular crimes is neither a new, nor a distinctively American, phenomenon. It was imported from England.[352] In the US, several states adopted the practice right from the outset; over time, other states followed suit. The trend began to reverse in the late twentieth century, when a number of states loosened the restrictions, typically by reducing the length of the ineligibility. In part, as Alexander Keyssar observes, these relaxations were a reaction to the extraordinary, and growing, size of the US prison population: "Between 1972 and 2003, the number of persons in prison or jail [in the U.S.] increased tenfold, from 200,000 to more than two million."[353] In combination with the number who had already been released, the result was that in the year 2000, some 4.7 million US citizens were rendered ineligible to vote because of criminal convictions.[354]

Despite the liberalizing trend in several states, the prison population continued to grow. By 2008, the number of citizens disenfranchised because of criminal convictions had soared to a record 5.3 million.[355] Since then, the number has pretty much plateaued; as of 2020, it was estimated to be roughly 5.2 million.[356]

Today, every state except Maine and Vermont disenfranchises citizens who have been convicted of specified categories of crimes.[357] The specifics vary widely. The two main variables are which crimes trigger disenfranchisement and when, if ever, the voting rights are restored.

As of June 2022, the main categories of qualifying crimes include the following: any felony; any felony or election-related crime; any felony or election-related crime or treason; any felony under the laws of the disenfranchising state (as opposed to convictions in federal court or other states' courts); and any felony, or any misdemeanor that leads to any incarceration.

Depending on the state law, the right to vote might be restored upon release from incarceration (either automatically or upon the citizen's application); upon release followed by completion of all probation or parole requirements; upon release followed by completion of all probation or parole requirements and payment of all required fines, fees, or victim restitution; only two years after both release and the

---

[352] It had also been prevalent on the European continent and even in ancient Rome. Keyssar, Right to Vote, note 70, at 50.

[353] *Ibid.*, at 274.

[354] *Ibid.*, at 274–75.

[355] *Ibid.*, at 276–77.

[356] Jean Chung, The Sentencing Project, *Voting Rights in the Era of Mass Incarceration* (July 2021), www.sentencingproject.org/app/uploads/2022/08/Voting-Rights-in-the-Era-of-Mass-Incarceration-A-Primer.pdf, at 1.

[357] U.S. Dept. of Justice, *Guide to State Voting Rules that Apply after a Criminal Conviction* (June 2022), www.justice.gov/voting/file/1507306/download. Two territories – Washington DC and Puerto Rico – similarly place no crime-related restrictions on the right to vote. *Ibid.*

completion of all probation or parole requirements; upon release followed by the earlier of five years or completion of all probation or parole requirements; or never (depending on the particular felony and sometimes subject to a gubernatorial power to dispense relief). In some states, the length of the disenfranchisement depends on such variables as the number of felonies, whether any of them were violent, and the dates and places of the convictions.[358]

Four states – Florida, Tennessee, Alabama, and Arizona – deny convicted felons the right to vote, even after release from incarceration and completion of all probation or parole requirements, until they have also repaid all fines and fees. Tennessee additionally conditions the restoration of voting rights on payment of any legally required child support. Some have compared the practical effects of such financial conditions to those of now-prohibited poll taxes.[359]

The impacts of these laws have been borne grossly disproportionately by African American men. Although African Americans comprised only 12.9 percent of the US population in 2000,[360] "[a]lmost half of the prison and parole populations were African American; ... In some states more than 15% of adult African American men were disenfranchised."[361] By 2020, there were at least seven states (all Republican-controlled) in which more than one out of every seven African American adults was disenfranchised.[362]

The disproportionate suppression of the African American vote has not always been a mere side effect of laws that add disenfranchisement to the penalty for commission of a crime; too often, the special impact on African Americans has been the very point. As Jeanne Chung has noted, "[i]n the post-Reconstruction period, several Southern states tailored their disenfranchisement laws in order to bar Black male voters, targeting those offenses believed to be committed most frequently by the Black population."[363] Keyssar points out that in the late nineteenth century "[c]riminal exclusion laws ... were altered to disenfranchise men convicted of minor offenses, such as vagrancy and bigamy. ... The overarching aim of such restrictions, usually undisguised, was to keep poor and illiterate blacks – and in Texas, Mexican Americans – from the polls."[364] That trend continued in the early twentieth century, when southern states passed additional restrictions that "were often more detailed and included lesser offenses, targeting minor violations of the law that could be invoked to disenfranchise African Americans."[365]

---

[358] *Ibid.* See also Chung, note 356.
[359] Chung, note 356, at 2.
[360] Jesse McKinnon, U.S. Census Bureau, *Census 2000 Brief: The Black Population: 2000* (Aug. 2001), www.census.gov/library/publications/2001/dec/c2kbr01-05.html#:~:text=Census%202000%20 Brief%3A%20The%20Black%20Population%3A%202000,-August%202001&text=Of%20the%20 total%2C%2036.4%20million,one%20or%20more%20other%20races.
[361] Keyssar, Right to Vote, note 70, at 275.
[362] Chung, note 356, at 2.
[363] *Ibid.*, at 3.
[364] Keyssar, Right to Vote, note 70, at 89.
[365] *Ibid.*, at 131.

In this century, as with the other voter restrictions discussed in this section, crass partisanship continues to drive criminal disenfranchisement laws. In Keyssar's words, "[b]oth Democrats and Republicans assumed, probably correctly, that most ex-felons – coming from poor or working-class backgrounds and being disproportionately African American – would vote Democratic. Many Republicans were consequently reluctant to support legislation that could hurt their own electoral fortunes, and they regarded Democratic support for liberalization as transparently partisan."[366]

Are racism and partisanship the only motives for criminal disenfranchisement, or are there meritorious arguments for it? Keyssar notes persuasively that the traditional arguments for criminal punishment lend no support to criminal disenfranchisement:

> [T]here was no evidence that it deterred crimes; it was an ill-fitting form of retribution; it did not limit the capacity of criminals to commit further crimes [a function that criminologists call "specific deterrence"]; and it certainly did not further the cause of rehabilitation. Indeed, many critics argued that it did just the opposite, preventing ex-felons from resuming a full and normal position in society.[367]

I would add that it obviously does not serve the additional criminal function of incapacitation – isolating the offender from society.

My view is that, if a legislature considers the criminal punishment allowed by law sufficient to achieve all the legitimate penal functions, then adding disenfranchisement is superfluous. And if it thinks the existing criminal penalties are insufficient for any of those purposes, it has a much more tailored remedy – increase the penalty for the particular crime. Either way, disenfranchisement serves none of the traditional goals of criminal justice.

Disenfranchisement, of course, is not the only civil disability that attaches to criminal convictions. People convicted of various crimes might be barred from carrying firearms, or excluded from particular occupations, or (if not US nationals) removed from the United States. The usual justification for civil disabilities is that the crime of which the person was convicted makes them unsuitable for the particular function. We don't want people convicted of violent crimes to walk around with guns. We don't want people convicted of drunk driving to pilot airplanes. We don't want people convicted of assault with a deadly weapon to become police officers. But no otherwise eligible voter – not even one who has been convicted of a serious crime – endangers anyone by voting.

So what, exactly, is the harm that we fear their voting would cause? Historically, one argument offered by defenders of criminal disenfranchisement is that ex-felons might vote for prosecutors or other officials who were perceived as soft on crime, or even vote to repeal the criminal laws entirely.[368] Apart from the lack of any empir-

[366] *Ibid.*, at 276.
[367] *Ibid.*, at 246–47.
[368] *Ibid.*, at 131–32, 247.

ical evidence to support those assumptions, there is nothing inappropriate about a person choosing to vote his or her self-interest. In a democracy, you get to do that.

That leaves us with what appears to have been the favored justification offered for criminal disenfranchisement in the late nineteenth century – to "preserve the purity of the ballot box." Letting ex-felons vote, the argument went, "would corrupt the electoral process."[369]

One might bristle at the brazenness of legislators who have no inhibitions about enacting a whole range of partisan-inspired voter suppression laws daring to invoke the purity of the ballot box in the first place. Regardless, a single wrongful act does not conclusively define a person's moral character. Perhaps most importantly, in a democracy, the right to vote should be seen as a fundamental attribute of citizenship, not a privilege dependent on legislators' speculative judgments about the intrinsic morality of their constituents.

C THE INDEPENDENT STATE LEGISLATURE THEORY

1 Electing Congress

Article I, Section 4, Clause 1 of the US Constitution (commonly referred to as the "elections clause") reads: "The Times, Places and Manner of holding Elections for Senators and Representatives, shall be prescribed in each State by *the Legislature* thereof; but the Congress may at any time by Law make or alter such Regulations, except as to the Places of chusing Senators ..." [emphasis added]. This clause has given rise to a legal argument known as the "independent state legislature theory" (the ISLT). In its pure form, the ISLT posits that the phrase "the legislature" means "only the legislature." Under that theory, the power that the elections clause confers on a state legislature is not constrained by the state's constitution, the state's courts, the state's governor, the state's voters, or any other organ of the state.

The ISLT has never gained a solid foothold in either federal or state courts. But it has become the Harold Stassen[370] of the electoral distortion movement, popping up with astonishing regularity only to be shot down every time before being trotted out yet again. And despite an important 2023 Supreme Court decision that will be

---

[369] *Ibid*.

[370] For younger readers, Harold Stassen was the youngest governor in Minnesota history before serving in the Eisenhower Administration. He was famous, and continually mocked, for having unsuccessfully sought the Republican presidential nomination no fewer than nine times, during the period from 1948 to 1988. The comparison ends there, however, for Stassen – unlike the ISLT – actually commanded wide respect as a thoughtful politician who spent an entire career trying to nudge the Republican Party toward more moderate positions. See Albin Krebs, The New York Times, *Harold E. Stassen, Who Sought G.O.P. Nomination for President 9 Times, Dies at 93* (Mar. 5, 2001), www.nytimes.com/2001/03/05/us/harold-e-stassen-who-sought-gop-nomination-for-president-9-times-dies-at-93.html.

discussed presently,[371] the ISLT remains a major threat to the integrity of congressional, as well as presidential, elections.

The ISLT made its first major appearance in 1916. The Ohio state constitution authorized statewide popular referenda approving or disapproving laws passed by the legislature. When the voters passed such a referendum disapproving their state legislature's congressional districting map, aggrieved citizens asked the courts to disregard the referendum. They argued that the elections clause of the US Constitution gives the state legislature the sole authority to draw congressional districting maps. The Ohio Supreme Court disagreed, holding that the legislature's power under the elections clause is subject to the state constitution and that the referendum results would therefore stand. The US Supreme Court affirmed unanimously.[372]

The Court was similarly unanimous in 1932, when it decided *Smiley* v. *Holm*.[373] There, the Court upheld a gubernatorial veto of the legislature's congressional districting map. The state constitution authorized the governor to veto legislation and the Court again held that the legislature's exercise of its elections clause power was subject to the state constitution.

More recently, the Court held yet again that the state legislatures' powers under the elections clause are subject to the limitations in their states' constitutions. In *Arizona State Legislature* v. *Arizona Independent Redistricting Commission*,[374] the challenge was to a state constitutional provision that transferred the congressional redistricting function to an independent commission. But by this time the Court had become more conservative and far more partisan, with the result that the state constitutional provision survived only by a tenuous margin of 5-4. All four dissenters were Republican appointees.

Support for the ISLT has not been limited to gerrymandering issues. In *Republican Party* v. *Degraffenreid*,[375] a Pennsylvania state statute allowed mail-in ballots for the 2020 elections, but only if they arrived by 8:00 pm on Election Day. In light of the COVID-19 pandemic and the accompanying long postal delays that were beyond the voters' control, the state supreme court understood that that time limit would result in significant numbers of even timely mailed ballots arriving too late to be counted. It thus interpreted the state constitution's requirement of "free and equal" elections to require a more realistic receipt date. For that purpose, the court extended the deadline for the ballots' arrival for three days. The Republican Party petitioned the US Supreme Court to review the decision, and the Court declined.

---

[371] *Moore* v. *Harper*, 143 S.Ct. 2065 (2023).
[372] *Ohio ex rel. Davis* v. *Hildebrant*, 241 U. S. 565 (1916).
[373] 285 U.S. 355 (1932).
[374] 576 U.S. 787 (2015).
[375] 141 S.Ct. 732 (2021).

But three Justices dissented. Justice Thomas hinted at support for the ISLT;[376] Justice Alito, in an opinion joined by Justice Gorsuch, endorsed it more fully, though not by name. Justice Alito wrote

> The provisions of the Federal Constitution conferring on state legislatures, not state courts, the authority to make rules governing federal elections would be meaningless if a state court could override the rules adopted by the legislature simply by claiming that a state constitutional provision gave the courts the authority to make whatever rules it thought appropriate for the conduct of a fair election.[377]

Justice Alito's dismissive language, especially the term "simply by claiming," minimizes what happened in this case. The state supreme court had carefully explained why, under the unusual conditions created by COVID, failing to count ballots that were likely delayed by postal logjams would violate the state constitution's requirement of "free and equal elections."

That brings us to the Supreme Court's landmark 2023 decision in *Moore v. Harper*.[378] As was discussed in Section A, the North Carolina Supreme Court – with Democrats then holding a 4-3 majority – had struck down the legislature's congressional districting map and had approved a new map, affirming the trial court's finding of intentional, extreme, partisan gerrymandering. The Republican Speaker of the North Carolina House and others asked the US Supreme Court to invalidate that remedial map.[379] Their argument rested on the independent state legislature theory. The elections clause, they maintained, should be interpreted as insulating state legislatures' congressional districting plans from all constraints otherwise imposed by state law, including state constitutions. Since the US Supreme Court in *Rucho* had barred federal court review of partisan gerrymandering claims just four years earlier,[380] embracing the state legislature's argument would have meant that partisan gerrymandering could not be constrained by any courts at all.

The Supreme Court declined to overrule its previous decisions rejecting the ISLT. By a 6-3 vote, it rejected the theory once again – in its pure form. Quoting from the *Smiley* case, the Court held that "[a] state legislature may not 'create congressional districts independently of [requirements imposed] by the state constitution with respect to the enactment of laws.'"[381] Quoting historical sources, the Court relied

---

[376] Justice Thomas laments that, despite the elections clause, "nonlegislative officials in various States took it upon themselves to set the rules instead." *Ibid.*, at 732 (not mentioning that in the present case those "nonlegislative officials" were state supreme court justices interpreting their state constitutions).

[377] *Ibid.*, at 738.

[378] *Moore v. Harper*, 143 S.Ct. 2065 (2023).

[379] While their request was pending, the midterm elections produced a Republican court majority. The newly constituted court promptly overruled its predecessors' earlier decision, while temporarily leaving in force the remedial map that had already been approved. In the US Supreme Court, therefore, that map remained the subject of the legislators' challenge. See *ibid.*, at 2074–76.

[380] *Rucho v. Common Cause*, 139 S.Ct. 2484 (2019).

[381] *Harper*, 143 S.Ct. at 2083.

heavily on the framers' understanding that state legislatures "are the mere creatures of the State Constitutions. ... [T]hey owe their existence to the Constitution: they derive their powers from the Constitution: It is their commission; and, therefore, all their acts must be conformable to it, or else they will be void."[382]

So far, so good. For now, the Supreme Court has contained the fire. And that is a big deal. But rather than extinguish the blaze completely, the Court has left the embers burning. It is one thing, the Court essentially says, to hold state legislatures to the limitations imposed by their state *constitutions*. But that, the Court explains, doesn't mean the legislatures are limited by their state supreme courts' *interpretations* of their state constitutions. In the Court's words, "Although we conclude that the Elections Clause does not exempt state legislatures from the ordinary constraints imposed by state law, state courts do not have free rein." It then cites Chief Justice Rehnquist's concurring opinion in *Bush* v. *Gore* for the proposition that the Court may disapprove state supreme court interpretations of state law if the latter "distorted" the state law "beyond what a fair reading required." Later, it adds: "We hold only that state courts may not transgress the ordinary bounds of judicial review such that they arrogate to themselves the power vested in state legislatures to regulate federal elections." Finally: "[F]ederal courts must not abandon their own duty to exercise judicial review. In interpreting state law in this area, state courts may not so exceed the bounds of ordinary judicial review as to unconstitutionally intrude upon the role specifically reserved to state legislatures by [the Elections Clause]."[383]

At least at this writing, no one knows what that means. What are the "ordinary" constraints of state law? What are the "ordinary bounds of judicial review?" If states don't have "free" rein, how much rein do they have? What will it take for federal judges to decide that they not only disagree with a state supreme court's interpretation of its state's laws, but think the state court "distorted" its state's law or that its reading of state law wasn't "fair" or that the state court "arrogated" the state legislature's power under the elections clause or that the state court "unconstitutionally intruded" on the legislature's elections law powers?

Readers of the Court's opinion waited in vain for answers to these questions. The Court declined to provide them: "We do not adopt these or any other test by which we can measure state court interpretations of state law in cases implicating the Elections Clause." That is because "[t]he questions presented in this area are complex and context specific."[384]

Perhaps, upon reaching this stage of the Court's opinion, some readers assumed that at least limited guidance would be provided once they got to the part where the Court tells us whether the North Carolina Supreme Court's interpretation of its state's law in the present case passes muster. But no: "We decline to address

---

[382] *Ibid.*, at 2083–84.
[383] *Ibid.*, at 2088–90.
[384] *Ibid.*, at 2989.

whether the North Carolina Supreme Court strayed beyond the limits derived from the Elections Clause. The legislative defendants did not meaningfully present the issue ..."[385]

Justice Kavanaugh joined the majority opinion and wrote a separate concurrence to consider what standards future federal courts might employ in deciding how far is too far. Ultimately, he expressed a preference for the Rehnquist standard described above.

When the Supreme Court tells us this many times in the same opinion that federal courts may still reject state supreme courts' interpretations of their own states' constitutions when reviewing their legislatures' congressional districting maps, we have to assume the Court really means it. And Chief Justice Roberts, the author of the majority opinion, is anything but sloppy. He has proven quite adept at giving conspicuously with one hand while taking back subtly with the other. In this case, I find the theory of democracy expert Richard Pildes highly plausible. His take is "that a majority was cobbled together among conservative and liberal justices by agreeing to decide this part of the case in the narrowest terms." The result, as Pildes points out, is simply "a weaker version" of the ISLT, one that he fears will infect the 2024 elections.[386] I will term this tamed-down version "ISLT-lite."

The US Supreme Court unquestionably has the power, and arguably the responsibility, to interpret the elections clause of the US Constitution. It does so here, rejecting the argument that the elections clause insulates state legislatures from the constraints imposed by their state constitutions. Once the Court has decided that federal constitutional issue, there is only one remaining question: Does the North Carolina constitution empower the state supreme court to review claims that the legislature's districting map reflects impermissible partisan gerrymandering? And that is purely a question of state law. I am at a loss to understand what business any federal court, including the Supreme Court, has in second-guessing a state supreme court's interpretation of its state's law. More perplexing still is that, as in *Bush* v. *Gore*, this same usurpation of a state supreme court's authority is endorsed by three of the Justices who consistently trumpet their fidelity to federalism and states' rights.

And yet, for at least two of the dissenting Justices, even ISLT-lite was not enough. Justice Thomas, in an opinion joined by Justice Gorsuch, dissented primarily because he felt the case was moot, but secondly because he disagreed on the merits. As to the latter, these two Justices adopted the extreme version of the ISLT, acknowledging only those state supreme court decisions that interpret the word "legislature." The decisions in cases like *Hildebrant* and *Smiley*, discussed earlier, tied their hands

---

[385] Ibid.

[386] Richard H. Pildes, Opinion, The New York Times, *The Supreme Court Rejected a Dangerous Election Theory. But It's Not All Good News* (June 28, 2023), www.nytimes.com/2023/06/28/opinion/supreme-court-independent-state-legislature-theory.html?campaign_id=39&emc=edit_ty_20230628&instance_id=96215&nl=opinion-today&regi_id=13788254&segment_id=137848&te=1&user_id=e16deb82e8516f294a4077a86c02f5c2.

on that score, since those decisions had recognized popular referenda and gubernatorial vetoes as part of the legislative process. But state constitutions, they maintained, cannot place *any* substantive limitations on the scope of state legislatures'
powers under the elections clause.[387]

Interestingly, Justice Alito joined only the mootness section of the Thomas dissent, not the ISLT portion of that opinion. But there is no doubt where he stands.
His embrace of a full-throated ISLT in dissenting from the denial of certiorari in
Degraffenreid has already been noted. And when the Republican state legislator
plaintiffs sought an emergency stay of the state court-approved remedial districting
map at issue in this very case, Justice Alito invoked the substance of the ISLT once
again, dissenting from the majority's refusal to grant the requested stay.[388]

How much damage can ISLT-lite do? Quite a bit, as it turns out. Earlier discussion asked what terms like "fair reading" and "exceed the bounds of ordinary judicial
review" mean. But that was a rhetorical question, for every Supreme Court scholar
knows the answer. It means whatever five members of the Court say it means. Given
the propensities of the current Justices, one can hardly be confident that the Court
will constrain state legislatures when they enact various measures testing the limits
of the Supreme Court's willingness to overturn state supreme court rulings on their
legislatures' exercise of their election clause powers. For that matter, there is no way
to know the ultimate fate of even the North Carolina legislature's extreme partisan
gerrymander, much less similar efforts by other states, because the Court declined
to say.

There are additional reasons to fear that we are not yet out of the woods. With
the current more solidly conservative, more Republican, and more activist Supreme
Court, Justices who embrace even the extreme version of the once-unthinkable independent state legislature theory can no longer be laughed off. The Court's current
Republican majority has not hesitated to overrule precedent when doing so furthers
its politically conservative views or the electoral welfare of the Republican Party, as
previous discussion has already demonstrated.[389] Three of the current Justices have
already signed on to a potential absolutist version of the independent state legislature theory. Overruling *Moore* would require just two more votes. They could come
from new appointments. Or they could come from either a change of mind or a
specific application of the Court's amorphous restrictions on state supreme court
interpretation powers by the Chief Justice or Justices Kavanaugh or Barrett, or some
combination of both.

Finally, not every case reaches the Supreme Court. And even those that do
will not always reach the Supreme Court in time for its ruling to affect a pending

---

[387] *Moore v. Harper*, 143 S.Ct. at 2100-04 (Justice Thomas dissenting).
[388] *Moore v. Harper*, 142 S. Ct. 1089, 1090 (2022) (observing that the language of the elections clause
"specifies a particular organ of a state government, and we must take that language seriously.")
[389] See Chapter 2, Section D.

election. Federal district and court of appeals judges whose mindsets are similar to those of the three dissenters in *Moore* – and as previous discussion showed, their ranks are plentiful – have many ways to circumvent the holding in *Moore*. They can interpret elastic terms like "ordinary" and "fair" creatively. Or they could slow the process enough to ensure that extreme gerrymandering or voter suppression laws are not struck down until after a pending election, knowing that undoing an election after the fact is exceptionally difficult. As the same previous discussion also showed, the easy availability of judicial forum shopping – and of dependable lower court judges willing to shape their legal analyses to fit their own ideological agendas – can give cynically motivated state legislatures the cover they need.

Leaving any state government officials free to disregard the constraints of their state constitutions and the legal interpretations of their courts would be dangerous enough. Here, though, an earlier point is worth repeating: Despite public perceptions, state legislatures are often profoundly counter-majoritarian to begin with – in the words of Miriam Seifter, "the least majoritarian branch" of state government.[390]

2 Electing the President

Might the independent state legislature theory apply to presidential elections? Article II, Section 1 of the US Constitution (the "electors clause") reads:

> … 2. Each State shall appoint, *in such Manner as the Legislature thereof may direct*, a Number of Electors, equal to the whole Number of Senators and Representatives to which the State may be entitled in the Congress … 5. The Congress may determine the Time of chusing the Electors, and the Day on which they shall give their Votes; which Day shall be the same throughout the United States [emphasis added].

The differences between this provision and the analogous provision governing congressional elections are notable. As the preceding subsection points out, state legislatures decide not only the manner, but also the times and places, of congressional elections, but Congress may supersede all of those choices. When it comes to presidential elections, only the state legislatures decide the manner of selecting presidential electors, and only Congress decides the date on which those electors must be chosen.

In the early years of the republic, several state legislatures chose their presidential electors themselves, rather than leave the decision to the people.[391] But for at least

---

[390] Seifter, note 16. See also Bulman-Pozen & Seifter, note 47; Karlan, note 23.
[391] *Bush v. Gore*, 531 U.S. 98, 104 (2000); *McPherson v. Blacker*, 146 U.S. 1, 28–33 (1892); James W. Ceaser & Jamie Raskin, National Constitution Center, *Article II*, Section 1, *Clauses 2 and 3*, https://constitutioncenter.org/the-constitution/articles/article-ii/clauses/350.

the past 150 years, the laws of every state provide for presidential electors to be cho-sen by popular vote.[392]

Could state legislators today resume the historical practice of naming their own preferred presidential electors instead of letting their constituents decide? The thought is disconcerting, and the question is an open one.

The Supreme Court's 1892 decision in *McPherson v. Blacker* takes a broad view of the state legislatures' powers under the electors clause. Upholding the Michigan legislature's decision to allocate its electoral votes via district-by-district elections, the Supreme Court described the legislature's power in sweeping terms. The power to decide the manner in which the state's presidential electors are chosen, the Court said,

> is conferred upon the legislatures of the States by the Constitution of the United States, and cannot be taken from them or modified by their State constitutions … Whatever provisions may be made by statute, or by the state constitution, to choose electors by the people, there is no doubt of the right of the legislature to resume the power at any time, for it can neither be taken away nor abdicated.[393]

Two points stand out. First, in contrast to the Court's analogous congressional election decisions, the Court says that the legislature's power to decide the manner of choosing presidential electors is not subject to the state's constitution. Second, the Court declares, even when a state statute or state constitution provides for pop-ular election of the presidential electors, the legislature has the right "to resume the power at any time" – meaning that the legislature can change the law and decide to name the presidential electors itself, regardless of what the state constitution says.

To be clear, both those statements are nonbinding dicta, for neither issue was before the Court in *McPherson*. There was no state constitutional provision alleg-edly prohibiting the legislature's districting plan; the challenge had been grounded in provisions of the US Constitution. Nor had the legislature attempted to substitute its own electors for those chosen by the people.

Nonetheless, the language in *McPherson* has had an impact. The Congressional Research Service concluded that "state legislatures still retain the constitutional option of taking [the election of presidential electors] out of the voters' hands, and selecting electors by some other, less democratic means." That very option, in fact, was "discussed in Florida in 2000 during the postelection recounts, when some members of the legislature proposed to convene in special session and award the state's electoral votes, regardless of who won the popular contest in the state."[394]

---

[392] See Thomas H. Neale, Congressional Research Service, *The Electoral College: How It Works in Contemporary Presidential Elections* (May 15, 2017), https://sgp.fas.org/crs/misc/RL32611.pdf.

[393] 146 U.S. at 35.

[394] Congressional Research Service, *Electoral College Reform: 110th Congress Proposals, the National Popular Vote Campaign, and Other Alternative Developments* (Feb. 9, 2009), https://crsreports .congress.gov/product/pdf/RL/RL34604/7, at 6.

That radical step proved unnecessary. As discussed earlier, a 5-4 majority of the Supreme Court in *Bush* v. *Gore* awarded Florida's electoral votes, and with them the presidency, to Republican nominee George W. Bush. The five Justices in the majority (all Republicans) ultimately decided that the differing standards employed in various Florida counties during the recount violated the equal protection clause of the US Constitution.

But in that case, Chief Justice Rehnquist wrote a separate concurring opinion, which was joined by two of the other majority Justices (Scalia and Thomas). In it, these three Justices offered an additional reason to overturn the decision of the Florida Supreme Court. Ordinarily, federal courts defer to state courts' interpretations of their states' laws. But because the US Constitution's presidential election clause left the manner of choosing the electors to the state legislatures, these three Justices believed that the Florida Supreme Court's interpretation of laws on that subject was not entitled to the usual deference. These Justices didn't specifically say that the state legislature is immune from any constraints imposed by the state constitution. Still, these Justices' explicit refusal to defer to the state supreme court – which is typically, also, the ultimate arbiter of what the state constitution means – comes perilously close to endorsing the ISLT and extending it to the presidential realm.[395]

Moreover, the majority – not just the three concurring Justices – took pains to emphasize the teachings of *McPherson* on this subject. "The individual citizen has no federal constitutional right to vote for electors for the President of the United States unless and until the state legislature chooses a statewide election as the means to implement its power to appoint members of the Electoral College [citing article II, section 1]." Citing *McPherson*, the Court added that

> the State legislature's power to select the manner for appointing electors is plenary; it may, if it so chooses, select the electors itself, which indeed was the manner used by State legislatures in several States for many years after the Framing of our Constitution. ... The State, of course, after granting the franchise in the special context of Article II, can take back the power to appoint electors.[396]

Dissatisfied with the results of the 2020 presidential election, "the Trump campaign was seriously considering asking several of the Republican-controlled state legislatures to select Trump electors."[397] Trump campaign lawyer John Eastman, in fact, discussed precisely that strategy with Pennsylvania Republicans.[398]

---

[395] *Bush* v. *Gore*, 531 U.S. 98, 111–22 (2000).
[396] *Ibid.*, at 104.
[397] The Conversation, *Could a Few State Legislatures Choose the Next President?*, https://theconversation.com/could-a-few-state-legislatures-choose-the-next-president-146950.
[398] Andy Craig, Cato Institute, *State Legislatures Can't Overturn Presidential Election Results* (May 11, 2022). See also Columbia Law School, *Five Questions on the Independent State Legislature Theory for Elections Expert Richard Briffault* (Nov. 16, 2022), www.law.columbia.edu/news/archive/five-questions-independent-state-legislature-theory-elections-expert-richard-briffault.

There is at least one fairly clear legal limit on such a strategy – timing. It is true that the Supreme Court in both *McPherson* and *Bush* v. *Gore* opined, albeit only in nonbinding dictum, that the US Constitution would permit state legislatures to reassert the power to select the presidential electors rather than let the voters decide. But Congress retains exclusive authority over the time when the electors are chosen. And it has chosen the first Tuesday after the first Monday of November in even-numbered years. Thus, in the minds of some, legislatures could not constitutionally substitute their own electors for the ones that the voters had selected on Election Day. By then, it would be too late.[399]

I'm not so sure. It does seem clear that state legislators could not take such action *after* Election Day. Nowadays, however, in the vast majority of states, the major television networks can project the winners of the electoral votes on election night. And even without a formal projection, state legislators might feel that the results are not looking good or simply that the outcome looks too close to leave to chance. In any of those scenarios, what legal barrier would there be to the legislature convening before midnight on election night, making any necessary rules changes to permit immediate action, amending its statute to allow legislative selection of its state's presidential electors (this assumes the governor is on board), and then choosing those electors? With that strategy, the legislature might argue that it is complying with the requirement that it choose its electors on the date designated by Congress.

My hope is that if such a strategy were attempted, even the current Supreme Court would reject the ISLT in much the same way that it rejected its application to congressional elections in *Harper*. The Court would simply need to read the Constitution's electors clause as assuming that the state legislatures, being creatures of the state constitution, are constrained by it. If the right of the people to select presidential electors is part of the state's constitution, and not merely statutory, this would not be a heavy lift. There are judicial dicta to the contrary, but no binding holdings.

Still, the same uncertainties exist. Three members of the current court are already on record as endorsing the ISLT; forming a majority would take only two more votes, from either new appointments or changes of minds by existing members. When the presidency hangs in the balance, *Bush* v. *Gore* teaches us that Republican Supreme Court Justices' allegiance to states' rights can be quite flexible.

The greater constraint, many others have argued, would be strong political headwinds. One can imagine the outrage were a state legislature to reject the votes of the people on an issue so important and so emotionally absorbing.[400] Then again, partisan polarization being as acute as it now is, one hesitates to make even that assumption.

---

[399] *Ibid.* Accord, Fred Wertheimer, Brookings, *Democracy on the Ballot – The "Independent State Legislature Theory" Will Not Empower State Legislatures to Override Presidential Election Results* (Nov. 4, 2022), www.brookings.edu/articles/the-independent-state-legislature-theory-will-not-empower-state-legislatures-to-override-presidential-election-results/.

[400] See, for example, The Conversation, Could a few, note 397; Wertheimer, note 399.

D INTIMIDATION OF VOTERS AND ELECTION OFFICIALS

Intimidating voters at the polls has been a storied ritual in the United States.[401] Even after passage of the Fifteenth Amendment, which prohibits the denial of the franchise on account of race, intimidation was one of the (many) tactics used to deter African Americans from voting.[402] In more recent times, as one observer notes,

> [T]here is dangerous historical precedent for groups using weapons as badges of potentially oppressive authority to intimidate voters. Over thirty years ago, the Republican National Committee had to answer in court after it deployed a 'National Ballot Security Task Force' of off-duty police officers wearing revolvers, arm bands and two-way radios to patrol polling sites with threatening signs and to challenge voters.[403]

So voter intimidation is not new. Since the 2020 elections, however, the problem has escalated sharply.[404] In 2022, multiple incidents of voter intimidation by partisan poll watchers (private observers) occurred even in the typically less bellicose primary elections.[405] In a Reuters survey taken days before the 2022 midterms, "Two in five U.S. voters [said] they [were] worried about threats of violence or voter intimidation at polling stations."[406]

The scare tactics are not confined to the polling stations. Volunteers, some of them reportedly armed, went door-to-door in Colorado hoping to find evidence of voter fraud; they allegedly knocked on up to 10,000 voters' doors.[407] In Arizona they targeted ballot drop boxes:

> In suburban Mesa, Arizona, people staked out an outdoor ballot drop box, taking photos and videos of voters dropping off ballots. Some wore tactical gear or camouflage. Some were visibly armed. Others videotaped voters and election workers at a ballot drop box and central tabulation office in downtown Phoenix. They set up lawn chairs and camped out to keep watch through a fence that had been added

---

[401] Katie Friel & Jasleen Singh, Brennan Center for Justice, *Voter Intimidation and Election Worker Intimidation Resource Guide* (Oct. 28, 2022), www.brennancenter.org/our-work/research-reports/voter-intimidation-and-election-worker-intimidation-resource-guide.

[402] Library of Congress, *Voting Rights for African Americans*, www.loc.gov/classroom-materials/elections/right-to-vote/voting-rights-for-african-americans/.

[403] Everytown Law, *Election Protection: Preventing and Responding to Illegal Armed Voter Intimidation and Election Interference*, https://everytownlaw.org/report/election-protection/.

[404] See Eileen Sullivan, N.Y. Times, *Election Workers Face Flood of Threats, but Charges Are Few* (Apr. 13, 2024), www.nytimes.com/2024/04/13/us/politics/election-workers-threats.html?campaign_id=56&emc=edit_cn_20240415&instance_id=120247&nl=on-politics&regi_id=13788254&segment_id=163550&te=1&user_id=e16deb82e8516f294a4077a86c02f5c2; Friel & Singh, note 401.

[405] *Ibid.*

[406] Moira Warburton & Jason Lange, Reuters/Ipsos, *Exclusive: Two in Five U.S. Voters Worry about Intimidation at Polls* (Oct. 26, 2022), www.reuters.com/world/us/exclusive-two-five-us-voters-worry-about-intimidation-polls-reutersipsos-2022-10-26/.

[407] Friel & Singh, note 401.

around the facility for safety after 2020 election protests. Some voters claim the observers approached or followed them in their vehicles.[408]

Nor are voters the only targets. Increasingly, extremists are threatening and endangering election officials and election workers. The victims have run the gamut from secretaries of state to on-the-ground poll workers, and the threats arrive through phone calls, mail, and social media.[409] In the first few months of its existence, a Justice Department task force launched in 2021 had already reviewed over 1,000 reports of "harassing contacts" with election workers.[410]

In the leadup to the 2022 midterms, Colorado Secretary of State Jena Griswold received hundreds of threats. "'Watch your back,' said one Facebook message. 'I KNOW WHERE YOU SLEEP, I SEE YOU SLEEPING. BE AFRAID, BE VERY AFRAID.' ... 'Penalty for treason? Hanging or firing squad. You can pick Griswold,' said one Instagram comment" [emphasis in original].[411]

During the same period, the workers in charge of counting ballots received a stream of threats on other sites, including Gab and the .win forums. "On Gab, people shared images of guns with captions like 'When it takes too long to count the ballots and it goes into another day' and 'When the windows are covered to count illegal ballots.'"[412]

In March 2022, the Brennan Center for Justice surveyed 596 local election officials from all parts of the country and all political affiliations. The results were eye-opening: One out of every six local election officials reported having personally received threats. Of those, 53% had been threatened in person, 73% over the phone, 37% through social media, and 25% by mail.[413]

The same survey revealed the resulting fears of the election workers and the potential implications for future staffing. "Nearly 2 in 3 local election officials believe that false information is making their jobs more dangerous."[414] After 2020,

---

[408] Rachel Leingang, The Guardian, *"We're Watching You": Incidents Of Voter Intimidation Rise as Midterm Elections Near* (Nov. 4, 2022), www.theguardian.com/us-news/2022/nov/04/voter-intimidation-midterm-elections-arizona. See also Friel & Singh, note 401; Rocio Fabbro, CNBC, *Election Officials Combat Voter Intimidation Across U.S. as Extremist Groups Post Armed Militia at Some Polls* (Nov. 6, 2022), www.cnbc.com/2022/11/06/election-officials-facing-armed-militia-presence-at-some-polls.html.

[409] Friel & Singh, note 401. See also Shannon Currie et al., Brennan Center for Justice, *Local Election Officials Survey* (Mar. 10, 2022), file:///C:/Users/legomsky/Downloads/Local_election_official_poll_March2022.pdf; Cat Zakrzewski, Washington Post, *Election Workers Brace for a Torrent of Threats: 'I KNOW WHERE YOU SLEEP'* (Nov. 8, 2022), www.washingtonpost.com/technology/2022/11/08/election-workers-online-threats/; Jane C. Timm, NBC News, *The DOJ is Investigating Dozens of Threats against Election Workers* (Mar. 25, 2024), www.nbcnews.com/politics/elections/doj-investigating-dozens-threats-election-workers-rcna145014?taid=66023a45f4ed320001801oe9&utm_campaign=trueanthem&utm_medium=social&utm_source=twitter.

[410] Zakrzewski, note 409.

[411] *Ibid.*

[412] *Ibid.*

[413] Currie, note 409.

[414] *Ibid.*

86% of election officials reported that they were "worried" about future political interference in the election process, including 36% who said they were "very" worried.

These fears have serious implications for the functioning of our election system. One in five local election officials reported they were "very unlikely" or "somewhat unlikely" to continue serving through 2024. Three in five were concerned that "threats, harassment, and intimidation against local election officials will make it more difficult to retain or recruit election workers in future elections."[415]

An array of federal laws, as well as the laws of every state, make the intimidation of voters and election workers (and several related actions) a criminal offense.[416] In addition, Justice Department officials, officials from other US departments, and state officials monitor many polling places in person on Election Day.[417] Those efforts are helpful, but the available resources are no match for the ever-increasing threats.

The vast majority of these threats to our democracy come from private individuals, political parties, and candidates for elected office or their campaign staffs – not from government officials. So, one might ask, what does this have to do with states?

The answer is that many of the violations are either direct, purposeful state actions or, more commonly, consciously state-enabled. Examples of direct, purposeful state action include two kinds of interventions described well by the Brennan Center's Katie Friel and Jasleen Singh. One strategy centers on the state-employed poll workers:

> Voters and election workers also face increased threats from official actors, such as poll workers and law enforcement. Across the country, organizations that spread false conspiracy theories about the 2020 election are attempting to recruit and train thousands of poll workers this year. In a poll worker training hosted by the Wayne County GOP the day before the Michigan primary, attendees were instructed to ignore election laws and were referred to as "undercover agents." At other recruitment events, speakers have outlined combative strategies for poll workers to challenge voters and question routine election processes.[418]

The authors go on to describe the use of state law enforcement officers for this purpose: "There are numerous signs that politicized law enforcement officials could pose new threats in 2022. A national association of sheriffs who falsely claim the authority to ignore laws they deem to be unconstitutional has encouraged its members to investigate election fraud."[419]

---

[415] *Ibid.*

[416] Friel & Singh, note 401.

[417] U.S. Dept. of Justice, *Justice Department to Monitor Polls in 24 States for Compliance with Federal Voting Rights Laws* (Nov. 7, 2022), www.justice.gov/opa/pr/justice-department-monitor-polls-24-states-compliance-federal-voting-rights-laws.

[418] Friel & Singh, note 401.

[419] *Ibid.*

Other state-assisted intimidation strategies are less direct. Since 2020, several states have passed laws ostensibly designed to "protect" poll watchers (private observers), including laws that insulate them from restraints by official election staff.[420] The vast majority of states have no laws that ban the open display of guns at polling stations, and the majority of the voters nationwide live in states that contain no explicit restrictions at all on bringing guns (openly or otherwise) to polling places.[421] And while as noted earlier the Justice Department sends monitors (usually lawyers) to polling stations, they may not go inside those stations without permission from local election officials. At least two states – Florida and Missouri – expressly forbade Justice Department monitors from entering polling stations during the 2022 midterms.[422]

When state legislatures or officials want to intimidate elections officials, threats of physical violence are not their only weapon of choice; threats to job security can also do the trick. In 2023, the Texas legislature passed two laws that open the door to state partisan takeovers of the local administration of elections. One of those laws allows the secretary of state (at the time, an appointee of the Republican governor) to remove local election officials for "good cause," which can include "something as minor as a voting machine malfunction." The other law abolishes the position of local election administrator entirely. But here's the twist: both bills are specifically drawn so as to apply to only one county in the state – Harris County.[423] This county is heavily Democratic; President Biden won it by thirteen points in 2020 and people of color comprise a majority.[424]

I do not claim that the kinds of state actions just described typify the state officials and the state and local workers who administer elections. To the contrary, I have no reason to doubt that the overwhelming majority perform their duties with integrity and professionalism. Regrettably, however, those traits are not universal. And in our closely divided nation, where so much can turn on the votes in a single state, renegade actions by state and local officials can have major national impact. For these and other reasons, my preference would be to shift the actual administration of our elections from the political control under which it currently functions to an organ of the national judiciary. That proposal is taken up in Chapter 6, Section B.3.

---

[420] *Ibid.*

[421] The authors include the positive observations that "at least 10 states" do ban guns at polling places and that "over 40 percent" of the voting-age population lives in states that have enacted explicit restrictions (though not necessarily complete bans). *Ibid.*

[422] Tim Craig et al., Washington Post, *Florida, Missouri Tell Justice Department Voting Monitors to Stay Outside Polling Places* (Nov. 8, 2022), www.washingtonpost.com/politics/2022/11/08/justice-department-monitors-florida-desantis/.

[423] The bill applies only to counties with populations of more than four million. Tex. Senate Bill 1933, § 31.018 (signed into law June 18, 2023). Only Harris County meets that requirement. World Population Review, Population of Counties in Texas (2023).

[424] Ari Berman, Mother Jones, *Republicans are Trying to Seize Control over Voting in Texas' Largest Democratic County* (May 23, 2023), www.motherjones.com/politics/2023/05/texas-republicans-just-passed-bills-to-takeover-voting-harris-county-houston/.

E STATE AND LOCAL CERTIFICATION OF ELECTION OUTCOMES

The 2020 presidential election focused America's attention on the Electoral College process generally and the congressional certification component in particular. As noted earlier, the Electoral Count Reform Act has reduced, though it hasn't eliminated, the risk of congressional sabotage. But some of the greatest threats to the integrity of the certification process arise at the state and local levels, before the Electoral College votes and before Congress becomes involved.

In every state, elections are administered by a combination of state and local authorities. The procedures vary. Local implementation might be at the municipal level or the county level, and the local authority might consist of a board, a single official, or both. That local authority counts and tabulates the ballots (this process is called a "canvass"), certifies those local results, and transmits them to the state election authorities.[425]

The job of the state election authorities is to aggregate the numbers from the various local canvasses and certify the final results. The state's certifying authority might be a board of elections or a single official, usually the secretary of state. In the case of federal elections, the certification must ultimately be signed by the governor or other official designated by state law.[426]

The preceding subsection outlined some of the ways in which state and local election officials have been victims of intimidation tactics. Unfortunately, they can also be perps. In 2020, several Republican state or local officials attempted to withhold certification of the presidential votes, falsely claiming the ballots had been tainted by voter fraud. In Michigan, for example, the two Republican members of the state's bipartisan Board of Canvassers initially refused to certify the election results in Wayne County, which comprises heavily Democratic Detroit and its surrounding areas.[427]

In the 2022 midterms, election officials in several states – including Arizona, Pennsylvania, North Carolina, Nevada, and New Mexico – refused to certify presidential vote totals, without any legal justification. Some of these officials were outvoted by their Democratic colleagues. Some, but not all, later reversed their decisions under threats of criminal sanctions or loss of their offices, or under direct court orders to perform their legal duties. In the end, all the 2022 electoral outcomes were certified, but the fear is that the general lack of personal consequences for these officials' violations of law will embolden similar actions in future elections.[428]

---

[425] Democracy Docket, *After Election Day: The Basics of Election Certification* (Nov. 29, 2021), www
.democracydocket.com/analysis/after-election-day-the-basics-of-election-certification/.

[426] *Ibid.* See also U.S. Election Assistance Commission, *Election Results, Canvass, and Certification*,
www.eac.gov/election-officials/election-results-canvass-and-certification.

[427] Public Interest, *Wayne County Canvassers Don't Certify Election Results in 2-2 Vote* (Nov. 18, 2020),
www.mlive.com/public-interest/2020/11/wayne-county-canvassers-dont-certify-election-results-in-
2-2-vote.html.

[428] Doug Bock Clark, *Some Election Officials Refused to Certify Results. Few Were Held Accountable* (Mar.
9, 2023), www.propublica.org/article/election-officials-refused-certify-results-few-held-accountable;
Jane C. Timm, NBC News, *Arizona Election Deniers Indicted and Charged with Holding Up Midterm*

Apart from these actual decertification efforts by state or county officials, 2020 witnessed losing candidate President Trump and high-ranking Republican officials unsuccessfully pressuring state legislators and state and local election officials to refuse to certify, or in one case pressuring them to actually alter, the actual vote totals. These entreaties included Trump's now famous request to the Georgia secretary of state to "find" the additional 11,780 votes needed to win the state.[429]

Partisan pressures can also emanate from state legislatures. "In 2023, Arkansas made it a criminal offense for an election worker to send even *applications* for absentee ballots to any voters who had not proactively requested them.[430] South Dakota similarly prescribed criminal penalties for election workers who engaged in previously acceptable conduct."[431]

Related to both decertification and improper pressuring, and requiring separate mention, have been the recent attempts by losing candidates and sympathetic state and county officeholders to weaponize the machinery for auditing electoral outcomes. A comprehensive, thoroughly documented report by William Adler, for the nonpartisan Center for Democracy and Technology, describes these fake audits (commonly called "fraudits") in some detail.[432]

As the report makes clear, election audits can add real value. They can confirm the accuracy of the initial outcome or expose procedural problems that can then be corrected before the next election. Either way, audits can bolster public confidence in the electoral process, a critical ingredient in any democratic system.

But that assumes the auditing is on the up and up. The auditors need to be experienced and unbiased, and the procedures need to be fair, accurate, and transparent. When those conditions are not met, the audits not only fail to bolster public confidence in the electoral process; they undermine it.

Results (Nov. 29, 2023), www.nbcnews.com/politics/elections/arizona-election-deniers-indicted-holding-2022-results-rcna127225?taid=6567d0f7db166200012aff76&utm_campaign=trueanthem&utm_medium=social&utm_source=twitter (noting that in 2023 two of Arizona's election officials refused to certify the valid results of the 2022 midterm elections until a court ultimately ordered them to do so). Even before the 2024 elections, Republicans were formulating plans to get officials to refuse certification of elections that Republicans lose. Jim Rutenberg & Nick Corasaniti, *Unbowed by Jan. 6 Charges, Republicans Pursue Plans to Contest a Republican Defeat* (July 13, 2024), www.nytimes.com/2024/07/13/us/politics/republican-election-campaign-2024.html.

[429] See Wikipedia, *Attempts to Overturn the 2020 United States Presidential Election*, https://en.wikipedia.org/wiki/Attempts_to_overturn_the_2020_United_States_presidential_election.

[430] Matthew Brown, Washington Post, *Ahead of 2024 Election, Several States Overhauled Voting Laws* (May 15, 2023), www.washingtonpost.com/politics/2023/05/15/2024-state-voting-laws/?utm_campaign=wp_post_most&utm_medium=email&utm_source=newsletter&wpisrc=nl_most&carta-url=https%3A%2F%2Fs2.washingtonpost.com%2Fcar-ln-tr%2F3a04d29%2F646255335dfb5222c4ba80 9d%2F5976f9099bbc0f6826be4986%2F23%2F72%2F646255335dfb5222c4ba809d.

[431] *Ibid.*

[432] William T. Adler, Center for Democracy and Technology, *De-Weaponizing and Standardizing the Post-Election Audit* (Oct. 2022), https://cdt.org/wp-content/uploads/2022/10/2022-10-26-CDT-fraudit-report-final-rem.pdf.

The report contains two sections worth highlighting here. In one section, it surveys the most significant "fraudits" that followed the 2020 presidential election, in which Joe Biden defeated Donald Trump. These included the most publicized of the fraudits, in Maricopa County, Arizona,[433] as well as others conducted in Fulton County, Pennsylvania; Mesa County, Colorado; and Coffee County, Georgia.

Those four examples had several things in common: All were initiated by state or local office holders; all of those who initiated the fraudits had publicly cast doubt on the election results; all of the auditing firms they chose were run by similar election deniers;[434] none of those companies had had any prior experience in election auditing; the work was done in secret; and in at least three of the four cases the auditors shared highly confidential information, including the voting machine software and data. (In one of the four cases, Fulton County, the secrecy made it impossible to determine who had access to the software and data and with whom they might have been shared.) As a result, the voting machines in all four counties were compromised and had to be replaced, at taxpayer expense.[435]

Another section of the report summarizes the many harmful effects of fraudits. These include the undermining of trust in the accuracy of election results; the spread of disinformation; gross violations of voter privacy, including the proliferation of individuals' social security numbers and birthdays; and the release, to people with less than trustworthy motives, of information such as usernames, passwords, other sensitive data, and machine software that destroys the security of the county's machines and requires their replacement at the cost of millions of taxpayer dollars. Further, because the same machine models are used in hundreds of other counties, those machines are now vulnerable to hacking and other attacks by others, including foreign countries such as Russia with a history of disrupting the election systems of the US and other nations.[436]

I repeat my earlier concession: Only a tiny fraction of the nation's election officials, and hopefully only rare presidential candidates and their staffs, engage in these types of misconduct. The overwhelming majority of US election officials perform their legal duties with integrity and professionalism. But in a country where elections at all levels of government have so frequently been nail-biters, one cannot

---

[433] See especially Barry C. Burden & Trey Grayson, States United Democracy Center, *Report on the Cyber Ninjas Review of the 2020 Presidential and U.S. Senatorial Elections in Maricopa County, Arizona* (June 22, 2021), https://statesuniteddemocracy.org/wp-content/uploads/2021/06/6.22.21-SUDC-Report-re-Cyber-Ninjas-Review-FINAL.pdf.

[434] The owner of Cyber Ninja's, the company that the Arizona Republican legislators sought out to conduct the Maricopa County audit, had issued a stream of public comments claiming that the election had been stolen. For a detailed account, see Ryan Randazzo et al., Arizona Republic, *Who is Looking at Your Ballot? These are the Companies Involved in the Arizona Election Recount* (June 16, 2021), www.azcentral.com/story/news/politics/elections/2021/06/03/arizona-audit-these-companies-are-looking-at-maricopa-county-ballots/5256982001/.

[435] Adler, note 432, at 18–21.

[436] *Ibid.*, at 25–28.

ignore the potential for even infrequent transgressions by election officials to thwart the popular will.

Of course, just as the final national totals have to be certified by someone, so too must an official or board in a position of public trust be responsible for certifying and transmitting the local results to that national authority. In the stateless country envisioned by this book, all national elections – both presidential and congressional – would be run by the national judiciary, as proposed in Chapter 6, rather than by elected officials with partisan and often overtly counter-majoritarian interests in the outcomes.

F STATES' USURPATION OF LOCAL GOVERNMENT FUNCTIONS

States wield enormous control over their local governments. The constitutions and statutes of all states grant various powers to local governments, but the range of those powers and the corresponding degrees of local autonomy vary widely.

Many states, by either state constitutional provision or statute, adopt some version of "home rule." The term is not always used consistently, and it can take several different forms. Most states' home rule provisions delegate a list of specific powers to their local governments.[437] In those systems, the enumerated powers (and whatever it takes to implement them) are the only powers the local government has, and the exercise of even those powers is subject to any contrary state law or constitutional provision. Since the same can be said about a non-home-rule state (i.e., the local government has only whatever powers the state affirmatively delegates to it), this kind of home rule is a matter of degree; the more comprehensive the set of delegated powers, the more likely it is that the state will be described as a home rule state.

Other states, typically via state constitutional provisions, go a step further. Rather than limit the local governments to a list of specific powers, these states grant the local governments all the powers over their respective territories that the state possesses statewide, though still subject to any contrary state statute or constitutional provision.[438] A few states go further still, carving out certain local government powers that even the state legislature may not preempt.[439]

---

[437] Many such provisions authorize local governments to adopt their own charters. Richard Briffaut, *The Challenge of the New Preemption*, 70 Stan. L. Rev. 1995, 2011 n.111 (2018).

[438] Daniel R. Mandelker *et al.*, State and Local Government in a Federal System 111–12 (9th ed. 2021); Jeffrey S. Sutton, Who Decides? States as Laboratories of Constitutional Experimentation 309 (2022); Ballotpedia, *Home Rule*, https://ballotpedia.org/Home_rule.

[439] For a good, detailed description of these various arrangements, see Mandelker *et al.*, note 438, at 87–170. An example of the third type of home rule is Colorado. Its constitution gives every municipality "every power theretofore possessed by the legislature to authorize municipalities to function in local and municipal affairs." Colorado Const. Art. XX, § 6. The state legislature may not interfere with those powers unless they affect "significant" statewide interests. *City and County of Denver v. State*, 788 P.2d 764, 766 (Colo. 1990).

Amidst all these variations, the one constant is that all the powers of the local government emanate from the state. More specifically, each state decides "what local
governments there will be; the proper allocation of powers to and among them; their
functional assignments; their internal structure, organizations, and procedures for
local operations; their fiscal options in regard to revenue, expenditures, and debt;
the extent of the interlocal cooperation; how their boundaries can be expanded or
contracted; and to some degree their land use patterns."[440]

In the leading case of *Hunter v. City of Pittsburgh*, the Supreme Court described
these state powers in breathtaking terms:

> Municipal corporations are political subdivisions of the State, created as conve-
> nient agencies for exercising such of the governmental powers of the State as may
> be entrusted to them. ... The number, nature and duration of the powers conferred
> upon these corporations and the territory over which they shall be exercised rests
> in the absolute discretion of the State. ... The State, therefore, at its pleasure may
> modify or withdraw all such powers, may take without compensation [municipal]
> property, hold it itself, or vest it in other agencies, expand or contract the territorial
> area, unite the whole or a part of it with another municipality, repeal the charter
> and destroy the corporation. All this may be done, conditionally or uncondition-
> ally, with or without the consent of the citizens, or even against their protest. In all
> these respects the State is supreme, and its legislative body, conforming its action
> to the state constitution, may do as it will, *unrestrained by any provision of the
> Constitution of the United States*. ... The power is in the State and those who leg-
> islate for the State are alone responsible for any unjust or oppressive exercise of it
> [emphasis added].[441]

Despite the Court's claim that in these matters the state is "unrestrained by any
provision of the Constitution of the United States," subsequent court decisions have
occasionally carved out exceptions. They have held that certain constitutional requirements – including the supremacy clause and the Fifteenth Amendment prohibition of
racial discrimination in voting – put at least some limits on what states may do to their
local governments. And as Nestor Davidson has demonstrated, in actual practice direct
partnerships between the federal and local governments have qualified the principle
of literally unlimited state authority over their local governments.[442] But the general
thrust of the *Hunter* opinion – that all local governments are creatures of the state and
subordinate to the state – remains at least roughly intact.[443]

It was not always this way. During much of the nineteenth century, courts often
denied states the power to interfere with local governments' "inherent right" of

---

[440] Mandelker *et al.*, note 438, at 7, quoting Advisory Commission on Intergovernmental Relations,
Report, *State and Local Roles in the Federal System* 151 (1982).

[441] 207 U.S. 161, 179 (1907).

[442] Nestor M. Davidson, *Cooperative Localism: Federal-Local Collaboration in an Era of State Sovereignty*,
93 Virginia L. Rev. 959, 96–1000 (2007).

[443] See Mandelker *et al.*, note 438, at 53–60 (providing a good summary of the case law).

self-governance. Over the years, however, that doctrine gradually disappeared from view.[444] It is now accepted that local governments may act only pursuant to powers granted, explicitly or implicitly, by the state – ordinarily in the form of state constitutional provisions, statutes, or local charters.

A separate but related question is how courts should go about interpreting the scope of the powers conferred by the state. In 1872, Justice John Dillon of the Iowa Supreme Court published the first known book on local government law.[445] In it appears what would become known as "Dillon's Rule." Municipalities, he declared, possessed only those powers that were expressly granted, implied or incident to those powers, and those that are *essential* to the declared objects and purposes of the [municipality] – not simply convenient, but *indispensable* [emphasis added]." Any interpretive doubts, he added, should be resolved against the municipality.[446]

Superimposing Dillon's Rule on the doctrine of state absolutism meant that the authority of local governments was doubly constrained. Not only were their powers limited to those that the state gave them; the powers that the states chose to give them were to be narrowly construed. Today, Dillon's Rule is still with us but applied inconsistently, in ways that have given rise to perceptions that its application is more result-oriented than principled.[447]

Importantly too, even when local governments are held to possess authority over a given subject area, it does not follow that that power will be exclusive. The state may pass legislation preempting a given exercise of that power.

So the states' powers over their local governments are vast. How have the states exercised those powers in practice?

Recent years have seen a marked increase in state legislative preemption of local ordinances.[448] "More than 700 such bills were introduced in state legislatures in

---

[444] *Id.* at 90–92; see also Gerald E. Frug, *The City as a Legal Concept*, 93 Harv. L. Rev. 1059 (1980) (tracing this change in thinking to the emerging distinction between public corporations, including municipalities, that were creatures of the state and private corporations that were created by individuals).

[445] John F. Dillon, Municipal Corporations (1st ed. 1872).

[446] *Ibid.* § 55.

[447] See, for example, Hugh Spitzer, *"Home Rule" vs. "Dillon's Rule" for Washington Cities*, 38 Seattle Univ. L. Rev. 809 (2015).

[448] See, for example, Sutton, note 438, at 324; Seifter, note 16, at 1750; Lauren E. Phillips, Note, *Impeding Innovation: State Preemption of Progressive Local Regulations*, 117 Colum. L. Rev. 2225 (2017); Opinion, The Editorial Board, The New York Times, *States Are Silencing the Will of Millions of Voters* (June 3, 2023), www.nytimes.com/2023/06/03/opinion/texas-preemption-bill.html?algo=combo_als_clicks_decay_96_50_ranks&block=5&campaign_id=142&emc=edit_fory_20230605&fellback=false&imp_id=292898246&instance_id=94288&nl=for-you&nlid=76642304&pool=fye-rotating-opinion-ls&rank=1&regi_id=76642304&req_id=25297540&segment_id=134760&surface=for-you-email-rotating-opinion&user_id=2785b718e28912cce3f4ef8d2794344a&variant=0_best_algo; Margaret Renkl, Opinion, The New York Times, *This Is How Red States Silence Blue Cities. And Democracy* (Jan. 16, 2023), www.nytimes.com/2023/01/16/opinion/nashville-city-council-tennessee-republicans.html?algo=combo_als_clicks_decay_96_50_ranks&block=5&campaign_id=142&emc=edit_fory_20230117&fellback=false&imp_id=330746648&instance_id=82957&nl=for-you&nlid=766423

2023, and at least ninety-two had passed as of October of that year."[449] Of these, the vast majority were enacted "by Republican lawmakers to curb policymaking in cities run by Democrats."[450] One leading scholar has pronounced this a phenomenon of "epidemic proportions."[451]

The examples are legion. Texas has been particularly busy. Having already prohibited cities from banning discrimination against low-income renters or reducing the sizes of their police forces, Texas added a welter of new restrictions in 2023. Under the first of these 2023 laws,

> no city could prohibit discrimination against L.G.B.T.Q. employees, as several Texas cities have done. No city could adopt new rules to limit predatory payday-lending practices. No city could restrict overgrown lots or unsafe festivals or inadequate waste storage. Cities would even be barred from enacting local worker protections, including requiring water breaks for laborers in the Texas heat, as Dallas, Austin, and other cities have done after multiple deaths and injuries.[452]

As discussed earlier,[453] the Texas legislature struck again later that same year. It passed a law that allows the Texas Secretary of State (a Republican) to take over the local administration of elections in one specific county – heavily Democratic Harris County.

Similar laws are now popping up regularly, almost exclusively in red states. There are state laws preempting local environmental ordinances, including especially local bans on plastic grocery bags;[454] laws that permit state takeovers of local police forces and laws that prohibit municipalities from reducing the sizes of their police forces;[455] laws restricting local action on immigration, gun safety, and pandemic protocols;[456] so-called "bathroom" laws that prohibit local governments from allowing transsexuals to use the public restrooms designated for their particular gender identities;[457] laws that bar local governments from prohibiting sexual orientation

---

04&pool=pool%2F459f4697-9859-45a3-b805-02773acebb03&rank=1&regi_id=76642304&req_id=48176129&segment_id=122768&surface=for-you-email-rotating-guestessays&user_id=2785b718e28 912cce3f4ef8d2794344a&variant=0_best_algo; Molly Hennessy-Fiske, Washington Post, *Antagonisms Flare as Red States Try to Dictate How Blue Cities are Run* (Nov. 27, 2023), www.washingtonpost.com/nation/2023/11/27/red-states-blue-cities-preemption-control/.

[449] Hennessy-Fiske, note 448. As to this pattern, see also the other sources cited in note 448.

[450] *States are Silencing*, note 448.

[451] Seifter, note 16, at 1750.

[452] The New York Times, States Are Silencing, note 448.

[453] See notes 423=24 and accompanying text.

[454] See, for example, Bowman *et al.*, note 21, at 334; Sutton, note 438, at 324; Seifter, note 16, at 1750.

[455] Kevin McDermott, The New York Times, Opinion, *St. Louis is the Struggling Downtown You Haven't Heard of – and Right-Wing Policies Are Making Things Worse* (June 27, 2023), www.nytimes.com/2023/06/27/opinion/st-louis-downtown-doom-loop-pandemic-return-to-office.html?campaign_id=39&emc=edit_ty_20230627&instance_id=96119&nl=opinion-today&regi_id=13788254&segment_id=137746&te=1&user_id=e16deb82e8516f294a4077a86c02f5c2.

[456] Seifter, note 16, at 1750; McDermott, note 455.

[457] Phillips, note 448, at 2225; Bowman *et al.*, note 21, at 330–31.

discrimination;[458] laws that ban sanctuary cities and local minimum wage requirements;[459] laws restricting local taxation;[460] and laws stripping elected district attorneys of various powers and even removing them from office.[461]

Under a recent Florida law, when anyone asks a court to enjoin a local ordinance on grounds of state preemption, that ordinance will automatically be suspended until the litigation is completed.[462] The Republican-controlled Mississippi legislature substituted a separate system of criminal laws just for the Democratic-controlled city of Jackson, which is 80 percent African American – a system that includes prison, rather than county jail, for such misdemeanors as disturbing the peace.[463] And the incoming governor of Louisiana has threatened to cut off state funding for the water infrastructure of the City of New Orleans unless the local district attorney prosecutes women who try to obtain abortions that are prohibited by state law.[464]

Increasingly too, these laws are doing more than simply preempting these local actions; they frequently impose punitive sanctions on local governments that are found to be noncompliant. These sanctions include "attaching fines, liability, or removal from office for local government officials who attempt to regulate preempted matters, or terminating state aid to localities that do so."[465] A 2023 Florida law allows businesses to sue municipalities for passing ordinances found to be "unreasonable." Attorney fees are awarded to the business if it wins, but not to the municipality if it wins.[466] And after Nashville declined to host the Republican National Convention, the Republican legislature in Tennessee exacted vengeance by cutting the size of the Nashville Metro Council, altering the district maps to the disadvantage of minority groups, taking over the Nashville airport and the Nashville sports authority, and cutting off state aid to the city's convention center, though a court has put some of those laws on hold.[467]

In federalism debates, a common refrain among states' rights advocates is that states know their people's needs and political preferences better, and therefore can represent the distinct interests of their residents better, than the federal government. Probably so. But not as well as local authorities. Arguably, therefore, the very dependence of local governments on the will of a state legislature controlled by a party whose views can differ radically from those of the local population is inherently in

---

[458] Phillips, note 448, at 2226.
[459] Bowman *et al.*, note 21, at 330–31, 334; McDermott, note 455.
[460] Sutton, note 438, at 324.
[461] Hennessy-Fiske, note 448.
[462] *Ibid.*
[463] *Ibid.*
[464] *Ibid.*
[465] Seifter, note 16, at 1750.
[466] Renkl, note 448.
[467] *Ibid.*; Hennessy-Fiske, note 448.

tension with democratic norms. That states so aggressively assert that power, running roughshod over the attempts of local communities to govern themselves on a range of local issues, only amplifies that tension.

Of course, one may argue that the same is true of federal power to enact nation-wide laws that are at odds with the wishes of majorities of various state populations. Majority rule makes this problem unavoidable. After all, any geographic area with a population of three or more people will contain subgroups that might hold views different from the larger geographic area of which they are a part. Even municipalities will contain individual neighborhoods in which a majority of the residents are subjected to ordinances with which they disagree. Individual neighborhoods, in turn, will contain blocks of houses for which the same can be said. And so on.

We shall return to this problem in Chapter 5, Section B, which takes on more directly the argument that states play an important role in tailoring laws to the needs and preferences of the people. For now, the key point is that, when the issue is which subnational level is optimally suited to perform that tailoring role, it is nearly impossible to make the case that the state is the best choice. As is evident from both prior and later discussion, the differences in popular political preferences among the various local communities within a state – particularly the urban/rural divide – overwhelm the state-to-state differences.

For similar reasons, I recognize that, by railing against states' counter-majoritarian usurpations of powers that should rest with local governments, while simultaneously arguing that we should do away with state government entirely (and on top of that, eliminate the Tenth Amendment constraints on the federal government), I leave myself open to charges of hypocrisy. Just as local governments are closer to the people than states are, and thus better situated to tailor their policies to their constituents' political preferences, so too states are closer to the people than the federal government is and thus better situated to tailor their policies to their constituents' political preferences.[468]

At first blush, these positions might seem inconsistent. But only at first blush, for there are two important differences. The first one has already been noted. As many others have shown, the state-to-state variations in political preference are far less pronounced, and in fact they mask, the profound political differences among the various local governments *within* any given state. The urban/rural split is but the most dramatic example. Second, at any rate, I am not proposing a wholesale transfer of the states' current powers to the national government. Rather, I am advocating that *some* of those powers be reallocated to the national government and that others be reassigned to the local governments. At worst, therefore, the net effect of these transfers on the ability of government to effectuate the wishes of its constituents is a wash.

---

[468] See the discussions in Chapter 3, Section A and Chapter 5, Section B.

G EFFECTS OF COUNTER-MAJORITARIAN STATE LEGISLATURES

Previous sections show how extreme the counter-majoritarian compositions of state legislatures have become and have identified the forces that enable those results. What are the practical consequences of those outcomes?

One effect is intangible but quite real. The partisan divide today maps very closely onto a cultural divide. The contrast between the multiracial, multiethnic, generally progressive voters in the urban Democratic strongholds and the overwhelmingly white, conservative, rural and exurban voters in the Republican strongholds is more vivid than ever. The two sides, so thoroughly polarized, increasingly view each other as threats to their respective visions of the social order.[469]

Another result is that the party that gains control of the legislature despite losing the statewide popular vote acquires the ability to pass the very election laws – including gerrymandering and voter suppression – that can help it continue to control the legislature in future years. Too often, counter-majoritarian legislatures are thus self-perpetuating.

But it is not only election laws that they can pass. Control of the legislative process – particularly when the counter-majoritarianism is extreme enough to convert a simple majority into a veto-proof supermajority – allows the legislature to pass other laws as well, even those to which most voters statewide are firmly opposed.[470]

Intrastate preemption – a state's takeover of a power previously entrusted to local government – can be another consequence of a statewide voter preference that culminates in legislative control by the other party. I say "can be" both because it will not necessarily occur and because even genuinely majoritarian legislatures can seize power from local municipalities. But examples of such legislative actions have increased sharply in recent years,[471] and their rise is "closely linked with the rise of American political polarization and the urban-rural divide; it typically involves red state legislatures preempting blue cities."[472]

Resistance to direct democracy has been another common form of counter-majoritarian state action. Twenty-six states and Washington, DC have laws that allow their citizens to pass legislation or constitutional amendments directly, through initiatives and/or referenda.[473] These instruments are one way in which states *can* promote majoritarianism, and the sharp rise of partisan polarization has

---

[469] Karlan, note 23, at 2332–33.

[470] See the example of Missouri's concealed carry gun law, note 480 and accompanying text.

[471] A full discussion of intrastate preemption appears in Section F.

[472] Seifter, note 16, at 1750–51.

[473] Mandelker *et al.*, note 438, at 907–24; Elaine S. Povich, Stateline, *Lawmakers Strike Back against Voter-Approved Ballot Measures* (July 28, 2017), https://stateline.org/2017/07/28/lawmakers-strike-back-against-voter-approved-ballot-measures/; Ballotpedia, Initiative and Referendum, https://ballotpedia.org/Initiative_and_referendum. Initiatives are proposed by the citizens themselves; in referenda, citizens vote on whether to approve or disapprove laws or constitutional amendments already proposed or passed by the legislature. *Ibid.* The latter are of two types: "Popular" referenda are initiated by citizen

made initiatives ever more popular. But the same polarization has also spurred state legislatures and other state officials to override the results of those initiatives, block their full implementation, or erect procedural obstacles to future initiatives.[474]

A few examples are worth noting. In 2016, the citizens of Utah passed an initiative expanding Medicaid eligibility; a year later, the Utah legislature substantially reduced the coverage expansion.[475] South Dakota voters in 2016 passed an initiative to reform the laws on campaign finance, ethics, and lobbying; the legislature repealed that law the following year.[476] Also in 2016, Maine voters passed four different initiatives, including two that raised taxes on the wealthy and raised the minimum wage for restaurant workers; the next year, the Maine legislature repealed one and partially repealed the other.[477] In 2017, in Massachusetts, the legislature rewrote a recreational marijuana law that the voters had approved by initiative.[478] The same year, the Florida legislature "revised" a voter-approved initiative legalizing medical marijuana by, among other things, prohibiting "smoking" marijuana.[479]

The impact of counter-majoritarianism on gun safety was especially evident in Missouri in 2003, when the Republican legislature enacted a concealed carry law that the voters had specifically rejected four years earlier. The Democratic governor vetoed the bill. But, with supermajorities that in both legislative chambers were disproportionate to the statewide popular votes, the Republican legislature was able to override the governor's veto.[480]

Occasionally, the obstruction comes from the state's executive branch rather than from the legislature. The Republican governor of Maine refused to implement a Medicaid expansion passed by the state's voters. In that case, a state superior court judge ordered the governor to implement the law, but not all state courts have been willing to take similar action.[481]

Apart from overturning or blocking initiatives that the voters have passed, or enacting laws the voters have rejected, state legislatures have been known to make it harder to pass future voter initiatives. They have done this by creating procedural obstacles to getting initiatives on the ballot. These include "imposing signature requirements for popular initiatives that would make the ballot-qualification process nearly impossible; introducing super-majority approval requirements; and adopting

petition to approve or disapprove legislative acts; "general" referenda are placed on the ballot by the legislature for affirmative citizen approval of legislative enactments. Bowman *et al.*, note 21, at 101.

[474] Bulman-Pozen & Seifter, note 47, at 923–24; Povich, note 473.

[475] Bulman-Pozen & Seifter, note 47, at 929.

[476] *Ibid.*, at 927–28; Povich, note 473.

[477] Povich, note 473.

[478] *Ibid.*

[479] *Ibid.*

[480] Gabrielle Hayes, NPR, *Law Blocking Federal Gun Regulation Sows Confusion in Missouri* (Jan. 27, 2023), www.pbs.org/newshour/nation/law-blocking-federal-gun-regulation-sows-confusion-in-missouri.

[481] Bulman-Pozen & Seifter, note 47, at 928–32.

deadlines, mandatory reviews, and wording requirements for popular initiatives that do not apply to amendments the legislature itself proposes."[482]

As Jessica Bulman-Pozen and Miriam Seifter acknowledge, there can be both legal and policy justifications for a legislature to repeal laws passed by voter initiatives, just as they can pass laws repealing their own prior legislation.[483] Admittedly too, direct participation is not universally admired. Some fear that it can too easily reflect demagogically driven passions that lead to the denial of minority rights,[484] though in today's political climate it is hard to argue that state legislatures are immune from the same disease. Moreover, when the legislature is itself genuinely majoritarian, one can argue that substituting the legislative will for the decisions made by the people directly is not necessarily antidemocratic; it merely elevates one form of democracy – representative – over another form of democracy – direct. The same can be said when it is the governor (having been elected by a fair, statewide majoritarian vote) who effectively thwarts the implementation of the initiative.[485]

But even in those latter scenarios, rejecting the voters' explicit preferences is at least arguably counter-majoritarian. And when the legislature that repeals an initiative or referendum passed directly by the voters is itself counter-majoritarian, in the sense that it is controlled by a party that the statewide popular vote rejected, its repeal actions amplify the counter-majoritarianism.

The abolition of state government would not have to spell the disappearance of direct democracy. First, if state government were abolished, local initiatives (i.e., voter-originated) and referenda (legislatively originated) could take their place. They are already common and would, in fact, become even more widely available. At present, both statewide and local initiatives and referenda require affirmative grants of authority by either the state constitution or state legislation, and while most states authorize local referenda, only about half authorize local initiatives.[486] In the unitary nation proposed in this book, affirmative authority would no longer be required. Local initiatives and referenda would be permissible as long as neither the US Congress nor local law itself prohibits them.

---

[482] Jessica Bulman-Pozen & Miriam Seifter, *The Right to Amend State Constitutions*, 133 Yale L. J. Forum 191, 192 (2023); see also Bulman-Pozen & Seifter, note 47. at 925; Aaron Blake, Washington Post, *With Abortion Rights looming, Missouri GOP Advances Slanted Ballot Rules* (Feb. 24, 2024), www.washingtonpost.com/politics/2024/02/24/missouri-gop-abortion/?utm_campaign=wp_post_most&utm_medium=email&utm_source=newsletter&wpisrc=nl_most&carta-url=https%3A%2F%2Fs2.washingtonpost.com%2Fcar-ln-tr%2F3cdb75e%2F65da188ea6014d34b386d412%2F5976f9099bbc0f6826be4986%2F22%2F44%2F65da188e a6014d34b386d412 (describing the Missouri legislature's effort to defeat an abortion rights initiative by amending the state constitution to provide that passage of an initiative requires both a statewide majority and majorities in at least five of the state's eight districts); Povich, note 473 (Arizona and Maine).

[483] Bulman-Pozen & Seifter, note 47, at 930–32.

[484] See, for example, Issacharoff *et al.*, note 14, at 16. Additional criticisms, as well as defenses, are summarized in Mandelker *et al.*, note 438, at 910–11, 922–24.

[485] See Bulman-Pozen & Seifter, note 47, at 928, and the Maine conflict over Medicaid expansion, described in text accompanying note 481.

[486] Mandelker *et al.*, note 438, at 907.

Second, there is no obvious policy reason to bar nationwide initiatives. Administratively, they would be only marginally more unwieldy than statewide elections. To be sure, Congress has never legislated them and there has never been any explicit constitutional authorization for Congress to do so. Moreover, Article I, Section 1 of the Constitution says that "[a]ll legislative Powers herein granted shall be vested in a Congress of the United States ..." The issue would be whether a nation-wide initiative is a "legislative power" that this provision precludes. Opponents of national referenda might additionally argue that the Constitution implicitly incorp-orates the Madisonian view of a "republican" form of government based solely on representative democracy. But any constitutional amendment abolishing state gov-ernment could also explicitly authorize national referenda and initiatives if the lat-ter are felt to be worth keeping.

Bulman-Pozen and Seifter identify one last example of counter-majoritarian actions by state legislatures: convening lame duck sessions to pass laws that strip the powers of incoming executive officials who were just popularly elected statewide. The authors describe two such episodes. In one, the outgoing Republican legisla-ture of North Carolina transferred much of the incoming Democratic governor's power to a committee controlled by Republicans. The state supreme court ulti-mately struck down the statute, but only on narrow separation of powers grounds, not – as the authors would have preferred – on the basis of the toll that the lame duck legislature's actions would have taken on democratic principles.[487] In the other episode, the Republican-controlled Wisconsin legislature convened a lame duck session to transfer powers from the incoming Democratic attorney general, who had similarly been elected statewide, to a Republican-controlled legislative committee. The Wisconsin Supreme Court upheld the latter power grab.[488]

---

[487] Bulman-Pozen & Seifter, note 47, at 917–19. See also Rebecca Hersher, NPR, *North Carolina Governor Signs Law Limiting Power of His Successor* (Dec. 16, 2016), www.npr.org/sections/thetwo-way/2016/12/16/505872501/north-carolina-governor-signs-law-limiting-power-of-his-successor; Trip Gabriel, The New York Times, *North Carolina G.O.P. Moves to Curb Power of New Democratic Governor* (Dec. 14, 2016), www.nytimes.com/2016/12/14/us/politics/north-carolina-governor-roy-cooper-republicans.html.

[488] Bulman-Pozen & Seifter, note 47, at 919–21.

4

Fiscal Waste

Chapters 2 and 3 described the pernicious effects of state government on our demo-cratic foundations. This chapter will demonstrate that state government is also a need-less source of additional regulation, additional taxation, and inefficient duplication of functions – in short, a waste of taxpayer money and a pointless burden on the citizenry.

Section A of this chapter distinguishes between those state expenditures that would be avoided if states were abolished and those that would simply be shifted to other levels of government. It shows that the fiscal costs of the former – chiefly, those needed to support the legislative and central executive branches of state governments and those that duplicate the work of other levels of government – are substantial.

Sections B and C go on to argue that Americans get little or nothing back in return, as the functions state governments perform, while mainly essential, could easily be reassigned to other existing levels of government. For some such functions, the optimal level might be the national government, operating either directly or through specialized regional divisions; for others, it might be local governments, acting either alone or through partnerships with other local governments or the national government. These sections demonstrate that, without states, this redistri-bution of state governments' functions is entirely feasible. Section B develops lists of general factors for deciding to which levels of government the various functions currently performed by states would best be reassigned. Section C concludes with selected illustrations of how those criteria might be applied in practice.

A SAVINGS FROM ELIMINATING STATE GOVERNMENT

How would the elimination of state government translate into taxpayer savings? Here it is important not to get too carried away, for the savings, though significant, fall short of what might initially be assumed. United States Census Bureau data[1] for

---

[1] U.S. Census Bureau, *2019 State & Local Government Finance Historical Datasets and Tables*, U.S. Summary and Alabama–Mississippi, Table 1, www.census.gov/data/datasets/2019/econ/local/public-use-datasets.html.

fiscal year 2019 is probably the most informative, because at this writing 2019 is the last fiscal year for which there is published data that excludes the unusual distortions due to COVID-19-related federal grants and state expenditures. In that year, direct expenditures by the fifty states (not including local governments' expenditures) totaled just under two trillion dollars. By far the two largest state expenditure categories that year were education (elementary, secondary, and tertiary) and public welfare (including hospital and health care costs). Nationwide, these items accounted for 27.5% and 26.8% of all direct state expenditures, respectively. The next-highest expenditures were 7.0% for public safety (police, fire, corrections, and inspections), 5.8% for environment and housing, and 5.1% for highways.[2]

Absent fundamental changes in substantive national priorities, however, one can assume that without state government, the vast bulk of those essential costs would simply be shifted to either the national government or local governments. Admittedly, therefore, most of those costs would not be saved by eliminating state government.

Rather, the savings would come from two other kinds of state expenditures. First, there are certain costs (described presently) that every state must incur just to exist and function. Second, there are the costs that flow from fifty governmental entities having to duplicate the same tasks – as each other or as the national or local governments.[3] In the other direction, of course, the abolition of states would leave local governments as the optimal units for the exercise of many of those functions. Since there are so many more local governments than there are current states, it might initially seem that to that extent the abolition of states would actually increase the duplication rather than decrease it. But when a particular reassigned task is truly duplicative, in the sense that its exercise doesn't need to vary with local conditions or preferences, the factors developed in Section B would ordinarily push it to the national government, thus avoiding duplication.

Although there are, therefore, significant expenditures that the elimination of state government can fairly be assumed to avoid, it is nearly impossible to assign them a precise dollar value or even a rough estimate. That is because, despite

---

[2] I obtained these percentages by lumping together the dollar figures for combinations of related categories and dividing the resulting figures by the total direct expenditures of $3,978,545,199. *Ibid.* As of March 2019, state governments collectively employed 5.5 million full-time or part-time workers; local governments employed 14.2 million. Elizabeth Dippold *et al.*, U.S. Census Bureau, *Annual Survey of Public Employment & Payroll Summary Report: 2019* (June 30, 2020), census.gov/content/dam/Census/library/publications/2020/econ/2019_summary.pdf.

[3] The two op-eds I have found that similarly advocate the abolition of state government both identify bureaucratic inefficiency generally, and duplication of functions in particular, as the principal costs of our federal-state system. See Lawrence R. Samuel, Washington Post, *States Are a Relic of the Past. It's Time to Get Rid of Them* (Nov. 15, 2016), www.washingtonpost.com/news/in-theory/wp/2016/11/15/states-are-a-relic-of-the-past-its-time-to-get-rid-of-them/; Daniel Greenwood, *Why the States?*, New York Newsday (Jan. 3, 1991), https://sites.hofstra.edu/daniel-greenwood/why-the-states/.

the availability of several published breakdowns of state expenditures,[4] none that I could find disaggregate the portions of those expenditures that represent either the cost of running the states (i.e., fixed costs) or the cost of fifty states duplicating the same tasks.

That said, while dollar estimates might be elusive, the fixed costs for state government just to exist – and thus the amounts wasted by retaining state government – are clearly considerable. There is, first, the cost of the state legislature itself. Members of both houses have to be paid – salary, health insurance, pension contributions, other fringe benefits, and reimbursements for food, lodging, travel, and other expenses. Each legislator has a staff; they too need salaries and fringe benefits. And so do all the employees who are needed to clean, maintain, and repair the buildings and administer the legislative process.

Then there are the costs of the brick and mortar, the landscaping, the security, the furniture, the phones, the computers, the printers, the other office supplies, and all the other necessary equipment. Add in the continuing costs of the vital utilities – the lighting, the heating, the air-conditioning, the water, the sewage, the trash collection, and so on.

That's just the legislative branch. In the executive branch, the taxpayers bear the costs of supporting the governor, the lieutenant governor, and their staffs – again, the package of salary, fringe benefits, travel, and other reimbursements. Then there are all the capital costs of the governor's office building and the governor's mansion, in addition to the ongoing maintenance costs. Further, without state government, there would be no need for fifty state attorneys general, fifty secretaries of state, fifty state auditors, fifty state treasurers, and the like – and thus no need for fifty teams of assistants and other staff members for each of these offices. Nor would we need fifty sets of physical buildings, furniture, and equipment to finance and maintain for each of these state offices.

The same can be said for at least a portion of the costs of the officials, the employees, and the buildings and supplies of each of the many specialized administrative agencies operating in each state. Some portion of these – most likely, a sizeable portion – pays for functions that would otherwise have to be shifted to some other level of government. But another portion pays for work that entails either horizontal duplication of the work done by the other forty-nine states or vertical duplication of work done by the national government or the local governments. For many of these functions, in fact, there would be affirmative benefits to having one set of rules applicable nationwide. Professional licensing, life insurance, securities fraud,

---

[4]   For example, *ibid.*; National Association of State Budget Officers (NASBO), *State Expenditure Report*, https://higherlogicdownload.s3.amazonaws.com/NASBO/9d2d2db1-c943-4f1b-b750-0fca152d64c2/ UploadedImages/SER%20Archive/2022_State_Expenditure_Report_-_S.pdf; Urban Institute, *State and Local Expenditures*, www.urban.org/policy-centers/cross-center-initiatives/state-and-local-finance-initiative/state-and-local-backgrounders/state-and-local-expenditures.

banking, and driver's licenses – and many more subject areas[5] – would be better regulated by one agency than by fifty-one.[6]

Cutting all these expenditures would open multiple options. The cuts could be used to reduce taxes (or at least reduce tax increases) or to avoid or reduce other spending cuts. At present, those state taxes are substantial. In FY 2021, they accounted for 47 percent of the states' revenue nationally.[7] In that year, with dramatic variations from state to state, the main sources of state tax revenue nationwide were personal income tax (40%) and general sales tax (29%). The remaining 31% came mainly from a combination of selective sales taxes (e.g., gasoline, liquor), license fees, corporate income tax, and mining and other so-called "severance" taxes.[8]

States' rights advocates are often, if not typically, politically conservative advocates of minimizing government regulation, taxes, and spending. Eliminating state government would serve all those goals. Instead of three levels of regulation, there would be only two – national and local. And, since a significant chunk of states' expenditures are either to maintain state government itself or duplicate the work of the other forty-nine states or other levels of government, eliminating state government would also reduce – or at least limit increases in – aggregate government spending and therefore taxes.

Rodney Hall has advocated the abolition of the six Australian states. Except for an occasional aside, his book, "Abolish the States," focuses entirely on fiscal waste.[9] He asks "Why are colossal amounts of tax money spent propping up a state system which is never called upon to justify itself?"[10] Hall refers to the "duplication of support services for running our multiplicity of parliaments, a massive overload of bureaucrats, …"[11] By way of illustration, he notes Australia has "nine Education Departments [he is counting the six states, the two territories, and the national government], nine health departments, nine departments of transport/aviation, and so forth."[12] Through

---

[5] See Section C.3.
[6] For purposes of this discussion, I do not count the costs of the state judiciary. Except for the costs of staffing, financing, and maintaining its administrative headquarters, I assume here that the cases handled by the state judges and their staffs would need to be transferred to other courts if state government were abolished. That transfer would necessitate major changes to the process for appointing national judges, as discussed in Chapter 6, Section C.
[7] Pew, *Where States Get Their Money: FY 2021* (Mar. 21, 2023), www.pewtrusts.org/en/research-and-analysis/data-visualizations/2023/where-states-get-their-money-fy-2021. Another 37% of state revenues came from federal grants. The remaining 16% came from what Pew describes as service fees, "miscellaneous," and local funds. But in that fiscal year, as in fiscal year 2020, those percentages reflect the unusually high amount of federal aid in connection with the COVID-19 pandemic.
[8] Pew, *How States Raise Their Tax Dollars: FY 2021* (Apr. 28, 2023), www.pewtrusts.org/en/research-and-analysis/data-visualizations/2022/how-states-raise-their-tax-dollars-fy2021.
[9] Rodney Hall, Abolish the States – Australia's Future and a $30 Billion Answer to Our Tax Problems (1998).
[10] *Ibid.* at 5.
[11] *Ibid.* at 18.
[12] *Ibid.* at 24.

a series of elaborate calculations, Hall estimates that abolishing the Australian states would save approximately 30 billion Australian dollars per year, or $1,500 per year per resident.[13] Finally, he points out that when citizens move from one state to another, there are not only the bureaucratic costs to the state governments in changing driver's licenses, car registrations, and other documents, but also costs to the time of the citizen in all those areas, in addition to the need to cope with different laws, health care systems, and so on.[14] All those statements (except the specific dollar amounts) could equally be made about the current federal system of the United States.

Of course, merely noting that the functions states currently serve *could* be performed instead by either the national or the local governments doesn't mean that those functions *should* be so transferred. Chapters 2 and 3 of this book have demonstrated the harmful effects of state government on our democracy, and this chapter has now identified the main fiscal costs of maintaining fifty state governments. But it remains to be shown that abolishing state government and redistributing its functions between the national and local governments would be a net improvement. That showing turns on whether state governments provide affirmative benefits that outweigh their democratic and fiscal costs. Among other things, that inquiry raises the question of whether state governments are any *better* suited to perform their current functions than either the national or the local governments would be. That comparative question is reserved for Chapter 5, which concludes that the answer is no.

B REASSIGNING STATE FUNCTIONS: GENERAL FACTORS

This section considers a "who should govern?" issue: If states were abolished, which levels of government – national or local – would be better suited to take over responsibility for the various functions the states currently perform and the decisions they currently make?

There is an antecedent question: Who should decide who decides? That is, who should decide the reassignment of the current state functions? Congress? The state legislatures during the transition period between ratification of the required constitutional amendments and their effective dates? An independent commission? That antecedent question has two parts: First, who should decide how to reallocate the current state powers between the national government and the local governments? Second, who should decide how the latter functions are then parceled out among the jumble of local governments – municipalities, counties, townships, and special purpose districts – in addition to unincorporated areas? Possible approaches to these antecedent issues are deferred to Chapter 6.[15]

---

[13]   *Ibid.* at 24, 97–109.
[14]   *Ibid.* at 27.
[15]   See Chapter 6, Section A.

But if the resulting redistribution is to be both principled and coherent, then whoever is charged with that task will first need to identify the factors that the sorting of the various governmental functions depends on. What characteristics make a given subject area a good fit for national decision-making, and what makes it a good fit for local decision-making? My own thoughts on these questions are the subject of this section.

I start with a basic premise as to what should *not* drive the criteria: expected policy outcomes. I appreciate that this is a vain hope. Human nature will have to be remade before politicians of any partisan and ideological stripes set aside all calculations as to whether the policies they favor are more likely to emerge from assigning responsibility to the national government or the local governments. Who decides often determines what is decided. But it is imperative to try, if for no other reason than that predictions about long-term political winds are generally fraught.

Perhaps nothing illustrates the importance of that premise more than conservatives' historic reliance on the mantra of "states' rights." As noted in the Introduction, too often the argument that a given set of policy decisions should be left to the states has been driven by expectations that the states were more likely than the national government to produce desired outcomes. And too often those desired outcomes have been the perverse substitution of states' rights for individual rights.

Examples abound. Slavery was the claimed "right" that the confederate states asserted as a justification for secession. *New York Times* columnist Jamelle Bouie elaborates:

> To suppress antislavery agitation and secure the peculiar institution within their borders, slave state legislatures trampled over every right mentioned in the Bill of Rights. They banned the circulation of antislavery materials, banned public speech against slavery, banned religious gatherings among free and enslaved Blacks, allowed the arbitrary search and seizure of any Black person found outside the dominion of a master, and mandated cruel and unusual punishments for Black people who broke these and other laws.[16]

Edward Rubin and Malcolm Feeley offer several additional examples:

> During the Kennedy–Johnson era and the heyday of the Warren Court, states' rights became a rallying cry of those who opposed desegregation, social welfare, and controls on law enforcement agents. During the years of the Reagan and Bush

---

[16] Jamelle Bouie, *The Real Threat to Freedom Is Coming from the States* (May 26, 2023), www .nytimes.com/2023/05/26/opinion/freedom-states-rights.html?campaign_id=39&emc=edit_ ty_20230526&instance_id=93535&nl=opinion-today&regi_id=13788254&segment_id=133976& te=1&user_id=e16deb82e8516f294a4077a86c02f5c2. See also Jessica Bulman-Pozen & Miriam Seifter, *The Democracy Principle in State Constitutions*, 119 Mich. L. Rev. 859, 861 (2021) ("State majorities' invocations of sovereignty, in particular, are indelibly connected to slavery and persisting racial injustice.").

administrations and the Rehnquist Court, proponents of abortion, gay rights, and abolition of the death penalty became enamored of federalism for equivalent reasons.[17]

The pretextual nature of conservatives' reliance on states' rights arguments is exposed by the ease with which they will jettison that ostensibly central belief when doing so serves the strategic purpose of promoting almost any other conservative cause. The Supreme Court decision in *Bush* v. *Gore*[18] was one of the early clues. To install a Republican president, a majority consisting of five conservative "states' rights" Justices had to navigate around not just one, but two fundamental conservative orthodoxies: deference to state courts' interpretations of state laws and narrow interpretations of the equal protection clause.[19]

In *Altria Group, Inc.* v. *Good*,[20] a cigarette manufacturer was sued, under a Maine law prohibiting false advertising, for fraudulently representing its product as relatively safe. The company, represented by leading conservative lawyer Ted Olsen, argued strenuously that the Maine law was preempted by a federal law on cigarette advertising. In a 5-4 decision, the Supreme Court rejected that claim. But the four dissenters (Chief Justice Roberts and Justices Scalia, Thomas, and Alito – all card-carrying states' rights conservatives like Mr. Olsen) voted in favor of the tobacco company. To do so, they had to set aside their passion for states' rights and argue that Maine had impermissibly invaded federally preempted turf.

During the Trump presidency, conservatives suddenly acquired a taste for broad federal legislation to supersede state legislation, at least when that state legislation was progressive. President Trump's EPA Administrator, Scott Pruitt, objected to California's tough emissions standards. How best to balance environmental protection against compliance costs was a job for the federal government, he insisted.[21]

Antiabortion advocates spent decades protesting indignantly against *Roe* v. *Wade*.[22] They argued that abortion policy was properly a matter for the states, not the federal courts. Until the Court in *Dobbs*[23] overruled *Roe* v. *Wade*, that is. The ink on the *Dobbs* opinion was barely dry before hordes of antiabortion advocates did a sharp, collective 180, advocating federal legislation to prevent or restrict states from protecting abortion rights. Republican and staunch antiabortion Senator James Lankford of Oklahoma said that "a group of Republican senators has discussed at multiple meetings the possibility of [Congress] banning abortion at around six

---

[17] Edward L. Rubin & Malcolm Feeley, *Federalism: Some Notes on a National Neurosis*, 41 UCLA L. Rev. 903, 935 (1994).
[18] 531 U.S. 98 (2000).
[19] See the discussion of this case in Chapter 2, Section D.
[20] 555 U.S. 70 (2008).
[21] Donald F. Kettl, The Divided States of America: Why Federalism Doesn't Work 149 (2020).
[22] 410 U.S. 113 (1973).
[23] *Dobbs* v. *Jackson Women's Health Organization*, 142 S.Ct. 2228 (2022).

weeks."[24] The president of one leading antiabortion group reports that most of the ten potential Republican 2024 presidential contenders would not only support a national ban on abortions, but make that support a centerpiece of their campaigns.[25]

If cynical use of the states' rights banner and other result-oriented strategies are inappropriate guidelines for redistributing the current state functions between the national and local governments, what should the criteria be?

A few preliminary explanations might be useful:

First, the factors suggested below are just that – factors, not requirements or prohibitions. They would need to be weighed and balanced, and some might be found to command greater weight than others. Naturally, too, they will sometimes point in opposite directions. Moreover, even the application of a single individual factor can require personal judgment. Three of the factors favoring national authority, for example, involve fundamental rights, basic economic needs, and substantial national impact, respectively. Disputes can arise over whether a right is fundamental, an economic interest basic, or the national impact substantial. For both reasons, these calculations are malleable. And that means they are vulnerable to cynical political manipulation.

I concede this. In my defense, I don't see how the problem can be avoided. For the foregoing reasons, it seems impossible to formulate a hard-and-fast rule that would produce dispositive results in all possible subject areas. At least I have been unable to come up with one. But having a list of factors to consider can generate useful insights and at any rate can't be worse than having no guidance at all. In addition, it is precisely when a principle requires either the application of broad guidance to wide-ranging fact situations or the balancing of competing values that the resulting judgment call should be made by the people's elected representatives. Yes, some of those decisions will invariably fall prey to poor judgment or even bad faith, but that is what it means – and that is the price we pay – to live in a democracy.

For some subjects, the optimal arrangement might involve lodging concurrent policymaking authority in the national government and the local governments. Analogous systems of concurrent national and state government policymaking

---

[24] Caroline Kitchener, Washington Post, *The Next Frontier for the Antiabortion Movement: A Nationwide Ban* (May 2, 2022), www.washingtonpost.com/nation/2022/05/02/abortion-ban-roe-supreme-court-mississippi/.

[25] *Ibid.* See generally Jerusalem Demsas, *The Fate of States' Rights after Roe*, The Atlantic Daily (July 18, 2022), www.theatlantic.com/newsletters/archive/2022/07/republicans-expose-their-hypocrisy-on-abortion/670562/ (highlighting the hypocrisy of anti-abortion advocates who attacked *Roe v. Wade* on federalism grounds only to call for federal abortion legislation once *Roe* was overturned). Former President Trump's most recent position is that each state should decide its own abortion policy. Cecelia Smith-Schoenwalder, U.S. News, *Quotes: Comparing Trump's Stance on Abortion Over Time* (Apr. 8, 2024), www.usnews.com/news/national-news/articles/quotes-comparing-trumps-stance-on-abortion-over-time.

authority are in common use today.[26] In the event the policies conflict, the supremacy clause gives precedence to national law.

Moreover, within a given subject area, the broad policymaking function and the implementation function can be divided between two entities, as they frequently are today. There are many areas, some of them included as examples in Section C.3, that combine national policymaking with local administration.

Here I must acknowledge the obvious risks of vesting additional power in local governments. Nestor Davidson sums it up well: "For every instrumental argument in favor of bolstering local autonomy, there is a counterargument. Local governments often give life to the Madisonian fear of the tyranny of local majorities: they sometimes reinforce racial, ethnic, and economic segregation; exclude outsiders; and generate significant externalities for neighboring communities."[27]

That risk can never be fully eliminated, but there are ways to temper it. One way is to make sure that concern is adequately reflected in the factors that determine which levels of government should be responsible for which subject areas. One of the factors that I propose below as favoring national responsibility over a given subject area is that the subject area is likely to implicate fundamental rights. Another is that the area is one in which local control would create too high a probability of local governments adopting policies that shift the costs to other local governments or to the nation as a whole.

A second safeguard is that reassigning a current state function to local governments doesn't mean they have to go it alone. When collaboration is beneficial, they can form partnerships with other local governments or with the national government. They might not want to do so even when collaboration makes eminent sense, for example for reasons that relate to local self-interest or ideological differences. In those cases, Davidson suggests that Congress mandate or at least encourage such partnerships, as it has often done.[28]

Conversely, reassigning a function to the national government doesn't necessarily mean creating one monstrous, monolithic, unwieldy bureaucracy physically distant from the scattered local communities that it serves. In many subject areas, the national government can operate through geographic regions. That is precisely what it commonly does today. At any rate, modern transportation makes travel easier, and digital innovation often makes it avoidable entirely.[29]

---

[26] Federal and state governments operate their own criminal justice systems, for example. Both levels of government also enact environmental protection laws, consumer safety laws, firearms laws, and the like.

[27] Nestor M. Davidson, *Cooperative Localism: Federal-Local Collaboration in an Era of State Sovereignty*, 93 Virginia L. Rev. 959, 962 (2007).

[28] *Ibid.* at 962, 1026–29. See also the discussion of regional collaboration in Section C.2.

[29] The U.S. Environmental Protection Agency (EPA), for example, operates through its ten regional offices. EPA, *Regional and Geographic Offices*, www.epa.gov/aboutepa/regional-and-geographic-offices. The U.S. Consumer Financial Protection Bureau (CFPB) has four regions. CFPB, *Regional Directors*, www.consumerfinance.gov/about-us/blog/meet-our-regional-directors/. The National Labor Relations Board (NLRB) has twenty-six regions. NLRB, *Regional Offices*, www.nlrb.gov/about-nlrb/

Here, first, is my suggested list of six factors that, when present in a given subject area, favor national responsibility (illustrations to follow in Section C.3):

N1. The subject area is one in which fundamental rights or interests are at stake. As to this factor, the scholarly literature has approached, but not quite attained, universal consensus.[30] In my view, examples of interests fundamental enough to trigger this factor include voting; nondiscrimination based on race, ethnicity, religion, sex, sexual orientation, age, and other evolving lines of division; equal access to justice; fair procedure; and access to basic human needs, to name a few.

N2. National action is needed to address serious geographic economic inequality. Many communities are too poor to meet such basic human needs as food, health care, housing, and education. The importance of national regulation to address economic inequality has been well covered by others.[31]

N3. Either nationwide uniformity in and of itself is distinctively important in this subject area, or there is simply no affirmative reason that the policies in this subject area should vary by geographic location. Uniformity might have special importance, for example, when the subject is one on which it is especially vital that the nation speak to the world with a single voice. There are also subjects for which differing regulations would make interstate travel or transactions difficult or impossible to navigate, particularly for companies that do business in many areas of the country.[32] Convenience and efficiency aside, uniformity serves the goal of equal treatment.

N4. Local governments might achieve or at least perceive benefit from a given policy, but only by externalizing significant costs – that is, by shifting them either to neighboring populations or to the entire nation.[33] Local action that affects a wider region or even the entire country is increasingly common today, as people, products, pollutants, effluents, viruses, and other matter now travel easily across subnational boundaries. Some kinds of external costs – for example, lowering corporate tax rates or relaxing public safety restrictions – can take the form of a race to the bottom,[34] where the self-interested actions

---

who-we-are/regional-offices. As for the travel issue, see the text accompanying Chapter 1, notes 61–62 (describing the Antifederalists' concern that a single large republic would make the necessary travel infeasible, and the responses to their concerns).

[30] See Barry Friedman, *Valuing Federalism*, 82 Minn. L. Rev. 317, 409–10 (1997). As Friedman points out, some writers worry about entrusting civil rights enforcement to conservative national governments. *Ibid.* at 410 n.386.

[31] See the discussion in Chapter 5, text accompanying notes 38–40.

[32] Robert M. Ackerman, *Tort Law and Federalism: Whatever Happened to Devolution?* 14 Yale J. on Regulation. 429, 448, 451 (1996).

[33] See Friedman, note 30, at 406–407.

[34] Friedman identifies race to the bottom as a separate factor favoring federal action over state action, see *ibid.* at 408, but I subsume it here because, analytically, it is merely one specific type of external cost that the subpart is shifting to the whole.

of a single local government leave its competitive neighbors with little choice but to follow suit. No local government should be permitted to impose its will on other local governments or on the nation as a whole.

N5. The nation as a whole would benefit from government providing certain goods or services, but individual local governments (or even a group of local governments) ordinarily can't afford the cost.[35]

N6. Assigning the task to multiple local governments would duplicate resources or generate other inefficiencies.

Now, here are factors that favor assignment of particular subject areas to local authority:

L1. The subject is one in which concentrating the entire power in a single national government would be too dangerous.

L2. There is a particularly strong reason to vary the policies to reflect the distinctive needs or political preferences of the local populations. This factor is the flip side of a need for uniformity.[36]

L3. For this subject, knowledge of local conditions is imperative.

L4. Local governments have already amassed a great deal of experience in this area and might even have the necessary administrative structures already in place.[37]

L5. This subject presents a special need for social innovation or experimentation by multiple authorities.

C REASSIGNING STATE FUNCTIONS: SELECTED ILLUSTRATIONS

1 *What States Do*

As noted earlier, the states – unlike the federal government – have plenary power over any subject matter that the Constitution does not affirmatively delegate, explicitly or implicitly, to the federal government.[38] They also have whatever additional

---

[35] *Ibid.* at 406–407.

[36] The tension between these two competing visions – uniformity versus tailoring – is not new; it was a topic of considerable debate among the founding fathers. See especially Federalist 44 and Antifederalist 11, 17, 35, and 37.

[37] One author sums it up well: "Local governments in most ways mirror the structure of the national and state governments. They have charters, mayors, unicameral city councils, courts, and agency-like commissions. Separation of powers sometimes applies there too ..." Jeffrey S. Sutton, Who Decides? States as Laboratories of Constitutional Experimentation 308 (2022).

[38] That principle should be distinguished from the principle that, within a state, the powers of the legislature are (typically) plenary, that is, not confined to a list of powers affirmatively enumerated in the state constitution. The former is a federalism principle, the latter a matter of intrastate separation of powers. As to the latter, see generally Daniel R. Mandelker *et al.*, State and Local Government in a Federal System 28–37 (9th ed. 2021) and sources cited therein.

powers the federal government willingly entrusts to them or shares with them. Any of these state powers might in turn be delegated to local governments or shared with them.

Below I have compiled a long, albeit incomplete, list of functions that the states currently perform. To make the list manageable, I have sorted these functions into rough groups. Several of the functions would easily fit into two of more of these groups, but to avoid repetition I have listed each only once. The groups are not listed in order of importance.

Many of the state functions relate to public safety and public health. These include access to medical care; pandemic measures; disaster relief; police, fire, and ambulance services; traffic control; gun safety; environmental protection; vehicle inspections; child protection; consumer product safety; workplace safety; and tort law. Some functions are meant to provide a social safety net – for example, means tested public assistance, unemployment insurance, and worker's compensation.

States make major policy decisions relating to public elementary, secondary, and tertiary education. All three branches of state governments make important human rights decisions, particularly with respect to nondiscrimination and reproductive freedom. They are also the prime policymakers in matters of marriage, divorce, child custody, and other family law issues.

States perform several political functions: they set voter qualifications; decide the times, places, and manner of both state and congressional elections; choose presidential electors; administer elections; send representatives to the US Congress; and ratify US constitutional amendments. They also operate justice systems – civil litigation, including juvenile justice and the probate process, and criminal justice, including law enforcement, prosecution, probation offices, public defender systems, courts, and corrections.

The states have primary responsibility for land use and housing policies. These functions include city and town planning, zoning, eminent domain, conservation of natural resources, historic preservation, parks, housing codes, landlord–tenant law, and mining restrictions. They spend much of their time on infrastructure issues: transportation, including roads and bridges, trucking regulations, mass transit, bicycle trails, railways, waterways, and airports; public utility management and regulation, including telecommunications, energy, water, sewage, and other refuse; and acquisition and maintenance of state office buildings.

Another major state function is licensing – driver's licenses and motor vehicle registrations; occupational licenses; and hunting and fishing licenses. States are immersed in business regulation, including contract law, bankruptcy, usury, predatory lending, consumer fraud protection, corporate and securities regulation, labor law, agriculture, banking and insurance regulation, and promotion of tourism and economic development. They record vital statistics relating to births, marriages, and deaths, as well as real property transactions.

2 *What Local Governments Do*

As earlier discussion explained,[39] local governments for the most part have only whatever powers either their state constitutions or state legislatures affirmatively give them. Local governments are also quite diverse. Among other things, they vary by population, geographic area, legal status, and internal organization. Most importantly here, they also have different functions.[40] The various local governments are typically classified as either general purpose governments, which as their name implies provide a general range of services, or special purpose entities, which are created to perform (typically) just one specific function.

The general local governments include municipalities, which are incorporated, and counties, which are not.[41] In twenty states, counties also contain unincorporated "townships."[42] Municipalities commonly provide such services as "[roads], police and fire protection, parking, libraries, housing and urban redevelopment, and sewerage and sanitation."[43] Counties' functions overlap with some of the services provided by municipalities, but the main job of counties is to administer statewide programs. Common examples include "property tax assessment and collection, deed recording, law enforcement, jails, courts, highways, public works, welfare and social services, health care and Medicaid, and agricultural and economic development. Urban counties often provide additional services, such as mass transit, parks and recreation, airports, planning, zoning, and regional governance."[44] Townships' powers vary a great deal, sometimes approaching those of municipalities; in many cases, their principal function is to provide and maintain roads in the unincorporated areas that they cover.[45]

The various special purpose districts span a wide range. School districts are probably the most familiar, since education accounts for about one-third of all local government expenditures nationwide. Other special purpose districts are charged with "[f]ire protection, water supply, soil conservation, housing and urban renewal, and drainage." Some are the creations of municipalities; others are independent political subdivisions.[46]

The total number of local government units has been increasing steadily since at least the early 1970s. By 2017, they numbered more than 90,000. These included

---

[39] See Chapter 3, Section F.
[40] Advisory Commission on Intergovernmental Relations [ACIR], *Report*, State and Local Roles in the Federal System 227 (1982), excerpted in Mandelker *et al.*, note 38, at 37.
[41] ACIR Report, note 40, at 240, excerpted in Mandelker *et al.*, note 38, at 38.
[42] Mandelker *et al.*, note 38, at 40–41.
[43] *Ibid.* at 38. To that list, Judge Sutton would add zoning, eminent domain, and taxing. Sutton, note 37, at 304.
[44] Mandelker *et al.*, note 38, at 39.
[45] *Ibid.* at 41.
[46] *Ibid.* at 41–42, 76–85.

approximately 39,000 general local governments (of which roughly 20,000 were municipalities) and 51,000 special purpose districts.[47] Almost every state has counties or their equivalent.[48]

For several reasons, local governments have been increasingly inclined to partner with one another. Urban sprawl, combined with huge migrations from urban centers to suburbs, have made the resulting metropolitan areas the main locus of economic activity. Further, those large, expanding metropolitan areas typically comprise many municipalities with racially and economically diverse populations and uneven qualities of public services. Regional partnerships serve multiple goals – economies of scale, environmental protection, and social and economic justice.[49]

These regional partnerships take many forms. They range from formal mergers to informal cooperation, and the functions they combine or share can range from general governance to administration of specific programs.[50] There are jointly run transit systems, special purpose utility districts, and other common arrangements.[51]

For present purposes, the point is that without state-imposed constraints the local governments would be free to collaborate, and free to choose the precise form of collaboration, that they believe to be in the best interests of their combined populations. Moreover, many metro areas cross current state lines. Examples include Kansas City, Missouri and Kansas City, Kansas; Portland, Oregon and Vancouver, Washington; and St. Louis, Missouri, and East St. Louis, Illinois. For these kinds of twin city metro areas the abolition of state government has an additional benefit – eliminating any pointless barriers that the laws of either of the two states might currently pose.

3 *Specific Applications of the Reassignment Criteria*

As noted in Section B, the process of applying my suggested reassignment factors to the functions currently performed by states is not cut and dried. Most of the factors, when applied to many of the functions, are defined broadly enough to require judgment calls. In addition, for some functions, multiple factors will apply and will push in opposite directions. But in the selected examples below I have done my best, fully accepting that many will disagree with my bottom line results.

My other prefatory note is one of humility. I claim no specialized expertise in any of the subject areas that I have selected as examples. The armies of experts in each of these areas will no doubt find my summaries simplistic. I plead guilty. My

---

[47] Ann O'M. Bowman *et al.*, State and Local Government 274–76 (11th ed. 2022), citing U.S. Census Bureau, 2017 Census of Governments, Table 2; Mandelker *et al.*, note 38, at 42, 78.

[48] Connecticut and Rhode Island appear to be the only exceptions. Louisiana has "parishes" and Alaska has "boroughs." Bowman *et al.*, note 47, at 276.

[49] Mandelker *et al.*, note 38, at 171–77.

[50] See *ibid.* at 178–97.

[51] *Ibid.* at 172.

objective in offering them is merely to illustrate the meanings of the general factors from Section B and how they might favor the reassignment of a particular (current) state function to the national government or the local governments – *not* to weigh in dogmatically on the bottom line conclusions. For the latter, I defer to those who actually know what they're talking about.

For ease of reference, the general factors favoring either national or local responsibility are repeated here in abbreviated form:

Factors favoring national authority:

N1. Fundamental rights or interests are at stake.

N2. National action is needed to address serious geographic economic inequality.

N3. Either nationwide uniformity in and of itself is distinctively important in this subject area, or there is simply no affirmative reason that the policies in this subject area should vary by geographic location.

N4. Local governments might achieve or at least perceive benefit from a given policy, but the policy would have a significant impact on neighboring populations or the entire nation.

N5. The nation as a whole would benefit from government providing certain goods or services, but individual local governments (or even a group of local governments) ordinarily can't afford the cost.

N6. Local regulation would duplicate resources or generate other inefficiencies.

Factors favoring local authority:

L1. In the particular subject area, concentrating power in a single national government would pose special dangers.

L2. In this area, there is an especially strong reason to vary the policies to reflect the differing needs or political preferences of the local populations.

L3. Knowledge of local conditions is imperative.

L4. Local governments have already amassed a great deal of experience in this subject and might even have the administrative structures already in place.

L5. This subject presents a special need for social experimentation or innovation.

Now, some illustrations:

(i) Public health and safety: This broad grouping has several component parts. For the traditional police, firefighting, and ambulance services, the most salient factors all seem to point toward local control. Every community has different needs and preferences (L2), particularly with respect to the crime rates, the proper role of the police, and community relations. Knowledge of local conditions is essential (L3). The local governments have experience in all these areas and even, typically, have the necessary administrative structures already in place (L4). And with so much current controversy surrounding the subject of police, there is exceptional need for the kind of social experimentation and innovation that multiple policymakers can bring to the table (L5). By way of exception, national law enforcement agencies such as the FBI, the DEA, and BATF remain necessary for large-scale law enforcement operations that exceed either the reach or the resource capabilities of local governments (N5).

Consumer product safety is different. In this area, national regulation is critical. For one thing, uniformity assumes great importance (N3), because multiple conflicting standards would pose difficulties for manufacturers who produce items for nationwide sale. In addition, because products travel easily throughout the country and the world, the lax standards of one local government could cause harm to residents of another (N4).

For the same reasons, and more controversially, gun safety standards cry out for national regulation. Whatever one's view on the two most contentious issues – background checks and assault weapons – leaving those decisions to local governments would create the same problems that state regulation creates today. If one local government allows possession of assault weapons and its neighboring municipality does not, nothing prevents someone in the first locale from buying an assault weapon there and traveling to the second locale to commit a mass murder (N4). Conversely, someone who lives in a local area where assault weapons cannot be sold could easily drive to a nearby area where they are legally available and then return home to commit a violent crime. Rural local governments might counterargue that the popularity of hunting by their residents should allow them, not the national government, to decide how best to regulate guns (L2). But assault weapons are not used for hunting, and at any rate the popularity of local hunting is no reason to skimp on background checks.

Prevention of, and responses to, calamitous events that endanger entire communities typically demand the combined efforts of national and local authorities. Local governments, even in partnership with other local governments, lack the resources to singlehandedly respond to natural disasters, pandemics, foreign invasion, or terrorism (N5). But in all these areas they are essential partners to the national government. Their officials know their own local areas far better than national officials do (L3), and they have the preexisting experience and administrative structures to deal with several of those problems (L4).

For similar reasons, the national government is the optimal governmental unit for medical research to fight common fatal diseases, both directly and through grants to private sector researchers. Local governments lack the resources for that job (N5). Even if they had the resources, efficiency would not be served by 90,000 local governments all duplicating the same task (N6).

(ii) Public assistance: Some of the current welfare programs are currently funded by the federal government, some by state governments, and some by a combination of the two.[52] Some are administered by the federal government, some by the

---

[52] Urban Institute, Public Welfare Expenditures, www.urban.org/policy-centers/cross-center-initiatives/
state-and-local-finance-initiative/state-and-local-backgrounders/public-welfare-expenditures#:~:text=

states, and a few by local governments.[53] Because they are meant to cover such basic human needs as food, shelter, health care, and general or specific cash assistance (N1),[54] and because the nation's local communities are separated by such vast differences in wealth, national funding of these programs is the only realistic way to address the extreme inequalities (N2 and N5).[55] Administration, in contrast, calls for different attributes. The experiences of local governments in a range of face-to-face interactions with individuals equip them well to administer many of the various public assistance programs (L4).

One countervailing factor is that public assistance is a perennial hot-button issue. Demagoguery is never far away. And when issues are controversial, diffusing government power arguably takes on its greatest importance (L1). Separation of powers at the national level provides some diffusion, however, and the social imperative of addressing profound economic inequality is, for me, the decisive factor. It is an imperative that only the national government is realistically positioned to confront.

(iii) Justice: In the United States today, more than 90 percent of all court cases – civil and criminal – are handled by state courts.[56] The abolition of state government would thus require a major decision: Where should the current state court caseload be relocated?

In an American republic shorn of its states, all laws would be passed by either the national government or the local governments. My general view is that, in municipalities that choose to operate their own courts, those courts should continue to have jurisdiction over one narrow slice of cases – civil cases that arise under the ordinances of those municipalities. All other civil cases, and all criminal cases, should be heard in the national courts.

This massive transformation of the country's judiciary will require a number of decisions as to the method of selecting judges, the length of their appointments, court procedures, and the funding of these additional national courts. Those issues are deferred to Chapter 6, Section C, as part of the structure of the new American republic proposed here. For now, it is enough to consider which set of courts would be best suited for which categories of cases.

Since laws that affect the nation as a whole would generally be the province of the national government (N4), the kinds of civil cases left for the municipal courts under the proposed scheme would implicate only local affairs. For that reason, these cases will frequently require knowledge of local conditions and local laws (L3).

State%20agencies%2C%20rather%20than%20local,local%20governments%20administer%20these%20programs.

[53] *Ibid.*

[54] *Ibid.*

[55] See Kettl, note 21, especially at 131–42; Jamila Michener, *Fragmented Democracy: Medicaid, Federalism, and Unequal Politics* 13–14 (2018).

[56] Center for American Progress, *State or Federal Court?* (Aug. 8, 2016), www.americanprogress.org/article/fact-sheet-state-or-federal-court/.

Criminal cases present other issues. First, the seriousness of a criminal conviction means that fundamental individual interests are especially likely to be at stake (N1). That fact elevates the importance of procedural fairness. And procedural fairness is not the strong suit of the existing criminal municipal courts. One writer has described them as "kangaroo courts."[57] The leading article on those courts offers several key observations:

> Nationwide, there are over 7,500 such courts in thirty states. Collectively they process over three and a half million criminal cases every year and collect at least two billion dollars in fines and fees. Created, funded, and controlled by local municipalities, these courts – sometimes referred to as "summary" or "justice" or "police" courts – are central to cities' ability to police, to maintain public safety, and to raise revenue. At the same time, they often exhibit many of the dysfunctions for which lower courts have been generally criticized: cavalier speed, legal sloppiness, punitive harshness, and disrespectful treatment of defendants. Unlike their state counterparts, however, the U.S. Supreme Court has formally excused municipal courts from some basic legal constraints: judges need not be attorneys and may simultaneously serve as city mayors, while proceedings are often summary and not of record. ...
>
> As the 2015 U.S. Department of Justice (DOJ) investigation of Ferguson revealed, the revenue from municipal courts may supply a substantial percentage of a municipality's budget and thus incentivize systemic overcriminalization.[58]

Procedural fairness aside, the fundamental interests at stake also suggest uniform national policies (N1). Nor is there any particular reason that either the decision to criminalize particular behavior or the severity of the punishment should hinge on where the person lives (N3).

One countervailing factor is that decisions as to what behavior to criminalize, as well as decisions as to the appropriate punishments (particularly capital punishment), are highly controversial. As with welfare reform, demagoguery on this subject is commonplace and thus there is danger in concentrating excessive power in one place (L1). But separation of powers at the national level again provides some diffusion, and in the absence of states the only alternative – 90,000 sets of local criminal law codes – seems untenable.

Within the sphere of criminal justice, therefore, I would allocate the bulk of the legislative and judicial functions to the national government. The other components of the criminal justice system are a different matter. These include policing, prosecution, probation offices, public defender systems, and corrections. As already discussed under the heading of "public health and safety" above, these functions should remain the job of the local authorities.

---

[57] Shawn Ossei-Owusu, *Kangaroo Courts*, 134 Harv. L. Rev. Forum 200 (2021).
[58] Alexandra Natapoff, *Criminal Municipal Courts*, 134 Harv. L. Rev. 964, 965, 969 (2021).

Chapter 3, Section F earlier highlighted the increased zeal with which state legislatures have begun to preempt local government policymaking in a wide range of subjects that have traditionally been the subject of municipal governance. As that discussion showed, the pattern has been highly asymmetrical – in the vast majority of cases, it has been Republican legislatures narrowing the authority of Democratic-run cities. In an age of renewed public attention to police violence and its racial implications, many local governments have revamped their law enforcement policies and reordered their police and prosecutorial priorities. State legislatures have often responded by preempting such local decisions. Not surprisingly, a good deal of modern scholarship has been devoted to advocating a greater role for the local governments on such matters as police staffing, prosecutorial discretion, and other elements of the law enforcement process.[59] Those writings emphasize various goals: reducing racial disparities, accommodating differences in local fiscal capacities, and democratizing the administration of criminal justice.

(iv) Education: This subject ticks almost all the factor boxes, and the collaboration of national and local governments is crucial. For public elementary and secondary education, the national government should set certain uniform minimum curricular requirements. First, education in modern day America and throughout the world rises to the level of a fundamental individual interest (N1). Moreover, in our increasingly homogeneous and highly mobile society, employers should not need to wonder whether job applicants have missed out on a well-rounded education that included all the basics of a common knowledge base (N3). At the same time, local governments should be encouraged to enrich the basic curriculum in ways they believe to be beneficial, particularly if the needs and conditions of the local area suggest either extra priority on specific elements of the basic package or additions of locale-specific subject matter. Pupils who remain in the geographic area will benefit from the enhancement (L2), and the local educators will know more than their national counterparts about local conditions (L3). The professional educators in the local governments should have broad discretion over teaching methods; among other things, education is an area in which the benefits of experimentation and innovation (L5) are valuable and new insights are constantly evolving.

Standards for teacher training and licensing should be uniform nationwide. When talented, well-educated teachers are shut out from teaching jobs because they were educated in a different geographic region, everyone suffers – the teachers themselves and the pupils and school districts that are deprived of their service. There is simply no reason that a school should be barred from hiring a teacher

---

[59] For example, William J. Stuntz, The Collapse of American Criminal Justice (2013); Joshua Kleinfeld, *Manifesto of Democratic Criminal Justice*, 111 Northwest. Univ. L. Rev. 1367 (2017); Rick Su, Marissa Roy & Nestor Davidson, *Preemption of Police Reform: A Roadblock to Racial Justice*, 94 Temp. L. Rev. 663 (2022); Anthony O'Rourke, Rick Su & Guyora Binder, *Disbanding Police Agencies*, 121 Colum. L. Rev. 1327 (2021).

because the teacher received his or her education in a different geographic area (N3). Nor is there any good reason to introduce the inefficiency of teachers having to duplicate the training they have already received in order to obtain the required certification (N6).

National funding of education would need to be increased to reflect the loss of state funding. Ideally, it should be further increased to help equalize educational opportunity. Local governments would continue to pay much of the costs for their schools, but the fundamental interest in education (N1), the inequalities attributable to geographically unequal economic conditions (N2), and the practical inability of the more cash-starved communities to provide the education (N5) their students deserve are all reasons for a generous national role in shoring up the schools in economically depressed areas.

The former state institutions of higher education (colleges, universities, and technical and vocational schools) should become national institutions. There would no longer be a need for out-of-state students to subsidize the tuitions of instate students, because state lines would no longer have legal or political significance. The national government would establish maximum tuition rates for all such institutions; those rates could take account of the extra educational costs in particular disciplines (e.g., medical education and science labs) and geographic differences in the cost of living. And, of course, the maximum rates could be updated over time to reflect inflation. But they would not depend on the location of the student's hometown. Uniform maximum tuition rates would mean that students who are admitted to their preferred institutions could choose the institutions that are best for them (N3). By way of exception, every institution of higher learning would have the discretion to reduce their tuition rates below the national maximum, as well as the discretion to offer scholarships. Review of the current programs for government-provided financial aid might well be beneficial but is beyond the scope of this discussion.

(v) Land use, city and town planning, and infrastructure: This heading covers a broad variety of interrelated government functions, in all of which the states currently play significant roles. Traditional land use and planning services include zoning, eminent domain, housing codes, building and occupancy permits, urban development, local parks, and libraries. Perhaps recording of real property transactions could be considered under this heading as well. All of those services are mainly in the hands of local governments today, and there is no reason that the abolition of states would need to change that. These decisions have to reflect local conditions and the needs of the local population (L2). Local governments will also have far greater knowledge of those needs than the national government will (N3), and they will have had both the experience in meeting those needs and existing administrative structures already in place (L4). Current state parks and forests, as well as any future large parks and forests that serve wider areas, would be more properly regulated and managed by the national government. The fate of those natural areas affects wider populations and geographic areas (N4), and the costs of conserving and maintaining them would ordinarily exceed the resources of local governments (N5).

Infrastructure raises some different issues. Local governments, operating under state law, currently make decisions on projects such as local roads, local bridges, and local transportation, including mass transit (often with federal subsidies) and local bicycle trails. Without states, they should continue to do so. As with most other city and town planning decisions, there is good reason to tailor those policies to local needs and preferences (L2), local officials will have the most knowledge of those needs and preferences (L3), and they will have the experience and existing administrative structure to effectuate them (L4).

In the absence of state government, the more major infrastructure projects – those that serve wider areas and today are regulated by either the national government or the state governments or both – should remain with the national government. These include long-distance transportation, such as interstate and current state roads and bridges, trucking regulations, railways, navigable waterways, and airports. They also include most utility regulation – power grids, water and sewage treatment, telecommunications, and broadband. These projects too are often beyond the fiscal means of individual local governments (N5). National regulation also serves efficiency goals, as central control permits the shifting of resources when drought or other natural disaster temporarily alters the demands for energy, water, or the like (N6).

(vi) Environmental protection: Certain services that can be classified as environmental – for example, trash collection and disposal and recycling – have traditionally been performed by local government, and sensibly so. Yet again, the policies need to reflect the needs and preferences of the local population (L2), the requisite community knowledge resides in local officials (L3), and they have both the experience in providing these services and the administrative structure already in place (L4).

But major environmental regulation has rested with the national and state governments and, without state government, should remain with the national government. These include the restrictions on pollutants (including greenhouse gases), effluents, the conservation of soil, forests, and coral reefs, and the prevention of coastal erosion. Local governments could have perverse economic incentives to externalize costs by permitting factories to belch out pollutants that the prevailing winds carry to neighboring areas or permitting them to discharge effluents into waterways that will carry the effluents downstream (N4). And the adversely affected communities might be unable to afford measures that would avoid or minimize the resulting environmental damage (N5). Uniform nationwide regulation, therefore, is essential.

(vii) Licensing: Today, practicing any of a long list of professions or trades requires a license issued by the state in which one is practicing. These occupations include many different groups of health care workers – physicians, dentists, dental hygienists, registered nurses, occupational therapists, physical therapists, dieticians, pharmacists, and veterinarians; certain mental health professionals, such as psychologists,

clinical social workers, mental health counselors, and marriage and family therapists; teachers and principals in public elementary and secondary schools; certified
public accountants; attorneys; engineers; architects; barbers; cosmetologists; and
most funeral service workers.[60]

Many have criticized various occupational licensing requirements as unnecessar-
ily restrictive.[61] I won't wade into that debate, because my concern here is the "who
decides?" question: in the absence of states, should occupational licensing be the
responsibility of the national government or the local governments?

The case for transferring the licensing function to the national government is
overwhelming, mainly because of the benefits of uniformity (N3). There is simply
no reason that the required qualifications for a health care worker, an accoun-
tant, a barber, or one who works in any of the other fields for which licenses are
required should vary within the territory of the United States. Your physiology
doesn't change when you move from Philadelphia to Camden. Neither does your
hair, your mental health, or the needs of your pets. In our current state-based system, perhaps one could argue that attorneys need to master the relevant laws of
the states in which they practice. But that factor (i) is weak even today, since law
schools and law practice teach and require certain skills, not memorization of laws
that quickly change; and (ii) disappears entirely if state government is abolished.
Meanwhile, limiting one's professional activity to a narrow geographic area either
inhibits mobility or forces people to expend great effort to re-qualify in other
locales when they move – or when their practices would otherwise encompass
more than one locale. And every time they do practice in more than one locale or
want to practice in multiple locales, both they and the relevant licensing officials
must duplicate the task of establishing their qualifications (N6). Implementation
aside, the very need to formulate and continually update the requirements for
each licensed occupation is itself a pointless duplication of effort (also N6). The
situation would become even worse if each of the 90,000 local governments,
instead of fifty-one US jurisdictions, had to duplicate the same licensing tasks and
if the affected workers could no longer move even to an adjacent suburb without
the need to re-qualify. At any rate, local governments could rarely afford the costs
of formulating and updating the requirements for all the affected occupations and
administering the application process (N5).

Analogous observations apply to driver's licenses. There is no reason that the written tests, road tests, eye tests, and age requirements for obtaining a driver's license

---

[60] Genevieve Carlton, *What Jobs Require a Professional License?* (July 17, 2023), www.accreditedschools
online.org/resources/jobs-requiring-professional-license/. Certain occupations in the aviation indus-
try – pilots, airplane mechanics, and air traffic controllers – also require licenses, but those are issued
by the Federal Aviation Administration (FAA). *Ibid.*

[61] See, for example, Sabina Loving, Institute for Justice, Occupational Licensing (2023), https://ij.org/
issues/economic-liberty/occupational-licensing/; see also the sources cited in Mandelker *et al.*, note
38, at 710–13.

need to vary from one US location to another. And the affirmative case for a uniform national driver's license is a strong one. It would avoid the need for people to apply for a new license every time they moved from one local community to another, and it would avoid the duplication of effort for the government officials who have to process the applications (N3 and N6).

Unlike both occupational and driver's licenses, hunting and fishing licenses seem well suited for local policymaking and administration. Requirements for these licenses need to reflect the natural environment of the local area, including the wildlife and fishing stock (L2). In addition, local officials will be best acquainted with those conditions (L3) and might even have prior experience with the applicable regulations (L4).

(viii) Elections for national office: As discussed earlier, the Constitution invests the state legislatures with the power to decide "the times, places, and manner" of congressional elections, but it goes on to say that Congress may supersede those decisions. Congress has exercised that power several times.[62] The Constitution also provides that each state's presidential electors are to be chosen "in such Manner as the Legislature thereof may direct."[63] The Supreme Court has made clear that the states, not Congress, also have the sole power (subject to various constitutional constraints) to decide who is eligible to vote in congressional elections.[64]

All those principles, of course, would become moot if state government were abolished. But a different version of the question would emerge: Who would be better suited to decide the manner of elections for national office and the qualifications voters must have – the national government or the local governments?

These decisions have many component parts. How best to avoid racial and partisan gerrymandering is one of them. In addition, underlying every one of the voter suppression strategies described in Chapter 3, Section B is a legitimate issue that has to be decided: What should be the requirements, and the process, for voter registration? When is it OK to purge a name from the registration list? When should early voting start and stop? How many polling stations and how many ballot drop boxes should there be, where should they be located, and what should be the hours of operation for polling stations and the time periods for access to ballot drop boxes? And so on. Someone has to make these decisions. Who should that be?

As to the manner of choosing presidential electors, the abolition of states would also spell the end of the Electoral College. In Chapter 6, which sketches the shape of the proposed new unitary American republic, I support the arguments already made by many others for replacing the Electoral College with a national popular vote. So let's put off that issue until that final chapter.

---

[62] U.S. Const. Art. I, § 4, Cl. 1. Examples of congressional exercises of this power appear in Chapter 3, Section A and in Library of Congress, *Constitution Annotated, ArtI.S.4.C1.3, Congress and Elections Clause*, https://constitution.congress.gov/browse/essay/artI-S4-C1-3/ALDE_00013640/.

[63] U.S. Const. Art. II, § 1, Cl. 3.

[64] *Term Limits* v. *Thornton*, 570 U.S. 1, 16–18 (1995).

As for congressional elections, some might argue that the general factors developed earlier favor putting both the voting process and voter qualifications in the hands of the local governments, just as the current process assigns them to the states. After all, one of the main functions of each member of Congress is to promote the distinctive interests of his or her local constituents. Therefore, the argument would run, the local governments should decide how their own local representatives are to be elected and by whom (L2). But members of Congress are additionally bound to promote what they see as the best interests of the nation as a whole (N4). More important, while the candidate's prospective constituents have the right to vote for those who they believe will best serve their interests, it doesn't follow that they should get to decide which of them may do the voting in the first place.

There is, however, a more convincing argument for local government authority to decide the manner of congressional elections and the voter qualifications: Putting these decisions in the hands of a single national government is risky. Chapter 3 demonstrated how brazenly state legislators and officials have manipulated voting processes and voter qualifications for crass partisan gain. While there is no reason to assume that local politicians will be any less driven by partisan or ideological motives than their state counterparts have been, at least there will be other local governments that will not succumb to that temptation (or will act out of countervailing partisan motives). In contrast, a national trifecta – that is, simultaneous control of both houses of Congress and the White House – by an extremist party bent on subverting the electoral process could cripple democracy nationwide (L1).

I believe nonetheless that other factors outweigh that fear and counsel national responsibility for deciding both the voting process itself and the voter qualifications. That the founding fathers left these powers with the states is historical fact, but not a normative argument. In a democracy, voting is indisputably a fundamental interest (N1). Uniform rules are beneficial if not paramount; no democracy should design a system in which some citizens choose the members of the national legislature while other, similarly situated, citizens are shut out (N3). Moreover, the way the people of one locale vote affects the composition of Congress and, therefore, the entire nation (N4). Additionally, as just noted, there is no defensible affirmative reason that either the basic elements of the voting process or the voting qualifications need to vary from one locale to another (N3). And the fear of an unfettered national government abusing the electoral process for partisan gain can be largely – admittedly not entirely – eliminated by placing that responsibility within the judicial branch in the particular way described in Chapter 6, Section B.3.

With respect to the electoral process itself, uniformity would bring additional benefits. As it is, different voting rules and ballot tabulation procedures in different states already confuse the process and feed suspicions among the more conspiracy-minded sectors of the population. Surely, a hodgepodge of 90,000 different local governments deciding on their own voting and ballot tabulation procedures would create yet greater cynicism and chaos.

And then there is the matter of timing. Election night junkies have certainly noticed the extreme differences in the speed with which various states, and even various counties within a state, report vote counts. State-to-state differences in the timing of a given media network's projections of outcomes are understandable; among other things, close elections make for later projections. But why should there be such dramatic variations in the reporting of votes? Why is one state able to report 80 percent of the precincts within minutes after the polls close, while others need days to reach that point? There are only a few potential explanations for those differentials: Some states attach different relative weights to the competing values of accuracy and timeliness; some states invest more per capita resources – staffing, equipment, or technology – than others; or some states' counting processes are simply more efficient than those of others.

I can think of no reason that any of those factors – the optimal balancing of accuracy and timeliness, the amount of resources devoted to vote-counting, or the efficiency of the process – should be allowed to vary with geographic location (N3). Surely the voters of California (a state with notoriously long delays in reporting[65]) have as much right to accuracy and speed in the reporting of their votes, deserve to have the same resources invested in the counting, and have the same interest in the efficiency of the process as the voters of Florida (a state that reports its votes very promptly).[66] And if the existing state-to-state variations in vote tabulation speed are problematic, one can again assume that local-to-local variations would be greater still.

So the balance of factors tilts heavily toward national responsibility for deciding congressional election procedures and voter qualifications.[67] But what to do about actual on-the-ground implementation of those national policies – both the casting and the counting of votes – requires a different analysis.

On the one hand, local officials will know the most about the local population's needs (L2) and expected turnout by polling station; thus, they seem well positioned to estimate the necessary staffing and equipment needs of the various precincts (L3). They will also have had experience in managing the voting process in their own local areas (L4).

On the other hand, many if not most of the decisions that relate to either election procedure or voter eligibility concern the very areas in which the voter suppression

---

[65] Mike TeSelle, KCRA, *Why Does It Take So Long to Count California Votes from the Election?* (Nov. 10, 2022), www.kcra.com/article/counting-california-votes-from-the-election-sacramento-county-official-explains/41924837#.

[66] See, for example, Matt Sczesny, *Florida Hailed as Model after Successful Election While Other States Continue to Count Ballots* (Nov. 6, 2020), www.wptv.com/news/election-2020/florida-hailed-as-model-after-successful-election-while-other-states-continue-to-count-ballots.

[67] I defer for now the question of which branches of the national government would be responsible for which aspects of the policymaking process. In Chapter 6, I advocate substantial adoption of the highly successful system managed by the national judiciary in Brazil – a country that, like the United States, is a federation with a large population and a large geographic area.

strategies described in Chapter 3, Section B have taken root. For that and the other reasons already discussed, such issues as voter registration, purging of names from voter rolls, requiring photo IDs or documentary proof of US citizenship, early and mailing voting, restricting third-party collection of absentee ballots, and disenfranchising citizens because of specified criminal convictions all cry out for uniform national remedies (N3).

Other common voter suppression instruments – particularly those relating to polling stations and ballot drop boxes – are a closer call. Who should decide how many polling stations there will be, where they will be located, and their hours? Who should decide how many ballot drop boxes there will be, where they will be placed, and for what time period they will be available? This is where the line between policymaking and implementation begins to blur. On the one hand, local officials will generally possess greater knowledge of such relevant local conditions as voter demand in the various precincts, proximity of polling stations to residential areas, and the availability of public transportation (L3). They might also have prior experience and even preexisting administrative structures already in place for these purposes (L4). On the other hand, the fundamental nature of the right to vote (N1), together with the history of manipulating the stationing of polling places and the availability of ballot drop boxes for partisan ends, point toward national policymaking even on these issues. A middle ground might be having national officials issue detailed standards governing the numbers, locations, and opening hours of polling stations and the numbers, locations, and durations of ballot boxes, while leaving some limited degree of local discretion as to implementation.

Chapter 6, Section B.3 favors a third option: administration of all national elections by a nonpartisan body that is located within the national judiciary and operated through a network of regional and local offices.

(ix) Business regulation: This umbrella term takes in a broad collection of subject areas. Among them are commercial law, including laws governing the formation and enforcement of contracts and bankruptcy law; corporations law, including incorporation, shareholder rights, acquisitions and mergers, antitrust, corporate and officer liability, corporate finance, corporate taxation, securities regulation, and partnerships; banking laws; insurance laws, including minimum reserve requirements and new product approvals; international trade; labor and employment law, including unions, minimum wage, child labor, workplace safety, and prohibitions on specified forms of employment discrimination; and consumer protection, both financial and personal safety. At present, these areas are regulated by the national government, the states, or both.

In the absence of states, I suggest all of those areas would be better suited for national regulation than for local. The benefits of uniform treatment (N3) are especially evident here. Standards that vary from place to place make operations difficult for manufacturers of products that are sold nationwide or for corporations that do business in multiple geographic areas of the country. If local governments could offer lax regulation of corporate activity or consumer safety or worker protections, or give corporate tax breaks to lure large corporations, they might well benefit by doing so, but those benefits would come at the expense of other local governments and could spur a race to the bottom that harms local government nationwide (N4). The need for 90,000 local governments to develop, update, and enforce their own sets of laws on each of these varied subjects would also duplicate efforts (N6) and would exceed the resource capabilities of many local governments if not most (N5).

There are other important subjects of current state activity – family law, reproductive freedom, taxation, and ratification of constitutional amendments, to name just a few – but this list of illustrations has already grown long. Again, while bottom line opinions have been expressed, the priority here is not to advocate that any particular set of current state government functions be reassigned to any particular level of government. There is room for wide differences of opinion in each case. Rather, the objectives here have been to demonstrate that these important government functions can be well served without state governments and that there are ways to decide whether, for each such function, the national government or the local governments are better positioned to step in. Chapter 5 addresses a related question: Even if state government isn't essential, is it at least beneficial?

5

The Benefits of State Government

Chapters 2–4 described the major harms for which, it was argued, state government is largely responsible. But does state government supply important offsetting benefits? In this chapter, I have tried to locate or imagine every conceivable benefit that one might claim state government offers. I didn't have to look hard. Most of the claimed benefits I could think of, and some that I would not have thought of on my own, have already been asserted by others.

To be sure, these previously invoked benefits have not been packaged as arguments for the retention of state government; serious debate over whether to abolish state government simply has not taken place. Rather, these arguments have typically been presented in defense of federalism. And that is a different debate.[1] It is possible to have states or their equivalent without federalism, as the below discussion on decentralization illustrates. Indeed, unitary systems in which the various subunits are subordinate to the national government are plentiful in today's world. But it is not possible to have federalism without states or their equivalent. Thus, every one of the arguments for federalism presupposes, and therefore is necessarily also an argument for, state government.

---

[1] A small sampling of the thousands of thoughtful books and articles that explore federalism from descriptive, normative, historical, or comparative perspectives includes John Gerring & Strom C. Thacker, A Centripetal Theory of Democratic Governance (2010); Donald F. Kettl, The Divided States of America: Why Federalism Doesn't Work (2020); Jamila D. Michener, Fragmented Democracy: Medicaid, Federalism, and Unequal Politics (2018); Felix Morley, Freedom and Federalism (originally published in 1959, reprinted in 1981); David L. Shapiro, Federalism: A Dialogue (1995); Ronald L. Watts, Comparing Federal Systems (3rd ed. 2008); Jeffrey S. Sutton, Who Decides? States as Laboratories of Constitutional Experimentation (2022); Erik Wibbels, Federalism and the Market: Intergovernmental Conflict and Economic Reform in the Developing World (2005); Giovanni Bognetti & Matthew F. Shugart, Britannica, Unitary and Federal Systems, www.britannica.com/topic/constitutional-law/Unitary-and-federal-systems (undated); Heather K. Gerken, The Supreme Court, 2009 Term – Forward: Federalism All the Way Down, 124 Harv. L. Rev. 4 (2010); Frédéric Lépine, A Journey through the History of Federalism: Is Multilevel Governance a Form of Federalism?, 1 L'Europe en Formation 21, no. 363, (2012) www.cairn.info/revue-l-europe-en-formation-2012-1-page-21 .htm; Edward L. Rubin & Malcolm Feeley, Federalism: Some Notes on a National Neurosis, 41 UCLA L. Rev. 903 (1994).

As I will show, these arguments are far less convincing than they initially appear. Each of the claimed benefits either does not exist, exists but is very minor, or could be replicated at least as well and often better by some other level of government.[2] A common flaw in most of those defenses of states is that the state is simply too blunt an instrument to achieve the claimed benefits. The local governments, to which I favor transferring many of the states' functions, will be shown to be far more precise.

Some scholars – most notably Edward Rubin & Malcolm Feeley – have made the different point that you don't need a federation to realize the benefits often cited for it; decentralization alone, they say, would be just as effective.[3] I agree but go a step further. You don't need state government at all to achieve the advantages that *either* federation or mere decentralization is said to provide. As the discussion in this chapter will show, the same arguments that make mere decentralization preferable to federation make the abolition of state government better yet – as do additional arguments.

Of course, there are many insightful commentators – perhaps most – who do not share my dim view of states' value.[4] An otherwise thoughtful and highly informative book by political scientists Ann O'M. Bowman, Richard Kearney, and Carmine Scavo overflows with cheery, uplifting tributes to the behaviors and accomplishments of states. On one page alone appear extravagant references to the states' capacities for "innovation," their transformations into "viable and progressive political units," the "positive outcomes" states generate, and the "new directions" they have "creatively crafted."[5] Negative behaviors are unavoidably acknowledged on occasion but receive scant emphasis. Neither the modern tidal wave of voter suppression and other counter-majoritarian state actions nor the states' disingenuous defenses of those measures come across.

I concede the obvious: Among the fifty states, all of which have been with us for anywhere between several decades and more than two centuries, and each of which has legislated on thousands of subjects along the way, it is easy to find countless examples of exemplary actions. It is for the reader to judge whether the benefits that state government sometimes brings offset the damage, described in Chapters 2–4, that they have done to our democratic ideals and to the fiscally efficient operation of our multilevel government structure.

---

[2] Others, while not suggesting the abolition of state government, have similarly pointed out that most of the virtues ascribed to federalism are at least as present at the local government level, and usually more so. See, for example, Sutton, note 1, at 307, quoting Gerken, note 1, at 6 and Richard Briffaut, *The Challenge of the New Preemption*, 70 Stan. L. Rev. 1995, 2019 (2018).

[3] Rubin & Feeley, note 1.

[4] Some writers see multiple benefits in having states. For example, Morley, note 1; Sutton, note 1.

[5] Ann O'M. Bowman, Richard Kearney, & Carmine Scavo, State and Local Government 6 (11th ed. 2022). An exception is *ibid.*, chapter 12, in which the authors criticize states that have aggressively constrained the legislative powers of local governments. See also Sutton, note 1.

A DIFFUSING GOVERNMENT POWER

The most frequently cited benefit of states is that they prevent what would otherwise be an unhealthy concentration of power in the national government. Diffusing government power, the argument runs, enables the federal government and the states to check each other's excesses, thereby protecting individual liberties. In the words of the Supreme Court, "State sovereignty is not just an end in itself: Rather, federalism secures to citizens the liberties that derive from the diffusion of sovereign power."[6] The Antifederalists strongly agreed and cited additional benefits of diffusing government power, including their belief that it helps check corruption.[7]

In *Printz* v. *United States*,[8] the Supreme Court similarly invoked diffusion of government power as a central purpose of our federal system. Interim provisions of the federal Brady Act required the chief law enforcement officers of each jurisdiction to complete certain paperwork, and perform background checks, before firearms could be sold. In its 5-4 decision, the Court declared those requirements unconstitutional. The Court held (among other things) that requiring state officers to assist in federal law enforcement violated the principle of dual federal and state sovereignty. The principle that the federal government may not force the states to administer a federal program has come to be known as the "anti-commandeering doctrine."

The Court in *Printz* quoted James Madison:

> In the compound republic of America, the power surrendered by the people is first divided between two distinct governments, and then the portion allotted to each subdivided among distinct and separate departments. Hence a double security

---

[6] *Bond* v. *United States*, 564 U.S. 211, 221 (2011), quoting *New York* v. *United States*, 505 U.S. 144, 181 (1992) and *Coleman* v. *Thompson*, 501 U.S. 722 (1991) (Blackmun, J., dissenting). Accord, *Gregory* v. *Ashcroft*, 501 U.S. 452, 458–59 (1991). See also Bowman *et al.*, note 5, at 30; Morley, note 1; Barry Friedman, *Valuing Federalism*, 82 Minn. L. Rev. 317, 402–403 (1997); Rubin & Feeley, note 1, at 928. Daniel Mandelker *et al.*, State and Local Government in a Federal System 7 (9th ed. 2021), make the additional point that the state executive branches provide further dispersion by vesting powers in several independently elected state officials rather than placing all of the ultimate power in the hands of the governors. They contrast this arrangement with the unitary federal executive branch in which nearly everyone reports directly or indirectly to the president. Accord, Sutton, note 1, at 147–82; Miriam Seifter, *Understanding State Agency Independence*, 117 Mich. L. Rev. 1537, 1553 (2019). Of course, the plural state executive has a corresponding downside – the heightened challenge of keeping policymaking coherent.

[7] Antifederalist 3, 60. They added two other arguments that are now moot. Diffusing government power, they believed, would help offset the then-proposed Constitution's lack of a bill of rights. Antifederalist 60, 84. That concern was quickly remedied by the subsequent adoption of the Bill of Rights. They also pointed to the practical difficulty of citizens living too far from the seat of government. Antifederalist 14. The latter concern has been alleviated both by the greater ease of modern travel and by the fact that the Constitution creates a form of representative democracy, not a direct democracy in which participation in the lawmaking process would have required citizens to travel great distances.

[8] 521 U.S. 898 (1997).

arises to the rights of the people. The different governments will control each other, at the same time that each will be controlled by itself.[9]

While much of the Court's opinion comes very close to treating state sovereignty as an end in itself, the above passage disavows sole reliance on that notion, making one feeble attempt to add content to the supposed benefits of dual sovereignty. The Court – and Madison – say that our federal system gives the people double protection: Each of the two sovereigns will "control" the other, and each will be subject to additional internal controls (the latter being a reference to separation of powers).[10]

But fears that a unitary system would unleash an untethered national government are less concerning than might initially appear. As a preliminary matter, the abolition of states would end the distortions produced by the Electoral College, by equal Senate representation for states with wildly different populations, and by the endless parade of gerrymandering, voter suppression, and similar actions of partisan state legislatures. Without those substantial counter-majoritarian advantages, a radical, authoritarian trifecta at the national level (both houses of Congress and the White House) would be much less likely to start with.

Admittedly, though, it would not be impossible. So let's assume for the sake of discussion that, against the odds, such a government achieves precisely such a national trifecta even without the unfair advantages that flow from the status and the actions of state governments. Even then, there would be several reasons to discount either the need or the effectiveness of federalism as an antidote.

First, the diffusion benefits of federalism sound more consequential than they are. Yes, federalism diffuses power in the sense that the federal government handles some subjects and the states handle others. But within each of those two orbits, one level of government or the other will always have a virtual monopoly of power. When the federal government exercises a power that the Constitution gives it, there is nothing that federalism enables the states to do about it. Conversely, when a state exercises a power that the Constitution doesn't give to the federal government, there is nothing the federal government can do about it. Within each of the two spheres of operations, therefore, federalism does little or nothing to check the exercise of government power. And even when the federal government sees fit to partner with the states in the implementation of a federal program or otherwise share a particular governance function with the states, the supremacy clause ensures that the federal government will always have the last word. If it wants to be tyrannical, there's nothing the states can do to stop it (other than go to court, which either private citizens or, in my proposed unitary nation, local governments could also do). So

[9] *Ibid.*, at 922, quoting Federalist 51 (Madison). See also Sutton, note 1, at 2 (similarly citing this passage in defense of federalism).

[10] The Court makes the same point, *ibid.*, at 920, when it quotes its previous decision in *U.S. Term Limits v. Thornton*, 514 U.S. 779, 838 (1995) (Kennedy, J., concurring), for the proposition that each of the two levels of government (state and federal) is "protected from incursion by the other."

while federalism means that the various subjects of governmental regulation will be divided up between these two levels of government, the fact remains that, with due respect to Madison and the Supreme Court, on any given subject neither level of government will have any meaningful "control" over the other.[11]

I will concede two narrow exceptions to that assertion. Under the anti-commandeering doctrine, even when Congress regulates a subject area that the Constitution otherwise assigns it, states can generally refuse to provide affirmative help in implementing Congress's wishes. Thus, if the particular program is one that requires ground level implementation, Congress needs to find an alternative to mandating state partnerships. Fortunately, several such alternatives exist. Even in our current federation, one option is voluntary partnerships with willing states, though admittedly that solution offers no assurance of nationwide cooperation and at any rate gives states negotiating leverage. And that leverage can sometimes be constraining. More important, however, with or without states the national government can, as it often does today, administer the law through a network of regional offices of the relevant federal agency. And if state government were abolished, still another option would be to assign the implementation function to local governments, which would remain free to partner with other local governments when it is efficient to do so.

The other narrow exception relates to law enforcement. The recent criminal actions that state prosecutors have brought against former President Donald Trump reveal the potential utility of subnational enforcement authority. If a tyrannical national government were in power (not the case at the time of these state prosecutions), national prosecutors might be less likely to bring criminal charges against the president, other members of the administration, or members of the president's party in Congress. But one struggles to recount frequent instances in which state police or prosecutors have had to initiate criminal proceedings against federal government officials because the federal government was refusing to do so for political reasons. If anything, the reverse comes to mind more readily; the need for the federal government to send National Guard troops to Alabama to force Governor George Wallace and other state officials to enforce federal civil rights law is not so distant a memory.[12]

---

[11] There is one qualification, but it is now of only historical interest. From the ratification of the Constitution until 1913, state legislatures chose the members of the United States Senate. See U.S. Const. Art. I, § 3, Cl. 1. During that period, therefore, one could credibly argue that the states thereby had some measure of "control" over the composition of the federal government. But that weapon disappeared with the 1913 ratification of the Seventeenth Amendment, under which U.S. senators are elected by direct vote of the people.

[12] See, for example, Claude Sitton, The New York Times, *Alabama Admits Negro Students; Wallace Bows to Federal Force; Kennedy Sees "Moral Crisis" in U.S.* (June 12, 1963), https://archive.nytimes .com/www.nytimes.com/library/national/race/061263race-ra.html (President Kennedy, protecting school integration in 1963); American Public Media, *Lyndon B. Johnson: The Road from Selma*, https://americanradioworks.publicradio.org/features/prestapes/c3.html (President Johnson, protecting civil rights march led by Dr. Martin Luther King in 1965).

The good news is that, even if federalism meaningfully constrained central government overreach, we wouldn't need federalism for that purpose. The central government is already triply constrained even without it: by the constitutional provisions that protect individual rights, by constitutionally enshrined separation of powers principles (a check that, in the light of political parties' current roles, I do not want to exaggerate),[13] and by the political process (a constraint that, as just noted, should grow stronger once state government and its counter-majoritarian effects no longer distort electoral outcomes). In addition, there is no reason that popular initiatives and referenda could not be introduced at the national level. They would be no harder to administer nationwide than the national presidential vote proposed here and would add another valuable political check.

If even the combination of those multiple constraints is thought to be inadequate, there is yet another whole set of checks and balances – *internal* separation of powers. This strand of separation of powers operates on a vertical basis within the federal executive branch. Its principal form is review of federal agencies' significant regulatory proposals by the Office of Information and Regulatory Affairs (OIRA). That office is located within the Office of Management and Budget, which in turn is part of the Executive Office of the President.[14]

Jennifer Nou points out that OIRA review can be even more important than judicial review. The former is more systematic, less deferential to the agency, and earlier in the process.[15] Of course, no one likes to have their decisions reversed, and federal agencies are no exception. As Nou demonstrates, executive branch agencies currently have a variety of ways to insulate their decisions from OIRA review. They can, for example, choose particular regulatory instruments that are not subject to OIRA review at all or find ways to make OIRA's review more time-consuming or otherwise more costly, in order to discourage rigorous scrutiny. But as Nou proceeds to argue, presidents have ways to resist and to preempt those kinds of self-insulation strategies. That presidential control, while far from absolute, thus remains a valuable safeguard against runaway federal agencies – one that

---

[13] A superb article by Daryl Levinson and Richard Pildes demonstrates that the functions the framers envisioned for separation of powers have been displaced by the growth of today's internally cohesive and externally polarized political parties. As they explain, during times of unified government – that is, control of the White House and both houses of Congress by the same party – traditional separation of powers constraints yield to the cooperative impulses of the legislative and executive branches. And during times of divided government, the real constraints flow from the competition – often rising to the level of outright hostility – between the parties, not the branches. See Daryl J. Levinson & Richard H. Pildes, *Separation of Parties, Not Powers*, 119 Harv. L. Rev. 2311 (2006). In his book, *The Failure of the Founding Fathers: Jefferson, Marshall, and the Rise of Presidential Democracy* (2005), Bruce Ackerman digs up the details of the 1800 presidential election, similarly revealing the framers' failure to foresee the impact that political parties would come to have on the functioning of the Constitution.

[14] The White House, *Information and Regulatory Affairs*, www.whitehouse.gov/omb/information-regulatory-affairs/.

[15] Jennifer Nou, *Agency Self-Insulation under Presidential Review*, 126 Harv. L. Rev. 1755, 1757–59 (2013).

supplements the traditional separation of powers constraints imposed by Congress and the courts.[16]

Transferring a large chunk of the states' current responsibilities to the national government would, of course, require a massive increase in the sheer size of the national government. New national agencies would be required. While the management of those individual agencies should be no more difficult than the management of the analogous state agencies they would be replacing, the job of supervising and coordinating the whole would clearly pose additional challenges. This is not a concern about authoritarian or tyrannical government, but I concede that an expansion this significant would make OIRA's work even more vital. OIRA would need to add new branches, and the jobs of the OIRA Administrator and the president would become less enviable.

OIRA does, however, have help. Congress has found other internal (within the executive branch) ways to cabin federal agencies. When Congress wants agencies to take adequate account of values that are outside of, or even contrary to, an agency's mission, it often creates what Margo Schlanger has called "offices of goodness."[17] Schlanger limits the term to those offices that are advisory only (not operational), have a mission defined by specific values (e.g., civil liberties or fiscal efficiency), and are internal to and dependent on the agency. Her chief example is the Department of Homeland Security's Office for Civil Rights and Civil Liberties (which she headed).[18] And as Neal Katyal has pointed out, still other devices for checking the actions of executive branch agencies, though not possessing all the attributes of "offices of goodness," include Offices of the General Counsel, Offices of Inspectors General, Ombudsmen, and the career Civil Service.[19]

Finally, suppose one disagrees with all of the preceding points. Suppose, in other words, that one does not believe that abolishing all the state-related countermajoritarian distortions of the political process would appreciably diminish the chances of a radical authoritarian party achieving a national trifecta; that there is some way in which federalism enables the states to control the national government even when the latter is otherwise exercising one of its constitutionally enumerated powers; and that all the existing constraints on the federal government, even taken collectively, are insufficient. If one therefore believes that dividing functions between the national government and fifty states offers the essential benefit of diffusing power, then imagine how much more diffusion we would get by dividing the

---

[16] *Ibid.*, at 1815–22.

[17] Margo Schlanger, *Offices of Goodness: Influence without Authority in Federal Agencies*, 36 Cardozo L. Rev. 53 (2014).

[18] *Ibid.*, at 60–62.

[19] See Neal Kumar Katyal, *Internal Separation of Powers: Checking Today's Most Dangerous Branch from Within*, 115 Yale L. J. 2314, 2318 (2006).

functions between the national government and tens of thousands of local governments, as this book proposes.[20] That's diffusion on steroids.

True, one might reply, these functions *could* be taken on by the local governments. But if the enumerated powers doctrine is repealed, the national government
wouldn't *have* to let them do these things. And, as the antifederalists worried, the
natural tendency of those in positions of power is to look for ways to expand their
power, not reduce it.

Nor, I must acknowledge, is this fear of a runaway national government just a
concern of states' rights conservatives. What if the Electoral College were to install
another Donald Trump as president and a similarly inclined or compliant Congress
controlled by that president's party is also elected? If there are no states, and if the
national government is no longer limited to enumerated powers, what prevents the
latter from usurping subject areas best left to local governments? The constitutional
provisions that guarantee certain individual rights and require separation of powers
will continue to impose limits, but not on the national government's choice of subject areas to regulate. It could prohibit or severely restrict the zoning authority of
local municipalities, or mandate weekly garbage collections, or decide which street
corners should have stop signs. It could make it a criminal offense to teach elementary or secondary school students about, or even to mention, slavery or voter suppression or protests against particular wars or other material deemed "unpatriotic" – or
other taboo topics such as evolution or climate change or unionization or sexual
orientation or nonbinary gender or contraception or abortion.[21]

That would be the worry, and it is a legitimate one. As just noted, a unitary system
would reduce the chances of a radical party monopolizing the political branches of
the national government in the first place, but such an event would still be possible.

First, however, let's be clear about the scope of the concern. Eliminating the
enumerated powers constraint would have no effect on any national actions that are
already within its current enumerated powers. The only effect of lifting that constraint would be on those national actions that the enumerated powers doctrine currently precludes. Those powers are not trivial, but at least the broad powers already
exercised by the national government would not be expanded.

Second, while the chances of a future national government impinging on local
government in one or more of the ways the argument hypothesizes are not zero, they
are not high. In some of the examples, such as local decisions on zoning, garbage
collection, or street signs, one can safely assume the national government would have

---

[20] Rubin and Feeley make the analogous point that mere decentralization would serve the diffusion
objective at least as well, if not better, than federalism. See Rubin & Feeley, note 1, at 929–30.

[21] See, for example, Elizabeth A. Harris & Alexandra Alter, The New York Times, A *Fast-Growing
Network of Conservative Groups Is Fueling a Surge in Book Bans* (Dec. 14, 2022), www.nytimes
.com/2022/12/12/books/book-bans-libraries.html?campaign_id=9&emc=edit_nn_20221219&instance_
id=80582&nl=the-morning&regi_id=76642304&segment_id=120267&te=1&user_id=2785b718e2891
2cce3f4ef8d2794344a.

little interest. In most of the other examples, feared federal excesses would be expected to enrage local citizenries. The political costs would run both wide and deep. For those, the political process – especially one shorn of its counter-majoritarian blemishes – would offer the best medicine.

Finally, the current constitutional scheme gives the states just as much leeway to operate in those subject areas that are outside the federally enumerated powers as the federal government has to operate within them. In virtually all the examples given, one can say that if the federal government has no business imposing the particular policy on local governments, the state government doesn't either. For anyone who views any of those hypothetical directives as undesirable (and I certainly do), it's a question of "pick your poison." When it comes to the kinds of extreme measures that this defense of federalism conjures up, my view is that, if anything, it is state governments that pose the greater threat.

That is so because, without discounting the rightful fear of a radically authoritarian national government – we had one as recently as 2017–21, though only with the aid of such state-related counter-majoritarian institutions as the Electoral College and the Senate – radical *state* governments willing to intrude in the ways feared are far more likely. There are solid red states and solid blue states, but there is no solid national state. Together, the tightness of many nationwide elections and the knife-edge balance of power that so often grips one or both houses of Congress naturally push the federal government into political terrain somewhere between the reddest states and the bluest ones. As long as there are state governments that need answer only to populations in which solid majorities are either reliably progressive or reliably conservative, the political headwinds against radical state intrusions are far weaker than those faced by a national government that answers to a more heterogeneous, and more fluid, countrywide population.

This last point might initially appear to undermine my proposal to shift substantial power from the states to their local municipalities. After all, just as the national government is likely to be less extreme than the most extreme state governments, so too a given state's government is likely to be less extreme than the most extreme of that state's municipalities. Under the current system, states can check overreaching local policies; without states, only the national government would be able to do so. And if a radical national government were sympathetic to those local policies, it would be unlikely to step in.

I concede that danger. But the alternative poses a corresponding danger. Under the present system, whole states can – and often do – run roughshod over the decision-making authority of their local governments, as Chapter 3, Section F highlighted. In a unitary nation, that would no longer be the case.

The preceding analysis is addressed to one specific problem – a radical, authoritarian national government ready to impose its views nationwide and against the wishes of the majority. That government might or might not sincerely believe it is acting in the best interests of the nation. In contrast, in Federalist 10, James Madison considered a different but parallel worry – "factions." By this term, he was referring to groups of people willing to pursue their own self-interest even when doing so harms other citizens or the nation as a whole.

Madison maintained that a large republic, headed by a strong national government, is best situated to control such factions. His argument began with the premise that there's a certain optimal size of a legislative body – too large and it becomes confusing, too small and it can be disrupted too easily by legislators of bad will. That optimal size – or at least optimal range – doesn't vary appreciably with the size of the governed population. Therefore, in a large population, there are more good candidates to choose from, for roughly the same number of spots. In addition, "as each representative will be chosen by a greater number of citizens in the large than in the small republic, it will be more difficult for unworthy candidates to practice with success the vicious arts by which elections are too often carried." Moreover, he added, "Extend the sphere, and you take in a greater variety of parties and interests; you make it less probable that a majority of the whole will have a common motive to invade the rights of other citizens."

For those same compelling reasons, controlling a politically radical minority – whether or not it is motivated by self-interest – is easier in a large population unit like the nation than in a smaller population unit like an individual US state. Again, we have solid blue states and solid red states, but not – at least yet – a solid national state.

A slight variation of the diffusion of power argument is "What about the 'good' states?" Today, if the national government is bad, at least the good states can enact laws that benefit their own citizens.

Good and bad, of course, are in the political eyes of the beholder. My normative view is that, whatever one's general political leanings, all Americans of good faith should be in favor of reforms that restore democracy and reduce fiscal waste. Those ought to be consensus views. But I recognize that the reality is different. Today, many Americans are willing to sacrifice either of those benefits to achieve competing goals to which they attach higher priorities.

At any rate, this point cuts both ways. Yes, one who dislikes the national government will be happy that states can offset some of its policies, at least for their own citizens. But that coin has a flip side. One who likes the national government typically won't like the prospect of states undermining its policies.

Finally, as the next section elaborates, even in states that we think of as solid red or solid blue, the popular political preferences almost always vary dramatically from one area of the state to another, especially as between the urban and rural areas. Thus, in a unitary republic, if you don't like the national government you can still take solace in the fact that there will be many local governments in a position to adopt more agreeable laws. Moreover, unlike the case today, in a unitary system a local government will be so positioned even if it is located in what had previously been a state with polar opposite political leanings and a willingness to impose those ideological preferences on its local governments.

One last point deserves mention. Jessica Bulman-Pozen has argued that partisan motives frequently inspire states to push back against federal action.[22] As she makes clear, her point is mainly descriptive, not a normative argument for partisan federalism, which could be seen as either beneficial or harmful.[23] My view is that, even if these sorts of pushbacks are viewed as a beneficial check on the federal government in the system as it is currently configured, they would not be needed in a unitary American republic. At least for those pushbacks that take place in court, challenges to the federal government's authority could be brought either by the local governments to which many of the state powers would devolve, or by aggrieved private individuals.

B DISTINCTIVE NEEDS AND PREFERENCES

Another benefit often claimed for federalism stems from the state-to-state differences in their populations. Bowman *et al.* emphasize that "[s]tates and their communities have different fiscal capacities and different voter preferences for public services and taxes."[24] The Supreme Court has also invoked that idea in defense of federalism. At least twice, it has said that federalism permits "local policies more sensitive to the diverse needs of a heterogeneous society ..."[25]

Those observations have been the basis for two different arguments on behalf of federalism. One is that federalism makes it possible to tailor laws and policies to the specific needs – and, one might add, political preferences – of various, diverse state populations. That democracy-focused argument – honoring the will of the relevant electorate – is often referred to as the "voice" rationale. It is taken up in this section. The other consequence of such tailoring, invoked more explicitly by Bowman *et al.*,[26] is that citizens who are dissatisfied with the laws and policies of the states in which they live have the option of moving to a state with policies more to their liking. Thus, they argue, federalism creates a healthy competition among states to retain their citizens. That second argument – citizen choice and the resulting interstate competition for citizens – is often referred to as the "exit" rationale. It will be the subject of Section C.1.

Barry Friedman argues that "[s]tate *and local* governments can work to protect the safety, health and welfare of their citizens" [emphasis added]. They can often do this more effectively than the national government, he suggests, because they can account for local conditions and needs.[27] But by lumping state and local

---

[22] Jessica Bulman-Pozen, *Partisan Federalism*, 127 Harv. L. Rev. 1077 (2014).
[23] *Ibid.*, at 1081 n.7.
[24] Bowman *et al.*, note 5, at 25.
[25] For example, *Bond v. United States*, 564 U.S. 211, 221 (2011); *Gregory v. Ashcroft*, 501 U.S. 452, 458 (1991). Accord, Morley, note 1; Friedman, note 6, at 386–87.
[26] Bowman *et al.*, note 5, at 25; see also Rubin & Feeley, note 1, at 917.
[27] Friedman, note 6, at 400–404.

governments together, I fear, he gives state government a free pass. I say this for two reasons.

First, and perhaps counterintuitively, it is not a given that in practice state government is any more likely to tailor its laws to the people than the federal government is. Miriam Seifter has persuasively cast empirical doubt on the premise that state government is closer to the people (and thus better able both to tailor its policies to those preferred by the people and to partner with the federal government in the administration of federal laws). In large part, she shows, that is because civil society, while providing a strong check on the federal government, has been a relatively weak check at the state level.[28]

But second, even if, contrary to Seifter's argument, states are indeed better positioned than the federal government to tailor their laws and policies to the interests and political preferences of the various state populations, their ability to do so is rooted in the fact that states outnumber the national government 50 to 1. Their populations and their territories, therefore, are only fractions of the national population and territory. But local governments in turn outnumber the states 90,000 to 50, so if anything they can achieve the tailoring objective even better than states can.

In fact, Friedman's main examples of functions for which states and local governments are better suited than the federal government are instructive: "How many police shall there be, how shall they conduct themselves, and where shall they be stationed? Where shall schools be, and what shall they teach? Should we have light rail, or other means of assisting commuters?"[29] All of these are quintessentially local government decisions, rarely if ever laws that apply uniformly statewide. He then goes on to assume that without federalism these decisions would have to be made by the national government, which he (and I too) believe to be unsuited for those tasks. But it is hard to imagine Congress or federal agency officials having any interest in making those decisions, and he does not consider leaving them with local authorities even though that is where the cited decisions typically rest today.

The larger point is that, in some subject areas, one could reasonably posit a democratic norm that prescribes tailoring laws and policies to the political preferences of the relevant subnational constituencies. The question that norm begs, however, is which subnational constituency is optimal – the statewide population or the various local populations.

As to that, the reality – both historically and today – is that intrastate polarization eclipses interstate polarization. The vivid divide between urban America and rural America has been thoroughly documented by Jonathan Rodden and others.[30] I would be hard-pressed to identify any cultural, racial, political, or other similarities

---

[28] Miriam Seifter, *Further from the People? The Puzzle of State Administration*, 93 NYU L. Rev. 107 (2018).

[29] Friedman, note 6, at 400.

[30] See Chapter 3, Section A.

between urban and rural populations, other than at a level of generality so high as to leave them indistinguishable from residents of any other state. Ask Philadelphians with whom they have more in common when it comes to interests, needs, lifestyle, political views, party, or anything else: residents of Camden, who live right across the state line in New Jersey, or farmers in western Pennsylvania. Conversely, ask farmers in western Pennsylvania with whom they have more in common: other farmers who live across the state line in eastern Ohio, or their fellow Pennsylvanians who live in Philadelphia. The answers are not hard to guess.

Happily, we don't have to guess. Just look at the 2020 presidential election results in almost any state. Missouri and Illinois provide nice illustrations. In Missouri, Trump beat Biden by 15 percentage points statewide.[31] In Illinois, Biden beat Trump by 17 percentage points statewide.[32] By any measure, those are substantial margins, and it seems fair to describe these two states today as reliably red and reliably blue, respectively.

And yet, impressive as those victory margins were, they absolutely pale when compared to the differences in voting patterns *within* each of those states. In Missouri, Biden carried the City of St. Louis by sixty-six points. In the heavily rural counties located in the four corners of the state, Trump beat Biden by anywhere between forty-five points and sixty-seven points.[33]

Illinois followed the same urban versus rural pattern. In Cook County, home to Chicago, Biden defeated Trump by forty-seven points. The counties that form three of the corners of Illinois are rural counties, where Trump won by margins ranging from seventeen points to forty-eight points.[34] In the two rural counties that jut out to the west, Trump's victory margins were forty-seven points and sixty-four points.[35]

---

[31] American Presidency Project, *Statistics 2020*, www.presidency.ucsb.edu/statistics/elections/2020.

[32] *Ibid.*

[33] These city and county figures are the differences between the two candidates' percentages of the total statewide votes. The two candidates' individual percentages are taken from Politico, *Donald Trump Won in Missouri* (Jan. 6, 2021), www.politico.com/2020-election/results/missouri/. In the City of St. Louis, Biden captured 82.3% of the votes, to Trump's 16.1%. Trump won Pemiscot County (SE corner) 71.8% to 27.2%; McDonald County (SW corner) 82.5% to 15.9%; Atchison County (NW corner) 78.1% to 20.0%; and Clark County (NE corner) 78.7% to 20.0%. *Ibid.*

[34] Like the Missouri figures, these are the differences between the two candidates' percentages of the total statewide vote. The two candidates' percentages are taken from Caroline Hurley, Chicago Sun Times, *See How Each Illinois County Voted in the Presidential Election*, (Nov. 6, 2020), https://chicago.suntimes.com/elections/2020/11/5/21551366/illinois-presidential-election-results-2020-county-map. In Cook County, Biden received 72.89% of the votes, to Trump's 25.60%. Trump defeated Biden in Jo Daviess County (NW corner) 57.39% to 40.85%; in Pulaski County (SW corner) 64.75% to 33.96%; and in Massac County (SE corner) 73.39% to 25.29%. Since the point of this comparison is to highlight the contrast between rural and urban voting patterns, I did not count Lake County, which occupies the northeast corner of the state, on the shores of Lake Michigan. It houses the city of Waukegan and is not rural.

[35] Those are Adams County and Hancock County, where Trump won 72.34% to 25.69% and 81.07% to 17.01%, respectively. *Ibid.*

One can construct other arguments for the preservation of state government. They are considered in the other sections of this chapter. But as for the specific goal of tailoring laws and policies to the political preferences of the various subnational constituencies, I cannot identify any credible advantage to statewide tailoring over local tailoring. As the election numbers highlighted above amply illustrate, states are absurdly crude proxies for gauging the political preferences, and presumably therefore the needs and interests, of subnational populations. Thus, states are crude instruments for accomplishing the legitimate goal of tailoring laws and policies to those particularized needs and preferences. The mismatch is also unnecessary, because the local governments, to which many of the current state functions would be transferred under my proposal, are far better proxies for the varying preferences of different populations.

A separate argument for valuing the distinctive needs and preferences of individual states' citizens is that doing so creates a kind of steam valve, relieving pressure that would otherwise trigger internal strife. Antifederalist 7, by "Philanthropos," went so far as to suggest that for this reason too strong a national government could lead to civil war. One might even assume that it did indeed do so, though in that instance the moral price of avoidance would have been accepting the enslavement of an entire race. At any rate, the civil strife argument too is easily answered, and for the same reason that the democracy-based argument for subnational choice does not justify states: If the states are thought to be useful instruments for placating their citizens by recognizing their distinctive interests, then the local governments, which as noted above are far more precise proxies, would be better instruments still.

While the preceding discussion illustrates why local governments are better suited than state governments to accommodate subnational concerns, there are many areas in which the national government's ability to respond to diverse needs and interests also exceeds that of the states. As others (noted below) have documented, the states' differing resources have left them incapable of addressing serious state-to-state social and economic inequalities. In several respects, in fact, state government has only made those problems worse.

One striking example is the subject of a careful empirical study by Jennifer Karas Montes.[36] For every calendar year from 1970 to 2014, she correlated the average life expectancies of people living in each of the fifty states with the liberality or conservatism of those states in each of eighteen different policy domains. She found that "[m]ore liberal versions of policies related to abortion, civil rights, environment, gun control, immigration, LGBT rights, private sector labor, and tobacco tax, as well as a measure of policy innovation, predict longer lives." How much longer? "If all states enacted liberal policies across the 18 domains, our study estimated that U.S. life

---

[36] Jennifer Karas Montes, Research Brief No. 28, Lerner Center for Public Health Promotion, *Conservative State Policies Damage U.S. Life Expectancy* (Aug. 4, 2020), https://surface.syr.edu/cgi/viewcontent.cgi?article=1020&context=lerner.

expectancy would increase by 2.8 years for women and 2.1 years for men. However, if all states enacted conservative policies, U.S. life expectancy would decline by 2.0 years for women and 1.9 years for men." Moreover, widening political polarization in recent years has only increased the gap in life expectancies between states with liberal policies and those with conservative policies.[37]

While the point of that empirically comprehensive article was to highlight the health and life expectancy benefits of liberal policies, it also fortifies the point, more relevant here, made by writers like Donald Kettl and Jamila Michener: State-to-state policy differences generate dramatic geographic inequalities in the health, welfare, and life expectancies of their citizens.[38] All else equal, your chances of living a long and healthy life depend heavily on the policies of the state you live in. And that is a problem that too many states have proved either unable or unwilling to fix.

Of course, just as economic inequalities exist from state to state, so too they exist from one local area to another. What role the national government should play in addressing geographic economic disparities is an issue that would arise with or without states; it is thus beyond the scope of this book. The only observation I can offer is that, without states, the central government would remain the only actor with the capacity to end those sorts of geographic inequities. Nothing would force Congress to fulfill that responsibility even then, but federalism would no longer provide cover for its inaction.

I can think of one final argument that might be made as to why the surgically targeted policymaking that federalism purportedly permits is beneficial. Members of Congress are supposed to promote the welfare of both the nation and their own constituents. Those two obligations can conflict; what is best for the people of one particular state or one particular US House district is not necessarily best for the country as a whole. State legislators and state officials, patriotic as some might genuinely be, are less burdened by that dual loyalty. They can give top priority to the interests of their respective states.

That distinction, however, might be more theoretical than practical. Unless members of Congress plan to retire, the realities of reelection can never be far from their minds. And that means focusing intensely on the desires of one's own state or local constituents, just as their state legislative counterparts do.

---

[37] *Ibid.* Accord, Paola Scommegna, PRB, *Life Expectancy Is Increasingly Tied to a State's Policy Leanings* (Jan. 12, 2023), www.prb.org/resources/liberal-u-s-state-policies-linked-to-longer-lives/.

[38] Kettl, note 1 (focusing heavily on health care, infrastructure, education, and air and water quality, and linking these inequalities to the policy choices of different states); Michener, note 1, at 13–14 (making the point that state-to-state variations in Medicaid eligibility "are the product of policy choices made possible (but not necessitated) by federalism" and that these inequities undermine not just economic, but also political, participation). See also Paul Brest *et al.*, Processes of Constitutional Decisionmaking: Cases and Materials 331–420 (7th ed., 2018) (discussing the history of the Fourteenth Amendment and, in particular, the range of individual interests that at least some judges and commentators believed to be among the "privileges and immunities" protected by section 1 of the Fourteenth Amendment).

In addition, the local governments that would assume the lion's share of the localized functions currently performed by states would have at least as much incentive as state legislators currently have to prioritize local interests. They would likely have even greater incentives to do so, since, as discussed earlier, the political preferences of their local constituents might diverge sharply from those of individuals who live elsewhere in the state.

C INTERSTATE COMPETITION

States, it is sometimes said, are a source of healthy competition. Two different kinds of competition are commonly asserted: Through their differing laws and policies, states give people a choice of where to live. If you are dissatisfied with the laws of your current state of residence, or enamored of the laws of another state, you can vote with your feet. This so-called "exit" option incentivizes states to be responsive to their citizens' needs and desires. The other strand of the competition argument is that, similarly through their laws and policies, states compete to attract businesses that will benefit their economies.

1 *Competition for Citizens*

The exit option has been invoked frequently by courts and commentators. The Supreme Court has said that federalism "makes government more responsive by putting the States in competition for a mobile citizenry."[39]

But there are problems with that argument. The first one is reality. Ask yourself a simple question: Do I know a single person who has actually moved from one state to another solely, or even in large part, because they disagreed with the laws or policies of the state where they lived or were drawn by the politics of the state to which they moved? I myself do not know such a person. We might grumble, even passionately, about the politics of the state where we live, but that frustration rarely prompts us to pull up stakes and move to another state. Yes, we occasionally hear about exceptionally wealthy US citizens who either leave *the country* to avoid or reduce their income taxes or purposely domicile themselves in a state with no or low income taxes. Surely, however, we are talking here about a minute percentage of the national population. Rather, as others have pointed out,[40] inertia keeps most people moored to a given area. When people do move to a new state, it is usually for reasons related to work, study, family, climate, health, or other personal factors – not policy differences.

---

[39] *Bond* v. *United States*, 564 U.S. 211, 221 (2011), quoting *Gregory* v. *Ashcroft*, 501 U.S. 452, 458 (1991). Accord, Bowman *et al.*, note 5, at 25; Friedman, note 6, at 387; Gerken, note 1, at 7.

[40] For example, Friedman, note 6, at 387–88. Accord, Rubin & Feeley, note 1, at 918 (arguing that "the transaction costs of obtaining information and transplanting one's life may well overwhelm the utility gains from the selection process, particularly for people with limited resources.")

In contrast, dissatisfaction with governmental law or policy frequently spurs people to move, *within* a state, from one city or town to a neighboring political subdivision. They might, for example, move because they perceive the public schools to be better elsewhere, or because their property taxes will be lower. Rubin and Feeley point out that those kinds of local moves are more attractive, both because there are more local governments to choose from than there are states and because the new locations are closer and the moves therefore less disruptive.[41] And yet, as discussed earlier, states have increasingly limited the decision-making authority of their local governments. So if the objective is to foster a healthy competition for citizens, my proposed abolition of state government and attendant transfer of many state functions to local governments would serve that purpose better, not worse, than leaving that job to the states.

2 Economic Competition

The argument here is that states compete to attract businesses that will spur economic growth and that that competition benefits the entire nation.[42] Unlike in the above discussion of competition for citizens, one can safely assume that businesses indeed can be lured to states that offer various sweeteners. These might include lax corporate regulation or environmental regulation or labor standards, low state corporate tax rates, or property tax breaks. But as an argument for state government, this too falls short.

First, it is not at all clear that this kind of state-to-state competition benefits the nation. States that take these sorts of steps are externalizing their costs, simply shifting them to other states. Frequently, those costs come in the form of a race to the bottom.[43] Other states also eager to attract businesses might feel a need to respond by similarly relaxing their corporate, environmental, or labor regulations, to the detriment of the residents, consumers, and shareholders whom those regulations are meant to protect. Or, other states might have to reduce their corporate income tax rates in order to compete, with the result that they must either cut spending on important programs or raise other tax rates to compensate for the loss of corporate tax revenue. As discussed in more detail in Chapter 4, Section B, external costs, particularly if they amount to a race to the bottom, are frequently present and are a factor strongly favoring uniform national regulation.

Second, even apart from all these external costs to the people of other states and to the nation, the playing field is not level. As Donald Kettl has demonstrated, extreme state-to-state inequalities make it impossible for some states to match the resources of

---

[41] Rubin & Feeley, note 1, at 919.
[42] See Friedman, note 6, at 387; Gerken, note 1, at 6.
[43] See, for example, Friedman, note 6, at 387, 407–408, and sources cited at 387 n.299.

other states.[44] Rodney Hall, writing about an analogous problem with Australia's federal system, put the point well: "If we accept competition between the states, we must accept that people living where there are rich resources (minerals, agricultural land, population) will become far better off than those in states with poorer resources."[45]

D LABORATORIES OF INNOVATION

In 1932, Supreme Court Justice Louis Brandeis wrote: "It is one of the happy incidents of the federal system that a single courageous State may, if its citizens choose, serve as a laboratory; and try novel social and economic experiments without risk to the rest of the country."[46] Those oft-quoted words[47] have become part of the lore surrounding our federal system.

But there are major problems with that defense of states. To begin with, even on those occasions when state experimentation has produced seemingly positive results – and I don't deny there have been many such instances – the credit often belongs elsewhere. Charles Tyler and Heather Gerken have demonstrated that the real credit for innovation belongs not to the states, but to the third-party interest groups and funders who motivate the states and influence the federal framework.[48]

Perhaps more important, there are so many ways in which these "experiments" not only have failed to generate actual benefits, but have caused great harms. Michael Wishnie has decried "state anti-immigrant employment restrictions" as well as "state or local restrictions on immigrant access to student financial aid and free primary and secondary education."[49] What some euphemistically call laboratories of "innovation," Wishnie calls "laboratories of bigotry."[50]

---

[44] Kettl, note 1, at 5, 92–110, 131–42.

[45] Rodney Hall, Abolish the States – Australia's Future and a $30 Billion Answer to Our Tax Problems 72 (1998).

[46] *New State Ice Co.* v. *Liebmann*, 285 U.S. 262, 311 (1932) (Justice Brandeis, dissenting).

[47] For example, *Bond* v. *United States*, 564 U.S. 211, 221 (2011) (federalism "permits innovation and experimentation"); *Gregory* v. *Ashcroft*, 501 U.S. 452, 458 (1991) (federalism "allows for more innovation and experimentation in government"); Mandelker *et al.*, note 6, at xlix ("The rhetorical depiction of states as 'laboratories' of democracy has never rung more true."); Sutton, note 1, at 6 ([b]etter … to allow different governors to try different approaches and to watch the results in real time"); Friedman, note 6, at 397 ("Intuition suggests that with fifty different parallel state governments, *and countless substate governments as well*, innovations in governing or problem solving will occur" [my emphasis]). I'll return in a moment to the crucial importance of the phrase I've italicized here. *Cf.* Bowman *et al.*, note 5, at 25 (different states' "fresh policy ideas" provide "resiliency"); Kettl, note 1, at 143–69 (describing Congress's use of discretionary waivers that allow states to experiment, but pointing out that those devices often produce harmful inequalities).

[48] Charles W. Tyler & Heather K. Gerken, *The Myth of the Laboratories of Democracy*, 122 Columbia L. Rev. 2187 (2022).

[49] Michael J. Wishnie, *Laboratories of Bigotry? Devolution of the Immigration Power, Equal Protection, and Federalism*, 76 NYU L. Rev. 493, 553–54 (2001).

[50] *Ibid.*, at 553. To be sure, Wishnie's reference here is to "state *and local* laboratories of bigotry against immigrants" [my emphasis]. Since I argue below that local governments would serve the innovation

Other writers, referring to the wave of antidemocratic state actions, have also preferred alternative terms for these sorts of state experiments: "laboratories of [o]ligarchy," "laboratories of autocracy," and "laboratories of authoritarianism."[51] Similarly, Gowri Ramachandran & Matthew Germer have specifically criticized the spread of state actions auditing election results based on false claims of voter fraud.[52]

Indeed, in the very case in which Justice Brandeis uttered his famous laboratory of experimentation quote, the state "experiment" that his dissenting opinion would have sanctioned was Oklahoma's licensing requirement for anyone who wanted to sell ice. If the Court had let this Oklahoma law stand, the practical result would have been to allow the state to deny such licenses whenever it found that that state's one existing ice company was adequately serving the state's residents – in other words, the creation of a monopoly for one favored company.

Even Judge Jeffrey Sutton, a staunch fan of states' rights, chooses to use just one example to illustrate what he sees as the benefits of letting states innovate. Remarkably, the example he selects is the varying state responses to the COVID-19 pandemic. Commendably, he begins by conceding the obvious – that this example is "an unlikely candidate for illustrating how federalism works," because "[i]t's not a parochial problem with parochial effects; [i]t's an existential threat to everyone, all people, all American governments. And it's a problem that does not respect borders."[53]

Precisely. But he nonetheless lauds giving the states a wide berth in responding to COVID, arguing that "it's a problem in which borders add tools and flexibility for fixing the problem," mainly because no one leader has all the answers.[54] He neglects what for me stands out as the most tragic consequence of that devolution: the reckless, irresponsible policies of some states that fostered the spread of a dangerous and highly contagious disease throughout the nation. How many of the more than one million American deaths occurred needlessly because some governors and legislatures refused to regulate large public gatherings, or affirmatively discouraged

---

function better than states do, I emphasize that immigration is not one of the functions that I would reassign to the local governments. Both the need for the United States to speak to the world with a single voice on immigration matters and the fact that immigrants, like anyone else, are free to cross state lines strongly counsel exclusive national responsibility for immigration.

[51] Bulman-Pozen & Seifter, note 22, at 863, citing Matt Ford, New Republic, *The GOP's Laboratories of Oligarchy* (Dec. 4, 2018), https://newrepublic.com/article/152515/gops-laboratories-oligarchy, and Steven Levitsky & Daniel Ziblatt, How Democracies Die 2 (2018) ("laboratories of authoritarianism)." See also David Pepper, Laboratories of Autocracy: A Wake-Up Call from Behind the Lines (2021).

[52] Gowri Ramachandran & Matthew Germer, Brennan Center for Justice, *Bad-faith Election Audits Are Sabotaging Democracy Across the Nation* (Aug. 4, 2021), www.brennancenter.org/our-work/analysis-opinion/bad-faith-election-audits-are-sabotaging-democracy-across-nation. See the fuller discussion of manipulative audits (commonly called "fraudits") in Chapter 3, Section E.

[53] Sutton, note 1, at 5.

[54] *Ibid.*

vaccinations, or openly mocked those who wore masks? We shall never know. But if *any* issue cries out for uniform national regulation, surely it is the containment of a highly contagious fatal disease that flows like water across state lines.

Apart from the kinds of affirmative harms described above, Rubin and Feeley have provided an important insight into a problem inherent in the very concept of states innovating solutions to national problems:

> In a unitary system, the central authority will generally have a single goal, but it may be uncertain which of several policies will best achieve that goal. To resolve this uncertainty, it could order different subunits to experiment with different strategies until the best way to achieve the goal emerges. Experimentation of this sort is ... useful only when the subunits share a single goal. It is not particularly relevant to subunits whose goals are different from each other. But true federalism allows governmental subunits to choose different goals, not to experiment with different mechanisms for achieving a single one.[55]

Thus, the authors conclude, in a federation the different innovations don't help us solve common national problems.

That insight reinforces my final point. Local governments, lacking sovereignty, do not present the same obstacles that states currently do. Without states, the national government could formulate common goals on those issues that are suitable for national regulation. The innovations of local governments could therefore be directed to achieving those goals, not obstructing them.

Nor is it just a matter of sovereignty. There are more local governments than there are states – far more. If 50 political subdivisions are thought to provide the machinery for social experimentation, imagine what 90,000 would do. To the extent that the argument rests on there being multiple governmental units to experiment with a variety of approaches, therefore, we don't need states. Local governments could serve that function at least as well, especially without state governments tying their hands. Even Friedman, an enthusiastic proponent of the innovation rationale, is careful to couch his description as one of state "and local" experimentation.[56]

Sometimes, of course, the particular experiment will be too large a project for either the population or the geographic area of a single local government. In those instances, it can partner with the national government or with neighboring general or special purpose local governments – or, depending on the subject, even distant local governments. Thus, partnerships do more than exponentially expand the sheer number of possible collaborations; they can also make experiments economically or logistically more feasible.

---

55 Rubin & Feeley, note 1, at 924.
56 Friedman, note 6, at 397 (also referring to "fifty different parallel state governments, *and countless substate governments as well*) [my emphasis].

E ENCOURAGING CITIZEN PARTICIPATION

Another common refrain among federalism fans similarly rests on the premise that states are closer to the people than the national government is. This argument is that federalism thereby enables and encourages citizens to become more involved in the democratic process.[57]

But neither the premise nor the conclusion is self-evident. For starters, as Rubin and Feeley observe, "there is no theoretical or empirical reason to believe" that states are closer to the people in actual practice.[58] There is, in fact, reason to believe the opposite. As noted earlier, at least one prominent scholar, Miriam Seifter, demonstrates empirically that civil society has been a much weaker check on state laws and policies than on those of the federal government.[59]

Second, as Rubin and Feeley also point out, "[f]ederalism does not necessarily increase participation; it simply authorizes a set of specified political sub-units – states in our case – to decide for themselves how much participation is desirable. Some might choose to encourage participation but others might choose to suppress it."[60] Indeed. Although their 1994 article was written decades after the elimination of both poll taxes and literacy tests, the spread of state voter suppression measures discussed in Chapter 3, Section B has since reached epidemic proportions, making their observation even more salient today.

But most importantly, returning to a common theme, any argument that state government encourages citizen participation can be made *a fortiori* for local governments. Heather Gerken observes that, "[b]ecause states are so large, scholars who write about bringing governance closer to the people often segue into discussions of lower-level institutions."[61]

This is for good reason. For one thing, by virtue of their closer physical proximity, local officials will generally be more accessible and more easily held accountable than federal officials[62] and, I would add, than state officials. In addition, all else equal, voters might be expected to be inherently more motivated to participate

---

[57] See, for example, *Bond v. United States*, 564 U.S. 211, 221 (2011); *Gregory v. Ashcroft*, 501 U.S. 452, 458 (1991); *cf.* Richard Briffaut, *"What about the 'Ism'?" Normative and Formal Concerns in Contemporary Federalism*, 47 Vanderbilt L. Rev. 1303, 1305 (1994) (noting argument that federalism "increas[es] opportunities for political participation"); Friedman, note 6, at 389–90 (observing that states "and their substate local governments" are closer to the people than the national government is). Briffaut's observation requires further discussion below.

[58] Rubin & Feeley, note 1, at 916.

[59] Seifter, *Further From*, note 28.

[60] Rubin & Feeley, note 1, at 915.

[61] Gerken, note 1, at 21 n.56, citing as examples Shapiro, note 1, at 91–94; Friedman, note 6, at 389–91; Lewis B. Kaden, *Politics, Money, and State Sovereignty: The Judicial Role*, 79 Colum. L. Rev. 847, 853–54 (1979); Deborah Jones Merritt, *The Guarantee Clause and State Autonomy: Federalism for a Third Century*, 88 Colum. L. Rev. 1, 7–8 (1988); Andrzej Rapaczynski, *From Sovereignty to Process: The Jurisprudence of Federalism after Garcia*, Sup. Ct. Rev. 341, 402, 415–16, (1985).

[62] Friedman, note 6, at 395.

in local political affairs than in state or national affairs because their preferences –
whether expressed in the form of a vote or any other form of political participation –
are more likely to make a difference. Then too, many neighborhood citizen advisory
boards offer their local governments valuable ground level input into the needs and
preferences of the communities they serve.[63] For all these reasons, the transfer of
much of the states' decision-making to local governments would expand the terrain
over which this advantage could be realized.

Richard Briffaut has an interesting take on these issues. He readily acknowledges
that "the values said to be advanced by federalism are not distinctively associated
with the states. Many of these values [including political participation] may be
served better by local governments than by states." I fully agree. But he goes on
to argue that that's not the point. Preferring a formal approach to federalism over
a normative approach, he maintains that characteristics like fixed boundaries and
autonomy over spending (in those subject areas not reserved for the national government) leave the states better positioned than their constituent local subdivisions
to discharge the functions of federalism.[64] With that, I am not sure I agree. It is
unclear, for example, how either fixed boundaries (which local governments also
typically possess, for that matter) and partial spending autonomy render states better
suited than local governments to encourage political participation. But even if one
accepts Briffaut's factual assumption, his argument does not identify any value that
federalism serves. At most, it suggests that, *given* federalism, those functions that are
to be performed at some subnational level – or at least some of them – are better
performed by the states than by local governments. It does not explain why we need
federalism, or even state government, in the first place.

F CITIZENS' VOICE IN NATIONAL POLICIES

A state's congressional delegation, acting collectively, will generally have more muscle than a single member of either the House or the Senate. They can use that
extra muscle to call the attention of Congress or the Administration to a problem
that has arisen in their state and to push for a remedy that only the national government has the resources to provide. In that way, the argument might run, the current
federal-state system strengthens the voice of every state's citizens in the formulation
of national policy, especially on matters that affect them in distinctive ways.

But that assumes that the members of the state's congressional delegation share
a common incentive to spend their political capital on that problem. That assumption, in turn, ignores the fundamental demographic reality that makes the division
of our country into states so politically arbitrary to begin with. Common problems

[63] Mandelker *et al.*, note 6, at 197–204.
[64] Briffaut, note 57, at 1305.

and common political preferences are extremely unlikely to map so neatly onto the geographic territories of the states. To return to a recurring theme, a given problem is much more likely to be confined to one area within the state (often mainly urban or mainly rural), or common to parts of different states, or national in scope, than to be congruent with the area defined by the frequently arbitrary borders of a single state. Thus, the members of Congress who serve the affected geographic areas (or all of Congress if the problem is nationwide) will be a more receptive coalition than a delegation of members whose only connection to one another is that their districts happen to lie in the same state or states. We are back once again to the same familiar reality that casts doubt on most of the claimed benefits of states: When it comes to serving as proxies for the varying interests or political preferences of subnational populations, the states are no match for the local governments.

G STATE CONSTITUTIONS AND INDIVIDUAL RIGHTS

Judge Sutton points out that most state constitutions differ from the US Constitution in important ways. His more significant examples include popular election and retention of judges; a plural executive in which several state leaders, not just the chief executive and second-in-command, are independently elected; balanced budget requirements; initiatives and referenda; and a relatively easy constitutional amendment process.[65] Jessica Bulman-Pozen and Miriam Seifter identify some of the same examples and add others, including equipopulous Senate districts[66] and explicit recognition of the right to vote.[67] All this, they rightly point out, adds up to final constitutional products that are generally more majoritarian than their federal cousin.

The point of Bulman-Pozen's and Seifter's excellent article is to call attention to state constitutions' promotion of democratic norms. Judge Sutton's similarly

---

[65] Sutton, note 1, at 8–9. See also Jeffrey S. Sutton, 51 Imperfect Solutions: States and the Making of American Constitutional Law (2018) (arguing that the role of state constitutions and state courts in protecting liberty is underappreciated); William J. Brennan, Jr., *State Constitutions and the Protection of Individual Rights*, 90 Harv. L. Rev. 489 (1977). Some of the most sophisticated writing on state constitutions, and particularly on the ease of amending state constitutions, has been that of Jessica Bulman-Pozen and Miriam Seifter. In addition to Bulman-Pozen & Seifter, note 22, see Jessica Bulman-Pozen & Miriam Seifter, *State Constitutional Rights and Democratic Proportionality*, 123 Colum. L. Rev. 1855 (2023); Jessica Bulman-Pozen & Miriam Seifter, *The Right to Amend State Constitutions*, 133 Yale L. J. Forum 191 (2023) (focusing on the right, created by state constitutions, to amend those constitutions by popular initiative and observing, at 193, that voter initiatives amending state constitutions sometimes protect, but sometimes threaten, minority rights).

[66] Bulman-Pozen & Seifter, note 22, at 873–74.

[67] Ibid., at 861. See also Richard Hasen, The New York Times, *The U.S. Lacks What Every Democracy Needs* (Jan. 16, 2024), www.nytimes.com/2024/01/16/opinion/voting-rights-constitution-28th-amendment.html?campaign_id=39&emc=edit_ty_20240116&instance_id=112634&nl=opinion-today&regi_id=13788254&segment_id=155451&te=1&user_id=e16deb82e8516f294a4077a86co2f5c2.

thoughtful book seems aimed at a broader objective – to extoll federalism and to urge a broader role for state government in our federal system.

But whether or not so intended, in my view none of these differences between the federal and state constitutions strengthens the arguments for federalism or even for having states at all. Some of my reasons for saying this relate specifically to the individual examples; my other reasons apply more generally to all the examples.

Let's start with the specifics. Although there are reasonable arguments to be made both for and against the popular election and periodic retention of judges, I regard the practice as a serious weakness, not a strength, in the state systems that follow it. Still, I leave that discussion to Chapter 6, Section C, as part of the outline of my proposed new republic. Whatever one's preferred method of selecting judges, there are more general reasons, discussed below, not to view this feature as a benefit of having states.

As Bulman-Pozen and Seifter observe, the plural executive that most state constitutions require can be thought of as majoritarian in nature. But it is majoritarian only in the same sense that initiatives, referenda, and even popular selection of judges are majoritarian: all these measures exemplify direct democracy. And direct democracy is not the only form, or in the United States even the primary form, of democracy. In our representative democracy, the people delegate to their elected leaders the power not only to pass laws and make policy decisions, but also to choose other policymaking officials. Which of these officials should be elected, and which ones should be appointed by others who have been elected, is a question of degree and therefore a matter of opinion.

A constitutionally entrenched balanced budget requirement, in contrast, is not a majoritarian feature. To the contrary, it is explicitly counter-majoritarian, since it prohibits the people's elected representatives from enacting a budget deficit when they deem it beneficial to do so – for example, by cutting taxes or authorizing stimulus spending in times of recession. Economists will forever differ over the relative pros and cons of long-term budget deficits, but the point here is that the prohibitions contained in various state constitutions are not a majoritarian example.

Popular initiatives and referenda similarly have both pros and cons, but I agree with Bulman-Pozen and Seifter that they can be fairly characterized as majoritarian instruments. Still, they merely substitute direct democracy for representative democracy, and at any rate, the discussion in Chapter 3, Section F describes the modern trend of state governments overriding or preempting popular initiatives. Moreover, as discussed below, local governments also frequently allow popular initiatives and referenda. Under the model proposed in this book, they would remain able to do so, and national initiatives and referenda would be permitted as well.

The relative ease with which state constitutions can be amended is clearly a majoritarian feature, especially when accomplished by a direct vote of the people. But constitutions protect fundamental individual rights and essential institutions of government; they are not meant to be too casually altered. Some measure of durability, even though inherently counter-majoritarian, is important. While I argued in Chapter 2, Section E that the US Constitution tilts too heavily toward durability, my view is that the power to change state constitutions by simple majority vote tilts too heavily in the opposite direction. While I therefore don't see this feature of many state constitutions as an argument for keeping states, I acknowledge that those who favor an easy or more purely majoritarian constitutional amendment process might well feel otherwise.

Bulman-Pozen and Seifter point out that state Senates, unlike the United States Senate, are equipopulous. And they rightly regard that component as a prerequisite to political equality, which in turn is a basic pillar of a true democracy. Judge Sutton, tellingly, does not include that feature in his list of arguments for federalism or for states; to do so would have required an acknowledgment that the contrary composition of the United States Senate, necessitated by the notion of equal state sovereignty, is undemocratic. But before giving the states credit for adopting greater legislative majoritarianism than the federal government does, let us remember that it was the US Supreme Court, in *Reynolds* v. *Sims*,[68] that forced them to do so. At any rate, without states, the US Senate could, and under my proposal would, become similarly equipopulous, as discussed in Chapter 6, Section B.2.

As noted, many state constitutions commendably enshrine the right to vote. The US Constitution does not. It merely specifies certain impermissible forms of discrimination in voting.[69] Its only recognition of a right to vote is the Seventeenth Amendment requirement that US senators be "elected by the people" of each state.[70] My proposal envisions explicit recognition of a right to vote – directly for the president upon abolition of the Electoral College, and by a separate, similar provision for election of members of the Senate.[71]

Apart from these provision-specific responses, there are at least three general reasons that none of these distinctive characteristics of state constitutions is a persuasive argument for federalism or even for states. First, in the absence of state governments and the constraints they currently impose on their constituent local governments, the latter could decide on their governmental structures themselves. If the residents of one municipality wanted to choose their mayor and city or town council by direct election and let the mayor appoint all the other executive officials, while another municipality preferred direct election of the city or town manager, the city attorney, and any other officials, both of those municipalities could do as they wished. The

---

[68] 377 U.S. 533 (1964), discussed in Chapter 2, Section A.
[69] The vote cannot constitutionally be denied on the basis of race, sex, failure to pay a poll tax, or age (if over 18). See U.S. Const. amends. XV, § 1; XIX; XXIV, § 1; and XXVI, § 1.
[70] U.S. Const. Amend. XVII, Cl. 1. Several writers have advocated amending the US Constitution by explicitly adding a right to vote, as a way to repair many of the democratic gaps in the US elections laws. See especially Richard L. Hasen, A Real Right to Vote: How a Constitutional Amendment Can Safeguard American Democracy (2024). See also Levitsky & Ziblatt, note 51, at 232.
[71] See Chapter 6, Sections B.1 and B.2.

same is true of the decisions whether to require balanced budgets, or permit legislation by popular initiative, or make it relatively easy to amend the city or town charter, or enshrine the right to vote in the local government charter, or elect the city
or town or county legislative council through equipopulous districts, or provide for
popular election of municipal judges.[72] If democratic norms call for allowing each
state to choose its own governmental structure, then they call even more loudly for
local cities, towns, and counties to have the right to do so. Even Judge Sutton ends
a chapter with the following conclusion: "Democracy indeed may work most effectively at the local level today."[73]

Second, whatever one's view of the merits of each of those issues, it's hard to see
how those merits vary depending on the needs of the particular state. At either the
national level or the state level, do elected judges and elected attorneys general and
equipopulous Senate districts make more sense for residents of Michigan than for
residents of Alabama? Would the availability of popular initiatives, or easier amendments of a constitution, be better for folks in South Carolina than for those living in
Oregon? Are there states where people would be better off if the right to vote were
not recognized? Offhand, I can't think of anything one might find in the Wisconsin
waters that is lacking in the Colorado Rockies that makes it especially important to
elect judges and officials rather than let the chief executive appoint them, or to prescribe a plural executive, or to require balanced budgets, or to allow legislation by
popular initiative, or to ease the path to constitutional amendments.

Some might argue that that is not the point. Even if the merits of the competing
arguments don't depend on the distinctive needs of the particular state, the decisions should depend on the political preferences of that state's citizenry. That is,
after all, the essence of democracy.

Whatever force that argument is thought to have, it is not a reason to retain state
government, mainly because the needs and preferences of a given state are rarely
either internally uniform or externally distinctive. Again, the prevailing political preferences of Atlanta's citizens bear little resemblance to those living in rural Georgia.
When it comes to political polarization, the urban-rural divide is far sharper than
the divides among states.

Third, state constitutions are only as good as the interpretations that the states'
Supreme Court justices place on them. Who are those justices? In many states,
judges are elected (and retained or terminated) by the same voters who choose
whether to elect and reelect the state legislators. And the vast majority of states are
safe states – that is, reliably red or reliably blue. So one can reasonably assume that

---

[72] It is true that in the proposed model the current state judgeships would be replaced by national judgeships, some of which, like the existing national judgeships, would be filled by presidential appointment and Senate confirmation. But the president will have been popularly elected and the Senate
will have become equipopulous, as discussed in Chapter 6, Sections B.1 and B.2, thus eliminating the
objections to the current process discussed in Chapter 2, Section D.

[73] Sutton, note 1, at 327 (ending his chapter 9, on local government).

in most states the political views of the judges will generally not stray far from those of the legislative majority. That matters. As discussed in detail in Chapter 2, Section D, interpretation is often – and in the case of constitutions, usually – far from cut and dried. It requires judgment, and judgment is unavoidably affected by one's ideological – or, dare I say, partisan – inclinations. State constitutions can certainly be valuable tools. But for the task of taming counter-majoritarian state action, they are a thin reed on which to rely. Bulman-Pozen and Seifter cite decisions by the Supreme Courts of Pennsylvania and North Carolina striking down legislatively gerrymandered maps as violations of their respective state constitutions,[74] but it was not long afterward that a partisan shift in the North Carolina Supreme Court's majority prompted that court to overrule its earlier decision with breathtaking speed.[75]

H PERSONAL OR POLITICAL COMMUNITY

Some have argued that federalism provides a sense of community. As Rubin and Feeley explain, two main forms of community have been invoked in service of this argument. There are what some have called "affective" communities, in which "members feel a personal or emotional connection with one another," and there are "political" communities, in which members "engage in a collective decision-making process."[76]

But both strands of the community argument assume that a state's residents share some important commonality and that that commonality distinguishes them from the residents of other states. Rubin and Feeley debunk that assumption as well as anyone has. They point out that "affective communities necessarily consist of small groups."[77] States are not nearly small enough to serve that purpose. As for political communities, "Most of our states, the alleged political communities that federalism would preserve, are mere administrative units, rectangular swatches of the prairie with nothing but their legal definitions to distinguish them from one another."[78]

Recall that the federalism argument discussed in Section B relied on the claimed ability of states to tailor their laws and policies to the distinctive needs and preferences of their citizens. The federalism defense considered in this section relates to that same theme but is slightly different. Where the earlier defense focused on supposedly common interests and therefore preferences for particular laws and policies, this one focuses on community as a personal or political end in itself. Citizens of a given state are depicted as having characteristics that leave them bound to one another in ways that do not bind them to others. This, the argument runs, enables

---

[74] Bulman-Pozen & Seifter, note 22, at 862–63.
[75] See the discussion of that episode in Chapter 2, Section D.
[76] Rubin & Feeley, note 1, at 937. See also Rapaczynski, note 61.
[77] Rubin & Feeley, note 1, at 938.
[78] *Ibid.*, at 944.

them to forge bonds, and pursue community interests, that are not realistic for the much larger national population.

While the arguments considered in these two sections of the chapter differ slightly, they contain the same fatal flaws: the sheer sizes of states and the crudity of their boundaries as a proxy for delineating these groups. As Section B demonstrated, the most dramatic divides are not interstate, but intrastate. Let us assume for the sake of argument that states, presumably because of their smaller populations and geographic areas than the nation as a whole, are more likely *than the federal government* to foster – and protect – a sense of both political and personal community. If that is so, then the same attributes – smaller land masses and smaller populations – would suggest that local governments are still better suited to that purpose than states.

I STATES AS FEDERAL PARTNERS

Some scholars have touted, or at least acknowledged, the advantages of states partnering with the federal government to implement federal programs.[79] Bowman *et al.* identify states' closeness to the people as a reason that they can adapt public programs to local needs in ways that are administratively efficient.[80]

Of course, if closeness to the people is what makes states good partners in implementing federal programs, then local governments, being closer still, should make even better federal partners. Many of the concrete examples offered in Chapter 4, Section C.3 illustrate the value of national-local partnerships in discharging functions that would be reassigned to the local governments if state government were abolished. In addition, regional arrangements of local governments have an advantage as partners that states don't have: they can cross state lines. Those collaborations can be voluntary or, as Nestor Davidson has noted, accomplished with a nudge from Congress – as has been done in the past.[81]

Still, one might assume, it is a lot easier for the national government to deal with 50 state partners than to deal with 90,000 local partners. Yet, they do it all the time. Davidson refutes the conventional view that the only direct relationships

---

[79] Bowman *et al.*, note 5, at 30. This view has been expressed even by scholars who favor a much stronger national government role and share a negative view of federalism. For example, Rubin & Feeley, note 1, at 951 (taking a dim view of state sovereignty but acknowledging that "[s]tates serve a valuable function in our nation; they are the natural and convenient means to achieve the managerial benefits that flow from decentralizing certain governmental functions. ..."); Kettl, note 1, at 198 (acknowledging that "[t]he states can surely maintain their central role as administrators of intergovernmental programs" but that the federal government needs to drive the policymaking if economic inequality is to be meaningfully addressed).

[80] Bowman *et al.*, note 5, at 30.

[81] Nestor M. Davidson, *Cooperative Localism: Federal-Local Collaboration in an Era of State Sovereignty*, 93 Virginia. L. Rev. 959, 1026–29 (2007).

between two levels of government are federal-state and state-local. To the contrary, he shows,

> In practice, ... numerous federal regulatory, spending, and enforcement policies actively rely on the participation of local governments independent from the states. Indeed, direct relations between the federal government and local governments ... play a significant role in areas of contemporary policy as disparate as homeland security, law enforcement, disaster response, economic development, social services, immigration, and environmental protection, among other areas of vital national concern.[82]

Moreover, as noted in Chapter 4, Section B, the federal government can, and frequently does, operate through regional offices that interact with all the states in the region. In the absence of states, it could similarly interact with all the local governments in their respective regions. Additionally, there would be no need to provide each regional office with its own separate legislature, its own separate governor's office, and its own separate judiciary, attributes required for the states whom they now use as intermediaries.

These sorts of direct national-local relationships would be easier still in a unitary republic. There would be no state sovereignty and therefore no anti-commandeering doctrine. As discussed earlier, in the anti-commandeering cases the Supreme Court has prohibited the federal government from requiring states to help implement federal programs. Unless every state consents – not always the case in our increasingly polarized country – it can be virtually impossible to operate a nationwide program that relies on local implementation. In our current federal system that prohibition is absolute – no balancing of competing interests is involved – and is not limited to the law enforcement context.[83]

Without state government, there would also be no assertions of plenary state authority over local governments. In Davidson's view, local governments should not be held subservient to the states in which they are located. Rather, he argues, the national government can be both the source of, and the constraint on, local governments' autonomy.[84] I very much agree. But while Davidson's point is that the Supreme Court should embrace that view (rather than a more sweeping version of state sovereignty) as a matter of constitutional interpretation, I am suggesting, for all the reasons included in this book, that the US would do well to go two steps further. I would eliminate not just the concept of plenary state power over local governments, and not even just state sovereignty, but the entire institution of state government.

Jessica Bulman-Pozen argues that, when Congress enlists states as partners in the implementation of a federal program, the states play a useful separation of powers

---

[82] *Ibid.*, at 960. He elaborates on these examples, *ibid.*, at 968–74.
[83] See Chapter 1, notes 37–41 and accompanying text.
[84] Davidson, note 81, at 962–63.

role. They do this, she maintains, by challenging federal executive branch actions that the states believe exceed the executive's statutory authority.[85] It is an interesting thought, and I don't quarrel with it. For present purposes, it is enough to say that in the unitary American republic considered in this book, local governments would be equally well positioned to perform the function of challenging executive actions on those sorts of *ultra vires* grounds. In many cases, private parties who are adversely affected by the national executive branch actions would similarly be able to bring the case to court.

J METHOD TO THE MADNESS: BOUNDARY LOCATIONS

When this book was in its early stages, its thesis drew more than its share of skeptics. Most likely, it still does. One friend asked me (and I'm paraphrasing) "Why were the various state boundaries drawn where they were in the first place? Surely there must have been *some* rhyme or reason to the locations of those lines. And wouldn't the reasons for separating the states along those specific boundaries reveal reasons for having states in the first place?"[86]

It was an intriguing question. In searching for the answer, I stumbled upon an exceptionally helpful article by John Harrington & Grant Suneson.[87] The authors carefully researched and described the origins of each state and its boundaries. From the collection of those individual descriptions, I take the liberty of breaking the inquiry into two parts: How did each state become a state? And why were its specific boundary lines drawn where they were?

The technical legal answers to those two questions turn out to be the same: "it's a mishmash." As to the "how" question: The thirteen original states, of course, were formed out of the British colonies and became US states by ratifying the new Constitution. Some of the other states had been US territories or carved out of US territories. Still other states resulted from the partitions of existing states. Some states were admitted in pairs, one slave state and one free state. And some states (e.g., California and Texas) had been independent countries before being admitted to the Union.[88]

As to the "why" question: The explanations for the fifty states' precise boundaries are similarly diverse. Most of the thirteen original states simply retained their colonial boundaries. And most of those boundaries had been laid out in charters, deeds, or patents granted by the King, often in keeping with natural geographic

---

[85] Jessica Bulman-Pozen, *Federalism as a Safeguard of the Separation of Powers*, 112 Colum. L. Rev. 459 (2012).

[86] I thank JoAnne LaSala for this insight.

[87] John Harrington & Grant Suneson, *This Is How Each State Got Its Shape* (Apr. 3, 2021), https://247wallst.com/special-report/2021/04/03/this-is-how-each-state-got-its-shape/.

[88] *Ibid.*

barriers. Those natural barriers – seacoasts, gulfs, bays, lakes, rivers, mountains, and in the case of the Dakotas the edge of a plateau – would likewise determine the boundary lines of many of the subsequently admitted states. As the nation developed, canals and railroads began to surpass rivers as the primary means of both trade and travel; increasingly, they too became state boundaries. Stillother state boundaries were fixed by either latitude lines ("parallels") or longitude lines (meridians). Some of those were set so as to accommodate President Jefferson's predilection for states of similar size and shape, often a recipe for otherwise arbitrary boundaries.[89]

At least with respect to the drawing of the boundaries, this patchwork might be analogized to the European colonization of Africa and the ultimate division of that continent into its current independent nations. One scholar, recounting the history of African colonization, could as easily have been describing the origins of the American states when she said: "Lines of longitude and latitude, rivers and mountain ranges were pressed into service as borders separating the colonies. Or one simply placed a ruler on the map and drew a straight line."[90]

For present purposes, the key takeaway is that none of those determinants – royal charters, natural geographic barriers, canals and railroads, latitude and longitude lines, or a desire for states of equal geographic areas or similar shapes – had anything to do with the ethnicities, religions, interests, or political preferences of the state's inhabitants.

There are a handful of arguable exceptions. The populations of the slave states and the free states had sharply differing interests, and their admissions in pairs reflected political compromises. But those differences don't explain the precise locations of their boundary lines. Similarly, at least two early border disputes – Pennsylvania/Maryland and Virginia/West Virginia – were settled by separating the states along the Mason–Dixon line. California's eastern boundary could not be pushed further east because the Mormons were in the process of establishing a separate territory. And Rhode Island was shaped by Roger Williams's desire for a colony based on religious tolerance.[91]

But even if those few examples are seen as exceptions to the demographic randomness of the state boundaries, they are pretty much the only exceptions. And even

---

[89] *Ibid.*; see also Trip Trivia, *How the State Shapes Were Formed* (June 10, 2020), www.triptrivia.com/how-states-got-their-shapes/XqhcSlGOvwAGHmpg#:~:text=Influence%20of%20Canals%20and%20Railroads&text=Instead%20of%20mapping%20state%20boundaries,borders%20of%20some%20western%20states.

[90] Hilke Fischer, *130 Years Ago: Carving up Africa in Berlin* (Feb. 25, 2015), www.dw.com/en/130-years-ago-carving-up-africa-in-berlin/a-18278894#:~:text=In%201885%20European%20leaders%20met,that%20exist%20to%20this%20day.&text=The%20map%20on%20the%20wall,names%20and%20many%20white%20spots. (going on to observe the colonial powers' lack of concern over the splitting of tribal or ethnic communities and the direct link between that failing and the tensions plaguing the African continent to this day).

[91] Harrington & Suneson, note 87.

if most of the state lines had been drawn to accommodate demographic differences among the nation's people, demographics change over time – and with increased speed as technology makes interstate migration ever easier. For that reason too, the demographic differences are too transient to explain the need to divide the nation into fifty permanent states. Moreover, as the discussion in Section B makes clear, it is the local governments, not the states, that provide the better proxies for the differing interests and preferences of the nation's subnational populations.

6

A New American Republic

The preceding chapters make the case for abolishing state government in the United States. The functions that state governments have been performing up to now would be redistributed among the national government, the local governments, and inter-government partnerships. The national government would no longer have to link everything it does to one of the specific subjects listed in the Constitution. And the plenary power that the states currently wield over the local governments would instead lie with the national government.

While those are the direct effects, the abolition of state government would also necessitate several sets of secondary decisions. Four of them are basic enough to require elaboration:

A. Who decides the redistribution of the current state functions (i) between the national and local governments; and (ii) among the various kinds of local governments (municipalities, counties or their equivalent, townships, special purpose districts, and unincorporated areas)?

B. Today, state governments play multiple roles in national elections. Without states, someone else would have to discharge those or analogous functions. These include the following:

   1. In presidential elections, each state is assigned a certain number of members of the Electoral College. And if there is no Electoral College majority, the House of Representatives, voting by state delegation, selects the president. Without state government, the president could instead be directly elected by a national popular vote. But what if, as happens often, no single candidate receives a majority of the national popular vote? Should the candidate who wins a plurality become the president? Should the election go to the House of Representatives, as it now does (but with voting by members rather than by state delegations)? Or should the presidency be determined by ranked-choice voting or a run-off election?

   2. Redesigning and Electing Congress

    a. Without states, the main historical rationale for a bicameral Congress – a compromise between equal representation of states and equal representation of citizens – would no longer apply. Should the new Congress therefore be unicameral, or are there good, independent reasons to keep it bicameral?

    b. State legislatures currently draw the US House district lines. Who should take over that function (and the analogous function for the Senate if Congress remains bicameral)?

3. At present, state officials manage the ground level administration of all national elections, including the primaries. In its current form, the Constitution authorizes the state legislatures to decide the times, places, and manner of congressional elections but allows Congress to supplement or modify those decisions. The state legislatures decide the manner of conducting presidential elections. As argued earlier, without state government these responsibilities should be transferred to the national government rather than the local governments. But which branch of the national government should it be?

C. Under the current system, federal judges are nominated by the president and confirmed by the Senate. In contrast, the far more numerous state court judges are selected in various ways, in many states by a direct vote of the people. In the unitary system proposed here, those state court judgeships would be replaced by national court judgeships. The national judiciary would thus become orders of magnitude larger. How should the judicial appointment process adapt to that reality? Relatedly, over what subject matter should the national courts have jurisdiction?

D. Under the current process for amending the US Constitution, the final step is ratification by three-fourths of the state legislatures. Without state government, what should the process be?

These are questions that no one who advocates the abolition of state government can responsibly ignore. For present purposes, the analyses needn't be comprehensive and the conclusions needn't be definitive. But it does seem essential to show that, for these fundamental decisions, the abolition of state government would not leave the country without manageable options. Identifying those options is the task of this chapter.

In contrast, other important questions being debated today arise regardless of whether state government is retained. These are beyond the scope of this book: Who should have the right to vote? Should the size of the US House of Representatives be increased? Should we change the method of voting for members of the House from the current single-member district model to any of the alternative voting systems, such as proportional representation or at-large districts with either cumulative voting or "limited voting"? Should each party hold its own primary elections, and if so, should they be open to all or limited to members of that party?[1] Should our current system of sequential primary elections be replaced by a single nationwide primary?[2] If the Senate is retained, should its filibuster rule be preserved, repealed, or modified? Should the Supreme Court be expanded from its current nine-members? Should national judges continue to enjoy life tenure? Should the national government play a greater role than it now does in addressing the resource disparities among the current state and local governments? I leave all those critical issues on the table except for occasional brief mention.

Three more preliminary items: First, there is the matter of terminology. Without states, the name "United States of America" would need to change. If it is felt important to emphasize that the new name doesn't signal a lessening of our national unity, possible new names could include "the United American Republic" or "the United Republic of America." Or it could simply be "America." Any of those names risks offending the other countries of the Americas, but no more so than the existing "United States of America."

As noted in the Introduction, in a unitary republic the term "federal government" would also disappear. When discussing the elements of the hypothetical new republic, this chapter will therefore refer to the "central government" or the "national government."

Second, the proposed transformation would require a massive constitutional amendment or, more likely, a series of amendments. All the state governments – not just those whose legislatures ratified the amendments – would be abolished.[3] Many current constitutional provisions would fall prey. Apart from the substantive debate, our collective reverence for the "genius" of the framers' design would itself be a likely source of resistance.

Robert Dahl questions whether that collective reverence to the original Constitution is deserved. He calls out its most prominent antidemocratic features: its acceptance of slavery; its refusal to guarantee suffrage to women, African Americans, and Native Americans; the Electoral College; the selection of US

---

[1] For a summary of the ongoing debate, see, for example, Ashley Lopez, *The U.S. has a "Primary Problem," Say Advocates Who Call for New Election Systems* (Sept. 18, 2023), www.npr .org/2023/09/18/1199318220/nonpartisan-open-primaries-explainer.

[2] For a bibliography of writings arguing for or against a single national primary, see Debate US, *Resolved: On balance, a one day national primary would be more beneficial for the United States than our current presidential primary process*, https://debateus.org/resolved-on-balance-a-one-day-national-primary-would-be-more-beneficial-for-the-united-states-than-our-current-presidential-primary-process/.

[3] Under Art. VII, the original Constitution was binding only on those states that ratified it. The first thirteen states all did so, and all the subsequently admitted states similarly agreed to be bound by it. In turn, the Constitution by which they agreed to be bound lays out in Art. V the requirements for its amendment. Thus, as correctly noted by Justice Thomas, "[t]he people of each State ... agreed to be bound by constitutional amendments that they themselves refused to ratify." *Term Limits* v. *Thornton*, 514 US 779, 846 (1995) (Justice Thomas, dissenting from the Court's decision prohibiting states from putting term limits on members of their congressional delegations). I would simply add "even if, as advocated here, they would be agreeing to their own abolition."

senators by the state legislatures; and equal Senate representation for states with drastically different populations.[4] Dahl acknowledges that constitutional amendments have since corrected some of those elements, but he rightly laments not only how long it took for those corrections to be made, but also how entrenched other problematic features – especially the Electoral College and equal Senate representation for states – remain.

I would add one other point. The drafting of the original Constitution was completed in 1787 – at this writing, 237 years ago. The men who drafted it were understandably influenced by the then-prevailing cultural norms. They were further constrained by the then-contemporary political realities that limited their options if the Constitution were to have any chance of garnering the necessary nine state ratifications. No one would suggest that the framers should have tried to entrench the cultural and political norms that had prevailed 237 years earlier, in the year 1550. Why, then, should we assume that the framers, fully aware they were writing a constitution for a world that would evolve in unimaginable ways in the decades and centuries to come, intended to insulate us from the unknowable norms that would prevail 237 years into the future?

I don't offer these observations for the purpose of arguing against an originalist interpretation of the Constitution; that debate is well beyond the scope of this book. Rather, my more modest point is that to press today for a fundamentally rewritten constitution conveys no disrespect to those who drafted the original document. It simply reflects the reality, surely understood by the framers, that with the passage of time even foundational changes would be both desirable and inevitable.

Finally, changes of this magnitude would require a lengthy transition period that would not even begin until all the necessary constitutional amendments have been ratified. During this period, studies will be needed. Negotiations over the reassignment of the current state functions will be controversial and protracted. Congress will have to pass laws that codify the resulting reassignments.

And that's just the beginning. States regulate a wide swath of subjects, ranging from commercial law to the laws of property, torts, corporations, criminal law, and so many other areas. Congress will have to replace each of these fifty different sets of state laws with a single, uniform set of national laws. The local governments will have to do the same for those subjects that are sent their way.

Nor is it just a matter of enacting legislation. Enforcement mechanisms will have to be devised. National and local government budgets will need to be overhauled. New national and local administrative agencies will have to be created. New office facilities will be required. Both national and local workforces will have

---

4 Robert A. Dahl, How Democratic Is the American Constitution? 15–20 (2nd ed. 2003). His list additionally includes two more contestable examples of antidemocratic elements: judicial "legislation" and the absence of a federal power to tax income.

to be augmented. New employees will require training. New national judgeships will need to be filled.

I can't pretend that the work won't be overwhelming. But these are onetime costs. The end product will be a country that, in the long-term, will be far more democratic and significantly more efficient than the fifty-state system we know today. Moreover, it might not be such a bad thing to force government to undertake, once every 200 years, a comprehensive reexamination of laws that in many instances originated decades or centuries earlier. Still, while I regard the long-term democratic and fiscal benefits as greater than the admittedly daunting short-term transition costs, I acknowledge that that is a judgment call that others might well make differently.

A SELECTING A DECISION-MAKER

Who should decide how to reallocate the current state functions between the national and local governments? Chapter 4, Section B suggests general criteria for those decisions, but the deciding body would have to settle on its own criteria and apply them to the various state functions. Someone will also have to decide how those powers that are assigned to the local governments are further divided up among the various kinds of local governments – municipalities, counties and their equivalents, townships, unincorporated areas, and special purpose districts. Who should that someone be?

The short answer is that the final decisions would have to rest with Congress. There is really no alternative. It would be possible for the Constitution, rather than Congress, to lay out the list of subject areas for which the local governments are responsible, but that approach would simply create another federation, one in which the local governments effectively become sovereign entities with constitutionally enshrined autonomy over their designated turf. Rather, in a unitary republic shorn of the current enumerated powers constraints, Congress would possess plenary power over the local governments. Instead of local governments deriving their powers from the states in which they are located, as is now the case, they would derive their powers from the national government.

But if these decisions are to be at least largely principled, safeguards to minimize rank partisan abuse are essential. One constraint, of course, is the political process itself. The hope is that popular sentiment for local control would check Congress's most extreme partisan impulses. Still, if the decision-making is to be informed and partisanship is to be minimized (it cannot be eliminated), then more is needed. I suggest the creation of an advisory body charged with studying the universe of national, state, and local government decision-making; formulating general criteria for the redistribution of the current state functions (with the aid of the analysis in Chapter 4 if that is felt to be helpful); and presenting Congress with a comprehensive final report. That report would contain concrete recommendations as to both

(i) the distribution of functions between the national and local governments and (ii) the further distribution among the various kinds of local governments. Congress would have the last word, but it would have a structure to work with and a blueprint that could supply concrete starting points for bipartisan negotiations.

For the advisory body to be effective, its members would have to be collectively well-versed in national, state, and local government decision-making. It would have to be given adequate time and resources, including a professional staff with the requisite expertise. It should be politically independent and directed to function in a nonpartisan manner. The appointment of its members will be virtually impossible to insulate from congressional partisanship, but there are ways to assure that the membership itself, if not nonpartisan in actual practice, is at least truly bipartisan.

For that purpose, there is a useful model. In 1959, Congress created an independent federal agency called the Advisory Commission on Intergovernmental Relations (ACIR).[5] Its main job was to study and offer recommendations on issues concerned with the relations among the federal, state, and local governments. Its members included federal, state, and local officials as well as private citizens, and it had a professional staff that produced many helpful reports over the years. These included 130 "policy reports" with recommendations and 194 "information reports" without recommendations. But Congress defunded it in 1996 and it has never been resuscitated.[6]

The advisory body that I am proposing for present purposes would be a revived – and slightly revised – version of the ACIR. Congress could make it either a single-purpose entity that expires upon submission of its report to Congress or a continuing body that Congress could call upon to monitor and update its recommendations, for a fixed term or even permanently.

Either way, one significant revision would be desirable if not essential. ACIR had twenty-six members: six members of Congress, four governors, three state legislators, four mayors, three county officials, three federal executive branch officials, and three private citizens.[7] The resulting diversity of experiences was a real positive, but the appointments were not bipartisan. Rather, the congressional members were chosen by the leaders of the majority parties of the two houses of Congress. The president appointed the executive branch and private citizen representatives. The state and local officials were nominated by national organizations of state and local governments, but their ultimate selection was again that of the president.[8] To assure both expertise and bipartisanship, Congress should invite nominations from its own members, the president and executive agency heads, governors, mayors, and

5   Pub. L. 86–380, 73 Stat. 703 (Sept. 24, 1959).
6   Center for the Study of Federalism, *Advisory Commission on Intergovernmental Relations*, https://encyclopedia.federalism.org/index.php/Advisory_Commission_on_Intergovernmental_Relations.
7   Wikipedia, *U.S. Advisory Commission on Intergovernmental Relations*, https://en.wikipedia.org/wiki/U.S._Advisory_Commission_on_Intergovernmental_Relations.
8   *Ibid.*

national organizations of state and local governments. From those nominations, the appointments should be made in equal numbers by the leaders of the two main political parties in Congress – not solely by the majority parties. The members of the new commission would then select and organize their staff.

Once the advisory commission has submitted its report, Congress's first task would be to decide which of the current state functions it wants the national government to take on, either exclusively or in partnership with the local governments. In doing so, it would have the benefit of not only the commission's ultimate recommendations, but also the general criteria that the commission used in arriving at those recommendations. Congress would not have to individually specify the subject areas that it wishes to leave for the local governments. Those powers would be residual; the local governments would be empowered to regulate all subject areas not claimed by Congress, in much the same way that the states currently have power to regulate all subject areas not reserved for the national government. But unlike Congress's current inability to expand the list of its powers beyond those granted by the Constitution, Congress in this proposed unitary republic could constitutionally expand the scope of the national domain any time it wished. For that matter, at any time it could also do just the opposite, choosing to transfer responsibility for specific subject areas to the local governments or enact concurrent powers or administrative partnerships with the local governments. The changes Congress makes during the transition period need not be permanent. It could modify those assignments to reflect experience or changed circumstances.

For those subjects that are reassigned to the local governments, the further allocation of power among the various types of local governments is more complicated. As previously discussed, there are different kinds of local governments – municipalities, counties (and their equivalents), townships, special purpose districts, and unincorporated areas.[9] Moreover, not every state has the same system of local government. In some states, for example, counties control all the unincorporated areas within their respective territories, while in other states control over those areas rests with townships within counties.[10]

Fortunately, neither the commission nor Congress would have to reinvent the entire wheel. With respect to those subjects that are already within the ambit of local governments (and that Congress does not choose to take over), I do not propose disturbing the existence, boundaries, or powers of the current state subdivisions.

The complexities arise with respect to those powers that are currently exercised by state government but which Congress now elects to transfer to local governments. As to those, one option would be to assign all the new local powers to the

---

[9] See Chapter 4, Section C.3.
[10] Wikipedia, *County (United States)*, https://en.wikipedia.org/wiki/County_(United_States)#:~:text= Counties%20are%20usually%20governed%20by,city%2Fcounty%20or%20city%20affairs.

municipalities and, in the case of unincorporated areas,[11] to the counties or township that currently govern them. But that sort of one-size-fits-all strategy would likely be hard to square with the many existing state-to-state variations in the hierarchies of municipalities and counties. It would also leave the status of special purpose districts, particularly new ones that are created to administer any of the new local responsibilities, in some doubt.[12]

A better option, therefore, might be to operate state by state during the transition period. As part of its study of how best to reallocate the new local responsibilities, the advisory commission should assign a team of staff members to each of the current states. The final commission report could then include state-specific recommendations for reassigning the local functions among the various types of local governments.

B RESTRUCTURING NATIONAL ELECTIONS

As Chapters 1–3 of this book illustrate, the states currently play multiple roles in the national election process. Abolishing state government would thus mean transforming the entire electoral system. The most pressing of the decisions that would have to be made are the subject of this section.

1 Electing the President

Earlier discussion stated the case for scrapping the Electoral College.[13] A national popular vote would be the logical replacement. But what should happen when, as is often the case, no candidate wins an outright majority of the popular vote? This issue is not unique to the United States or, for that matter, to elections of the chief executive. Among the world's nations, and among the various states and local governments within the United States, several different methods have been used to decide elections in which the leading vote-getter wins only a plurality of the vote.[14]

The simplest option would be a "first-past-the-post" system, in which a plurality of the national popular vote is all it takes to become president. If this seems

---

[11] This is an important element. As of 2010, unincorporated communities housed an estimated 37 percent of the US population. Cristina Gomez-Vidal & Anu Manchikanti Gomez, NIH, National Library of Medicine, *Invisible and Unequal: Unincorporated Community Status as a Structural Determinant of Health*, 285 Soc. Sci. Med. 114292 (Sept. 2021), www.sciencedirect.com/science/article/pii/S0277953621006249?via%3Dihub.

[12] See Heather Gerken, The Supreme Court, (2009) *Term: Foreword, Federalism All the Way Down*, 124 Harv. L. Rev. 4 (2010) (arguing persuasively that, while some other scholars have rightly emphasized the roles of cities in our federal system, the debate should also include the roles of other substate entities – in particular, "special purpose institutions" like school boards and zoning districts).

[13] See Chapter 2, Section B.

[14] A separate choice is between single-member district elections and multimember at large elections. That issue arises only in the elections of multimember legislative bodies and is therefore discussed in Section B.2.

objectionable, we must consider that the current system already installs presidents who failed to receive outright majorities of the popular vote; on at least five occasions, in fact, candidates who had failed to win even a plurality of the popular vote landed in the White House.[15] For that matter, in forty-eight of the fifty states, all the electoral votes are awarded to the candidate who wins a mere plurality of the state-wide vote; majorities are not required. We also routinely elect governors, members of both houses of Congress, and members of both state legislative chambers on the basis of mere pluralities.

The earlier discussion addressed the argument that the Electoral College system lends "legitimacy" to the presidential selection process. It does this, its defenders say, by requiring a majority – not just a plurality – of the Electoral College. As that discussion demonstrated, however, the claimed legitimacy is a mirage. Since the Electoral College is an artificial construct, the fact remains that it can hand the presidency to the winner of a mere plurality of the American voters or, worse, as it did on five occasions, to a candidate who failed to manage even that. The Electoral College might well provide the illusion of legitimacy, but it can never supply the real thing.[16]

Still, if our willingness to accept a plurality president were to change, there are other options. Under the current system, the House of Representatives, voting by state delegation, chooses the president when no one achieves a majority of the Electoral College. With the abolition of states, of course, there would be no state delegations, but in that scenario, one option would be for the House, voting by membership, to choose the president when no candidate secures a majority of the national popular vote. I acknowledge that option in the interest of completeness, but I do not favor it. As earlier discussion demonstrated, the combination of residential patterns (especially urban versus rural) and single-member district elections frequently makes the House a counter-majoritarian body.[17] Besides, there are at least two better, majoritarian alternatives.

One of those options is a runoff election between the top vote-getters. Several countries use runoffs in presidential elections.[18] In the US, two states (Georgia and Louisiana) use them in general elections for congressional and most state and local offices, and ten US states use them for primary elections.[19] The specific features can

---

[15] Wikipedia, *List of United States Presidential Elections in Which the Winner Lost the Popular Vote*, https://en.wikipedia.org/wiki/List_of_United_States_presidential_elections_in_which_the_winner_lost_the_popular_vote.

[16] See Chapter 2, Section B.

[17] See Chapter 3, Section A.

[18] See Samuel Issacharoff *et al.*, The Law of Democracy – Legal Structure of the Political Process 1149 (6th ed. 2022). For examples, see Dahl, note 4, at 205 n.20; Sanford Levinson, Our Undemocratic Constitution: Where the Constitution Goes Wrong (And How We the People Can Correct It) 214 n.35 (2006).

[19] Ballotpedia, *Runoff election*, https://ballotpedia.org/Runoff_election. In one of the latter ten states – Vermont – a runoff election would be held only in the event of an exact tie. *Ibid.*

vary. Ordinarily, the runoff is held whenever no candidate initially receives a majority of the vote, but in at least one state – North Carolina – the required threshold is only 30 percent of the vote.[20] The runoff can be limited to the top two vote-getters, in which case a majority will be guaranteed, or it can be extended to the top three, in which case a specified plurality might still suffice.

In all of these variations, the central goal is for the candidates to appeal to a broader segment of the voters, by making it harder for extremist candidates to be elected. But runoff elections do have disadvantages: They prolong the already exhausting campaign season (for candidates, campaign workers, donors, and voters alike); they entail additional administrative costs for the relevant governments; and they delay the final outcomes. In the case of US presidential elections, the resulting delay would shrink the time interval between the certification of the final results and the January 20 inauguration date. The concern would be whether, during that reduced interval, there is enough time for the election officials to complete their work and for both the incoming and outgoing presidential transition teams to effect a smooth succession. If there is not, then a later inauguration date would have to be set.

Another alternative to first-past-the-post is "ranked choice voting" (RCV). Rather than vote for a single candidate, voters rank the candidates in order of preference. If no one wins a majority of the first-choice votes, then the last-place finisher gets lopped off and their first-choice votes are distributed to the candidates whom their voters ranked as their second choice. The process continues in that manner until one candidate has a majority. In elections for a single office, RCV is often referred to as "instant runoff voting"; in elections to fill multiple seats, it is often called "single transferable voting."[21]

RCV, like runoff elections, has the advantage (over first-past-the-post) of producing winners who are acceptable to a broader segment of the population. And unlike runoff elections, RCV doesn't delay the final outcome. Jesse Wegman identifies additional advantages: "Dozens of cities and towns around the country are already using ranked-choice voting to decide their local elections," and

> [n]early everywhere, voters seem happy with the system and no more confused than they are by standard single-vote elections. Studies of ranked-choice voting have found that it increases voter participation, reduces polarization, and elects leaders who better reflect what a majority of voters want. It also leads to campaigns that are more civil and less negative, because candidates realize that it's not a zero-sum game anymore.[22]

[20] *Ibid.*
[21] Issacharoff *et al.*, note 18, at 1172–89. For another detailed explanation, see *Dudum* v. *Arntz*, 640 F.3d 1098 (9th Cir. 2011).
[22] Jesse Wegman, Let the People Pick the President: The Case for Abolishing the Electoral College 232 (2020).

Apart from these advantages, both women[23] and racial minority candidates[24] generally benefit from RCV.

2 Redesigning and Electing Congress

As discussed earlier,[25] the historical impetus for a bicameral Congress was the compromise offered by Connecticut's Roger Sherman at the constitutional convention. Congress would consist of a lower house in which the people receive equal representation and an upper house in which the states receive equal representation. With the abolition of states, that rationale would no longer apply, but bicameral legislatures bring other independent benefits, as well as costs. The first question, then, is whether a unitary American republic should retain bicameralism.

The pros and cons of unicameral and bicameral legislatures are laid out comprehensively in a policy brief prepared by Tom Todd for the Research Department of the Minnesota House of Representatives.[26] I take the liberty of summarizing the main opposing arguments here:

Proponents of unilateral legislatures argue that they are generally more majoritarian; that they are more accountable to the people because their procedures are simpler and more transparent and because the legislators are unable to shift blame to another chamber; that they avoid the gridlock, additional fiscal costs, and duplication of bicameral legislatures; and that they can pass legislation more quickly and more efficiently.

Bicameralism advocates, for their part, observe that two houses give each citizen two representatives in the legislature rather than just one. That, they point out, means citizens have more opportunity for direct contact with a representative, a better chance to find one who will be responsive, and often a choice between members of different political parties. The upper chamber will inevitably consist of larger and therefore more diverse districts, which complement the greater number and smaller size of the lower house's districts. Bicameralism, it is further argued, better balances rival policy preferences; makes it harder for powerful interests to successfully lobby; leads to greater stability, restraint, and moderation in the resulting laws; affords a healthy opportunity for second thought; and diffuses government power.

The national legislatures of most of the world's democracies are bicameral, but exceptions include Finland, Israel, Luxembourg, Denmark, Sweden, and New

---

[23] Issacharoff *et al.*, note 18, at 1181.
[24] Deb Otis & Nora Dell, Fair Vote, *Ranked Choice Voting Elections Benefit Candidates and Voters of Color* (2021), www.fairvote.org/report_rcv_benefits_candidates_and_voters_of_color.
[25] See Chapter 2, Section A.
[26] Tom Todd, Minnesota House of Representatives Research Department, Policy Brief, *Unicameral or Bicameral State Legislatures: Policy Debate* (Aug. 1999), at 2–13, www.house.mn.gov/hrd/pubs/unibicam.pdf.

Zealand. All of Canada's provincial legislatures are unicameral, but in the United States the legislature of every state except Nebraska is bicameral.[27]

So there are fair arguments on both sides, and the world's nations and subdivisions furnish ample experience with both alternatives. Either would be perfectly workable in a new American unitary republic. But for purposes of discussion, let's assume the bicameral Congress is retained.

The question then is how to structure the elections of each chamber's members. At present, federal law mandates that each member of the US House of Representatives be elected from a single district – as opposed to at large multi-member districts.[28] The election of US senators can likewise be thought of as a single-member district process, even though there are two senators per state. That is because, whenever a given candidate is up for election or reelection to the Senate, the voter still casts one vote for one candidate, not multiple votes for two or more candidates running at large.

Would at large elections be a better way to choose the members of either house of Congress? That turns out to be a complicated question. For one thing, as explained below, that choice has huge racial and partisan consequences. For another, there are many different forms of at large voting, each with its own set of pros and cons.

This chapter, however, is not meant to address every possible reform of our electoral process – just those decisions that the abolition of states would necessitate. Whether to switch from single-member districts to at large elections is a decision that arises as easily in our current federation as it would in the proposed unitary republic. Even without a constitutional amendment, Congress could repeal the law that mandates single-member House districts. And even a federal system could be designed to make Senate districts equipopulous; no law of nature requires that they map onto state boundaries.[29] For either House, moreover, the endless varieties of alternative voting methods would be available whether or not the US were to abolish state government.

So I won't try to replicate the wealth of literature[30] describing, evaluating, and/or advocating the various forms of alternative voting. That subject is well beyond the scope of this book. A few comments will hopefully suffice.

---

[27] *Ibid.*, at 8 n1.

[28] Pub. L. 90–196, 81 Stat. 581 (Dec. 14, 1967).

[29] This statement requires qualification, because there is an issue as to whether the Constitution can be amended to alter the requirement of equal Senate representation for each state. The discussion in Chapter 2, Section E concludes that the answer is yes.

[30] Robert G. Dixon, Jr., Democratic Representation: Reapportionment in Law and Politics 503–27 (1968); David M. Farrell, Electoral Systems: A Comparative Introduction 1–2 (2d ed. 2011) (finding over 2,500 writings on the various voting systems); Issacharoff *et al.*, note 1, at 1147–1215; Arend Lijphart, Democracies: Patterns of Majoritarian and Consensus Government in Twenty-One Countries (1984); Arend Lijphart & Bernard Grofman (eds.), Choosing an Electoral System: Issues and Alternatives (1984); Douglas W. Rae, The Political Consequences of Electoral Laws (1967); Jonathan Rodden, Why Cities Lose: The Deep Roots of the Urban-Rural Political Divide, chapter 8 (2019).

First, as discussed in Chapter 3, the current single-member district system that governs election to Congress frequently produces counter-majoritarian results. As Jonathan Rodden explains, populations that tend to vote for Democrats – in particular, people of color – are overwhelmingly concentrated in urban centers, where large percentages of Democrats' huge victory margins become mere surplus.[31]

Second, even in those instances when single-member district systems don't prevent the majority from governing, the price for that governance is often the near exclusion of minority representation. In particular, an at large voting process is a prerequisite to proportional representation – today the single most prevalent form of consensus-based democracy (as opposed to majoritarian democracy).

The literature on proportional representation is especially vast.[32] The basic idea is that one votes for a political party, not for individual candidates. Each party is then allotted a percentage of the legislative seats equal to that party's percentage of the vote. There are many variations of this system. The percentages might be applied to the total national vote, or they might be applied region by region. The individual legislators might be selected from a list prepared in advance by each party ("closed list"), or they might be chosen by the voters ("open list").

Since the early twentieth century, proportional representation systems have been the norm on the European continent, but not in the UK or in most of its former colonies.[33] The consequences of those countries' differing choices have been dramatic. Rodden observes two patterns that have taken hold in the countries that retain single-member districts: Practically every important issue became "a battle pitting urban political parties of the left against exurban and rural parties of the right." In addition, "because of the geographic concentration of progressives in cities, the urban political parties have been systematically underrepresented relative to their share of the vote." In contrast, he points out, the European proportional representation systems have preserved multiparty representation in Parliament; "center-right governments almost always contain urban representatives." And as new issues arise, they haven't had to be bundled "into a single overarching urban-rural battle."[34]

The main disadvantage of proportional representation is that it forces the voters to choose political parties rather than specific candidates. For independents, as well as for members of those political parties that are too small to qualify for an allocation of legislative seats, that limitation can be frustrating. And even members of the larger political parties might occasionally have preferred to cross party lines for a particular candidate.

---

[31] Rodden, note 30; Miriam Seifter, *Countermajoritarian State Legislatures*, 121 Colum. L. Rev. 1733, 1761 (2021).

[32] A small sample includes Issacharoff *et al.*, note 18, at 1151–54; Lijphart, note 30, chapter 9 (1984); Lijphart & Grofman, note 30 (containing multiple essays on proportional representation); Rodden, note 30, chapter 8.

[33] Issacharoff *et al.*, note 18, at 1151; Rodden, note 30, at 227.

[34] Rodden, note 30, at 227–28.

At large systems can take other forms as well. One of those is "cumulative" voting. Each voter gets as many votes as there are seats, but with one added feature: You can cast two or more of your votes for the same candidate. For example, if there are five seats to fill, you can spread out your votes by casting one for each of the five candidates you like the most, or cast all five of your votes for the same candidate, or allocate your votes in any other way you choose. As Richard Pildes puts it, cumulative voting "enables voters to express not just their raw preferences, but the intensity with which those preferences are held."[35] For precisely that reason, cumulative voting has been touted as a way to increase the representation of both racial and partisan minorities.[36] Today, several local governments in the US use cumulative voting; so do corporations, for shareholder voting.[37]

Still another alternative is "limited voting." That system too utilizes multimember at large districts, but each voter gets fewer votes than the number of seats to be filled. In that way, unlike in a traditional at large election, the same majority doesn't get to fill every seat. Thus, a minority group, if well enough organized, can often win a seat.[38]

Under any of these systems, someone has to draw the district maps for both the House and, if it is retained, the Senate. At present, as discussed in Chapter 3, Section A, state legislatures draw the US House map. And the state boundaries fix the lines of the Senate map. Without state government, who should step in to perform these functions?

One might well question whether state legislatures should be drawing congressional maps even in the current federation. And if state government were abolished, I take as a given that the 90,000 local governments should not be tasked with getting together and somehow agreeing on a map. That leaves the national government. But which branch of the national government would be best suited to that job, and what should the process be?

As a preliminary matter, the House district lines – having been distorted by state legislative gerrymanders, with all the debilitating counter-majoritarian effects laid out earlier[39] – would need to be revisited. They have to be reassessed anyway at each decennial Census, so the first such Census after the adoption of the constitutional amendment(s) abolishing states would be the logical occasion for accomplishing

---

[35] Richard H. Pildes, The New Republic, *Gimme Five: Non-Gerrymandering Racial Justice* (Mar. 1, 1993), excerpt reproduced in Issacharoff *et al.*, note 18, at 1154–56.

[36] See Issacharoff *et al.*, note 18, at 1154–66 and their treatment of two judicial decisions that explore the cumulative voting issue in depth, *Dillard v. Chilton County Board of Education*, 699 F. Supp. 870 (M.D. Alabama (1988), and *McCoy v. Chicago Heights*, 6 F. Supp. 2d 973 (N.D. Ill. 1998). See also Lani Guinier, The Tyranny of the Majority 16, 152 (1994), excerpted in Issacharoff *et al.*, note 18, at 1154 (describing cumulative voting as "a solution that permits voters to self-select their identities" and a means to increase women's representation).

[37] Issacharoff *et al.*, note 18, at 1154 (corporations), 1168–72 (local governments).

[38] *Ibid.*, at 1189–97.

[39] See Chapter 3, Section A.

the essential de-gerrymandering. To be sure, gerrymandering is not the only culprit. Single-member district voting accounts for much of the counter-majoritarian tilt in both state legislative and US House elections; hence, the need to consider the various alternative voting systems discussed above. But gerrymandering makes the problem significantly worse.

With states no longer available to draw the district lines, the time would be ripe for transferring that responsibility to a constitutionally enshrined, independent, nonpartisan, national commission. The same commission would be responsible for drawing the Senate districts. It could create, say, 100 equally populated senatorial districts.

We don't have to live with gerrymandering. Practically nobody else does. Among the world's liberal democracies, the United States stands almost alone in entrusting the construction of legislative district maps to politicians.[40] In the vast majority of the other liberal democracies, that task is performed by nonpartisan or bipartisan commissions or their equivalent, with the result that gerrymandering is unknown. In the US as well, a number of states have recently assigned the redistricting of either congressional or state legislative districts, or both, to commissions that vary with respect to authority, independence, and other attributes.[41] And the Fairness and Independence in Redistricting Act, which has been introduced in every Congress since 2005, would mandate independent redistricting commissions in every state.[42]

Nonpartisan commissions insulated from partisan pressures provide clear benefits.[43] The goal of any political party that has firm control over a legislature will never be to draw a districting plan that promotes all the democratic norms theorized by academics. The party in control will try, first and foremost, to draw a map that maximizes the number of seats for that party, however extreme the result. So leaving these sorts of decisions to partisan politicians is never a good idea. And if a

---

[40] Nicholas O. Stephanopoulos, *Our Electoral Exceptionalism*, 80 U. Chi L. Rev. 769, 781 (2013) (pointing out that the practice of allowing politicians to draw legislative district lines – without court-imposed limits, admittedly a significant qualifier – exists only in "authoritarian states such as Cameroon, Kyrgystan, Malaysia, and Singapore"). In Malaysia, for example, the result of that policy choice is that "[t]he voters in rural districts are over-represented in Malaysia while the urban districts are under-represented. The largest parliamentary seat (Kapar) is nine times larger than the smallest one (Putrajaya). On average, the rural parliamentary seats are over-represented by six times compared to the urban seats." Wikipedia, *Apportionment by Country*, https://en.wikipedia.org/wiki/Apportionment_by_country#:~:text=The%20apportionment%20of%20seats%20in,is%20specified%20by%20negotiated%20treaty. See also Rodden, note 30, at 5–7.

[41] See, for example., Issacharoff *et al.*, note 18, at 741–43; Jessica Bulman-Pozen & Miriam Seifter, *The Democracy Principle in State Constitutions*, 119 Mich. L. Rev. 859, 914–15 (2021) (identifying approximately twenty US states that have adopted some form of districting commission).

[42] This bill is more fully described in *Rucho v. United States*, 139 S.Ct. 2484, 2508 (2019).

[43] For good discussions of those benefits, as well as the costs, see, for example, Emily Rong Zhang, *Bolstering Faith with Facts: Supporting Independent Redistricting Commissions with Redistricting Algorithms*, 109 Calif. L. Rev. 987 (2021); Jeffrey C. Kubin, *The Case for Redistricting Commissions*, 75 Texas L. Rev. 837 (1997).

legislature is drawing a district map for its own members – as is currently the case with the state legislatures and as would be the case if Congress were to take over that function for its own members in a new unitary republic – the incumbents will have the additional gerrymandering incentive to keep their own districts politically safe. Between the twin impulses of maintaining party control and protecting individual incumbency, politicians are in no position to make these essential decisions in a democratically objective manner.

I appreciate the irony of invoking majoritarianism as a rationale for taking a fundamental democratic function away from the people's elected representatives and handing it to a politically unaccountable body. As explained in Chapter 2, however, even in a democracy what appears to be majority rule must give way to legitimate exceptions and qualifications. One of those is the need to protect the essential elements of democracy itself. Majority rule would be self-defeating if it were deployed for the very purpose of overcoming the majority's choice of its own leaders – the precise point of gerrymandering.

The Supreme Court in *Arizona State Legislature* v. *Arizona Independent Redistricting Commission* upheld an independent congressional redistricting commission that the people had created via statewide initiative. To do so, it invoked John Locke's analogous reasoning: The people are the ultimate sovereign. The legislature is merely a "fiduciary" authorized to act on their behalf. So if the people find the legislature's actions "contrary to the trust reposed in them," then the people "may place it anew where they shall think best for their safety and security."[44]

Still, it is one thing to recommend an independent redistricting commission. The devil, as always, is in the details. Congress should enact guidelines that identify the general criteria to be applied by the Commission for both the initial districting and the periodic redistricting. There is ample room for debate over what those criteria should be. The existing districting commissions are constrained by laws that either require or prohibit consideration of specified factors in the drawing of the legislative map. The lists of required or prohibited factors vary from one jurisdiction to another, typically reflecting explicit or unstated philosophical priorities.

The Supreme Court, in *Rucho* v. *Common Cause*, offered a sampling of the criteria that appear in several of the current state or proposed federal statutes:

> Some [states] have outright prohibited partisan favoritism in redistricting. See … [the Iowa law] ("No district shall be drawn for the purpose of favoring a political party, incumbent legislator or member of Congress, or other person or group."); [the Delaware law] (providing that in determining district boundaries for the state legislature, no district shall "be created so as to unduly favor any person or political party"). … [T]he Fairness and Independence in Redistricting Act [FIRA] … [would] set forth criteria for the [required] independent commissions to use, such

as compactness, contiguity, and population equality. It would prohibit consideration of voting history, political party affiliation, or incumbent Representatives' residence.[45]

The choice of criteria is among the more consequential of the distinguishing variables. FIRA (above) is illustrative. Since the Supreme Court's 1964 decision in *Wesberry* v. *Sanders*,[46] population equality from one district to another has been a given. Compactness and contiguity have also been traditional factors in judging the legality of an alleged gerrymander. But by prohibiting consideration of voting history and political party affiliation, FIRA would (i) leave even deliberate gerrymanders easy to achieve while still difficult to prove and (ii) generate counter-majoritarian outcomes even in the absence of bad faith. That is because, as discussed in depth in Chapter 3, Democrats are heavily clustered in compact, contiguous districts in which they win majorities by massive margins that effectively waste large numbers of votes.

The Michigan law, in contrast, provides that "districts shall not provide a disproportionate advantage to any political party." As Issacharoff *et al.* point out, this provision bars more than affirmative partisan intent; it bars district maps that have even the unintended *effect* of creating a partisan advantage.[47]

Also open to debate are the availability and scope of judicial review of the commission's maps. Nicholas Stephanopoulos identifies an inverse correlation between the degree of independence the commission enjoys and the need for intensive judicial supervision of its work.[48] The more partisan pressure the commission is under, the more aggressive the judicial review of its maps tends to be.

Another variable is the composition of the commission. Stephanopoulos observes that "commissions are typically composed of nonpartisan government officials, judges, or academics, who receive their positions either ex officio or by appointment. For example, Australia's and New Zealand's commissions are made up mostly of technocrats such as surveyors, statisticians, and electoral officers, while Britain and Canada's rely more heavily on appointees such as judges and professors."[49]

My own preference is the technocrats.[50] There is no argument to be made for a map specifically designed to leave racial or partisan minorities with a disproportionately small share of the legislature. But reasonable arguments can be made either for a map that excludes all racial and partisan considerations or for a map that affirmatively seeks to assure racial and partisan minorities an opportunity for proportionate

---

[45] 139 S.Ct. 2484, 2507–508 (2019).
[46] 376 U.S. 1 (1964).
[47] Issacharoff *et al.*, note 18, at 743.
[48] Stephanopoulos, note 40, at 787–96.
[49] *Ibid.*, at 783–84.
[50] See, for example, Steven Levitsky and Daniel Ziblatt, Tyranny of the Minority 233 (2023) (similarly favoring election administration by nonpartisan professionals, though not specifying in which branch of government those officials would be situated).

representation. For either of those latter objectives, the work of constructing such a map is hypertechnically complex. And while a skilled support staff will do the groundwork, commission members with the training necessary to understand the methodologies and the implications of the multiple available digital models would be the optimal fit. They could be drawn from the ranks of respected demographers, statisticians, geographers, and the like. In contrast, it is not clear what training non-specialized government officials or judges would bring to that phase of the process.

One final issue: Who should pick the members of the Commission? To ensure that the members are chosen on the basis of their professional distinction and not their party affiliation, the selection should not be left with politicians. Section B.3 recommends putting the ground level administration of the national elections in the hands of a special entity within the national judiciary, operating through various regional bodies – as is done, with great success, in Brazil. If that system were adopted, the same entity could be charged with appointing the members of the redistricting commission.

3 Administering National Elections

We turn now to that broader subject – the overall ground level administration of the national electoral process. I am proposing here that both presidential and congressional elections be run by an independent entity within the national judicial branch. Its role would be to prescribe and administer the entire electoral process, including functions relating to the times, places, and manner of national elections.

Chapter 3 described the inherent temptations, consistent with actual experience, for politicians to introduce partisan and incumbency biases into legislative district maps. Section B.2 therefore recommended reassigning that function to an independent, nonpartisan redistricting commission. For the same reasons, extreme partisan bias is inevitable when politicians or their subordinates are in charge of election mechanics. Chapter 3 described countless ways in which state legislatures and state officials have worked actively to tilt the electoral playing fields in their favor: placing needless obstacles in the way of voter registration; selectively purging the voter rolls; requiring proof of US citizenship; manipulating the number and location of the election day polling places; aiding efforts to intimidate voters and election staffers; and refusing to certify clearly legitimate electoral outcomes. While it is true that these examples all implicate state actors, there is no reason to believe that either members of Congress or national executive officials are immune from the same temptations.

Despite my similar cynicism about the partisan neutrality of federal judges,[51] partisan motivation is relative. Absent evidence to the contrary, I make the assumption that the vast majority of federal judges, respectful of their assigned roles and

---

[51] See Chapter 2, Section D.

conscious of their reputations, feel far less free to let partisan preferences drive their decisions than do legislators and executive branch political appointees. The difference might be just one of degree, but surely that difference is substantial.

Neutrality aside, there is ample reason to trust the national judiciary's competence to run national elections. That confidence comes from what might seem an unlikely source: Brazil.

Let me explain. Like the United States, Brazil is a large country – the world's seventh-largest in population and fifth-largest in geographic area – and is a federation of states.[52] Like the United States, its national legislature consists of a lower house in which the districts are apportioned by population and an upper house in which each state has equal representation (three senators). And like the proposed new unitary American republic, Brazil elects its president through a national popular vote (with a runoff between the top two vote-getters if no one wins a majority in the first round).[53] There are some important differences in the ways the two countries conduct elections, but those particular differences don't have any apparent bearing on whether the national judiciary should be charged with election administration.[54]

Still, one might think, Brazil should not be our role model. There is "noticeable corruption, crime and social inequality."[55] On top of that, it has only recently been the scene of authoritarian rule and political violence eerily parallel to the saga that most of us in the United States want to erase from memory and banish from the future. Both before and after losing a close presidential run off election, incumbent President Jair Bolsonaro took a page out of President Trump's book, spreading false claims of election fraud and refusing to concede defeat. On January 8, 2023, a mob of his supporters stormed the Presidential Palace, the National Congress building, and the Federal Supreme Court building. With the goal of overthrowing the government, they vandalized and looted all three buildings, attacking the badly outnumbered police and journalists in the process.[56]

---

52 Wikipedia, *Brazil*, https://en.wikipedia.org/wiki/Brazil.
53 Wikipedia, *Elections in Brazil*, https://en.wikipedia.org/wiki/Elections_in_Brazil#Electoral_systems.
54 For example, in Brazil voting is compulsory (with some exemptions); Brazil has multiple political parties that are popular enough to make coalition governments common; and the lower house of its Congress is elected by proportional representation. *Ibid.* In contrast, in the United States voting is optional; there are only two major political parties; within the federal executive branch the concept of power-sharing by two or more parties is unknown (at least since presidents and vice presidents started running on the same ticket); and the lower house of Congress consists entirely of single-member districts. Whatever effects those differences might have on the arguments over any other election-related issues, I can think of no respect in which they enlarge or diminish the pros and cons of entrusting ground level election administration to the judiciary.
55 Wikipedia, *Brazil*, note 52.
56 Emma Bowman, NPR, *Security Forces Regain Control after Bolsonaro Supporters Storm Congress* (Jan. 8, 2023), www.npr.org/2023/01/08/1147757260/bolsonaro-supporters-storm-brazil-congress-lula; Wikipedia, 2023 *Brazilian Congress Attack*, https://en.wikipedia.org/wiki/2023_Brazilian_Congress_attack. In at least two respects, these events differed from the January 6, 2021 attack on the US Capitol. Brazil has a recent history of rule by military dictatorship; its democracy is therefore younger and

But let's give credit where credit is due. Unlike in the United States, where national election procedures are governed by the babel of laws enacted by fifty different state legislatures and implemented by assortments of state and local officials operating under different constraints, Brazil's 2022 presidential election was governed by a single, uniform set of laws and regulations and administered by one body – the national judiciary. And even amidst all the heightened political tensions and fears of violence, the national judiciary, through its specially constructed "Electoral Court,"[57] steered the country through the election process from start to finish without a hitch.

Perhaps most astounding, despite a very close race[58] in which each of the two main opposing candidates commanded passionate followings, the final results were available within hours after the polls closed – with no evidence of fraud.[59] Bolsonaro nonetheless claimed otherwise and ordered the military to investigate. To his disappointment, the military reported that they had been unable to find a single instance of fraud.[60]

The drama was not yet over, though. "[A]nalysts noted that the armed forces, which have been a key component of Bolsonaro's administration, appeared cautious not to displease the president as they maintained a semblance of uncertainty." And so, "[i]n a second statement …, the Defense Ministry stressed that while it had not found any evidence of fraud in the vote counting, it could not exclude that possibility." It cited "the electoral authority's internal network to process the machines' source codes, which they say augments the risk of external interference. The electoral authority says its network is safe."[61]

The Electoral Court's assurances about the security of the voting machines' source codes are credible. For one thing, "[t]he electronic voting machine is not vulnerable to external attacks. It is a stand-alone device, i.e., it has no mechanism for connecting to computer networks, such as the Internet. Moreover, it does not have the necessary hardware to connect to a network or even any form of wired or wireless network

---

more fragile than ours. And the Brazilian attack occurred after the inauguration of the new president; unlike President Trump, Brazil's newly elected President Lula da Silva immediately summoned security forces to put down the insurrection. Kenichi Serino, PBS News Hour, *Here's What's Different about the Brazil Attack Compared to Jan. 6* (Jan. 13, 2023), www.pbs.org/newshour/world/what-the-attack-in-brazil-says-about-far-right-movements-around-the-world.

[57] Superior Electoral Court, *Election Process in Brazil*, https://international.tse.jus.br/en/elections/election-process-in-brazil.

[58] No candidate won a majority in the initial round. In the runoff election, Lula da Silva defeated Bolsonaro, 60,345,999 to 58,206,354, or 50.9% to 49.1%. Wikipedia, *Elections in Brazil*, note 53.

[59] *Ibid.*

[60] Diane Jeantet & Carla Bridi, AP, *Report by Brazil's Military on Election Count Cites No Fraud* (Nov. 10, 2022), https://apnews.com/article/jair-bolsonaro-caribbean-brazil-rio-de-janeiro-ffc6206a16e2 6e192c87995430c4d17c. See also The Guardian, *Brazil Military Finds No Evidence of Election Fraud, Dashing Hopes of Bolsonaro Supporters* (Nov. 10, 2022), www.theguardian.com/world/2022/nov/10/brazil-military-finds-no-evidence-of-election-dashing-hopes-of-bolsonaro-supporters.

[61] Jeantet & Bridi, note 60.

connection."[62] For another, in the twenty-six years in which the machines had been in use, every accusation of fraud had been investigated and not a one had been confirmed.[63] Finally, whatever reservations there might be about any other Brazilian government institutions, its Electoral Court system has "recognized integrity, according to internationally prestigious initiatives, such as NEADA (National Elections Across Democracy and Autocracy) and GPEI (Global Perceptions of Electoral Integrity)."[64]

How do they do it? How can a country as large and diverse as Brazil manage to tabulate, certify, and disseminate the votes of the entire nation, and to do so reliably, within a matter of hours? And if they can do it, why can't we?

The key to Brazil's unique ability to count the votes so quickly and accurately is that all voting is electronic.[65] The voting machines sequentially perform three functions, all digitally – "voter identification, secure voting and tallying – … aiming to eliminate fraud based on forged or falsified public documents."[66]

But this means that all voting is in person, at polling stations, on election day. Voter identification requires either a government-issued ID card or biometric data. There is no absentee or mail voting.[67] Among other things, that means no third-party collection of absentee ballots. Allowing only in-person voting also eliminates ballot drop -off boxes.

In the United States, as discussed in Chapter 3, Section B, these have been among the practices most effectively used by partisan state legislatures and partisan officials to selectively suppress the votes of racial and partisan minorities. In Brazil, those kinds of disproportionate adverse effects are much less likely, because voting is mandatory (with some exceptions).[68] Unless the US were similarly to make voting mandatory (highly unlikely today – then again, so is the abolition of state government) – an all-electronic, in-person, same-day voting system would have the same pernicious effects as many of the current voter suppression strategies.

For that reason, again absent adoption of mandatory voting, the all-electronic system that enables Brazil to report the electoral outcomes within hours is not recommended for the United States. Rather, the component of the Brazilian system that is being touted here is the role of the national judiciary in the overall administration of the system. As that experience has shown, the judiciary has both the competence and the (relative) institutional integrity that the job requires. Unless one believes that

---

[62] Tribunal Superior Eleitoral, International Affairs Unit, *Practical Guide: 2022 Brazilian Elections*, at 82, https://international.tse.jus.br/en/assuntos-internacionais/guia-pratico-para-pessoas-estrangeiras_ingles_digital-1.pdf.

[63] *Ibid.*, at 83.

[64] *Ibid.*, at 42.

[65] Superior Electoral Court, Election Process, note 57; Tribunal Superior Eleitoral, note 61, at 10. As of 2023, Brazil is the only such country in the world. Wikipedia, *Elections in Brazil*, note 52.

[66] Wikipedia, *Elections in Brazil*, note 53.

[67] Tribunal Superior Eleitoral, International Affairs Unit, note 62, at 9–10.

[68] The minimum voting age is 16sixteen. Voting is mandatory for literate citizens ages 18–70. It is optional for those who are 16–18, over seventy, or illiterate. Wikipedia, *Elections in Brazil*, note 53.

US federal judges are either less competent or less trustworthy than their Brazilian counterparts – an assumption few would make, much less be able to support – there is no reason to doubt that our national judiciary could do just as exemplary a job in running our national elections.

The functions of Brazil's Electoral Court extend to practically every element of the election process:

> The Electoral Court organizes, supervises, and conducts elections by regulating the elections process, examining the accounts of parties and candidates in campaigns, monitoring compliance with relevant legislation during electoral periods and judging processes related to elections. Although the stages of voting, counting and dissemination of results are the best known, the electoral process has other very important stages such as voter registration, the candidacy stage, financial reporting, and electoral logistics. There is also the postelection phase, which includes, among other activities, the inauguration of elected officials.[69]

At the head of the system is the Superior Electoral Court. It has seven members – "3 Supreme Court Justices, 2 lower court judges, and 2 members chosen by the President from a list of 6 lawyers nominated by the Supreme Court."[70] Its network of regional courts and electoral boards includes more than 3,000 judges, 22,000 civil servants, and 2 million poll workers and assistants. Together, this workforce selects and operates over 460,000 polling stations in Brazil and more than 2,000 in other countries.[71]

In the United States, an analogous entity – let's call it the "Electoral Conference" for now – could perform the same functions that the Electoral Court does in Brazil. The Judicial Conference of the United States is the policymaking body for the federal courts.[72] Its members are the Chief Justice of the United States (presiding), and judges from the various lower federal courts.[73] Additionally, each of the federal judicial circuits has its own "Judicial Council," which makes "orders for the effective and expeditious administration of justice within its circuit."[74] The members of each of these Judicial Councils are the Chief Judge of the circuit and various other court of appeals and district court judges within the circuit.[75]

The functions of the proposed Electoral Conference would be very different from those of the Judicial Conference and the various Judicial Councils, and the scale

---

[69] Superior Electoral Court, Election Process, note 57.
[70] Superior Electoral Court, *Structure*, https://international.tse.jus.br/en/superior-electoral-court/structure.
[71] Tribunal Superior Eleitoral, International Affairs Unit, note 62, at 8.
[72] United States Courts, *Governance & the Judicial Conference*, www.uscourts.gov/about-federal-courts/governance-judicial-conference.
[73] United States Courts, *About the Judicial Conference*, www.uscourts.gov/about-federal-courts/governance-judicial-conference/about-judicial-conference.
[74] 28 U.S.C. § 332(d).
[75] 28 U.S.C. § 332(a)(1).

of its operations would require a far larger workforce, but it could operate through an analogous system of central control and regional courts or councils. In addition, like its Brazilian counterpart, the US Electoral Conference would require the use of local electoral boards for most of the groundwork. They could report to the regional circuit councils. The entire Electoral Conference staff would take over the functions currently performed by the armies of state and local election workers and officials, though initial grandparenting of most of the current state and local employees would be advisable and expected.

The proposed transfer of administrative responsibility to the national judiciary applies to both primary and general elections. As noted earlier, whether a nationwide primary would be better than the current system of sequential primaries is the subject of ongoing debate. So is the question whether primaries should be open or closed. Those would be live issues with or without state government and thus are beyond the scope of this book. But at present the primaries are held on a state-by-state basis. So if state government were eliminated, and the concept of sequential elections were retained, how would those sequences be arranged?

Again, there are manageable options. Primary elections could be held in each Senate district at staggered times. Depending on the number of Senate districts, however, that system could produce an unwieldy number of election days. An alternative would be to group the Senate districts into regions for this purpose. For that matter, it would not be necessary that all the primaries held on a given date be in the same region; they could be scattered around the country – as often happens today. Either way, the result would be something akin to today's Super Tuesdays, when several states hold primaries on the same day. And either way, the chronology could revolve with each election cycle so as not to perpetually advantage or disadvantage voters in the same districts or regions.

Given the partisan implications of its work, the judges who serve on both the national and regional components of the Electoral Conference should be appointed with the aim of minimizing both the reality and the appearance of partisan bias. One possibility would be to require, on each of those bodies, equal numbers of judges appointed by presidents who are from the major political parties – each set of judges selected by lottery, with further provision for ensuring participation from all three levels of court. To avoid the disarray of scores of third parties represented on either the Conference or the regional Councils, some specified minimum percentage of the national popular vote in, say, the preceding election, could be required. The members of both the Conference and the regional Councils should serve fixed, nonrenewable terms.

C RESHAPING THE NATIONAL COURTS

Without state government, the work currently done by the state courts would have to be shifted to other judges. This book has proposed that the lion's share of that work be reassigned to the national courts.[76] The municipal courts would have jurisdiction only over civil cases that turn solely on questions of local law.

This transfer would be a big deal. Over 100 million cases are filed in state trial courts every year. This compares to only about 400,000 annual case filings in federal trial courts. And the roughly 1,700 federal judges compare to 30,000 state judges.[77] That comes out to one federal judge for every eighteen state court judges. On the assumption that neither the average number of weekly work hours nor the number of hours the average case requires would change appreciably if the current state cases were instead decided by national judges, this means the national judiciary would have to expand to about nineteen times its current size.

The existing constitutionally mandated process for selecting federal judges – nomination by the president and confirmation by the Senate – would become untenable. Strained as it already is by a combination of gridlock, finite resources, and time constraints, the current process could not possibly bear the weight of such dramatically increased demands. What, then, are the options?

Together, the current federal and state systems provide several models to choose from. At least four different processes are in play for the selection and retention of state court judges. And within any given state, the methods can additionally vary from one level of court to another, particularly as between trial courts and appellate courts.

Of the four current state models, the two most common are elections (partisan or nonpartisan) by the people and "merit" plans. Both are described below. In a handful of states, the judges are appointed solely by the governor or solely by the state legislature.[78]

Debates over the relative merits of the various judicial selection systems tend to form two main philosophical battle lines. The opposing systems can generally be thought of as a majoritarian model and a justice model. The majoritarian model stresses public accountability; the justice model stresses decisional independence. Many of the states have hybrid systems that contain elements of both.

Equally important are the judges' terms of office. In contrast to the lifetime appointments of federal judges, almost 90 percent of state judges serve fixed terms that require periodic retention elections.[79] In addition, thirty-seven states have a mandatory retirement age, usually seventy.[80]

---

[76] See Chapter 4, Section C.3.

[77] Institute for the Advancement of the American Legal System, *Quality Judges Initiative, FAQs: Judges in the United States*, https://iaals.du.edu/sites/default/files/documents/publications/judge_faq.pdf.

[78] Ann O'M Bowman, Richard Kearney, and Carmine Scavo, State and Local Government 248–56 (11th ed. 2022); Jeffrey S. Sutton, Who Decides? States as Laboratories of Constitutional Experimentation 69–100, 375–79 (2022); Ballotpedia, Judicial Selection in the States, https://ballotpedia.org/Judicial_selection_in_the_states.

[79] Sutton, note 78, at 87.

[80] Bowman *et al.*, note 78, at 257.

Neither the selection nor the retention of judges has to be an all-or-nothing proposition. In particular, the methods for appointing trial judges and appellate judges
often differ, and for two reasons. Their numbers differ, and so do their functions.
So too, there can be good reasons that the judicial appointment process might vary
as between specialized courts and courts of general jurisdiction. These variables are
discussed at the end of this section.

Every method of selecting and retaining judges has its downside, so let's proceed by process of elimination. Probably the most controversial, and most widely
discussed, option is letting the people decide directly.[81] That subject is too large
for comprehensive treatment in a few pages, but the problems with popular election or retention of judges run deep and in the present context require a few basic
observations.

As a preliminary matter, I recognize the irony (once again) in criticizing the popular election and retention of judges in a book that bemoans the threats to democracy generally and majority rule in particular. But the two prescriptions are perfectly
consistent.

First, the main defense of elected judges is its supposed reflection of majoritarian
preferences. Among the arguments offered by Judge Jeffrey Sutton in defense of
popular election of judges is that "[i]t gave the people a direct rather than indirect
voice in who their judges are. It had the potential to give each judge a mandate
directly from the people."[82]

Ultimately, though, the judicial selection method is only as important as the effects
it has, if any, on the decisions that the judges hand down. And as Michael Klarman
(writing about judicial review generally, not the popular election method of judicial
selection) has argued, it is not necessarily counter-majoritarian for even unelected
judges to review the actions of elected legislatures. His "anti-entrenchment" theory
posits that, in practice, courts – even those whose judges are appointed rather than
elected – are often more majoritarian than the legislatures whose decisions they
are reviewing. Individual legislators might prioritize their own reelection goals over
the policy preferences of their constituents. Moreover, he points out, legislatures
that enjoy a temporary political majority might try to extend their control into the
future, long after that political majority has evaporated.[83] As Jessica Bulman-Pozen

---

[81] The debate over the pros and cons of the popular election of judges is longstanding. See, for example,
    ibid., at 250–53; Charles Gardner Geyh, Who is to Judge? The Perennial Debate over Whether to
    Elect or Appoint America's Judges (2019); Issacharoff *et al.*, note 18, at 947–58; Stefanie A. Lindquist,
    Countering the Majoritarian Difficulty, 96 Virginia L. Rev. 719 (2010); Sutton, note 78, at 79–87; G.
    Alan Tarr, Without Fear or Favor: Judicial Independence and Judicial Accountability in the States
    (2012); Steven P. Croley, *The Majoritarian Difficulty: Elective Judiciaries and the Rule of Law*, 62
    Univ. Chicago L. Rev. 689 (1995); Seifter, note 31, at 1771–74.
[82] Sutton, note 78, at 94.
[83] Michael J. Klarman, *Majoritarian Judicial Review: The Entrenchment Problem*, 85 Geo. L. J. 491,
    497–98 (1997).

and Miriam Seifter observe, other scholars too are less fearful of unelected judges imposing their will on the majority than of the converse – elected state court judges ruling against the interests of political minorities.[84] As explained below, they have good reason to worry.

And those are merely things legislators do after they've been elected. As both Chapters 2 and 3 have demonstrated, counter-majoritarian processes at both the federal and state levels are often what enable those legislators to get elected in the first place. Of special importance to the thesis of this book, that is particularly true of the state legislatures (despite having equipopulous Senates, unlike the US Congress). As Miriam Seifter demonstrates especially well, "state legislatures are typically a state's least majoritarian branch. Often they are outright counter-majoritarian institutions."[85]

To be fair, Judge Sutton's argument relies on more than the majoritarian advantages of electing and retaining judges. He is also emphasizing the distinction between direct and indirect expressions of the people's voice. But the appointment of judges by elected legislatures or elected executive branch officials is no less democratic than election by the people. The difference is simply between two different forms of democracy – direct versus representative. If selection of judges by elected officials is undemocratic, then so too are presidents appointing Department heads and, indeed, legislatures passing laws. In all these instances, the people are electing individuals directly and delegating to them the power to appoint other individuals or enact legislation – the precise point of the Madisonian model.

Judge Sutton also makes a slightly different argument: Popular election of judges "created independence from the appointing branches. ... And it advanced the goals of Jacksonian democracy and the Revolution – distrust of government, whatever the branch, whatever the function."[86] But what is the appointing (legislative or executive) branch from which independence is deemed crucial? And what is the government that these arguments assume the people hold in such distrust? They are the very officials whom the people themselves chose, and by the very process in which Judge Sutton places his confidence – popular election.

To this, one might counter that the public has ample reason to distrust even their own directly elected legislatures. As Chapters 4 and 5 of this book and the anti-entrenchment factors postulated by Klarman illustrate, Congress and the state legislatures can be counter-majoritarian in both their composition and their actions. And as Seifter points out, one of the oft-cited benefits of electing judges is that legislatures, in contrast, are perceived by many as corrupt.[87]

Still, while legislative counter-majoritarianism is real, it does not provide a rationale for popular election of judges. It supplies only an argument against legislative

---

[84] Bulman-Pozen and Seifter, note 41, at 904, citing, for example, Croley, note 81, at 694.
[85] Seifter, note 31, at 1735.
[86] Sutton, note 78, at 94.
[87] Seifter, note 31, at 1771–74.

appointment of judges. The discussion below will show that other available options are better than both. The perception of corruption in politics is also understandable. As will be seen, however, the popular election of judges inspires its own forms of corruption.

At this point, it is worth noting that the debate over the benefits of direct public input into the selection and retention of judges often hinges on which of two different judicial functions one emphasizes. The clearest function of courts is to resolve individual disputes between two or more specific parties. As will be argued below, the policy preferences of the electorate should be irrelevant to the exercise of that function. But in the process of deciding cases, judges sometimes express their reasoning in the form of binding precedential opinions. These precedents serve multiple functions, including consistency, equality, and efficiency. In every sense of the word, they ultimately create law. And lawmaking, defenders of judicial elections argue, should reflect the preferences of the majority. At the very least, they would contend, the public should have a direct voice in the selection of those who will be performing that lawmaking function.

The argument is a reasonable one, but it must be emphasized that only a minute percentage of lower court cases – federal or state – result in any precedential decisions at all. And only in some small percentage of even those cases will that precedent deal with subject matter so broad and so important that the general public demands a direct voice. To jettison an essential safeguard of fair dispute resolution in the overwhelming bulk of cases that come before the courts, just to assure a majoritarian voice in such a small number of precedent decisions (however important), seems like the tail wagging the dog. The US and state Supreme Courts are a different matter; there, precedent decisions are far more frequent and have more sweeping national or statewide impact. For those courts, the case for some form of majoritarian input into judicial selection – and arguably even judicial retention – admittedly is stronger. Even then, it will be argued here, popular election and retention of the justices is not the optimal form of majoritarian input.

At best, then, the benefits of electing judges – even Supreme Court justices – are debatable. Less debatable is the damage that this judicial selection method has caused. The harms have taken multiple forms.

First, the campaigns for elected judgeships have become unseemly. They have gradually morphed from subtle political messages to demagoguery, mudslinging, and unabashed partisanship. Candidates find ways to signal how they plan to decide cases that have not even been filed yet, much less briefed and argued. The political parties have supported this growing partisanship by pouring grotesque sums of money into the campaigns of their party's judge candidates, often by purchasing advertisements that openly mock the other party's elected leaders.[88]

---

[88] See, for example, Ruth Marcus, The Washington Post, *The Biggest and Least Known Fight of the 2022 Election* (Oct. 30, 2022), www.washingtonpost.com/opinions/2022/10/30/state-supreme-court-races-importance/?utm_campaign=wp_post_most&utm_medium=email&utm_

In 2023, Wisconsin was the scene of the most expensive campaign for a state Supreme Court seat in history; it appears to have more than doubled the amounts spent by the candidates in any previous such race. With the existing justices split 3-3 between Democrats and Republicans, the stakes were high. It was clear that the election would determine the fate of both that state's restrictive abortion law and its gerrymandered legislative map. The winning candidate, Democrat Janet Protasiewicz, made no attempt to hide her intention to strike down both of those measures. The losing candidate, Republican Dan Kelly, attacked his opponent as soft on crime. The opposing rhetoric was harsh and unforgiving.[89]

Just weeks later, a similar state Supreme Court campaign unfolded in North Carolina. *New York Times* reporter Michael Wines noted that it reflected "a national trend in which states that elect their judges – Ohio, Kentucky, Wisconsin, Pennsylvania and others – have seen races for their high court seats turned into multimillion-dollar political battles, and their justices' rulings viewed through a deeply partisan lens."[90] The authors of a leading text on state and local government law observe that "[j]udicial races have become increasingly politicized, with candidates engaged in demagoguery on legal issues and slinging mud at their opponents."[91]

It gets worse, because the impact of this spending orgy is not theoretical. Although popular election of judges is often lauded as a way to reduce corruption, all too frequently it does just the opposite. Studies show that elected judges have frequently been influenced to hand down decisions in favor of major campaign donors.[92] In

---

source=newsletter&wpisrc=nl_most&carta-url=https%3A%2F%2Fs2.washingtonpost.com%2Fcar-ln-tr%2F383f25e%2F635e9b9ef3d9003c581f0bcd%2F5976f9099bbc0f6826be4986%2F18%2F72%2F635e9b9ef3d9003c581f0bcd&wp_cu=46ff53dcffa9ac52f667b1c4cc42a07c%7C476A9E883480308EE05301 00007FF804.

[89] See, for example, Reid J. Epstein, The New York Times, *Costly Court Race Points to a Politicized Future for Judicial Elections* (Mar. 28, 2023), www.nytimes.com/2023/03/28/us/politics/ wisconsin-supreme-court-race.html?algo=combo_lda_channelsize5_unique_edimp_fye_ step50_diversified&block=1&campaign_id=142&emc=edit_fory_20230328&fellback=false&imp_ id=4062221&instance_id=88867&nl=for-you&nlid=76642304&rank=3&regi_id=76642304&req_ id=434999942&segment_id=128995&surface=for-you-email-wym&user_id=2785b718e28912cce3f4e f8d2794344a&variant=0_combo_lda_channelsize5_unique_edimp_fye_step50_diversified; Reid J. Epstein, The New York Times, *Liberal Wins Wisconsin Court Race, in Victory for Abortion Rights Backers* (Apr. 5, 2023), www.nytimes.com/2023/04/04/us/politics/wisconsin-supreme-court-protasiewicz .html?campaign_id=60&emc=edit_na_20230404&instance_id=0&nl=breaking-news&ref=cta&regi_ id=13788254&segment_id=129604&user_id=e16deb82e8516f294a4077a86c02f5c2; Shawn Johnson, Wisconsin Public Radio, *For the First Time in 15 Years, Liberals Win Control of the Wisconsin Supreme Court* (Apr. 4, 2023, www.npr.org/2023/04/04/1167815077/wisconsin-supreme-court-election-results-abortion-voting-protasiewicz-kelly.

[90] Michael Wines, The New York Times, *North Carolina Gerrymander Ruling Reflects Politicization of Judiciary Nationally* (May 2, 2023), www.nytimes.com/2023/04/28/us/north-carolina-supreme-court-gerrymander.html?campaign_id=60&emc=edit_na_20230428&instance_id=0&nl=breaking-news&ref=cta&regi_id=13788254&segment_id=131629&user_id=e16deb82e8516f294a4077a86c 02f5c2.

[91] Bowman *et al.*, note 78, at 251–53.

[92] *Ibid.*

particular, the empirical data make clear that campaign contributions from business interests especially influence judicial outcomes.[93] In contrast, federal judges, with all the admitted shenanigans that have so contaminated the confirmation process in recent years, are at least free to exercise their independent professional judgment once they are on the bench.

Retention elections (as distinguished from judges' initial elections) pose special problems. Judge Sutton describes two of the more notable voter purges of state court judges. Probably the most famous was the 1986 election in which Chief Justice Rose Bird of the California Supreme Court and two other Justices (Cruz Reynoso and Joseph Grodin) on the seven-Justice court were voted off the bench. All three were known for their generally liberal leanings.[94] Bird was the central figure, unacceptable to "Republican politicians, business leaders, [and] law-and-order activists," especially on death penalty issues.[95] So her opponents enlisted an Orange County consulting firm to organize a successful $10 million campaign against her that relied heavily on television ads.[96]

In 1996, the voters similarly removed Justice Penny White from the Tennessee Supreme Court. Her transgression was voting not to impose the death penalty in a highly sensational case.[97] And in 2010, three Iowa Supreme Court Justices, including the Chief Justice, were voted out amidst a public uproar over the court's unanimous decision a year earlier to recognize same-sex marriages.[98]

One's instinctive reaction might be that perhaps those results were deserved. Certainly, Judge Sutton's description reveals his clear belief that the ousted Justices had only themselves to blame. They took it upon themselves to issue unpopular decisions, and the majority spoke.

I don't doubt that in a well-funded, high-PR-oriented campaign that features specific, controversial judicial decisions, the voters will often come away with a general sense of a given Justice's positions on the highlighted issues. And those positions might indeed be unpopular among the majority of voters. But one explanation Judge Sutton offers in defense of the voters' decision not to retain the California Supreme Court Justices is hard to swallow:

> The norm in the state courts [as opposed to the federal courts] tends to be a greater correlation between language and interpretation. And I suspect that if the courts ignore that tradition in the future, as the California Supreme Court did during the

[93] See, for example, Michael S. Kang & Joanna M. Shepherd, *The Partisan Price of Justice: An Empirical Analysis of Campaign Contributions and Judicial Decisions*, 86 NYU L. Rev. 69, 100, 121 (2011) (empirically correlating campaign contributions from business interests with subsequent rulings favoring those interests); Seifter, note 31, at 1773.

[94] Wikipedia, *Rose Bird*, https://en.wikipedia.org/wiki/Rose_Bird.

[95] Sutton, note 78, at 89.

[96] *Ibid.*, at 89–90.

[97] Bowman *et al.*, note 78, at 255.

[98] Sutton, note 78, at 91–92.

decade or so before 1986, the people will tend to replace the judges and change the constitution to prohibit future like-minded innovations.[99]

For me, the notion that the general public has any earthly idea as to the language of the statutes and constitutional provisions that the Justices are interpreting, much less "the correlation" between that language and the court's interpretive rationale, is a nonstarter. Nor are the voters likely to know much about the judges' rulings, or the quality of their analyses, in the vast majority of the less sensational cases.[100] And even if they did, the exceptionally low turnout for most judicial races[101] makes it impossible to take the electoral outcomes as a proxy for majority sentiment.

My view is that reasonable job security is a precondition to decisional[102] independence and that decisional independence, in turn, is a precondition to adjudicative fairness.[103] Human nature being what it is, judges who must constantly look over their shoulders for fear of alienating a majority of the electorate are not well positioned to administer blind justice. The data support that proposition. In Miriam Seifter's words: "On the empirical side, some accounts indicate that state court judges face 'the majoritarian difficulty' and are highly susceptible to public opinion, especially in criminal or high-salience cases."[104]

Elsewhere, I have argued that contemporary societal values influence judicial decision-making in two ways: The judges' own policy preferences, like those of anyone else living in a society, can be shaped consciously or unconsciously by the views of those around them. When they must decide controversial cases, shutting out their own deeply held beliefs is not easy. In addition, whether or not the judge personally shares the majority's opinions on a given issue, the judge might have all kinds of reasons to avoid antagonizing that majority.[105] In the case of judges who will have to face retention votes, those reasons can be compelling.

So the problem is not merely that the lay population rarely knows the first thing about the professional calibers of the individual judges. It is that the judiciary is not supposed to be one of the political branches of government in the first place.

---

[99] Ibid., at 96–97.
[100] See, for example, Stephen B. Burbank, *The Architecture of Judicial Independence*, 72 South. Calif. L. Rev. 315, 316 (1999) (noting the public's "abysmal knowledge base about the judiciary").
[101] See Bowman *et al.*, note 78, at 250–51.
[102] Decisional independence refers to a judge's insulation from political pressure to rule for particular parties in individual cases. It differs from "institutional independence," which relates more to separation of powers and, in particular, the insulation of the entire judiciary from the other branches of government. See generally American Bar Association, *Overview*, in An Independent Judiciary: Report of the ABA Committee on Separation of Powers and Judicial Independence (1997).
[103] See Stephen H. Legomsky, *Deportation and the War on Independence*, 91 Cornell L. Rev. 369, 385–403 (2006).
[104] Seifter, note 31, at 1773 & n.266, citing Croley, note 81, at 693.
[105] See Stephen H. Legomsky, Immigration and the Judiciary: Law and Politics in Britain and America 241–53 (1987) (describing ways in which contemporary societal attitudes can, and do, influence judicial decision-making).

On the contrary, it is supposed to be a neutral arbiter of the facts of the cases and the interpretation of the law. One three-judge federal district court panel, holding that elections of state court judges need not observe the principle of one-person-one-vote, put the point this way: "Judges do not represent people, they serve people."[106]

Of course, the reality is different. Notwithstanding the usual claims of neutrality,[107] no serious observer today could doubt that judges routinely bring their own ideological preferences to bear in reasonably close decisions. Nor is it clear that judges are immune from the ideological pressures of public opinion. But they are supposed to at least try to be policy-neutral. They are supposed to decide cases based on their objective evaluation of the evidence and their honest interpretations of the law, not on the basis of which policy statements will attract the most votes and, later on, which case outcomes will best assure their retention. If I were in court, I would not want my case to be decided by judges who believe that a decision in my favor would jeopardize their jobs, derail their careers, or destroy their long-term professional ambitions. That is the aptly named "majoritarian difficulty," and it is why judges need to be insulated from political pressures – an impossibility when their appointments and job security both hinge on currying the support of the public.[108] And it is the very reason that the US Constitution affords life tenure to federal judges (with the rarely used exception of impeachment for "high crimes and misdemeanors").

Most of this simply boils down to basic procedural fairness for the parties before the court. That alone should give pause, but still more is at stake. Fears of public backlash can distort both the outcomes for the specific parties and the precedents that bind others in ways that fail to protect unpopular individuals, racial or partisan minorities, other groups, or political viewpoints. Worries of getting booted from the bench can also steer judges away from decisions that are controversial but necessary. The same concerns can discourage good lawyers from seeking judgeships. The political nature of the retention elections can diminish the appearance of justice in the eyes of the public generally and the parties to a given case. There is also what I have termed "reverse social Darwinism," whereby those judges with the weakest backbones survive retention elections and prosper, while those with the courage and the integrity to speak truth to power are culled from the herd. And there are other

---

[106] *Wells v. Edwards*, 347 F. Supp. 453 (M.D. La. 1972), aff'd, 409 U.S. 1095 (1973), quoting *Buchanan v. Rhodes*, 249 F. Supp. 860 (N.D. Ohio 1966).

[107] See especially the claims of Chief Justice John Roberts and Justice Neil Gorsuch at their Senate confirmation hearings, in Chapter 2, text accompanying notes 219–20.

[108] See especially Lindquist, note 81, and the many sources cited therein (describing the ways in which the popular election of judges undermines the rule of law in the name of protecting democracy). See also J. Clifford Wallace, *An Essay on Independence of the Judiciary: Independence from What and Why*, 58 NYU Ann. Surv. Am. Law 241, 242 (2001) ("[T]he independence of the judiciary from political pressures is an essential aspect of justice at any level.").

harms as well.[109] For all these reasons, it is not surprising that almost nowhere else in the world are judges elected by the people.[110]

One last distinction should be noted. Asserting that judges need to be independent begs an important question: independence from whom? Proponents of judicial elections argue that decisional independence might well require insulation from the other branches of government, but that it does not require insulation from the people. To the contrary, they maintain, one of the historical arguments for judicial elections is that it gives judges greater independence from the political branches than would a system of legislative or executive branch appointments.[111] But that does not explain the need for retention elections, and it does not refute any of the above arguments even with respect to the appointment process.

If the ability and the willingness to pander to public opinion are not the ideal qualifications for a judge, what are? Drawing on the American Bar Association's 2000 report on the methods of selecting state court judges,[112] Bowman *et al.* provide a nice summary:

> [J]udges should be chosen on the basis of solid professional and personal qualifications, regardless of their political views and party identification. Criteria for choosing judges should include experience, integrity, professional competence, judicial temperament, and service to the law and contribution to the effective administration of justice. They should be good listeners. ...
>
> An appellate or general trial court judge should also have relevant experience in a lower court or as a courtroom attorney.[113]

These are not the sorts of individual professional attributes that the general public is in a position to evaluate. For that and all the other reasons just given, the popular election of judges would seem no more sensible in a unitary republic than under the present system. That is not to say popular judicial elections couldn't be part of the mix; after all, none of the alternatives is perfect either. But electing judges comes with enough heavy baggage that in a newly constructed system it should be avoided if at all possible.

Where does this leave us? At present, the same system of presidential nomination and Senate confirmation is used for all three levels of the federal courts – district courts, courts of appeals, and the Supreme Court. If all three levels of national judges had to be appointed through a single process in the proposed stateless republic, the numbers alone would make certain judicial selection methods unworkable. The president could not reasonably be expected to fill the huge number of annual

---

[109] Legomsky, Deportation, note 103, at 394–401 (articulating ten theories of decisional independence).
[110] Bowman *et al.*, note 78, at 250–51. As this book was going to press, Mexico amended its constitution to provide for the popular election of judges.
[111] Sutton, note 78, at 94.
[112] American Bar Association, Standards on State Judicial Selection (July 2000).
[113] Bowman *et al.*, note 78, at 248–49.

judicial vacancies, and the Senate could not be counted on to confirm that number of nominees.

A congressional appointment process analogous to the gubernatorial appointment process in place in South Carolina and Virginia[114] would be even less feasible. And not just because of the numbers. Given cronyism, legislative appointments tend invariably to result in awarding judgeships to former legislators as rewards for their service. As Bowman *et al.* observe, "[l]egislative experience has little connection to the demands of a judgeship" and for that reason "[f]ew people other than legislators approve of legislative election."[115]

That leaves merit plans. They come in different forms. In the typical merit plan, the process begins with a nominating commission that most commonly consists of a judge, one or more state bar association representatives, and one or more laypersons appointed by the governor. The commission investigates the records of potential candidates and submits a list of three nominees to the governor, who makes the final selection. The judge is subjected to a retention election after a year or two, and then periodically thereafter.[116]

Merit plans, like the other alternatives, have pros and cons. Their goal is to produce judges who are chosen because of their professional qualifications for the bench rather than for political reasons. And often they do just that. But not always. As Bowman *et al.* points out, they have not succeeded in banishing politics from the process. The governor's handpicked commission members are typically individuals chosen because they know the governor or share the governor's preference for particular candidates. The lawyer members tend to be either pro-plaintiff or pro-defendant, and those inclinations color their decisions. In addition, the retention election is subject to all the criticisms laid out earlier. Nor have merit plans in practice produced judges who are any more qualified, more diverse, or less likely to be disciplined once on the bench.[117]

Still, in the newly constructed system proposed here, the merit plan would not need to operate in the same way it currently does in the states. The flaws that Bowman *et al.* identify could be avoided or at least greatly mitigated by making four modifications. Appointment of lay commission members by a politically motivated chief executive could be eliminated. Judges, rather than self-interested pro-plaintiff or pro-defendant lawyers, could select the members of the commission. The commission could actually appoint judges rather than simply nominate them. And the final step in the current typical state merit plan – retention elections – could also be eliminated. Without retention elections, judges would be appointed either for life or for a fixed, nonrenewable term, one that preferably lasts until a specified

[114] *Ibid.*, at 250.
[115] *Ibid.*
[116] *Ibid.*, at 253–54.
[117] *Ibid.*, at 254–55.

mandatory retirement age. With those revisions, merit plans could be administered within each of the individual judicial circuits.

Is there a way to put these various puzzle pieces together? As hinted at the beginning of this section, my view is that the different levels of national courts call for different appointment methods, because district judges differ from appellate judges in two important ways. First, there are many more of them; there are also many more circuit judges than there are Supreme Court Justices. Processes that are protracted or resource-intensive can be tolerated when they are needed only on a few isolated occasions, as in filling Supreme Court vacancies. They become less manageable when they must be applied in large numbers on a continuous basis, as in filling district court vacancies.

Second, appellate judges differ from trial judges in their overall missions and, therefore, their day-to-day work. They perform different tasks in different proportions. Appellate courts are said to have two basic functions – resolving disputes between the opposing parties in individual cases and creating law for the disposition of future cases. Trial courts, in general, are concerned almost exclusively with the dispute resolution function.

Partly because of that basic difference, appellate judges and trial judges also differ in the proportions of time they spend on fact finding and legal interpretation. Trial judges spend the bulk of their time evaluating evidence and making findings of fact, at least in nonjury trials. Institutional constraints prevent them from becoming major players in the creation of national law. Appellate judges, in contrast, are limited almost exclusively to interpreting and applying the law. In particular, when interpreting the often vague, broadly worded provisions of constitutions and statutes and the similarly general prescriptions of judicial precedents, appellate courts are routinely called upon to make decisions that require judgment and discretion. The precedents established by those decisions create binding legal rights and obligations.

I don't mean to exaggerate these distinctions. Trial judges are more than factfinders, even in nonjury cases; they are also interpreters of the law. They are frequently required to rule from the bench on the parties' various motions. In addition, they constantly exercise discretion, especially in criminal sentencing. Typically, however, those discretionary decisions affect only the parties to the case and, indirectly, other specific individuals affected by those decisions. As discussed earlier,[118] federal trial judges have also become increasingly aggressive in their use of nationwide injunctions to block executive actions of presidents of the opposing political parties. But that practice has been confined to a small percentage of trial judges, and even when it occurs, the decisions are at least subject to appeal. Conversely, even though appellate judges have only infrequent occasion to make formal findings of fact, they routinely have to determine whether the findings of trial judges or

---

[118] See Chapter 2, Section D.

administrative agencies are adequately supported by the evidence. Overall, though, the ratios of legal interpretation and lawmaking time to fact finding and dispute resolution time are undeniably greater for appellate judges than for trial judges – and highest of all for the Supreme Court.

For these reasons, the argument for factoring majoritarian policy preferences into the process for selecting and retaining appellate judges is stronger than it is for trial judges. And within the appellate judiciary, the benefits of considering majoritarian preferences are stronger for the Supreme Court than for the courts of appeals. The Supreme Court has the last word, and the direct impact of its precedents extends nationwide, not just to the territory covered by a single judicial circuit.

How do these differences in the sizes and missions of the three levels of national courts translate into judicial selection methods? One possibility would be to use judge-appointed merit commissions for the selection of national trial judges while retaining the current process of presidential nomination and Senate confirmation for national appellate judges. Or, if the number of court of appeals judge vacancies is expected to be greater than what the current process can competently handle in a timely fashion, then those judgeships too could be filled by judge-appointed merit commissions, with the current process reserved for the appointment of Supreme Court Justices.

It is true that the earlier discussion[119] identified multiple counter-majoritarian ingredients of the current process for selecting all federal judges, as well as numerous examples of the partisan extremes that have resulted. But the proposals in this chapter would largely cancel those counter-majoritarian effects. If presidents were elected by a national popular vote, *and* the Senate districts were made equipopulous, *and* the Senate district lines were drawn by an independent nonpartisan commission, *and* elections were run and voter suppression strategies erased by an independent, nonpartisan entity within the national judiciary, then the current process for selecting federal judges would no longer systematically bias any one particular political party.

Admittedly, we would not be entirely out of the counter-majoritarian woods even then. While no one political party would be systematically advantaged, a longitudinal source of counter-majoritarianism would persist. The selection of national judges would still depend on the timing of the judicial vacancies. The number of vacancies that happen to occur during the term of any particular president would determine how much long-term impact that president would have on the national bench. For that reason, for a period of years or even decades, the will of the majority at the time of one president's election would count more than the will of the majority at the times of other presidents' elections.

This would not be a significant problem for lower court appointments. There are enough of them that the law of large numbers would assure a roughly constant

[119] See *ibid.*

turnover. At any rate, the proposal here does not call for a majoritarian selection method for trial judges; the recommended modified version of the merit plan would work well for trial judge appointments. The problem would be the Supreme Court, which currently has only nine Justices. That number could be increased, but any expansion dramatic enough to trigger the law of large numbers is unrealistic. The inequity is minor compared to those of the current selection system, but it is a factor worth taking into account.

In choosing a method of selection or retention, it would also be possible to distinguish specialized courts from courts of general jurisdiction. Today, a diverse array of specialized courts play key roles in both the federal[120] and state[121] systems. In allocating limited resources, Congress might wish to reserve the more labor-intensive processes for those specialized courts that have jurisdiction over subject areas in which particularly great interests are commonly at stake. Congress might also wish to tailor the process to the degree of specialized expertise that the particular subject matter demands. And there are other subject matter attributes, which I have considered elsewhere,[122] that make specialized adjudication particularly suitable or unsuitable.

Those considerations aside, it's not just the total caseload of the national courts that will increase. The range of subject areas will also expand. Contracts, property, torts, corporations, probate, and other specialties that have been governed primarily by state law would now become the responsibility of national judges. The greater variety of legal subjects is a lot to ask the judges to become conversant with. There is something to be said for easing the burden through the greater use of specialized courts.

One final point concerns the transition. Out of fairness to the current state court judges, and to speed the transition process for the system as a whole, those judges could be grandparented into temporary national judgeships, perhaps after cursory background checks to identify any obvious disqualifying factors. All those appointments would automatically expire at the end of their current terms. At that point, like anyone else, they could choose to become candidates for the longer-term national judgeships. For this purpose, the state trial judges would be grandparented into national trial judgeships; judges on both the state Supreme Courts and the state intermediate appellate courts would be grandparented into the national courts of appeals – not the US Supreme Court.

As the discussion in this section shows, manageable solutions exist. And as with the issues considered in the preceding sections of this chapter, there is more than one alternative for which a fair case can be made.

---

[120] See generally Stephen H. Legomsky, Specialized Justice: Courts, Administrative Tribunals, and a Cross-National Theory of Specialization 20–32 (1990).

[121] Common examples of specialized state courts include juvenile courts, traffic courts, police courts, probate courts, domestic violence courts, veterans courts, and small claims courts. Bowman *et al.*, note 78, at 245.

[122] Legomsky, Specialized Justice, note 120, at 20–32.

D DEMOCRATIZING THE CONSTITUTIONAL AMENDMENT PROCESS

Earlier discussion accepted the premise that a constitutional amendment should require more than simple majority approval. Constitutional provisions that protect fundamental individual rights or the basic institutions of government should not be subject to majority overreach and should not change back and forth with every shift in the political winds.

At the same time, that discussion criticized the multiple layers of counter-majoritarianism in the current process as excessive. It called particular attention to the requirements of a two-thirds vote in a House of Representatives already dis-figured by a combination of gerrymandering, single-member district elections, urban/rural residential patterns, and voter suppression laws; a two-thirds vote in a Senate in which a citizen of one state receives sixty-nine times the representation of a citizen of another state; and ratification by three-fourths of the state legislatures, which in many cases are individually counter-majoritarian as a result of the same forces that shape the US House and which also have equal say in the amendment process regardless of their respective population sizes. The argument specifically highlighted the counter-majoritarian effects of giving the states a degree of power out of all proportion to their populations – in the process, arguably making the US Constitution the hardest constitution in the world to amend.[123]

In a unitary American republic, the process could begin as it does now – with a two-thirds vote by both houses of Congress – if the other reforms recommended else-where in this book were implemented. These include a House de-gerrymandered by an independent, national, nonpartisan commission of demographers, statisticians, and similar nonpolitical actors; the replacement of the current single-member dis-trict system by a more majoritarian election method such as proportional represen-tation; and an equipopulous Senate.

As for ratification, there would be at least two options that don't require states. One option would be simply to dispense with ratification entirely. The requirement of a two-thirds vote in both of the newly majoritarian chambers of Congress might well be enough to assure both the stability of the Constitution and a fair representa-tion of national sentiment.

Alternatively, ratification could be left to a nationwide referendum. I would favor requiring approval by a specified supermajority (perhaps 60 percent, perhaps two-thirds) of the people. Rather than privilege the citizens of small states over those of large states, as the current system does, either of these procedures would give every citizen an equal voice. At the same time, it would preserve the requirement

---

[123] Chapter 2, Section E. As that discussion also notes, the Constitution offers alternative amendment processes. These include "applications" filed by two-thirds of the state legislatures and ratification by constitutional conventions held in three-fourths of the states. U.S. Const. Art. V. To date, those alter-natives have never been used.

of a substantial supermajority to protect the fundamental individual rights and basic building blocks of a government of the people.

* * *

For more than two centuries, the United States has survived and prospered as a federation of states. This must be acknowledged. With or without state government, and even amidst the fierce centrifugal forces and swirling rage that too often pit us against one another, I don't doubt that America's economic and military might will assure its continuation as a sovereign country well into the future.

But there is no reason to settle for mere survival. Remaining a democracy – or, perhaps more accurately, *becoming* a true democracy – is the more urgent challenge. This book has suggested that state government stands in the way. It has been, is today, and unless abolished will remain, the single greatest obstacle to genuine democratic rule. It is also a needless source of fiscal waste. Together, these harms far outweigh any benefits that state government might be claimed to supply.

The preamble to the US Constitution conveys the dream of "a more perfect union." But it reserves that dream for "the People of the United *States* [my emphasis]." Our goal should be more ambitious. Rather than settle for a union of the state populations, let us aspire to something simpler and more meaningful – a union of the American People.

Index